Advergaming Developer's Guide: Using Macromedia® Flash™ MX 2004 and Director® MX

Advergaming Developer's Guide:

Using Macromedia® Flash™ MX 2004 and Director® MX

Rod Afshar, Duke Banerjee,
Clifford Jones

CHARLES RIVER MEDIA

CHARLES RIVER MEDIA, INC.
Hingham, Massachusetts

Publisher: Jenifer Niles
Production: Publishers' Design and Production Services, Inc
Cover Design: The Printed Image
Cover Image: epic software group, inc.

CHARLES RIVER MEDIA, INC.
10 Downer Avenue
Hingham, Massachusetts 02043
781-740-0400
781-740-8816 (FAX)
info@charlesriver.com
www.charlesriver.com

This book is printed on acid-free paper.

Rod Afshar, Duke Banerjee, Clifford Jones. *Advergaming Developers Guide: Using Macromedia Flash MX 2004 and Director MX.*
ISBN: 1-58450-316-5

Library of Congress Cataloging-in-Publication Data
Afshar, Rod, 1984-
Advergaming developer's guide : using Macromedia Flash MX 2004 and Director MX / Rod Afshar, Duke Banerjee, Clifford Jones.
p. cm.
ISBN 1-58450-316-5 (alk. paper)
1. Computer games—Programming. 2. Flash (Computer file) 3. Director (Computer file) 4. Advertising—Brand name products. 5. Brand name products. I. Banerjee, Duke, 1979- II. Jones, Clifford, 1982- III. Title.
QA76.76.C672A35 2004
794.8'0285—dc22

2003026506

Printed in the United States of America
04 7 6 5 4 3 2 First Edition

CHARLES RIVER MEDIA titles are available for site license or bulk purchase by institutions, user groups, corporations, etc. For additional information, please contact the Special Sales Department at 781-740-0400.

Requests for replacement of a defective CD-ROM must be accompanied by the original disc, your mailing address, telephone number, date of purchase and purchase price. Please state the nature of the problem, and send the information to CHARLES RIVER MEDIA, INC., 10 Downer Avenue, Hingham, Massachusetts 02043. CRM's sole obligation to the purchaser is to replace the disc, based on defective materials or faulty workmanship, but not on the operation or functionality of the product.

Contents

Acknowledgments

It takes a great deal of time and effort to put together a book like this. Many people contributed to the content and design, whereas others provided encouragement and support.

When I founded the epic software group, inc. in 1990, I realized the most successful projects would be team efforts, in which each person would contribute his best work. And that was indeed the case with the *Advergaming Developer's Guide*. Without a doubt, it would have remained just another interesting idea had it not been for the combined efforts of this talented team. I would like to offer my heartfelt appreciation to everyone who helped in taking an idea and turning it into a book we are all proud of.

First and foremost, I would like to thank our three authors, Rod Afshar, Cliff Jones, and Duke Banerjee. Each has a talent for taking a complex concept and explaining it in terms we can all understand.

Next, I must thank Robert Bailey, our Sr. Multimedia Director Project Manager. Robert has "lived" in Macromedia® Director® for over five years. He does not simply write programs, he attacks them.

Many of the 3D graphics in the book were created by Danny Duhon, our Creative Director and Lead 3D Artist. Derek Hughes is our 2D Artist. It is wonderful to watch concepts from a brainstorming session magically appear in pencil sketches, storyboards, illustrations, and vector animations. I am very proud of their work. Thanks guys for all the wonderful eye candy.

One of the most important aspects of any software book is getting the details right. Our proofreader, Sharon Howerton, kept us in line by checking and rechecking every line of copy in the book.

Perhaps the folks we have to thank the most are our friends at Charles River Media, Jenifer Niles, the Publisher, and the production staff, including Meg Dunkerley and Bryan Davidson.

Vic Cherubini
President
epic software group, inc.

Rod Afshar–

I would like to thank my dad, mom, and sister for all the support they've given me over the years. A special thanks to Vic Cherubini for the opportunities he has provided me from my early days as a high school intern to the present. The support of my friends has also been great—that's you, Steph, Vic, and Trev. I am also thankful that God has given me the will and the ability to undertake such a huge project.

Cliff Jones–

I would like to thank all my friends and family for putting up with me and often doing without my wit and charm while I was immersed in the development of this book, and the lovely Miss Tina Vivar for sharing hers with me whenever I had a free moment.

Duke Banerjee–

First of all, I would like to thank Vic and the epic crew for giving me the opportunity to write this book. I really had a great time with it. But, it was an insane amount of work, with plenty of all-nighters and Exxon coffee to meet those tight deadlines. I am greatly indebted to my parents and particularly my wife Anamika for the support and comfort in those times when I was eating, sleeping, and breathing nothing but this book. And thank *you* for picking up this book. I only hope that you can create something wonderful using the knowledge and experience we have attempted to put into words.

Introduction to the World of Advergaming

For years, advertisers have tried ingenious ways to make consumers pay attention to their products and services. Everything from billboards, to newspaper ads and TV commercials, to radio spots are used to tout the latest new products. Years ago, astute brand managers learned that when their products were shown in a popular movie, people paid attention and often bought the product. When Katharine Hepburn dumped Gordon's® London Dry Gin overboard in the 1951 classic *The African Queen*, sales increased dramatically. Products strategically placed or mentioned in a film help to bring the character or product to life. James Bond wears a Rolex®, E.T. loves Reese's Pieces®, and Tom Hanks, as Forrest Gump, delivers a slam dunk when he announces that his favorite thing about meeting the president was that he could have as much Dr. Pepper® as he wanted. Today, products, carefully placed in movies, represent millions of dollars in ad revenues to studios, and often return far more in sales to the companies that own the products.

It should come as no surprise that these same companies discovered that product placements in video games could yield similar results. The video game industry is *huge*. Sales for 2001 were $6.35 billion as reported by the Interactive Digital Software Association (IDSA), the trade group for the U.S. computer and video game industry. What is even more significant is that in 2001, for the first time, total revenues for video games also exceeded the take at the box office.

With gaming being such a huge industry, it is no surprise that ad placement is now becoming commonplace. Advertisers have realized that there are a large number of people playing all sorts of games from 3D shooters to arcade games, and they want to get in on the action and reap the rewards. The first time I encountered advertising in video games was back in the early 1990s when I would play *Teenage Mutant Ninja Turtles* on the original Nintendo®. The advertising space that Pizza Hut® obtained for the TV show spilled over into the video game as the turtles would fight with Pizza Hut signs in the background. Since then, more and more advertising has populated games to the point that companies such as 7-UP® began releasing games featuring their product. In *7-UP Cool Spot*, you played as the red 7-UP spot and explored worlds loaded with their products. This game was one of the first of many games specifically made to advertise a product and generate profits. These programs fit into a small but rapidly growing market segment known as *Advergames.*

WHAT IS AN ADVERGAME?

" '*Advergaming*' is the use of interactive gaming technology to deliver embedded advertising messages to consumers. While many sites use free games to encourage traffic and may offer banner ads surrounding the game, Advergaming goes much further by incorporating branding directly into the gaming environment. In short, the advertising message is central to gameplay."

Welcome to the world of Advergaming! Interactive games are one of the fastest growing forms of entertainment, and video games of all kinds are on track to exceed movie box office ticket sales. When you have revenues measured in "billions" of dollars, you know it's bound to attract the attention of advertisers seeking new venues to promote their brands. Although most commercial games released today are created specifically to be sold as retail products, Advergames are free. And they are not embarrassed by their crass commercialism because they exist for a specific purpose—to promote a company, its brand, and its products. With an Advergame, the brand is not simply inserted into the game, but the game is built from the ground up around the brand. This level of integration dramatically increases the relationship between the brand and the consumer.

A significant number of companies are choosing to use these brandcentric games to supplement and, in some cases, replace the traditional branding methods (print ads, billboards, TV and radio spots, etc.) that have been used for decades. Whereas most advertising techniques provide little entertainment value, Advergames have the power to keep a viewer absorbed. With other methods, such as watching television or listening to the radio, people are prone to tuning out commercials or taking care of other tasks until their show comes back on. As if that wasn't bad enough for TV advertisements, the popularity of TiVo® brings really bad news for commercials. TiVo is a service that keeps track of your favorite TV shows and automatically records them on a Digital Video Recorder that saves everything on a hard drive without any commercials. As TiVo spreads to more and more households, people will be opting to catch their shows later and without commercials, making it even harder to make someone actually see a TV advertisement. Games, on the other hand, have the ability to grab players and keep them involved in the action, causing them to do what every marketer hopes for—tune everything else out. Advergames use a variety of methods to grab and hold a player's attention. Stunning graphics, addictive gameplay, and multiplayer capabilities immerse players in the activity and keep them engaged. In Chapter 21, "Interview and Case Study—AGENCY.COM," you'll read about the Miller Lite® NASCAR® *Fantasy Car Challenge* game that allows players to create their own team of drivers and puts them head-to-head with other players around the world for an entire season. The Advergame is so successful at drawing people into it, that entire communities are formed around these fantasy NASCAR teams and loyalty to their sport (and the brand) skyrockets.

Advergames are proving to be an excellent way to channel Web surfers to a site and keep them there. By providing visitors with a call to action, such as registering to play the game for prizes, a company can build a massive database of names. This database can be used to contact prospects and fans with additional e-mail or direct mail offerings.

Advergames can also incorporate information about a product's features and functions that differentiate it from the competition, and use the game to educate consumers while entertaining them. To call attention to their high-speed Internet service, BellSouth® used an Advergame called *BellSouth FastAccess DSL Racing*. The game was developed by Leviathan™ Games, and the splash screen is shown in Figure 0.1. The object of the game is to obtain the fastest racing time, but you need to "Avoid 56K Dial-up Potholes" and steer clear of "Cable Modem Speed Bumps."

Advergames can either be created as a small, entertaining game, such as a simple arcade game for the Web or a CD-ROM, or a full-sized game that requires a full team, working collectively, to produce something that takes players hours to complete. Although this book focuses on the first category—games that either an individual or a small team of artists and programmers can produce—we take a peek behind the curtain at some of the larger games as well. By working through the *Advergaming Developer's Guide*, you learn how to create anything you want from the ground up—even if you have no prior game development experience.

WHERE WILL YOU FIND ADVERGAMES?

Advergames are distributed in a variety of ways. Of course, you can find them online, but they may also turn up on your cell phone (see the Heineken® UK case study in Chapter 21), as a CD-ROM offer on your box of breakfast cereal (see Figure 0.2), embedded in your e-mail, and in a number of other strange places. There are Web sites that act as portals for Advergame enthusiasts (*www.zeeks.com*, *www.kewlbox.com*, *www.shockwave.com*). These sites are specifically created to

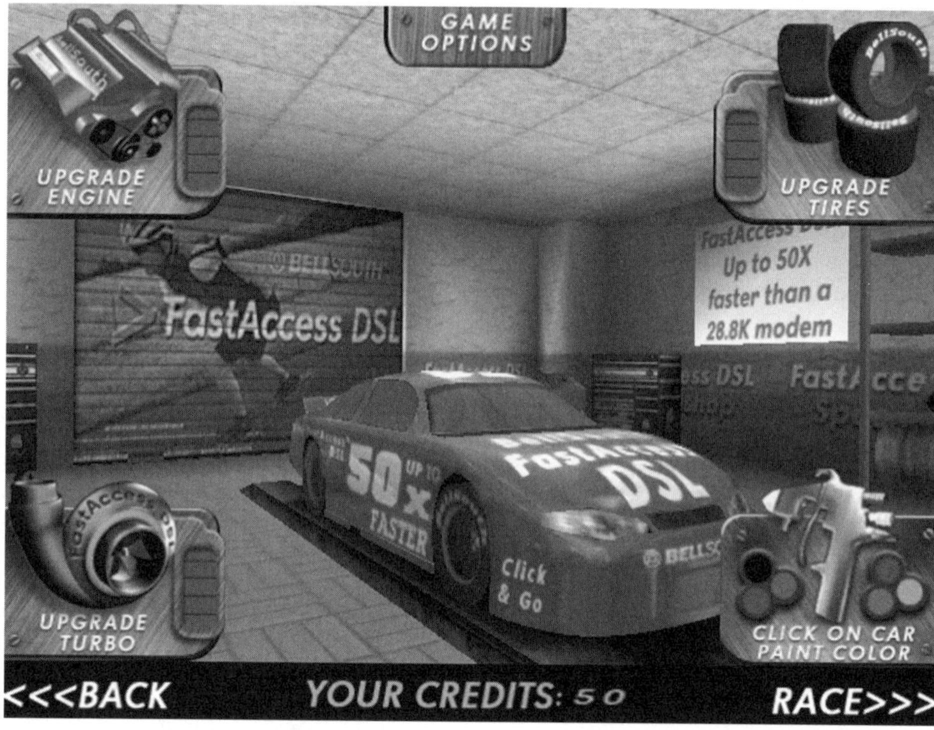

FIGURE 0.1 The *BellSouth FastAccess DSL Racing Game* Advergame, developed by Leviathan Games. © 2003. Reprinted with permission from Leviathan Games.

showcase new games and provide a variety of options to visitors of all ages. One visit to Candystand.com by Nabisco® helps you understand just how effective (and addictive) these game clustered sites can be.

You'll often find Advergames on the site of the company for which they were created. Everyone can use a little diversion from the pressures of the day—so why not provide some relief in the form of an entertaining game? Making a site "sticky" by keeping visitors engaged is a great way to get your company in the "Favorites" folder of a prospect who (with a return visit or two) may soon become a customer.

Although the concept of "Viral Marketing" may initially sound distasteful, the idea of having one user pass an Advergame on to a friend is perhaps the pinnacle of advertising success. "Word of Mouse" is a powerful means of publicity that is controlled (and paid for) by fans who want to share a game experience with a friend. Advergame developers make it easy by including a "Challenge a Friend" e-mail form that enables you to send your high score to a fellow game player, along with a link directly to the game.

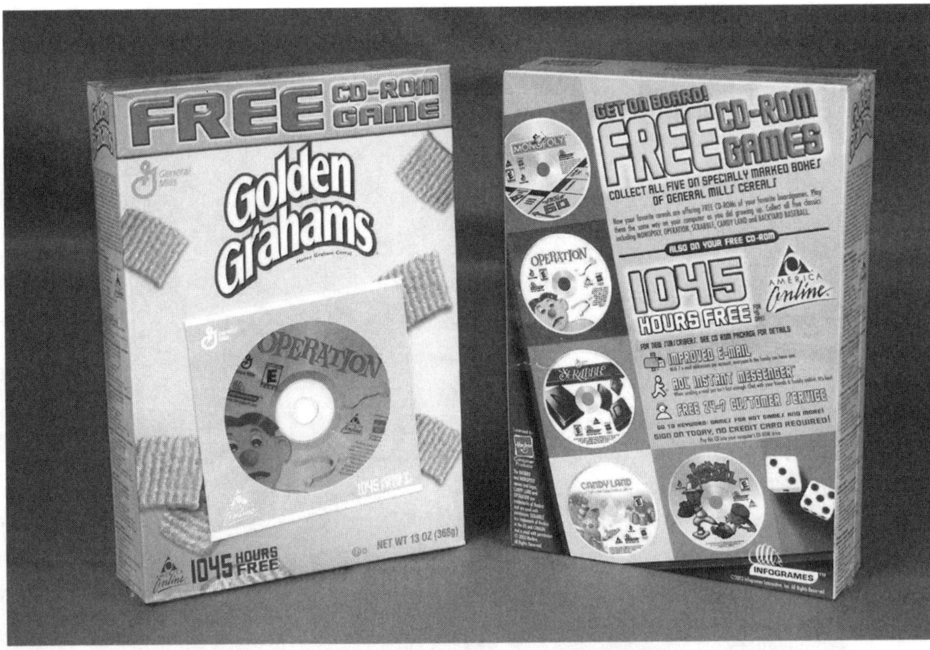

FIGURE 0.2 Buy this box of Golden Grahams® and get a free CD-ROM. Photo by Vic Cherubini, epic software group, inc.

For those games that require multiple players, a sense of community is created and players feel they are part of something more important that just the game itself. Game enthusiasts—who may not find your message in more traditional media easily—seek out hot new games and quickly drive traffic to your site.

Although banner ads have not fulfilled the expectations of those who paid dearly for them, pop-up Advergames appear to be more successful. Challenging the viewer's knowledge and competitive nature, a game can often be tempting enough to take a shot at winning (Figure 0.3).

WHO DEVELOPS ADVERGAMES?

Advergames are becoming very common today for two reasons. First, businesses are increasing their demand for this new advertising method. Second, just about anyone can create them. Advergame budgets can range from a few thousand dollars to well into six figures. Everybody from major game development companies, to multimedia studios, to amateur computer users, to serious teens, can successfully develop an eye-catching and entertaining game—the only roadblock people face is lack of knowledge about how to go about creating one. That's where this book

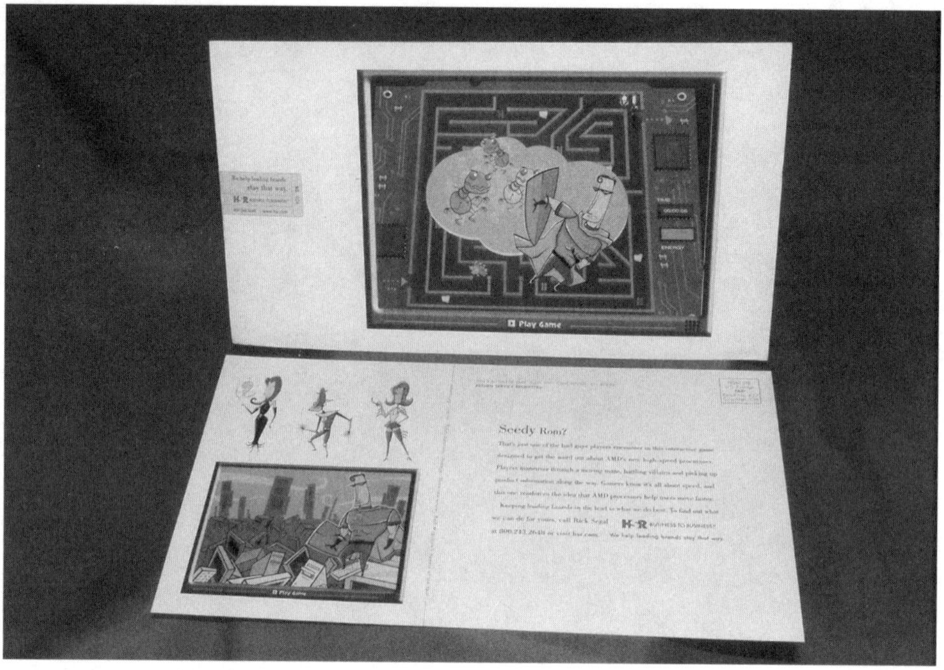

FIGURE 0.3 Postcard created by the HSR Agency—"Seedy ROM" is just one of the bad guys players encounter in this AMD Advergame. Photo by Vic Cherubini, epic software group, inc.

comes in. You don't have to be a professional, nor do you have to be the village geek to learn the process. This book has been created to teach you what tools you will need, how to use the software to create your games, and the conceptual process every game developer needs to go through to create a successful project. We introduce you to some of the major Advergaming developers, and give you a chance to build nine games from concept to completion. If you are thinking about having an Advergame built for your company, or are a budding game developer looking for a job, our directory introduces you to the key players. Most people who read this book will want to get dirty in the details to learn the finer points of Advergame creation. So, before we go much further, let's take a look at the two programs that are used to develop most Advergames—Macromedia® Flash™ MX 2004 and Macromedia® Director® MX.

WHAT TOOLS ARE USED TO DEVELOP ADVERGAMES?

ON THE CD

The two most popular tools used for developing Advergames are Macromedia Flash MX 2004 and its big brother, Macromedia Director MX. Evaluation copies of both programs are found on the CD-ROM that accompanies this book. In Chapter 2, Tools of the Trade: Macromedia Flash MX 2004 and Director MX, we provide you with the information you need to understand each program and to determine which is best for the Advergame application you want to build. In some cases, you find the best way to build your game is by using both tools, so we have devoted a separate chapter for each design to get you quickly into these programs.

OVERVIEW OF THE CHAPTERS

Chapter 1, Advergaming Components, introduces you to the components that make up an Advergame. The chapter discusses the two main aspects—branding and gameplay—followed by a case study to illustrate a real-world Advergaming situation that takes these two key components into account.

Chapter 2, Tools of the Trade: Macromedia Flash MX 2004 and Director MX, is an introduction to the tools available for Advergaming development. The chapter focuses on two programs, Macromedia Flash MX 2004 and Director MX, and provides useful information that can be used to determine which application is best for your Advergame.

Chapter 3, Macromedia Director MX, is a basic introduction to Macromedia Director MX. The chapter takes you through the program and introduces you to the graphical interface and the Director MX programming language, Lingo™.

Chapter 4, Macromedia Flash MX 2004, is a basic introduction to Macromedia Flash. The chapter takes you through this powerful program and introduces you to the graphical interface and the Macromedia Flash scripting language, ActionScript™.

Chapter 5, The Concept: Conceptualizing an Advergame from the Ground Up, begins the actual process of creating an Advergame. The chapter focuses on the conceptual half of the development process, in which all the planning occurs. It discusses everything from identifying your product through choosing a game and designing its interface.

Chapter 6, The Creation: Building an Advergame, focuses on the actual development of the game. It begins with a guide on how to organize the game and guides you through converting your conceptual ideas into an actual product.

Chapter 7, The Launch: Getting the Word Out on Your Game, brings your game around to the crucial part of deploying your Advergame. You are introduced to the various mediums available for distribution, along with the advantages and disadvantages of each. The chapter also discusses techniques for publishing your game within Macromedia Flash MX 2004 and Director MX.

Chapter 8, The Results: Tracking Site Activity and Measuring Success, is a resource for understanding and evaluating the effectiveness of your Advergame. First, the various statistics for evaluating your game are discussed, and then the available technologies are discussed.

Chapter 9, epic Cosmetics, takes you through the development process of the epic Cosmetics game. epic Cosmetics is an Advergame that showcases a new line of makeup that has recently been released by allowing the player to "make over" a virtual model.

Chapter 10, epic Realtor's Strongest Link, takes you through the development process of epic Realtor's Strongest Link. The Strongest Link game was created to increase awareness about the company, its history, and its services through a quiz game show.

Chapter 11, Mutt Chow Match-Up, takes you through the development process of Mutt Chow Match-Up. Mutt Chow Match-Up is a memory game that has the player flip over cards to create matching pairs of dogs and dog food products.

Chapter 12, Spray a Bug, takes you through the development process of Spray a Bug. Spray a Bug is a "Whack-A-Mole" style game in which the player wields a can of Bug Bee Gone bug spray and uses it on various insects that pop out of holes in the machine.

Chapter 13, Cellular Shuffle, takes you through the development process of Cellular Shuffle. Cellular Shuffle is a puzzle game in which the player has to slide tiles to create a graphic of a new line of epic Cellular Phones.

Chapter 14, Tasty Tic-Tac-Toe, takes you through the development process of E&E's Tasty Tic-Tac-Toe. E&E's Tasty Tic-Tac-Toe is a classic game of tic-tac-toe that is played with E&E candies instead of the traditional Xs and Os.

Chapter 15, epic Holiday Shoppe, takes you through the development process of epic Holiday Shoppe. epic Holiday Shoppe is a memory game that has the player follow a sequence of notes that are sung by a set of nutcrackers to earn a coupon for a discount at the store.

Chapter 16, High Voltage Pinball, takes you through the development process of High Voltage Pinball. High Voltage Pinball is a pinball machine that showcases the power of epic Batteries.

Chapter 17, Blasteroids, takes you through the development process of Blasteriods. Blasteroids is a tribute to the arcade classic *Asteroids* that involved a spaceship flying around and destroying asteroids with its lasers. The Blasteroids game harnesses the power of epic Drill Bits as you fly a ship that launches bits to destroy asteroids.

Chapter 18, Advergaming Developer's Guide, is the Advergaming Developer's Guide that goes into finding a company to develop an Advergame for you or going into the business yourself. This chapter includes a case study of an independent Advergame developer who shares some tips, tools, and techniques he has learned over the years.

Chapter 19, Interview and Case Study—Blockdot, is an interview with Blockdot, a development company that has earned multiple distinctions over the past eight years. Their founders boast many successes and work with over a score of Fortune 500 companies.

Chapter 20, Interview and Case Study—YaYa Media Inc., is an interview with YaYa Media Inc., who is responsible for creating the games you may have played on the Chrysler®, Siemens®, Paramount®, K-Mart®, Burger King®, Honda®, and Pepsi® Web sites.

Chapter 21, Interview and Case Study—AGENCY.COM, is an interview with AGENCY.COM, a company that provides services for electronic advertising. AGENCY.COM has offices all over the world and has created unique Advergames for a variety of platforms, including the Web and cell phones.

Chapter 22, A Guide to Advergame Development Companies, is a directory of Advergaming development companies that provide services in creating custom Advergames for businesses. If you want to have an Advergame developed for your company and would rather not do it yourself, this is the chapter for you!

1 Advergaming Components

In this chapter, we take a closer look at the two key aspects of both Advergaming branding and game development. If you are a game developer, the branding section helps you understand the basics and why building a brand is important to your customer (who is most likely a product or marketing manager). You learn the language of branding and why a company works so hard at creating and maintaining their brands. If you are a marketing manager planning to use an Advergame to promote your brand, the section on what makes a compelling game provides you with a number of ideas about how you can best showcase your product or service.

WHAT IS A BRAND?

> "In a world of information overload, brands become ever more important. Icons with virtual memory, brands save time. I may have intelligent agents that can go out and assemble pages of reports on every camcorder on the market, but I don't have time to read them. I'll buy Sony."
>
> —Steve Hayden, as quoted in *Advertising Age* magazine

A brand is a promise made by a company to consumers. It is a set of expectations and may foster a relationship that creates consumer preference. The purpose of creating a brand is to achieve consumer perception that your product or service is different and will deliver a sustainable competitive advantage for your company. A brand generates loyalty, even when your product or service is similar (in many cases, identical) to the other choices available to the consumer. A strong brand identity can help you outperform your competitors by providing the customer with an unspoken shorthand—a signpost. We are all busy, and when we are faced with making decisions, a well-regarded brand provides us with a level of confidence that is missing in a generic or unknown alternative.

The brand helps us quickly position the offering and determine if the cost of the product relative to the competition is a good value. It speeds up the decision-making process. Brand imagery can serve as a reminder the next time the customer is in a similar buying situation. A product or company logo can trigger a subconscious response to repeat the buying action. This can lead to brand loyalty and increased sales. Brands are built upon impressions received by the consumer over time. Every time a person reads an ad, hears a radio spot, sees a billboard, talks to a friend, or visits your Web site, you have a chance to build your brand image. These impressions must be clear, concise, and sustained consistently over time. Multiply this by thousands of people viewing them, and a brand is born.

Ask people about a brand, and they will typically describe a company's logo. Think "Coca-Cola®" and immediately the red and white flowing letters around their distinct bottle appear in your mind's eye. The logo is simply the image that has come to represent an entire experience and it is reflected in everything the brand does. The Coca-Cola brand has a well-earned reputation because it has a history of offering value, convenience, choice, relevance, reassurance, and satisfaction.

Branding is everywhere, and can be used by a variety of organizations:

- Nonprofit groups to garner gifts and donations
- Municipalities to build support for a bond issue
- Companies to increase sales and profits
- Cities to attract business investment or tourists
- Schools to attract the best facility and students, and to gain support from their alumni

Branding is all about building a relationship with your customer. It's a positive relationship based on trust rather than someone just trying to sell you something. And once your customers have used your brand and the product is delivered according to their expectations, you can use the brand itself to reinforce and help develop an ongoing relationship.

Although entire books have been written about the subject, we just touch on some of the more common terms and aspects of branding that you'll likely come across.

Brands are built around a *core proposition* that ties together everything you want your customer to understand and remember about your brand. Your core proposition includes the positioning, the brand personality, and what makes the product unique. (Brand managers use the term *USP*, which stands for *unique selling proposition.*) When customers can relate to your product, understand why it is distinct, and, at the same time, understand how it meets their functional and emotional needs, your core proposition is a solid one.

In addition, brand managers often use the term *brand equity* to represent the monetary sum for the intangible brand value that is separate from the worth of a given product or service. When a company decides to sell a division, the premium it receives from a willing buyer over the cost of the physical assets being sold is the brand equity. Branding is so valuable that it sometimes appears on a company's balance sheet. To drive home the point, it is estimated that the Coca-Cola brand alone is worth an additional $70 billion over the underlying value of its assets (bottling plants, trucks, and so on)!

Companies often build strong *corporate brands* by identifying or creating characteristics that apply to all their product lines. On the other hand, some firms choose *individual brand* identities for each of their products. Proctor & Gamble is an example of a company that does both well. All of their products benefit from their strong corporate brand, but each individual product also enjoys its own clear identity and personality, appealing to a specific market segment (Crest®, Max Factor®, Head & Shoulders®, and so on).

There are also *national, multinational,* or *global brands.* A brand owner with a product that is distributed in more than one country may use different brand names for the same product in different regions of the world. Others prefer to use a single brand name and a single market positioning in every country in which the product is distributed. For example, Volvo®'s brand is synonymous with vehicle safety in countries around the world.

When the promise and impression of a brand do not match, you have a problem known as *brand gap*—the difference between what you were promised or led to believe about your purchase and what was actually delivered. When a promise is broken, consumers act in a very predictable way—they turn to alternative products they know and trust. And it is difficult to win them back, so avoiding any brand gaps is essential to a strong brand identity.

Building a Brand

In most cases, Advergaming clients have a well-established brand, and want to use the Advergame to build upon the messages already delivered through traditional media (print, TV, radio, and so on). Some clients also use an Advergame as part of their initial launch strategy. To understand how this works, it is helpful to review how a brand is established.

If consumers were to choose products in a strictly rational way, and all things were equal, only the least expensive products would be purchased. However, the world around us clearly shows this is not the case. A customer's rational needs are just one factor in the selection process. The way a customer perceives a product does not always occur at the conscious level. If you ask a customer why he or she purchased a specific product, he or she might typically give a rational answer. But if you were to probe deeper, you would find that feelings about products are often difficult to put into words. Often, there is a relationship that has been formed over a period of time that is purely emotional. Marketing managers conduct research to probe into the subconscious of consumers to uncover what is driving their buying decisions. A strong brand offers the consumer intangible benefits beyond the product itself. The brand has a personality, and a company must continuously support the brand personality to make it clear and consistent over time. If the brand offers the buyer something that is valued and the customer believes it is superior to other products, you now have the basis for brand preference. Now, let's take a closer look at these two equally important considerations—the functional and emotional aspects of the consumer's decision.

Functionally, the product has to be well-suited to perform the task at hand. The product must deliver functional benefits to meet the need, at least as well as the competition. A product cannot survive for the long run without performance. Although it may be easier to focus on the functional needs of your customer, do not underestimate the power of emotions in the buying process. The emotional needs include how the product fits with the customers' own beliefs about themselves and their world. Companies do not buy products—people buy products. A strong brand addresses the fear factor that comes with a buying decision. People buy products and services that reflect the lifestyle and activities that are in tune with their own self-image (or the self-image they hope to project). If you are trying to project a perception of being hip and cool with your brand, everything about your Advergame should echo these qualities. Doing anything less with your game simply dilutes your other brand-building activities and confuses the consumer. A well-designed Advergame emotionally reinforces the brand image. By ensuring that the theme of the game, along with the visual elements and gameplay, are in concert with the brand image, an Advergame can be a very powerful tool in the arsenal of any brand manager.

The process of identifying customer needs is of fundamental importance in developing a new or existing brand. Focus groups, surveys, and listening carefully to the customer, with no preconceived opinions about what is important, should help uncover those needs. When building a brand, it is important to include a tone and personality that demonstrate your understanding of your customers' needs.

Branding Resources

Looking for more information on branding? Here are three resources worth checking out:

- For brand managers trying to meet with the movers and shakers in the world of branding, there is no better place than the BrandSlam Summit. This "By Invitation Only" conference is hosted by Marcus Evans, and is designed to facilitate networking and information exchange among the select group of attendees. Conference sessions include speakers from companies such as Coca-Cola, Gillette Company, Levi Strauss & Co., Bank of America Corporation, and dozens of other high-profile advertisers. Check out details about upcoming summits at *www.brandslam-summit.com.*

- To learn about the latest developments in branding, get a subscription to *BrandWeek Magazine*, or check them out on the Web at *www.brandweek.com*. You'll read about the latest marketing campaigns and find a number of helpful marketing resources. For example, the Brandweek Directory is an excellent reference source for information on U.S. consumer brands and their marketing companies. It contains over 6,700 brand identities with important information, such as key personnel, media expenditures, and creative agencies of record.
- One exhaustive online resource for branding information is Interbrand's Web site (*www.brandchannel.com*). You can join in on lively debates about brand issues on the discussion board, read reviews about books on branding, find a job in the industry, or search through hundreds of papers on the subject.

Successful branding requires all aspects of communication to agree with each other and align with corporate identity standards. When the message is focused and consistent across all media, your brand will be as strong as possible. Consumers will naturally try to determine and define your brand. Remember—if you do not manage the branding process, your customers and competitors will. Now that we have a basic understanding of branding, let's take a look at the second most important element of an Advergame—the game itself.

WHAT MAKES A GREAT COMPUTER GAME?

Think back to the time when you first discovered video games—the thrill and excitement of actually interacting with some element on the screen was enthralling. Now, stop and think about your favorite video game. What made it so special? Was it the graphics, the action, the story, the music, or a combination of things that simply immersed you in the experience? Why would you spend hour after hour in front of your computer screen being transformed into an altered state? You can almost hear your mom calling from the other room "Stop playing that stupid game and do your homework. No one is going to pay you to play video games!" Today, you can indeed make a living playing computer games, and even though it is hard work, developing computer games can be very rewarding. Let's take a look at some of the elements that go into great game design and answer the question—"What makes a great computer game?"

Gameplay

Ask veteran gamers to describe in a single word what makes their favorite game, and, most likely, they will say, "Gameplay." Gameplay describes the interaction between the player and game. Simply put—it's the overall experience you get from playing the game. A great game is engaging, not too hard to learn, visually appealing, and, most of all, fun to play. If you dream about the game when you are away from the computer, or click the Replay button even when your eyes are closing and your head is nodding off from lack of sleep, you know this game has great gameplay. A great example is the granddaddy of all video games—*Pong*. On its basic level, *Pong* is a game that is simply four walls, two lines to represent paddles, and a ball that bounces back and forth around the screen. The game was simple, straightforward, weak on graphics, but had amazing gameplay that kept people lined up at arcade machines. You become immersed in the experience. If asked how long you have been playing, your guess may actually be half of the real time you have been in front of the screen.

It may be easy to confuse gameplay with screen graphics, a specific game engine, or the underlying story, but these are mere elements to the game. Gameplay equals interactivity. Gameplay is a series of challenges that provide you with choices that result in rewards or consequences. Often, you are provided with incomplete information, so both luck and logic may play a role in your success. Keep in mind that gameplay is very subjective in nature, and one person's definition of a great game may be far different than another's.

The concept of gameplay applies to every game in existence, from the newest 3D shooter to the now-ancient, 8-bit video and arcade games. Advergames are no different. The gameplay must be just as addicting, if not more so, compared to the newest games around. They cannot rely on fast computers and the latest hardware to become amazing, but instead must work on a broad range of machines, while remaining fun to play. The gameplay involved in Advergames tends to be simpler and more straightforward when compared to regular games. All users in your target audience must be able to quickly learn the controls of your game and be able to enjoy it.

Graphics

Although gameplay may be the most important aspect of your game, graphics also play a crucial role in capturing attention and getting someone to try it out. In today's gaming world, graphics and gameplay go hand in hand when creating those addictive games that keep you mesmerized. Graphics serve two purposes: first, to create a stunning appearance that attracts the attention of new people, and second, to help create an immersive experience that users love. Today's greatest games don't look like a mass of copied and pasted art, but rather involve a cohesive design that was created specifically to work with the game. Dark characters are placed in gritty settings, whereas cartoon characters are placed in simpler, more colorful atmospheres. To create an appealing game, a designer has to ensure that nothing is out of place and everything is aesthetically pleasing. Never underestimate the importance of great "eye candy."

Advergames are not expected to have the same quality artwork that is seen in games today. As with regular game designs, graphics are used to set up the atmosphere of a game and to help provide an immersive experience. Whereas regular games are using real 3D layouts and complex layouts, Advergames can and, depending on your layout, should utilize attractive, yet simpler art. Incorporating complex 3D models into an Advergame pushes the game's file size higher and higher, resulting in longer download times for online Advergames. In addition, regular games tend to place high demands on a computer's processing power, often utilizing 100% of both the processor and graphics card while taking up a lot of RAM. With an Advergame, there is no room for taxing system resources, as most people are looking for Advergames that are easy to start and also allow them to have other things going on in the background. Finally, the problem of accessibility still exists. If everyone had a fast computer released in the last year, 3D models would not be a problem; however, many people are still using older computers or working with slow Internet connections. If you create a game that is too intensive for these machines to handle, you're immediately limiting your audience and crippling the effectiveness of your Advergame.

Music and Sound Effects

The next time you play your favorite video game, turn off the sound. Immediately, the mood changes, and the game has lost something very special. The addition of sound effects and carefully selected music gets the player emotionally involved in the action. When the music matches the level of action on-screen, it's truly a beautiful thing. Try playing a video game with the express purpose of listening to the music and hearing how the developer enriched the experience through the addition of sound. For additional inspiration, pay close attention to movie scores, and see if you notice that some of the same techniques used in films are applied directly to video games. Unlike a scene in a film, game music has to evolve and adapt to reflect the player's actions. Sometimes, sound quality is sacrificed for the flexibility that comes with triggering digital sounds directly from the computer's sound chip. "Interactive music" must be flexible enough to be looped, and unlike a movie, it may vary in length from player to player. The key is to keep the momentum up and not make it boring.

The only difference that exists with sound and music between Advergames and real games is the quality at which it is delivered. In regular games, sound can be offered at the highest quality, in a variety of methods, including quadraphonic and surround sound, but in Advergames, you typically have the same restraints that exist with graphics. Advergames deployed online need to remain wary of file size, and all Advergame developers need to keep in mind the users' system capabilities. The tools used to create Advergames may also be very limiting, not even supporting higher-quality sound.

Storyline

Another aspect that gamers look at is the game's storyline. Does it have a long, involved story that becomes an immersive experience, or does it completely lack a story and rely solely on gameplay and graphics to keep players interested? Depending on gamers' moods, they tend to go for one or the other. A storyline is most commonly achieved through one of two ways. The first is to create a game that takes hours to complete, with a storyline so developed that it is almost like reading a book. The game ensnares users by keeping them immersed in an ever-developing plotline with twists and turns that mimic the cliff-hangers in best-selling novels. They rely on the desire to "find out what happens next" to keep the gamer coming back. The other option is to create a series of games that build a story. This method is much more ideal for an Advergame because you can create installments to keep people coming back to see the next game. This technique is used in Webisodes and Web comics that release a new episode or strip on a regular basis. It is most effective if you have offers or content that changes often and want your clients to remain aware of what is going on.

CASE STUDY

Now that you have a basic understanding of the two key elements of an Advergame—branding and game design—let's take a quick look at a case study example. Back in 1999, Deepend developed a classic Advergame for the advertising agency Michaelides & Bednash and their client Tango®. Tango is a soft drink company that wanted to generate awareness and promote their brand. Deepend created a Macromedia® Shockwave® game called *Gotan Goes Fizzy* (*www.deepend.com/deny/games/*), shown in Figure 1.1, for this purpose. The following list states the six key objectives the team established at the beginning of the project. Notice how both branding and game design elements were incorporated into the application:

- To create a fun Web experience with "sticky" content
- To drive consumers through to purchasing and trial
- To generate both brand and product loyalty
- To maximize awareness of the Tango brand on- and offline by:
  - Creating a need and desire for repeat visits and to generate public interest
  - Creating an effective viral game that would appeal to the specified target audience (age 16 to 34)
- To integrate, leverage, and support this campaign with all other marketing and advertising materials
- To drive gamers through affiliate and partner media (Web sites and publications)

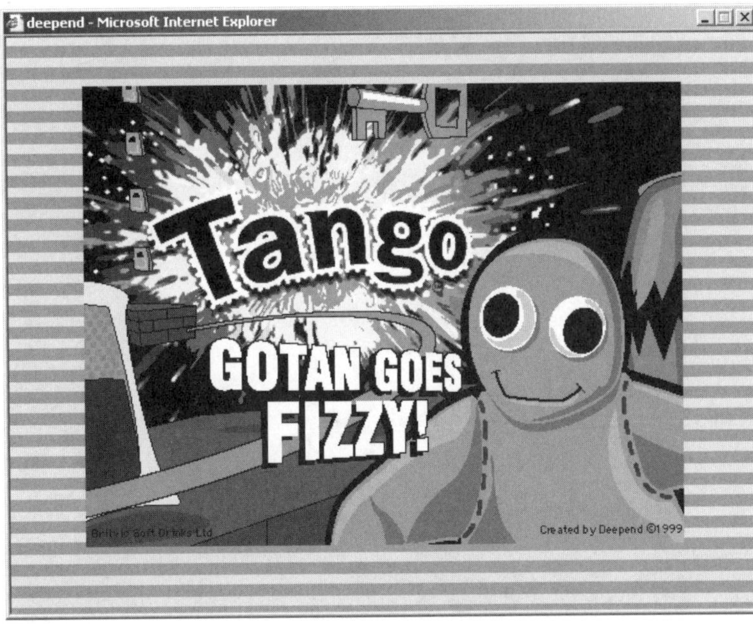

FIGURE 1.1 Tango splash page. © 2003. Reprinted with permission from Deepend.com.

Deepend created a fun Web experience in line with the objectives of this project by driving gamers through affiliated Web sites and through promotions in magazines such as *FHM*. On the partner Web sites were "keys" needed to unlock later levels of the game. It was crucial for a game player to visit these sites to progress through the game shown in Figure 1.2.

The results of the Tango Advergame included:

- An increase in average browsing time from 4 to 15 minutes
- An average game player involvement of 32 hours
- A significant increase in brand exposure time
- A marked increase in traffic through all affiliate and partner sites

SUMMARY

By embedding a brand into a video game, marketers are discovering a new way to draw attention to their products and services. Understanding branding and the el-

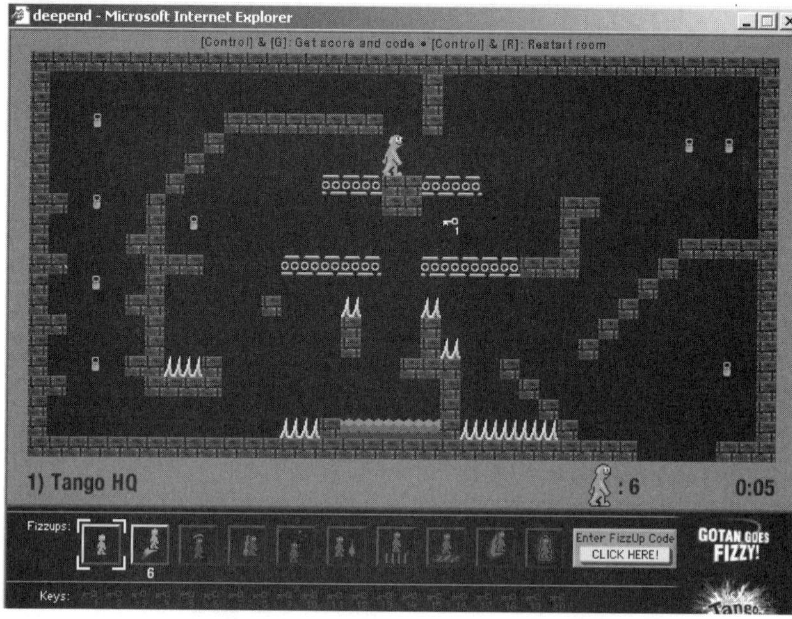

FIGURE 1.2 Tango game interface. © 2003. Reprinted with permission from Deepend.com.

ements of a great video game are critical to success. Advergaming blends branding with interactive video games and is quickly becoming an important tool in the arsenal of product and marketing managers.

Advergames are a form of viral marketing in which "word of mouse" rewards customers when they help with some of the heavy lifting that comes with releasing a new product or promoting an existing brand. At one extreme is a game that simply slaps a logo on the screen or displays a banner ad. At the other extreme is a game that is created from the ground up, specifically to showcase the unique features of the brand and immerse the player in the message.

Advergames represent a great opportunity for individual game developers trying to break into the industry, as well as multimedia development companies that want to extend their offerings into the game arena. This emerging sector of the game industry also merits serious consideration by advertisers who are looking for addictive content to build brand awareness and sales.

In the chapters that follow, we demonstrate how to use the basic concepts of branding and video gaming covered in this chapter. Read, experiment, design, develop, play, and, most important, have some fun creating your brand-focused game. In the end, having fun and building a buzz about a brand is what Advergaming is all about.

PART

I The Tools

2 Tools of the Trade: Macromedia Flash MX 2004 and Director MX

When undertaking a project, whether it is building a house or a barbeque grill, the most fundamental and important part is having the right tools. If you don't have the proper sized nails or wrenches, any attempts you make will be futile. Advergaming is no different. To successfully develop and capitalize off of an idea, you must be able to present it in the strongest and most efficient way possible. With Advergaming, Macromedia Flash MX 2004 and Director MX are the two main pieces of software that are used to create games. Both programs give you the power to create fluid multimedia applications with dynamic events and unparalleled interactivity for both the Web and CD-ROMs.

WHAT'S THE DIFFERENCE?

You may be asking, "Why does it matter, don't they both do the same thing?" The answer is both yes and no. Although either program is capable of creating the game you want in most situations, each title has its own strengths and weaknesses that should be taken into account. Picking the program that works best for you and your audience is crucial, so don't jump in blindly; we've done the research for you—all you need to do is read.

Both programs have recently undergone major overhauls in their layout interfaces. They use a panel organizational system, as shown in Figures 2.1 and 2.2, that devotes individual panels to sets of tools. These panels can easily be arranged, grouped, and docked to arrange your workspace exactly as needed.

Macromedia Flash MX 2004 and Director MX use a timeline-based layout in the authoring mode in which everything exists in a linear progression off the main timeline. From there, each program allows you to branch out and add any level of

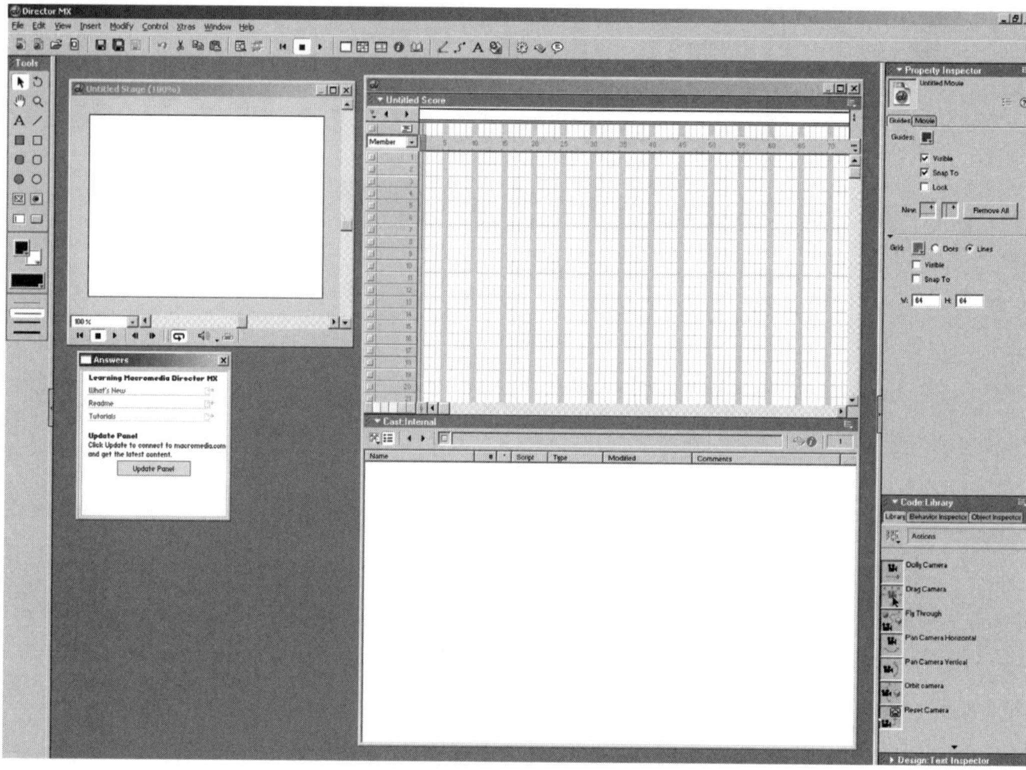

FIGURE 2.1 Default Director MX interface.

interactivity you want. In addition, they both have the ability to import graphic and sound files to be implemented onto the timeline. Both of them allow you to export movies for the Internet, and view them with a player or in a standalone executable. Throughout this book, we refer to the Director MX and Flash MX 2004 files as "movies," much like you refer to Microsoft Word® "documents" and Microsoft Excel® "worksheets." With so many shared features, the two seem like nearly identical programs; however, the next couple of sections explain the uses and applications of each program.

Macromedia Director MX

Macromedia Director MX has been used for years in kiosks and CD-ROMs. Its powerful features make it an ideal program to create interfaces and complex programs because it supports a broad range of imported media, including photo-quality images, long video and audio, animations, and even 3D models. Director MX moves beyond simply playing back imported media, and provides ways to con-

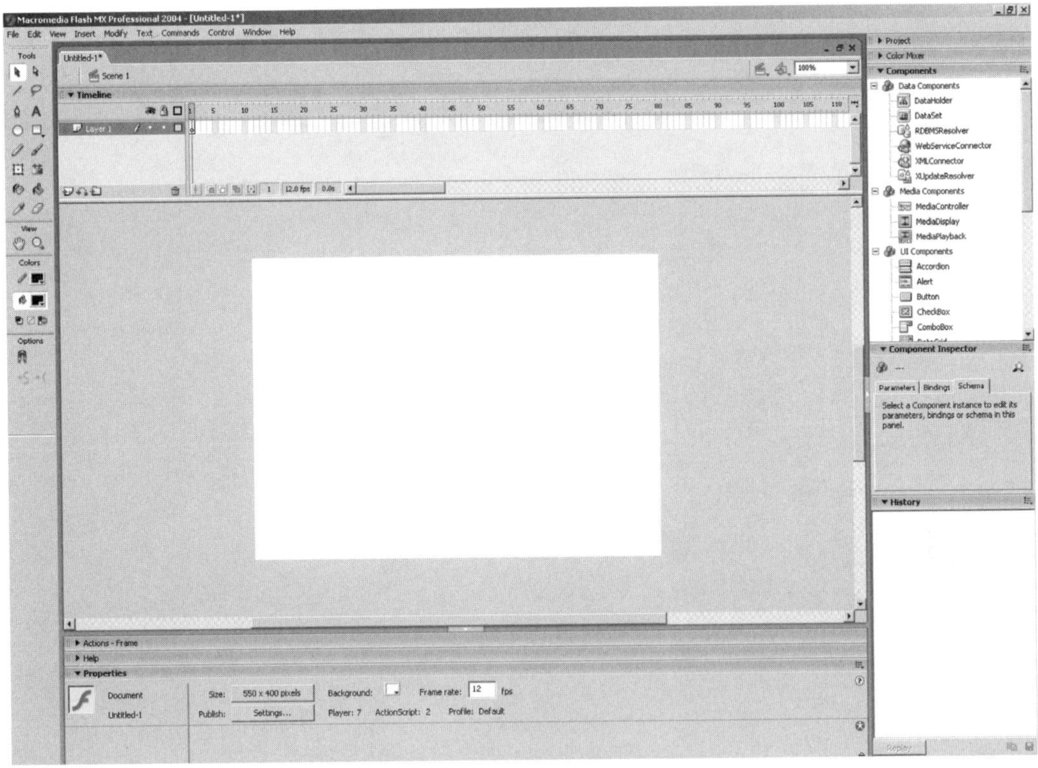

FIGURE 2.2 Default Macromedia Flash MX 2004 interface.

trol almost every aspect using Lingo, the programming language in Director MX. It is typically used for very involved presentations and databases because it is able to hold and display hundreds of megabytes of data and media without bringing the application to a halt for end users. Director is rarely used to create content, but is instead used to manipulate and arrange many multimedia files into one cohesive presentation. It also provides access to the user's hard drive and peripherals, such as joysticks, to provide maximum flexibility in anything you need. One of the newest features is its support for 3D models and animation. Now, you can actually import the models you create from any major 3D modeler and use Lingo to manipulate them.

On the programming side of things, Director has a very easy-to-understand language for professional programmers and people who have never touched code in their life. Lingo has been developed for many years and has been influenced by a host of other languages, including JavaScript and Visual Basic. As a result, Lingo has become a very logical language that allows a programmer to "read" code much like

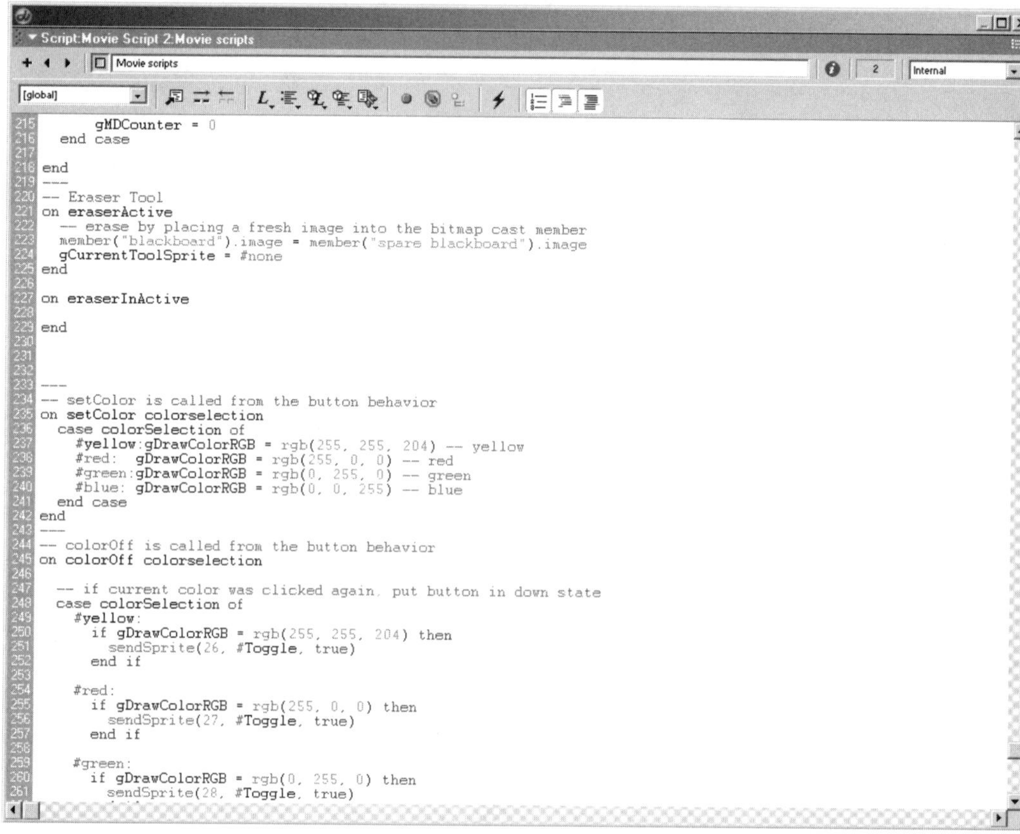

FIGURE 2.3 An example of Lingo code.

they would read English, as you can see in Figure 2.3. Rather than focus on symbols to direct code, it uses conversational English in many situations. One might think that a programming language that based itself around a written language would be limited in nature, but the opposite is true. Lingo is the most robust and powerful language available when compared to similar applications—it allows full manipulation of the timeline, interactivity, data tracking, animations, effects, animations, and 3D models.

When it comes to Advergames, Director MX allows you to include stunning sound, video, and 3D in your games that cannot be achieved using any other tool.

Macromedia Flash MX 2004

Macromedia Flash MX 2004 is the ideal program for Web authoring. It is a vector-based application that has been designed to create small files for presentation on the

Web. In addition to its small size, the content can be streamed, allowing the end user to view your movie as it downloads. Unlike Director, Macromedia Flash MX 2004 has a strong focus on the creation side of application development, allowing you to create all your graphics and drawings easily, right inside the program. Newer versions of Flash MX 2004 have stressed the need to provide powerful tools for programmers and developers by improving the capabilities of ActionScript, the scripting language used within Flash MX. Flash MX also allows you to import video so that you can add interactivity and take it to new levels. Flash is ideal for almost any situation in which your target audience will be viewing your Advergame over the Web.

Unlike most software on the market today, Flash utilizes a different technology to create its drawings and graphics. Traditional imaging software creates images as raster graphics, which are graphics that are a mosaic of pixels with various color and alpha values. A vector graphic is composed of a series of vectors that can be scaled to any resolution and never lose quality because they are mathematically based. Figure 2.4 illustrates the difference between a raster and vector graphic. When viewing them normally, the graphics are nearly identical; however, when you zoom in closer, the raster graphic becomes pixilated, whereas the vector graphic remains perfect.

As with Lingo, ActionScript has come a long way over previous versions. It has evolved from a weak method of navigating around the timeline to a full language with a dedicated editor and powerful capabilities. Because Macromedia Flash MX 2004 is a Web-oriented application, it is no wonder that Macromedia chose to

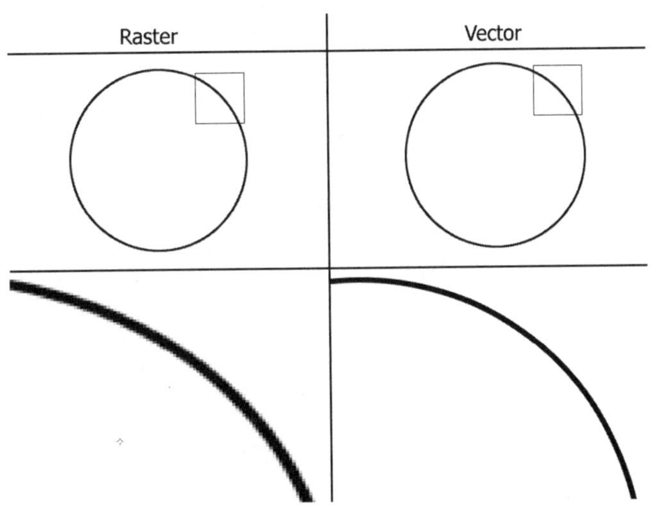

FIGURE 2.4 A comparison of raster and vector graphics.

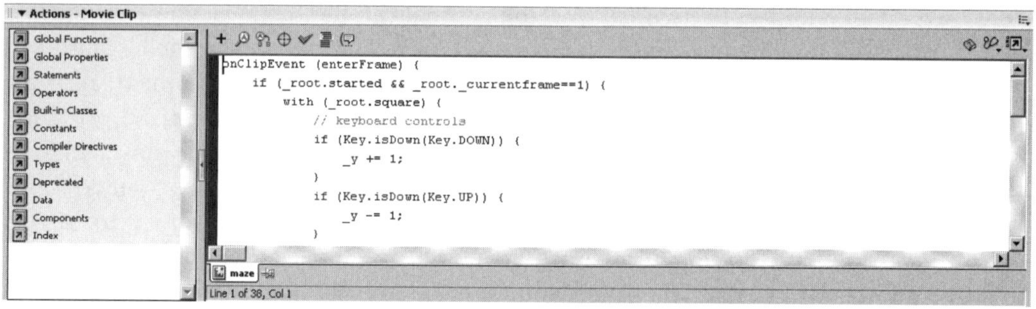

FIGURE 2.5 The ActionScript editor.

completely base the language off of the ECMA-262 Specification—the standard for JavaScript coding. Basing ActionScript off of JavaScript allows the core group of users to have an easy time adjusting to the language. ActionScript is a straightforward language that lets you learn however much you need to get by. You need not learn everything there is to know about it in order to use it. The editor comes in two modes, Normal Mode and Expert Mode. Normal Mode is a simple interface that allows you to choose your actions from a list, and fill in blanks to implement your code, as shown in Figure 2.5. This is useful for people who are new to programming because it makes the entire process a series of mouseclicks. Flash is an amazing tool with powerful features that will not leave you underpowered.

A SIDE-BY-SIDE COMPARISON

Although both programs may seem perfect for your game, several factors will help you decide which is best for you. Often, after trying both programs, people develop an affinity for one and begin to use it all the time. Table 2.1 will help you determine which program you want to use.

TABLE 2.1 Features of Macromedia Flash MX 2004 and Director MX

Macromedia Flash MX 2004	*Macromedia Director MX*
Vector-based (smaller file size)	Raster graphics
Great for creating graphics	Best with imported media
Best for Web	Best for CD-ROMs; good for Web
No 3D support	Real-time 3D support
Handles small video	Handles video of any size very well

TRYING OUT THE SOFTWARE

ON THE CD

Knowing the differences between the two programs is one thing, but you may not want to pick one until you actually get your hands dirty and see how they work. On the CD-ROM that accompanies this book, you will find trial versions of both Macromedia Flash MX 2004 and Macromedia Director MX. These trials are exactly the same as the full programs, but have a 30-day time limit from the first use. Chapters 3 and 4 (Macromedia Director MX and Macromedia Flash MX 2004, respectively) of this book give you a basic introduction to the workings of each program, so don't feel intimidated by either one. Even if you already know one program, install the other, try it out, and see what you can do—you might be surprised!

SUMMARY

For now, think of Macromedia Flash MX 2004 as a tool that is used by over a million professionals to deliver high-power multimedia presentations over the Web. Applications developed in Flash require the Flash Player to be installed on the user's computer, and the good news is that over a half-billion machines have the Flash Player loaded and ready to go.

Macromedia Director MX is a full featured authoring tool that has been the program of choice for CD-ROM developers for over 10 years. With the advent of the Internet, Macromedia released a feature within Director MX that was specifically created to deliver rich content (animation, high-quality graphics, and sound) at a fraction of the file size needed for a traditional Director program over the Web. They called it "Shockwave," and just like Flash, the Shockwave Player must be installed on the user's machine.

Flash and its big brother, Director, are the two most popular tools used for developing Advergames. In the next two chapters, we provide you with the information you need to develop a foundation in each program. In some cases, you will find the best way to build your game is to use both tools—utilizing the graphical strengths of Flash and the interfacing strengths of Director.

3 Macromedia Director MX

Macromedia Director MX is a powerful, yet surprisingly simple, authoring tool that allows users to create interactive Web content and/or standalone applications with minimal effort. Most multimedia development utilities are set up to produce either simple, noninteractive presentations or powerful applications that require a great deal of skill and effort to develop. Macromedia Director MX falls somewhere in the middle, requiring comparatively little programming knowledge to produce multimedia applications of varying complexity. As is the case with most authoring environments, the interface of Director MX can be split into two parts: the graphical user interface (GUI) and the application programming interface (API). In the remainder of this chapter, we discuss both parts in detail to ensure that you have a good working knowledge of Director.

LEARNING THE GRAPHICAL USER INTERFACE

With all its various parts, the interface of Director MX might seem overwhelming at first glance. But if you familiarize yourself with the GUI one piece at a time, you'll see that it's really not so complicated. Each major component serves a specific and unique purpose. You do not need every window open all the time, but because they work so closely together, you should try to make room for at least the Stage, Score, Cast, and Property Inspector windows.

Like most applications, Director MX features a set of menus at the top of its GUI that gives access to virtually all its commands. Notice that many of the menu options have keyboard shortcuts listed along the left side of the menus. If you find yourself frequently selecting a particular option from the menu system, you may want to save yourself some time and memorize that command's keyboard shortcut. The Toolbar provides another way to access some of the more common commands. To save your Director MX movie source file at any time, you can choose Save from the File menu, hold down the Control key and type "S," or click the Save button on the Toolbar. You should try to save your movie as often as possible to minimize the chance of losing work in the event your computer crashes or shuts down unexpectedly.

Using the Stage

The Stage is like a canvas that contains all the visual elements of a Director movie. Much like its theatrical counterpart, the Stage of Director is the part of a finished application that contains all the elements visible to the audience, or in this case, the user. The Stage itself is simply a solid rectangle that appears behind the movie's visual components, or sprites. As you work within Director, you will probably notice the Stage being the focus of your attention more often than not. If you do not see the Stage window within Director MX, click the Stage button on the Toolbar, as shown in Figure 3.1.

To play any Director movie, you must first create at least one sprite. A sprite is a media item (such as a text field or an image) that exists on the Stage. One simple method of creating sprites is to use the Tool Palette. If you cannot find the Tool Palette within your workspace, select Tool Palette from the Window menu. To add a text sprite to the Stage, click the Text button on the Tool Palette, and then click on the Stage. This creates the sprite and allows you to enter some text. If you want to change the appearance of your text, select it and choose Font from the Modify menu. Director opens the Font dialog box, as shown in Figure 3.2.

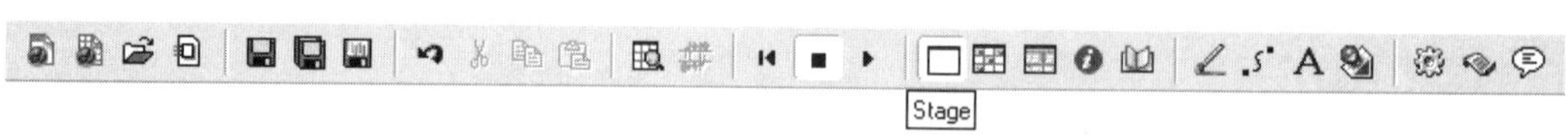

FIGURE 3.1 The Toolbar's Stage button.

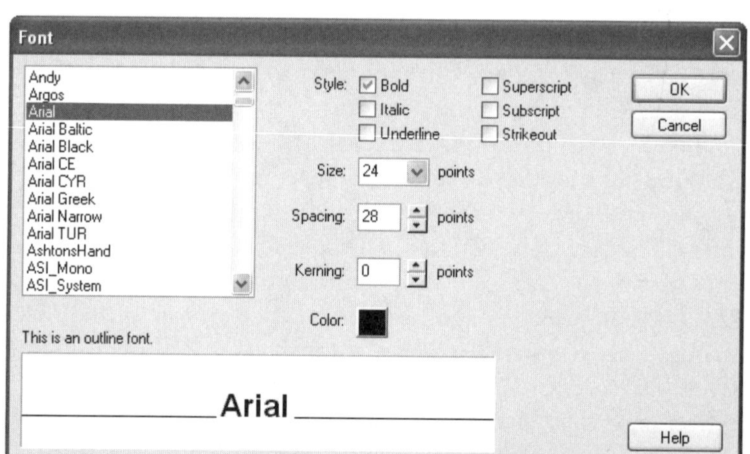

FIGURE 3.2 Modifying your text through the Font dialog box.

When you have finished editing the text, click an empty part of the Stage, and Director MX deselects your new sprite. Try dragging your sprite around the Stage to change its location and dragging its corners to change its dimensions. Notice, however, that you cannot directly change its height. This is because your text sprite has the default framing style of "Adjust to Fit." The easiest way to change this is through the Property Inspector.

Using the Property Inspector

The Property Inspector allows you to customize the properties of anything and everything within Director MX. You will probably use the Property Inspector at least as much as any other visual component of Director MX. You can choose to view the Property Inspector as a normal, free-floating window or docked, probably on the right side of your screen. If you do not see the Property Inspector within Director MX, click the Property Inspector button on the Toolbar, as shown in Figure 3.3.

Before you get too involved in creating your Director MX movie, you should make certain your Stage is set up the way you want it. Click the Movie tab of the Property Inspector to display such options as Stage size and color. You can choose any Stage size you want, but keep in mind that the resolution of some monitors is often as low as 640 by 480 pixels. Therefore, you should avoid making your movies any larger than this.

The Property Inspector can do much more than just modify your movie's global properties. You can also use it to modify sprites such as the text you created earlier. Select your text sprite within the Stage, and then click the Text tab of the Property Inspector. From here, you can change text properties such as framing style, as mentioned earlier. Now click the Sprite tab to display the more general sprite properties, and then click the Moveable button, as shown in Figure 3.4. This allows the user to drag the text around the screen as your movie plays.

To name your text field, click the Member tab of the Property Inspector and enter something into the Name field. You are not required to name such media elements in Director MX, but as your movies become increasingly complicated, you'll be glad that you developed the habit of keeping things nice and organized.

After making any major change to a movie in Director MX, you generally need to make certain it still functions as expected. Clicking the Play button on the Toolbar is a quick way to test your movie. Director MX uses the Stage to display your

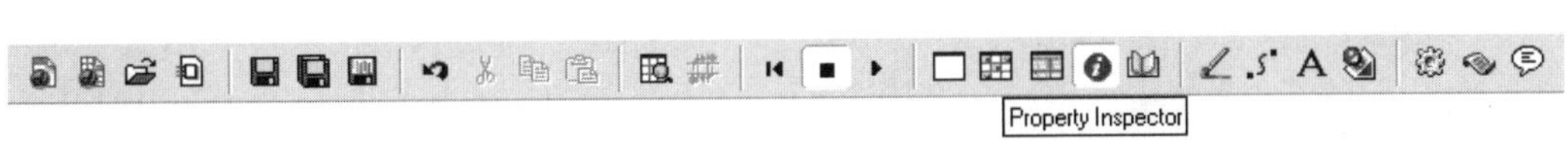

FIGURE 3.3 The Toolbar's Property Inspector button.

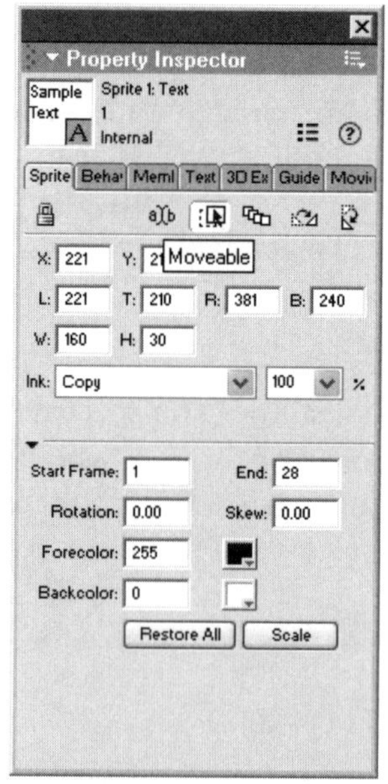

FIGURE 3.4 The Moveable button within the Sprite tab of the Property Inspector.

modified movie just as if it were an executable projector or Shockwave content on a Web site. Try playing your movie and making certain you are able to drag the text sprite. If your movie doesn't loop automatically, make certain the Control menu's Loop Playback option is selected. We more thoroughly cover testing and publishing later in this chapter.

Using the Score

The Score is the part of Director MX that separates it from ordinary application development tools. You can think of the Score as the place where Director MX stores all the sprites used in a particular movie. Furthermore, the position of these sprites within the Score determines when and in what order they will become active. The sprites themselves can be said to determine their position and appearance on the Stage, as these values are stored in sprite properties, which you can modify through the Property Inspector. From this perspective, the Score is quite essential. If you do not see the Score window within Director MX, click the Score Window button on the Toolbar, as shown in Figure 3.5.

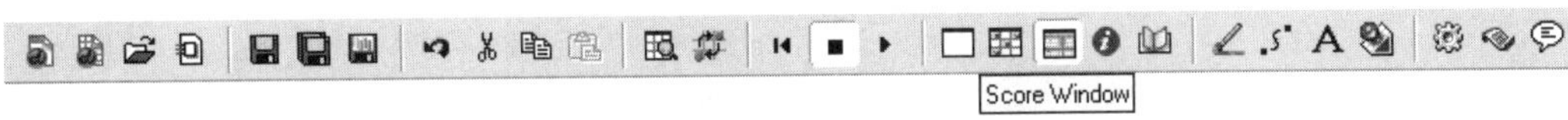

FIGURE 3.5 The Toolbar's Score Window button.

The Score consists of a large matrix of cells, each of which has the potential to contain a different sprite. The numbered rows of this matrix are called channels and are used to determine the layering of sprites and, if applicable, the order in which their attached programming code is executed. If you find yourself running low on sprite channels while working on a movie, this is an easy problem to correct. Simply go to the Movie tab of your Property Inspector and edit the Channels field. The Score updates its number of channels accordingly.

As a movie plays, the Score's playhead moves through its columns, or frames, displaying the contents of each on the Stage, one after another. Therefore, by changing the position or appearance of a sprite from one frame to the next, you can produce the effect of animation. In fact, by using the Score effectively, you could create an entire multimedia presentation without any programming knowledge. Generally speaking, however, the more interactive you want your final product to be, the more you will rely on programming code over simple frame-by-frame animation. Still, the Score is a very important tool for layering and organizing your movie's sprites.

To move a sprite using the Score window, it must be under the exclusive control of the Score. By default, all sprites are under Score control. However, the text sprite you created earlier is draggable and, therefore, is under the control of the user. Director MX ignores any movement you specify in the Score for this sprite unless you first disable its ability to be dragged. To do this, simply return to the Property Inspector's Sprite tab and click the Moveable button once more.

Now that you have returned your sprite to Score control, perform the following steps to create an animation using two keyframes.

1. Click the frame of the Score that lines up with the rightmost cell of your sprite (most likely frame 28), as shown in Figure 3.6.
2. Right-click the active cell of your sprite and choose Insert Keyframe.
3. Click a frame of the Score somewhere in the middle of your sprite.
4. Right-click the active cell of your sprite and choose Insert Keyframe.
5. Within the Stage, drag your sprite to a new location.

Return your movie to its first frame by clicking the Rewind button on the Toolbar and then play the movie to test it out. You should see your text sprite moving back and forth between its original location and the one you specified for the second keyframe you created.

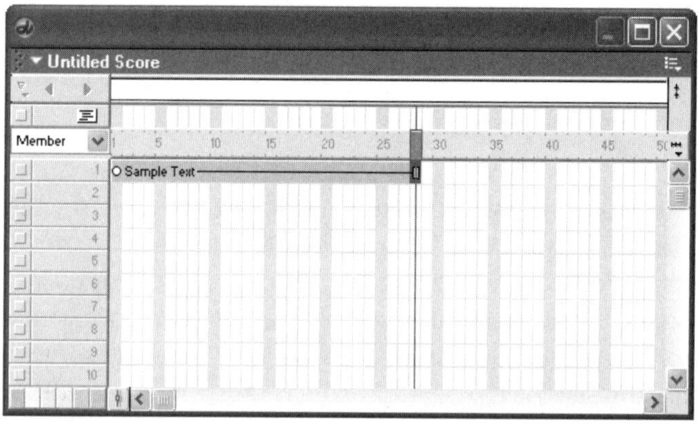

FIGURE 3.6 Moving the playhead to frame 28 of the Score.

Try creating more keyframes and changing the rotation and skew angles of your sprite at different keyframes. You can edit these values through the Rotation and Skew fields of the Behavior Inspector's Sprite sheet. Director MX creates a smooth transition, or tween, between your keyframes, provided they are far enough apart. You can tell Director MX exactly how to create these transitions by right-clicking your sprite and choosing Tweening.

By now, you may be wondering exactly which window stores the media elements with which you've been working. You know that the Stage cannot store media because its contents can vary from frame to frame. The Score can't either because programming code can create, change, and/or destroy sprites while a movie is playing. The component of Director MX that actually stores elements, such as text and graphics, is called the Cast window.

Working with Cast Members

Director MX uses groups called casts to store a movie's media elements and programming scripts. These items are called cast members. In every new movie, Director MX creates an empty cast named Internal. Until you get a bit more experience working with Director MX, you'll be alright just storing everything in the Internal cast. If you do not see the Cast window within Director MX, click the Cast Window button on the Toolbar, as shown in Figure 3.7.

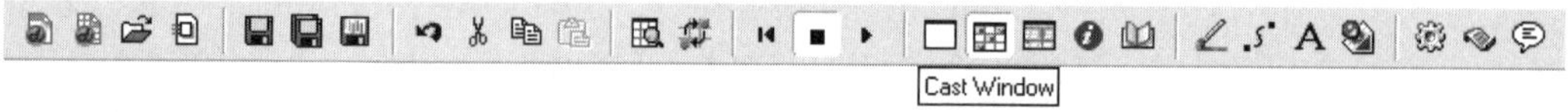

FIGURE 3.7 The Toolbar's Cast Window button.

Within the Cast window, you should see a cast member for the text you created earlier. Up to now, you've only been looking at a sprite instance of this cast member through the Stage and the Score. You can make as many sprites as you want from a single cast member. If you edit a cast member, all sprites created from it are affected. Along the same vein, deleting a cast member results in its sprites going blank. This may seem confusing at first, but you'll get the hang of it in no time.

The Cast window offers two display styles to suit your needs. The Thumbnail view arranges small previews of the cast members in numerical order. The List view sorts cast members by name and displays no thumbnail images. List view is more useful for finding a specific cast member by name, but should not be used all the time. You should keep your cast members organized in Thumbnail view, especially if you want your movie to access a cast member by number through programming code, as we discuss later in this chapter.

Although Director MX offers its own tools for creating various types of media and allows you to paste items directly into the Cast window, importing is often still the best method. For example, if you want to create a large number of cast members from image files, pasting each image into the Cast window separately would be extremely inconvenient. To import one or more media files into your Director MX movie, perform the following steps.

1. Click an empty spot in the Cast window.
2. Click the Import button on the Toolbar, as shown in Figure 3.8.
3. Navigate to a media file on your hard disk or this book's companion CD-ROM and double-click it to add it to the File list. Repeat this step to import multiple files.
4. Click Import.

ON THE CD

If you selected any image files, you may be presented with one or more Image Options dialog boxes. You may want to clear the Trim White Space checkbox and/or select the Same Settings for Remaining Images checkbox. When you import a media element into your movie, Director MX creates a cast member based on its filename. You may want to rename a cast member to ensure that it agrees with your standard naming conventions. It's a good idea to name all your cast members in a uniform manner so that you can later access them by name without running into trouble.

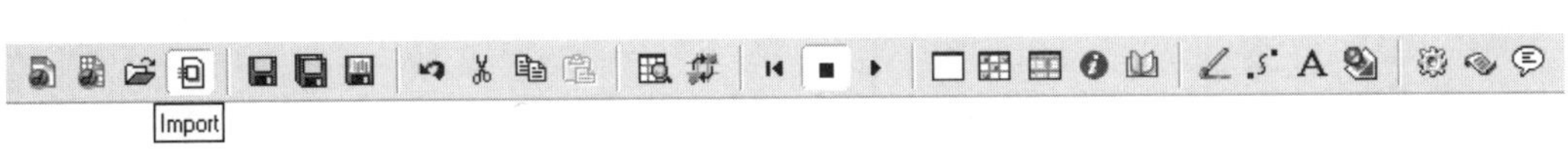

FIGURE 3.8 The Toolbar's Import button.

Creating and Using Lingo Scripts

The programming language used within Director MX is named Lingo. You learn more about writing Lingo scripts later in this chapter. For now, just type the Lingo code you are given and don't worry about trying to understand it. You will find, however, that most Lingo is simple enough to understand without any programming experience. This is by design.

When you begin writing Lingo code for your movies, you'll probably just be using two kinds of scripts: movie scripts, which are global in scope, and behaviors, which can affect only the sprites and/or frames to which they are applied. To create a movie script, perform the following steps.

1. Click an empty spot in the Cast window.
2. Click the Script Window button on the Toolbar, as shown in Figure 3.9.
3. Type the following code in the Script window.

```
on prepareFrame
    (the stage).bgColor = rgb(random(128), random(128), random(128))
end
```

4. Type "Main" into the Cast Member Name field, as shown in Figure 3.10, and close the Script window.

This is all you must do to create and implement a movie script. As soon as it exists as a cast member, its code should execute as part of your movie. Occasionally, Director MX seems to have trouble with this part and needs to be restarted, but this is simply a bug and an exception to the rule. In general, anytime that Director MX is giving you trouble, just save your work and restart the program. Try playing your movie to make sure your script works. You should see the movie looping as the background color of the Stage flashes randomly.

Now that you have seen a very basic movie script in action, you can move on to what really gives Director MX its power: the behavior script. This sort of script makes object-oriented programming highly intuitive and surprisingly fun. Object-oriented programming, or OOP, is simply a programming method that involves assigning properties (local variable data) and functions (bits of programming code also called methods) to items called objects. In this case, the objects are the sprites

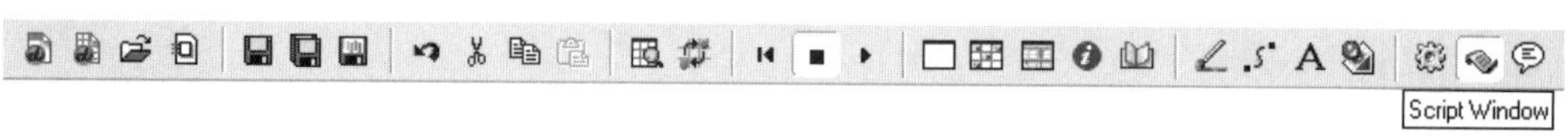

FIGURE 3.9 The Toolbar's Script Window button.

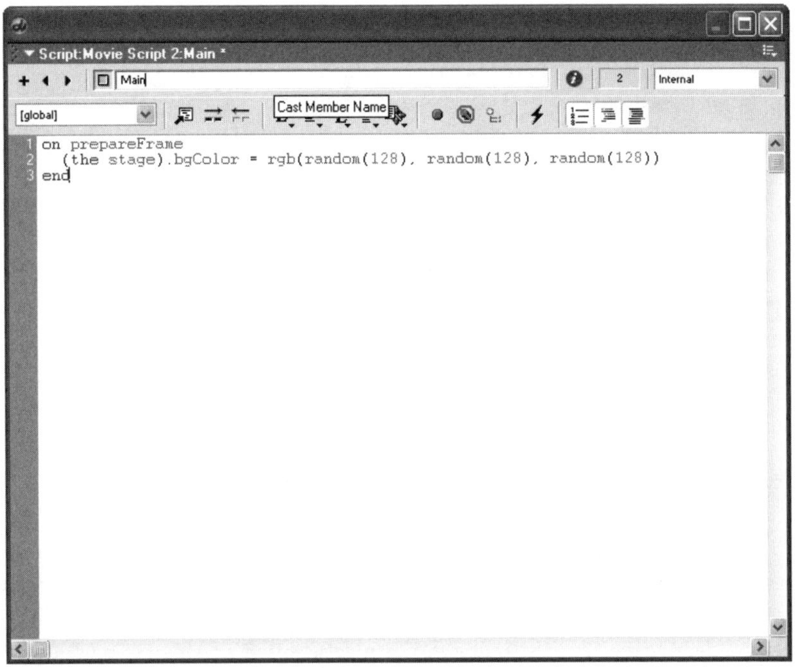

FIGURE 3.10 Naming the new Main movie script.

that make use of behaviors. To create a behavior script and apply it to a sprite, perform the following steps.

1. Click an empty spot in the Cast window.
2. Click the Script Window button on the Toolbar.
3. Type the following code in the Script window.

```
property my, r, stepR

on beginSprite me
    my = sprite(me.spriteNum)
    r = 0
    stepR = 0
end

on prepareFrame
    stepR = stepR*0.9
    r = r+stepR
```

```
    my.rotation = r
end

on mouseDown
    stepR = stepR+50
end
```

4. Click the Script tab of the Property Inspector.
5. Choose Behavior from the Type drop-down list.
6. Within the Script window, type "Spinner" in the Cast Member Name field and close the window.
7. Drag one of your graphical cast members from the Cast window into the Score.
8. Drag the Spinner behavior from the Cast window onto the sprite you just created in the Score.

Play your movie and see what happens. At first, your new sprite should simply sit in the middle of the screen doing nothing. But if you click on the sprite, it should spin for just a moment. The faster you click, the faster it spins. The Spinner behavior is sensitive to mouseclicks simply because of the `on mouseDown` portion of its code. If all this new code seems a bit overwhelming, don't worry. By the time you've finished reading this entire chapter, you should feel quite a bit more comfortable in Lingo.

As mentioned earlier, you can apply behaviors to frames as well as sprites. Such a behavior script acts much like a movie script but is only active while the playhead rests within its frame. To apply a behavior to a particular frame, perform the following steps.

1. Click an empty spot in the Cast window.
2. Click the Script Window button on the Toolbar.
3. Type the following code in the Script window.

```
on exitFrame
    play the frame
end
```

4. Click the Script tab of the Property Inspector.
5. Choose Behavior from the Type drop-down list.
6. Within the Script window, type "Wait" in the Cast Member Name field and close the window.
7. Drag the Wait behavior from the Cast window into cell 1 of the Script channel of the Score, as shown in Figure 3.11.

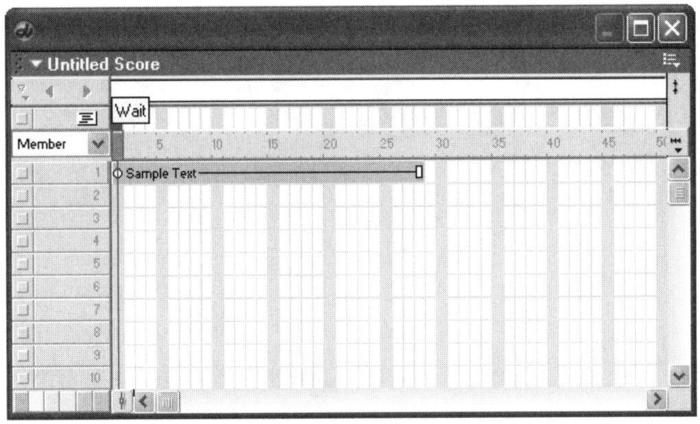

FIGURE 3.11 Applying the Wait behavior to frame 1.

Play your movie once more from the beginning. If your Wait behavior is working correctly, you will see the Score's playhead sticking on the movie's first frame. Your movie is not actually stopped, but is looping on a single frame. Try moving your Wait behavior to another frame and check the results.

Lingo programming is really what makes Director MX so much fun. It's all about trying new things and seeing if they work. At this point, you may be tempted to skip ahead and jump right into playing around with Lingo. Be patient; you're almost finished with the GUI section. After you have finished, you'll be able to dive into Lingo as deep as you want without worrying about what it was you so hastily skipped over.

Arranging Your Workspace

Now that you have explored the major components of Director MX, you need to start thinking about the best way to arrange them on your screen. If possible, you should keep the Stage, Score, Cast window, and Property Inspector fully visible at all times. Such a goal may be difficult to reach at a resolution of 800 by 600 pixels and perhaps impossible at 640 by 480. If you're having trouble fitting all the windows on your screen, you might consider adjusting your available screen area. You can accomplish this task through your operating system's Control Panel. Your goal is to give yourself as much room to work as possible without shrinking everything down so far that small text is blurry and illegible. Choose a resolution that is convenient for you.

After you have settled on a resolution that gives you enough screen space (without giving you eyestrain), you can start moving your windows around to find the best arrangement for you. As a general rule, you should leave the Stage window in

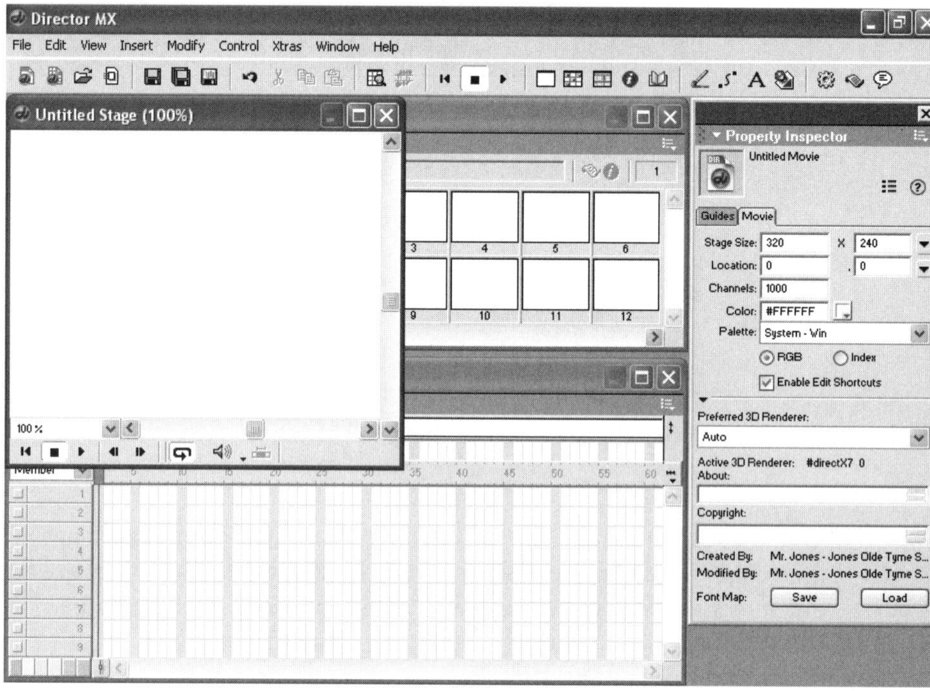

FIGURE 3.12 Macromedia Director MX at 800 by 600 pixels.

the top-left corner of Director MX. If your Stage is currently somewhere else, do not drag the window into the corner. Just choose Upper Left from the Location menu of the Property Inspector's Movie sheet. Figures 3.12, 3.13, and 3.14 show some possible workspace arrangements for Director MX at various resolutions.

Testing and Publishing

You've already tested your Director MX movie several times simply by playing it. Although this gives you a good idea of how it will behave once it's compiled into an executable projector or Shockwave DCR file, some inconsistency may occur. For example, certain Lingo commands are ignored in Shockwave files for security over the Internet. Also, both projectors and Shockwave files can be compressed to varying degrees, which can affect the appearance of graphics and possibly the quality of audio. The best way to test out your Director MX movie is to publish it and view it as any other user would, preferably on a variety of computers.

One way to publish your movie is to create a projector. A projector can effectively turn your Director MX movie into a standalone application. Projector files are executable, meaning that all a user must do is double-click, and your movie

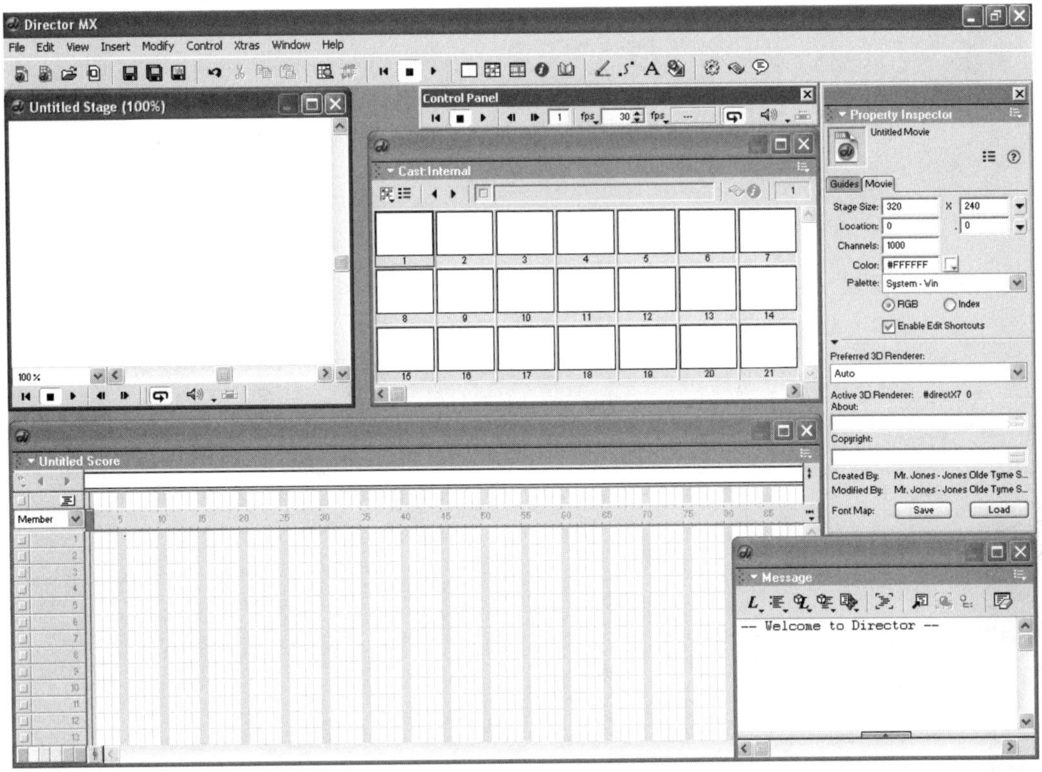

FIGURE 3.13 Macromedia Director MX at 1024 by 768 pixels.

plays. Users do not need your original source file. However, any external files that your movie requires have to be distributed along with the projector. To create an executable projector file, save your work and then perform the following steps.

1. Choose Create Projector from the File menu.
2. Navigate to the movie that you want to publish and double-click it to add it to the File list.
3. Click Options.
4. Customize the playback and compression of your movie, and then click OK.
5. Click Create.
6. Specify a name and location for your projector file, and then click Save.

Projector files do have one major drawback. After you build a projector file on your computer, those using a different operating system than yours may be unable

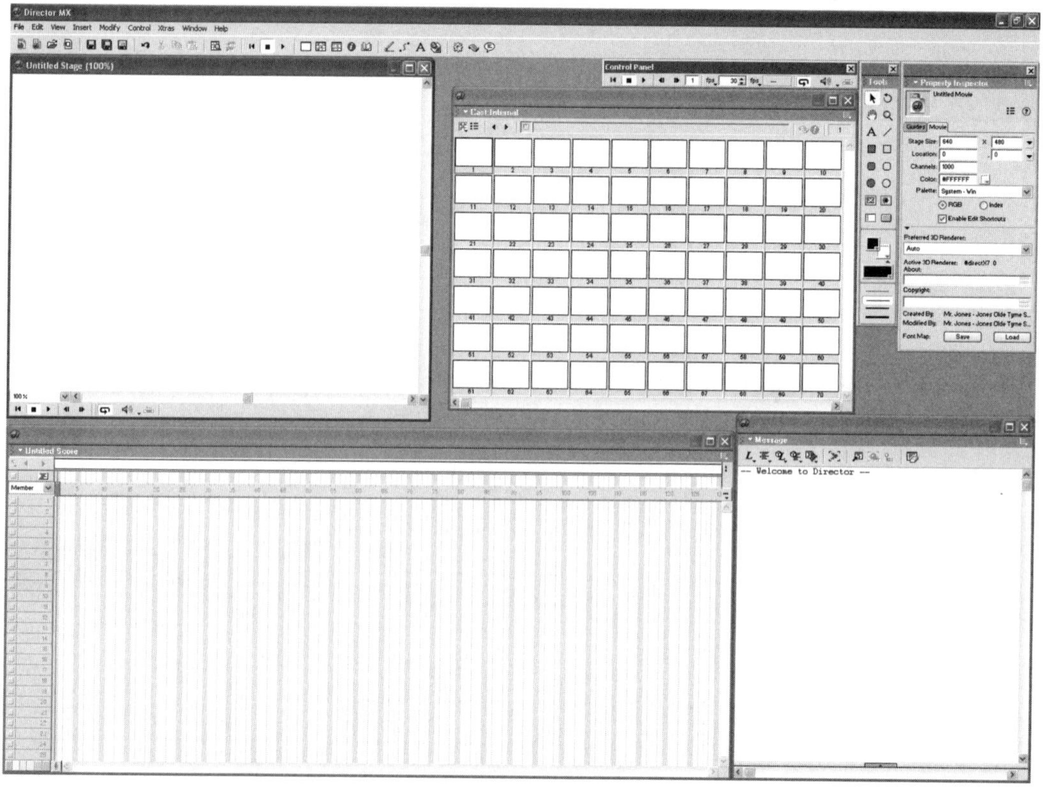

FIGURE 3.14 Macromedia Director MX at 1600 by 1200 pixels.

to view your movie. One simple solution is to build two projectors, one using Windows and one using a Macintosh. Of course, people using other operating systems such as Linux may still be unable to run your movie. For the widest possible audience, you must publish in Shockwave format.

What sets Macromedia Director MX apart from most other multimedia development tools is not that it can be used to create powerful applications with ease or that it produces interactive Web content, but that it can do both. The name Shockwave is used to refer both to Director MX movies created for the Internet and to the browser plug-ins that play those movies. When using Shockwave compression, a movie's file size can be much smaller than it would be as a standalone projector because the code for the player is not included. Director offers a variety of publishing options to allow you to find just the right balance between compression and quality.

To create a compressed Shockwave applet, or miniature application, perform the following steps.

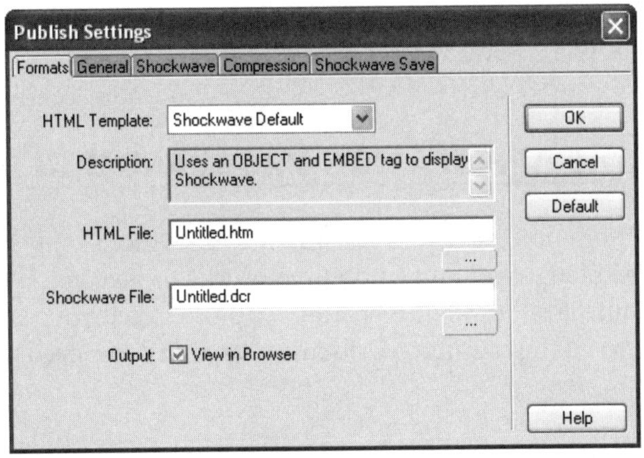

FIGURE 3.15 The View in Browser checkbox within the Publish Settings dialog box.

1. Choose Publish Settings from the File menu.
2. Click the Default button to reset all publish settings to their default values.
3. Select the View in Browser checkbox, as shown in Figure 3.15.
4. Click the Compression tab.
5. Select the Standard Image Compression option button.
6. Customize any other options and then click OK.
7. Save the changes to your movie, and then click the Publish button on the Toolbar, as shown in Figure 3.16.

For a user to view your movie as a Shockwave applet, he can run the Shockwave DCR file directly or load an HTML page containing a reference to that file. Either way, the file must run through a Web browser with an appropriate Shockwave plug-in. Each time you open the Publish Settings dialog box, you see various options having to do with creating an HTML file. If you choose to create an HTML page, Director MX places it in the same folder as your source file by default. View this HTML file in a text editor. To place your Shockwave movie on an existing Web page, you can copy the section of HTML code enclosed in an object or embed tag from the HTML file created by Director MX and paste it into the body of your sec-

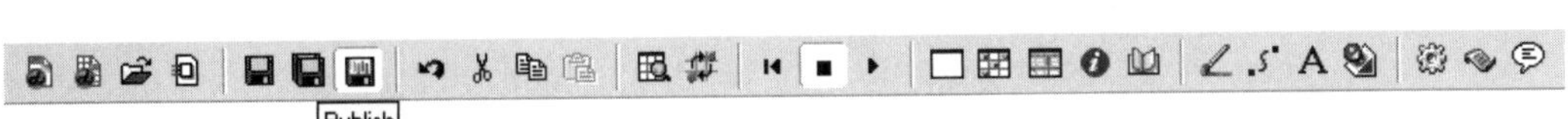

FIGURE 3.16 The Toolbar's Publish button.

ond HTML page. As long as your Shockwave DCR file is in the same directory as this page, your movie should appear just fine.

LEARNING THE APPLICATION PROGRAMMING INTERFACE

The API of Director MX is essentially synonymous with Lingo. Lingo is the programming language built into Director MX to give you complete control of your movie during runtime. It is the tool you use to tell your movie what to do. In the remainder of the chapter, we discuss everything you need to start programming in Lingo.

The Flexibility of Lingo

Lingo's original designers wanted the language to be intuitive and appealing to nonprogrammers. They decided that Lingo should use real English words instead of mathematical symbols as often as possible. The goal was to let developers communicate with the computer much as they would with other people. And for years, Lingo programmers typed commands like

```
set the rotation of sprite 3 to 45
```

instead of shorter, more mathematical commands like

```
sprite(3).rotation = 45
```

Eventually, Lingo's developers realized that their little experiment was just not as successful as they'd hoped. For communication with machines, English is simply not the best way to go. They developed an alternative design that more closely resembled other programming languages, such as C++ and BASIC. With the new syntax, a command as cumbersome as

```
set userName to word 4 to 7 of line 12 of the text of the member of
sprite 5
```

could be translated to

```
userName = sprite(5).member.text.line[12].word[4..7]
```

Lingo still includes the option to use the old, verbose syntax, but most programmers feel more comfortable with the new, dot syntax. This is especially true as the C++/Java style of coding continues to emerge as the world standard. Dot syntax makes code organization more obvious and often requires less typing. The difference may not seem like a big deal, but it adds up over time.

Lingo Syntax

As you begin writing code in Lingo, certain questions about spacing may arise. The only time you are actually required to type a space into your code is when two words must be separated. The following lines are totally equivalent.

```
newHeight = (sprite(2).height + 5)*10
newHeight=(sprite(2).height+5)*10
newHeight = ( sprite ( 2 ) . height + 5 ) * 10
```

Although spacing does not matter to Lingo, using appropriate spacing can make your code easier to read and, therefore, more convenient for you and any other developers who may work with your code in the future.

Unlike most programming languages today, Lingo is not case sensitive. This means that as far as Lingo is concerned, the terms `rightMouseDown`, `Rightmousedown`, and `rightMOUSEdown` are all equivalent. Because many terms in Lingo are made up of more than one word, most programmers use camel notation in their code. Camel notation is the method of using capital letters to separate words in the names of functions, properties, and such. Long words are often abbreviated to cut down on typing. A property that represents a new student identification number might appear as follows.

```
newStudentIDNum
```

Because of its optional verbose syntax, loose spacing requirements, and case insensitivity, Lingo offers programmers an unusual amount of freedom when it comes to developing their own styles. But when it comes down to it, Lingo is still just one language. Many elements of the language remain the same no matter who is doing the typing. The following operators are a vital part of Lingo's programming syntax.

- `+` **(plus):** Finds the sum of two numbers in an addition problem.
- `-` **(minus):** Finds the difference of two numbers in a subtraction problem.
- `*` **(asterisk):** Finds the product of two numbers in a multiplication problem.
- `/` **(slash):** Finds the quotient of two numbers in a division problem.
- `&` **(ampersand):** Concatenates, or combines, two text strings.
- `=` **(equal to):** Finds whether two expressions are of equal value.
- `<>` **(not equal to):** Finds whether two expressions are of unequal value.
- `>` **(greater than):** Finds whether the first expression is greater than the second.

`>=` **(greater than or equal to):** Finds whether the first expression is greater than or equal to the second.

`<` **(less than):** Finds whether the first expression is less than the second.

`<=` **(less than or equal to):** Finds whether the first expression is less than or equal to the second.

`#` **(hash):** Indicates a symbol when placed directly before a combination of characters not starting with a number.

`\` **(backslash):** Indicates a statement continuation when placed at the end of a line.

`–` **(comment):** Disables, or comments out, any code following it in the same line. Programmers use comments to explain ambiguous code or to temporarily disable lines of code to aid in debugging.

`and` Finds whether two expressions are both true.

`or` Finds whether at least one of two expressions is true.

`not` Reverses the truth value of an expression.

`(...)` **(parentheses):** Indicate a group of parameters or expressions.

`"..."` **(quotes):** Indicate a text string. Several characters may be placed inside the operators.

`[...]` **(brackets):** Indicate a list. Several values may be placed inside of the operators separated by commas. Brackets may also be used to indicate the number, or subscript, of a list item.

Try not to be overwhelmed by all the operators, functions, and properties listed in this chapter. Certainly, becoming familiar with such things will make you a better Lingo programmer, but it is not imperative that you memorize everything before moving on. Just remember that these lists are here for your reference should you need them.

Event Handlers

Lingo is an event-driven language. This means events such as a mouseclicks and keystrokes can be set to trigger sections of programming code stored within event handlers. Think of event handlers as empty bags that Lingo sets aside for you to fill with code. Any commands not stored within some sort of handler (or function) produce an error message and keep your program from running properly. An event handler should appear as follows. Only the italicized text will change.

```
on eventName
    command(s)
end
```

Most event handlers work with any type of Lingo script, but some events deal specifically with a particular sprite or the movie as a whole. Accordingly, these handlers are only valid within behavior and movie scripts, respectively. The following event handlers are called automatically throughout the run of a movie and are listed in the order that they normally execute.

`prepareMovie:` Executes once just before a movie begins playing. Its common usage is to initialize global variables. This handler is only valid in movie scripts.

`beginSprite:` Executes once when a sprite first appears in the Score. Its common usage is to initialize property variables. This handler is only valid in behavior scripts.

`prepareFrame:` Executes just before the beginning of each frame.

`startMovie:` Executes once at the beginning of a movie's first frame. This handler is only valid in movie scripts.

`enterFrame:` Executes at the beginning of each frame.

`exitFrame:` Executes at the end of each frame.

`stopMovie:` Executes once at the end of a movie's last frame. This handler is only valid in movie scripts.

`endSprite:` Executes once when a sprite last appears in the Score. This handler is only valid in behavior scripts.

If several scripts refer to the same event handler, Lingo executes the behavior scripts applied to sprites one after another starting with the sprite in channel 1 and moving down the Score. If a sprite uses more than one behavior with the handler, the behaviors execute in the order shown on the Property Inspector's Behavior sheet. After all the sprites' behaviors have been checked for the event handler, Lingo looks in the file's movie scripts.

Some event handlers wait for user interaction to execute their code. This type of handler is what makes event-driven programming so convenient. The following event handlers are triggered in some way by the user's mouse or keyboard.

`mouseEnter:` Executes each time the mouse cursor moves within the bounds of an associated sprite. This handler is only valid in behavior scripts.

`mouseWithin:` Executes constantly while the mouse cursor is within the bounds of an associated sprite. This handler is only valid in behavior scripts.

`mouseLeave:` Executes each time the mouse cursor moves outside the bounds of an associated sprite. This handler is only valid in behavior scripts.

`mouseDown:` Executes each time the user presses the left mouse button. If this handler is used in a behavior script, the mouse cursor must be within the bounds of an associated sprite.

`mouseUp`: Executes every time the user releases the left mouse button. If this handler is used in a behavior script, the mouse cursor must be within the bounds of an associated sprite.

`rightMouseDown`: Executes each time the user presses the right mouse button. If this handler is used in a behavior script, the mouse cursor must be within the bounds of an associated sprite.

`rightMouseUp`: Executes each time the user releases the right mouse button. If this handler is used in a behavior script, the mouse cursor must be within the bounds of an associated sprite.

`keyDown`: Executes each time the user presses a key. This handler does not work in a behavior script unless it is that of an editable text field.

`keyUp`: Executes each time the user releases a key. This handler does not work in a behavior script unless it is that of an editable text field.

Although these handlers function well for most situations, Lingo provides additional methods of testing the state of the user's mouse and keyboard. A variety of options are available to suit virtually any situation. However, you should first gain a better understanding of Lingo programming in general before concerning yourself with these methods.

Variables

A variable is a letter or a word that can represent a changing value. A variable can be accessible throughout the run of a movie or only in specific areas depending on how you define it. To create a local variable (one that is accessible only within the handler or function in which it was created), you need only set, or assign, it to a value. To assign a variable's value, you must type the name of the variable, an equal sign, and then the value that you want the variable to represent. If Lingo does not recognize the variable name you type, it assumes that you want to create a new local variable (as opposed to editing the value of an existing variable). A variable assignment should appear as follows.

```
variableName = value
```

A variable can represent all different types of data but only one type at a time. To tell Lingo which type of value that a variable represents, you must sometimes specify the type's name followed by an opening parenthesis, the value that you want to change, followed by a closing parenthesis. This process is called type casting. The resulting value functions just as if it were a constant value, such as a number or a text string. A type cast should appear as follows.

```
variableName = typeName(variableName)
```

A constant string value must always be enclosed in quotation marks. If it is not, Lingo assumes you are referring to the name of a variable. Number values do not require quotation marks because no variable name can begin with a number. Therefore, Lingo never confuses a constant number value with a variable name. The following data types can replace `typeName` in the preceding code example:

Integer: Returns the integer, or whole number, value of a specified expression

Float: Returns the decimal number value of a specified expression

String: Returns the text string value of a specified expression

Another data type's variables can hold one of only two possible values. A truth value may be equal to either the true or the false keyword. The number zero translates to false, and any other number translates to true. This data type is especially useful when dealing with conditionals and loops, as you discover later in this chapter.

To define a property variable (one that is directly accessible only within the script in which it was created), you must type the property keyword followed by the name of the variable at the beginning of the script that you will use the variable in, as shown in the following code.

```
property variableName

on eventName
    command(s)
end
```

To define a global variable (one that is accessible to any of a movie's scripts), you must type the global keyword and then the variable's name at the beginning of each script that you want to give access to it.

```
global variableName

on eventName
    command(s)
end
```

Almost every program requires the use of variables to keep track of its different values. In fact, Director MX uses all sorts of variables behind the scenes to control everything from sprite locations to a movie's frame rate. To access a property variable from a remote script, you must type the name of the sprite that contains that property, a dot, and then the name of the property variable you want to access. Assigning a variable to the value of a property of sprite 5 should appear as follows.

```
variableName = sprite(5).propertyName
```

Each sprite within a Director MX movie automatically contains a number of predefined properties. The following sprite properties can replace `propertyName` in the preceding code example.

`bgColor`: Indicates the background color of a particular sprite.

`blend`: Indicates the translucency of a particular sprite. Its value can range from 0 (transparent) to 100 (opaque).

`bottom`: Indicates the location of the bottom edge of a particular sprite.

`color`: Indicates foreground color of a particular sprite.

`flipH`: Indicates whether a particular sprite is mirrored.

`flipV`: Indicates whether a particular sprite is flipped.

`height`: Indicates the height of a particular sprite in pixels.

`left`: Indicates the location of the left edge of a particular sprite.

`loc`: Indicates the location of a particular sprite within the Stage in the form of a point value.

`locH`: Indicates the horizontal location of a particular sprite within the Stage.

`locV`: Indicates the vertical location of a particular sprite within the Stage.

`locZ`: Indicates the layer of a particular sprite within the Stage. Sprites with a higher `locZ` value appear in front of other sprites. If two sprites have the same `locZ` value, their channel numbers determine their order.

`member`: Indicates the cast member being used by a particular sprite.

`memberNum`: Indicates the number of the cast member being used by a particular sprite.

`puppet`: Indicates whether a particular sprite is under Lingo control.

`quad`: Indicates the coordinates of the top-left, top-right, bottom-left, and bottom-right corners of a particular sprite in the form of a list containing four point values.

`rect`: Indicates the locations of the borders of a particular sprite in the form of a rectangle value.

`right`: Indicates the location of the right edge of a particular sprite.

`rotation`: Indicates the degree of rotation of a particular sprite.

`skew`: Indicates the degree of tilt of a particular sprite.

`spriteNum:` Indicates the channel number of a particular sprite.

`top:` Indicates the location of the top edge of a particular sprite.

`visible:` Indicates whether a particular sprite is visible.

`width:` Indicates the width of a particular sprite in pixels.

Lingo also allows access to a number of system properties. All system properties are preceded by the "the" keyword to distinguish them from ordinary variables and are accessible from within any of a movie's scripts. The following system properties are useful when dealing with user interaction.

`the clickLoc:` Indicates the location in the Stage last clicked by the user in the form of a point value.

`the clickOn:` Indicates the channel number of the last sprite clicked by the user.

`the commandDown:` Indicates whether the user is holding down the Control key (the Command key on Macintosh).

`the doubleClick:` Indicates whether the user has just double-clicked.

`the key:` Indicates the string value of the last key pressed by the user.

`the keyCode:` Indicates the integer value of the last key pressed by the user.

`the keyDownScript:` Indicates, in the form of a string value, the commands to execute each time the user presses a key within a movie.

`the keyUpScript:` Indicates, in the form of a string value, the commands to execute each time the user releases a key within a movie.

`the mouseChar:` Indicates the number of the character directly under the mouse cursor within a text field. If the mouse cursor is not over a character, the result is –1.

`the mouseDown:` Indicates whether the user is holding down the left mouse button.

`the mouseDownScript:` Indicates, in the form of a string value, the commands to execute each time the user presses the left mouse button within a movie.

`the mouseH:` Indicates the horizontal location of the mouse cursor within the Stage.

`the mouseItem:` Indicates the number of the item directly under the mouse cursor within a text field. If the mouse cursor is not over an item, the result is –1.

`the mouseLine:` Indicates the number of the line directly under the mouse cursor within a text field. If the mouse cursor is not over a line, the result is –1.

`the mouseLoc`: Indicates the location of the mouse cursor within the Stage in the form of a point value.

`the mouseMember`: Indicates the number of the cast member used by the sprite directly under the mouse cursor within the Stage. If the mouse cursor is not over a sprite, the result is void.

`the mouseUpScript`: Indicates, in the form of a string value, the commands to execute each time the user releases the left mouse button within a movie.

`the mouseV`: Indicates the vertical location of the mouse cursor within the Stage.

`the mouseWord`: Indicates the number of the word directly under the mouse cursor within a text field. If the mouse cursor is not over a word, the result is –1.

`the optionDown`: Indicates whether the user is holding down the Alt key (the Option key on Macintosh).

`the rightMouseDown`: Indicates whether the user is holding down the right mouse button.

`the rollOver`: Indicates the channel number of the sprite the mouse cursor is currently over.

`the shiftDown`: Indicates whether the user is holding down the Shift key.

The predefined sprite and system properties listed here are by no means all that Lingo has to offer. Basically, everything that has to do with your movie is customizable through Lingo. These properties are just enough for you to begin creating powerful scripts for your movies.

Lists

Another way to store values in your Lingo scripts is by creating lists. A list is actually a type of variable that can hold several different values at once. The simplest way to retrieve a value from a list is to access it by number. To get a specific value from within a list, type the name of the list variable, an opening bracket, the number of the value that you want to access, and then a closing bracket. The resulting value functions just as if it were an ordinary variable name. Assigning a variable to the value of the fifth item in a list should appear as follows.

```
variableName = listName[5]
```

To assign a set of values to a list variable, type the name of the list, an equal sign, an opening bracket, any number of values separated by commas, and, finally, a closing bracket. Assigning a set of values to a list might appear as follows.

```
listName = ["string value", 3, variableName]
```

Property lists store not only values, but also property names. For instance, a car variable might have a year property and a model property. You can treat property lists just the same as ordinary, linear lists, or you can access their properties by name instead of by number by using dot notation. To assign a set of properties to a list, you use the same syntax as with other lists. The only difference is that, instead of just values, you type a number sign, or hash, the name of the property you are creating, a colon, and then the value that you want to assign to the property. Assigning a set of properties to a list might appear as follows.

```
listName = [#year: 1967, #model: "Beetle"]
```

Most predefined data types in Lingo (such as colors, points, and rectangles) consist of a property list with the properties already set up. For example, any color variable contains the properties `red`, `green`, and `blue`. Any point variable contains the properties `locH` and `locV`. Lingo defines several media types to make multimedia programming quite a bit more convenient than it is in many other languages.

Functions

Functions work almost exactly like event handlers. The main difference is that they execute only when they are told to do so by a call. You can define your own functions by using the same syntax as if you were using an event handler. Just be certain to pick a name for your function that hasn't already been reserved by Lingo. A function definition should appear as follows.

```
on functionName
    command(s)
end
```

To call a function, type its name, an opening parenthesis, and then a closing parenthesis in the part of your movie where you want the function's code to execute. After Lingo executes a function, it returns to the line directly after the function's call. A call might appear as follows.

```
functionName()
```

A function parameter (also called an argument) is a value that is passed to a function to be used as a local variable within that function. Parameters allow the programmer to create a single function that can perform a variety of different tasks.

For example, a function to move sprite 5 by a specified number of pixels might appear as follows.

```
on functionName stepX, stepY
    sprite(5).locH = sprite(5).locH+stepX
    sprite(5).locV = sprite(5).locV+setpY
end
```

To call a function that uses parameters, type the name of the function, an opening parenthesis, a value for each parameter of the function (separated by commas), and then a closing parenthesis. A function call that makes use of parameters might appear as follows.

```
functionName(-20, 15)
```

If a function returns a value, you can treat its call as if it were a variable representing that value. You can call the function normally, or you can assign or compare a variable to the call. To cause a function to return a value, you must type the `return` keyword followed by the value that you want the function to return at the point in the function where you want it to stop and return a value. If any programming code appears after the return line in a function, that code does not execute. A function that returns the product of two numbers might appear as follows.

```
on functionName first, second
    return first*second
end
```

A call of the preceding function would work just like a constant numerical value or a variable representing a number. Assigning a variable to the value returned by a function with two parameters might appear as follows.

```
variableName = functionName(2, 5)
```

To call a function or an event handler from a remote script, you must use the `sendSprite` command. This command is actually a function that accepts two parameters. The first parameter should be an integer value representing the number of the sprite whose behaviors you want to access. The second value should be the name of the function you want to call immediately preceded by a hash. Calling a function from a script applied to sprite 2 should appear as follows.

```
sendSprite(2, #functionName)
```

A good example of a function that accepts a parameter and returns a value is built into Lingo. The `keyPressed` function accepts a string or number value representing a key on the keyboard and returns a truth value indicating whether the specified key is currently being pressed. Setting a truth variable to store whether the user is pressing the spacebar should appear as follows.

```
variableName = keyPressed(" ")
```

It is not completely necessary that you create functions with parameters and return values because you can always just use global variables to pass values back and forth between scripts. However, these features greatly add to the convenience of Lingo programming, and learning to master them will make your code all the more elegant. By using local variables whenever possible, you will have fewer variables to keep track of and, thus, will reduce the risk of accidentally overwriting one value with another.

Conditionals

A conditional is a structure that keeps a section of code from executing unless a specified condition is met. The condition can be in the form of a mathematical equation, a group of equations, a truth variable, or anything else that can be interpreted as either true or false. If the final value of the condition is true, the enclosed programming code executes.

Lingo provides two conditional structures, each with its own advantages and disadvantages. The most popular and generally most useful of the two is the `if...then` structure. A basic `if...then` conditional should appear as follows.

```
if condition then
    command(s)
end
```

If only one command is enclosed within the `if...then` structure, the entire conditional can be placed on a single line. In this situation, the `end` command must be omitted. An `if...then` conditional on a single line should appear as follows.

```
if condition then command
```

To make `if...then` conditionals easier to use and understand, Lingo offers an optional `else` clause to be used when you want code to execute only if the preceding condition was not met. An `if...then` conditional with an `else` clause should appear as follows.

```
if condition then
    command(s)
else
    command(s)
end
```

To give `if...then` conditionals even more flexibility, Lingo allows you to expand the structure to include as many `else` clauses as you want. An `if...then` conditional with more than one `else` clause might appear as follows.

```
if condition then
    command(s)
else if condition then
    command(s)
else
    command(s)
end
```

The second conditional structure that Lingo has to offer is generally most useful for situations in which you want to test a single variable for a large number of possible values. The `case...of` structure is never completely necessary, as any `case...of` conditional could be replaced with an `if...then` conditional with a series of `else` clauses. However, you will run into situations in which `case...of` is simply more convenient. A `case...of` conditional might appear as follows.

```
case variableName of
    4: command(s)
    5: command(s)
    6: command(s)
end
```

The `case...of` structure has its own version of the `else` clause. If the `otherwise` keyword is typed in place of a value for the final condition, then its code executes only if no other conditions have been met so far. Think of the `otherwise` keyword as always being equal to the variable you are testing. A `case...of` conditional that uses the `otherwise` keyword might appear as follows.

```
case variableName of
    "red": command(s)
    "green": command(s)
    "blue": command(s)
    otherwise: command(s)
end
```

The reason that the `case...of` structure fits the definition of a conditional despite its unusual organization may be a bit difficult to grasp. Each time that Lingo reaches a value in a `case...of` conditional, it checks to see if the variable being tested is equal to that value. If this condition results in a value of true, Lingo executes the code that follows. Otherwise, Lingo moves on to the next condition. As soon as a condition is met, no more are tested.

Loops

Loops are very similar to conditionals. A loop repeatedly executes a section of code as long as its specified condition is true. Loops allow programmers to avoid typing similar statements over and over. A `repeat while` loop should appear as follows.

```
repeat while condition
    command(s)
end repeat
```

To make a loop execute a set number of times, or iterations, you must use a loop control variable. By incrementing, or adding to, the loop control variable each time the loop's code executes, you can count the iterations and end the loop when the variable is no longer below a certain value. However, Lingo handles the entire process for you if you use a `repeat with loop`. A `repeat with loop` that executes 50 times might appear as follows.

```
repeat with variableName = 1 to 50
    command(s)
end repeat
```

The loop control variable of a `repeat with loop` does not have to increase in value as the loop iterates. A simple modification to the loop structure causes its loop control variable to decrease in value, or decrement, as the loop progresses. A `repeat with loop` that counts from 50 down to 1 should appear as follows.

```
repeat with variableName = 50 down to 1
    command(s)
end repeat
```

When programming in Lingo, loops are generally most useful for dealing with lists or sequential sprites. Using a loop control variable, in place of integer constants in the preceding code examples, shortens 50 lines of code down to only three.

Controlling Movie Playback

One of Lingo's most convenient features is its ability to work with the Score window's playhead. Wherever the playhead moves, that frame's contents show up on the Stage. In addition to moving around with a Director MX movie, Lingo also offers commands for jumping to other movies, launching Web sites, and even running external applications. The following commands are used for navigation within and outside of Director MX movies.

`updateStage`: Updates the contents of the Stage immediately instead of waiting for the next frame

`play`: Tells Director MX to move the playhead to a specified frame in the form of an integer, marker in the form of a string, or external Director MX movie and begin playing

`go`: Tells Director MX to move the playhead to a specified frame in the form of an integer, marker in the form of a string, or external Director MX movie

`go next`: Tells Director MX to move the playhead to the next marker after the current frame of the movie

`go previous`: Tells Director MX to move the playhead to the previous marker before the current frame of the movie

`open`: Runs an external program from a specified path in the form of a string

`goToNetPage`: Opens the default Internet browser and loads a site from a specified URL in the form of a string

`appMinimize`: Minimizes a movie's window

`halt`: Stops a movie and closes its window

`restart`: Stops a movie and restarts the computer

`shutDown`: Stops a movie and shuts down the computer

Some Lingo commands, such as `appMinimize`, `restart`, and `shutDown`, are disabled in Shockwave applets made for the Internet. If you use these commands in a movie, you do not receive an error message. Lingo simply ignores the disabled commands and continues.

Debugging

As you begin to develop more and more complex movies within Director MX, debugging becomes increasingly important. If one of your scripts has a problem that disables it from running properly, Director MX stops and asks you what to do. You are given a short description of the error along with options on how to continue, as shown in Figure 3.17.

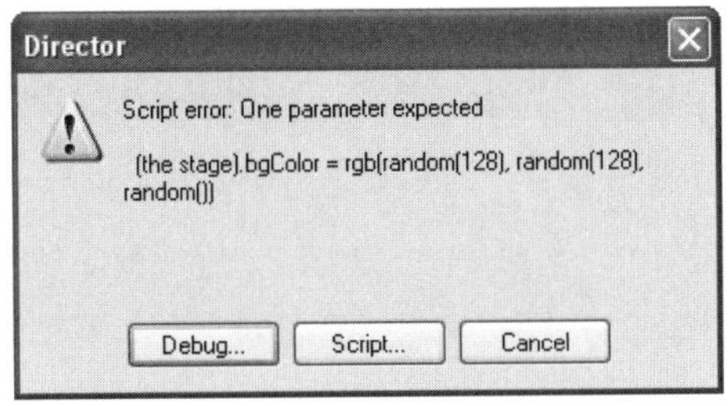

FIGURE 3.17 An error message indicating a problem with a Lingo script.

The dialog box's Cancel button simply stops the execution of your movie and gives you no further clues about why the error occurred. If you choose the Script button, Director opens the problematic Lingo script and moves the cursor to the line responsible for the error. Quite often, this is all you need to fix the error because many errors of this sort are simple typos. Sometimes, however, you may need a more in-depth analysis to discover why a given error occurred and how to fix it. If this is the case, you should click the dialog box's Debug button. This opens the problematic script in the Debugger window, as shown in Figure 3.18.

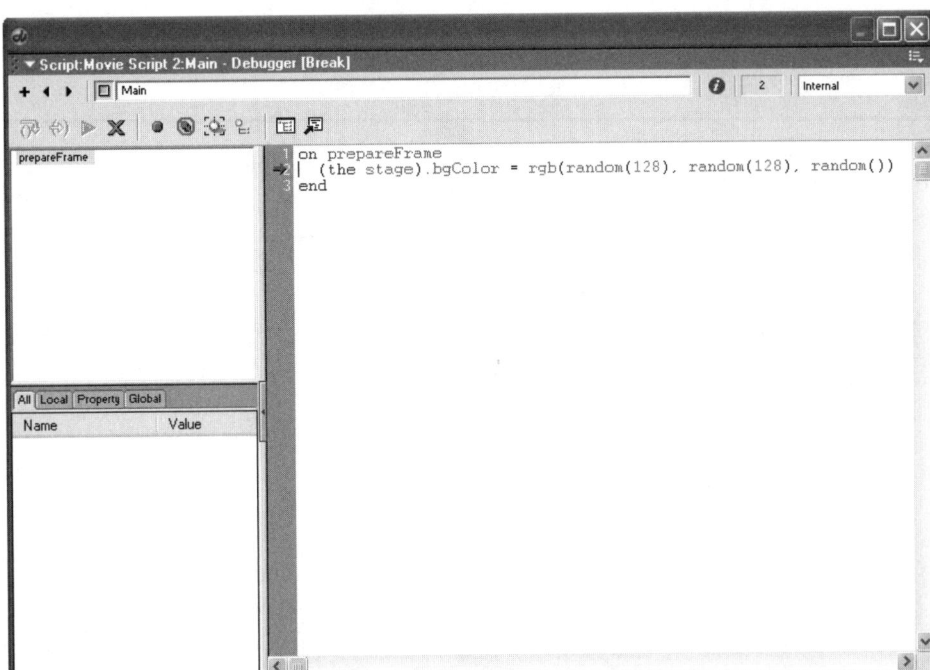

FIGURE 3.18 Using the Debugger window to analyze a runtime error.

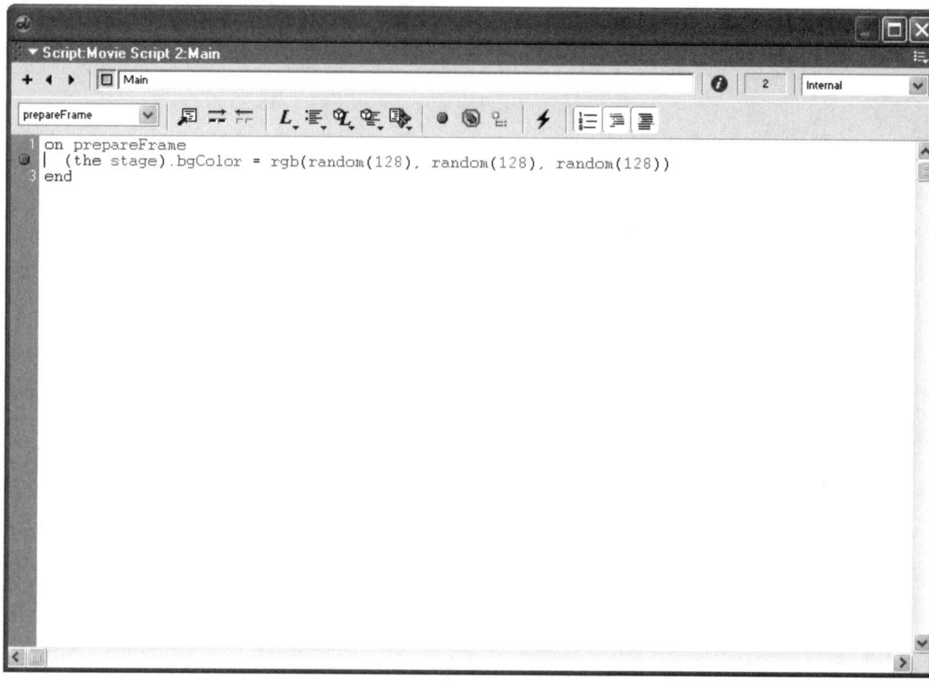

FIGURE 3.19 Inserting a breakpoint from within the Script window.

From the panel on the left side of the Debugger window, you can view the value of all variables stored in memory at the time of your movie's error. This is often quite helpful. If you want your movie to stop at a particular line of code even if no error occurs, you should enter a breakpoint. To do this, open the script in either the Script or the Debugger window, move the cursor to the line at which you want to stop, and click the Toggle Breakpoint button. You should see a red dot appear next to the line you chose, as shown in Figure 3.19.

Another method of debugging your scripts involves the Director MX Message window. At any given point in your code, you can type the `put` command with a string parameter, and the string shows up in the Message window when that line is executed. This is quite useful for checking the value of a variable over time because the `put` command won't interrupt the flow of your movie. To view the Message window, click the Message Window button on the Toolbar, as shown in Figure 3.20.

For more information on Lingo programming, choose Lingo Dictionary from the Help menu. All the major Lingo commands are explained in a system of pages complete with programming examples. At any time, you can click the Contents,

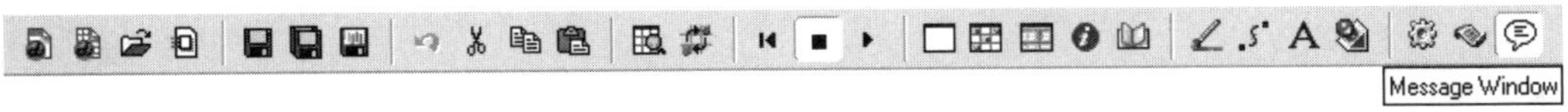

FIGURE 3.20 The Toolbar's Message Window button.

Index, or Search tab for a different browsing method. You might also want to visit the Director MX online support center for all sorts of tutorials, updates, and plug-ins. Just choose Director Support Center from the Help menu, and Director MX launches the site in your default Web browser.

SUMMARY

You should now have a basic understanding of how Director MX works. It is a vast program with many facets to explore—so don't limit yourself to what was taught in this tutorial, its purpose is only to teach the fundamentals of the program. By now, you should be able to work with both the GUI and API to perform simple tasks, create Lingo scripts, and manipulate the Score. With this knowledge, you will be able to understand the upcoming tutorials for games that have been created in Director MX.

4 Macromedia Flash MX 2004

Macromedia Flash MX 2004 is an essential software program that every artist, animator, and Web programmer should have. It's no wonder that over 516 million Internet users have the Flash Player installed with Flash and its unparalleled ability to provide crisp, clear animation at file sizes too small to believe. The development environment is one that envelops the user by providing tools that are customizable to each animator's and developer's preferences. Flash MX is being used on the Web today to provide stunning introductions, dynamic user interfaces and Web sites, learning software, online advertising, and even full-scale applications.

Before diving in and utilizing Flash MX, a basic foundation is required to unlock all of its powerful features. The software's interface can be broken down into two parts, the graphical user interface (GUI) and the application programming interface (API). Both parts integrate seamlessly to provide an authoring environment that satisfies everyone from amateurs to professionals and artists to programmers.

LEARNING THE GRAPHICAL USER INTERFACE

What is the GUI and what purpose does it serve? When Flash MX is opened, all of the visual elements from the menus to the toolbars and scrollbars make up the GUI. The *GUI*, simply put, is the graphical display that is seen in any program. Flash MX has an expertly designed GUI that allows maximum accessibility for anything that needs to be done.

The Workspace

The workspace is broken up into several different areas: the Stage, timeline, and panels. These three elements combine to provide you with control over the various *assets*—the various elements you use to create your movie—with which you will be working.

The Stage

Everything that appears in your final movie is created on the space in the middle of the screen. The Stage is where you compose each individual frame and arrange the assets of your Flash MX movie. You can draw, type, arrange, or import anything onto this surface and get exactly what you want in your final piece. Some of the most basic and important controls in Flash MX are specifically used for changing your view of the Stage. To change the amount of the Stage that appears on your screen, perform the following steps.

1. Choose Magnification from the View menu.
2. Choose the level of magnification you want.

You can also turn on grids, guides, and rulers to help you align and create your drawings in a very precise manner. To open, close, or edit grids and guides, perform the following steps.

1. Choose Grid or choose Guides from the View menu, and then choose Edit Grid or choose Edit Guides.
2. Select or clear the Show Grid or Show Guides and Snap To Grid or Snap To Guides checkboxes.
3. Next, type the values you want for horizontal and vertical spacing in the horizontal and vertical fields.
4. If working with guides, select or clear the Lock Guides checkbox.
5. Click the Snap Accuracy arrow and choose the accuracy you want.
6. Click OK.

To enable or disable the rulers, choose Rulers from the View menu.

To create a guide, perform the following steps.

1. Drag the mouse from a ruler onto the screen; a line appears as you drag.
2. Release the mouse where you want your guide to appear.

The Timeline

The dynamic and changing nature of Flash MX requires an extra dimension that isn't seen in graphics software—time. The passage of time is an important part in your movie because you want things to change and interact over time. Any sort of animation that occurs requires transitions that occur as the timeline progresses. You can customize the timeline in several ways (see Figure 4.1).

- To change the appearance of the frames in the timeline, click the Frame View button and choose your settings.

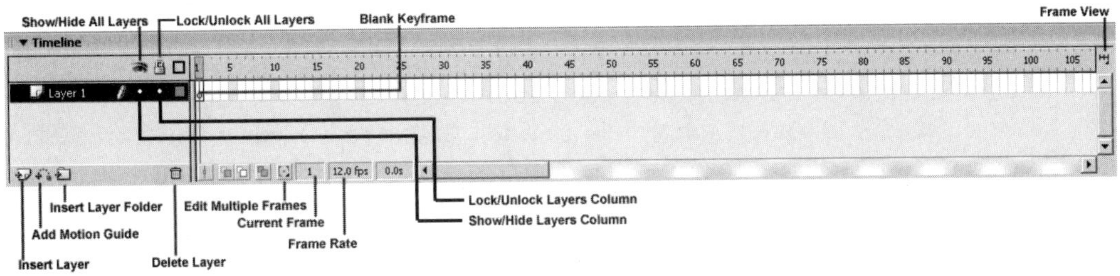

FIGURE 4.1 The timeline.

- To change the frame rate, double-click the frame rate, type a new frame rate into the Frame Rate field, and click OK.

Frames

The timeline is broken up into two elements, frames and layers. As you move horizontally across the timeline, you are advancing by frames. Each frame contains all of the assets that exist on the screen at one point in time. As the playhead advances, the current frame advances and the assets being displayed change at the frame rate specified in the movie. You can create different types of frames. Keyframes can be seen in Figure 4.1; they are frames that appear on the timeline as black dots and define changes in your animations. If a keyframe is empty, it appears as a white dot with a black outline, as shown in Figure 4.1. A regular frame contains whatever the preceding keyframe contained. You can perform the following actions with frames.

- Select frames by clicking and dragging across the desired frames.
- Move a keyframe by clicking a keyframe, and then dragging it to a new location on the timeline.
- Copy/Cut/Paste frames by right-clicking your selection and choosing Copy, Cut, or Paste.
- Insert a new keyframe by right-clicking a frame and choosing Insert Keyframe.
- Erase a keyframe by right-clicking a keyframe and choosing Clear Keyframe.
- Insert a frame by right-clicking a frame and choosing Insert Frame.
- Delete frames by selecting the frames you want to delete, right-clicking the selection, and choosing Remove Frames.
- Edit multiple frames by clicking the Edit Multiple Frames button. (See Figure 4.1.)

Layers

As you move vertically down the timeline, you are advancing by layers. Layers are the horizontal bars that go across the timeline in Figure 4.1. Each layer acts independent of the other layers and behaves as if it has a separate timeline from the rest of the movie. Each layer is transparent and may contain any assets you want to place there, with the layers at the top appearing over the ones at the bottom. To work on a specific layer, simply select a frame in that row. Folders can be created to help organize layers into groups. Several basic actions can be performed on layers:

- Select layers by holding down the Ctrl key and clicking the layers you want to select.
- Create a layer by clicking the Insert Layer button. (See Figure 4.1.)
- Copy/Cut/Paste layers by right-clicking your selection and choosing Copy, Cut, or Paste.
- Move a layer by dragging a layer to a new location.
- Delete a layer by right-clicking a layer and choosing Delete Layer.
- Rename a layer by double-clicking the layer name and typing a new name.
- Show/Hide a layer by clicking in the Show/Hide column. (See Figure 4.1.)
- Show/Hide all layers by clicking the Eye button. (See Figure 4.1.)
- Lock/Unlock a layer by clicking in the Lock column. (See Figure 4.1.)
- Lock/Unlock all layers by clicking the Padlock button. (See Figure 4.1.)
- Create a layer folder by clicking the Insert Layer Folder button. (See Figure 4.1.)

The Tool Panel

The Tool panel contains all of the tools used for drawing, shading, fills, control, sizing, zooming, and everything else that manipulates assets on your stage. It is organized into different sections that group tools of similar functions, as shown in Figure 4.2. The Tools section contains everything that is needed for drawing, painting, and selection. The View section contains tools for zooming and panning the Stage. The Colors section allows you to pick colors for the lines and fills of your shapes. The Options section contains specific modifiers for your tools.

Panels

Your workspace can be arranged however you want it. An important part of any work environment is the ability to make it your own. Everyone likes their tools organized in a unique manner that best suits their needs. For example, some people like to have everything docked on the side of the screen and have the Stage shrink, whereas others like to have everything floating on top of the Stage. To assist with the arrangement of your workspace, Flash MX uses a panel system. All of the panels that appear on the screen can be adjusted, moved, and combined on the screen. Because your panel layout may change based on what type of project you are working on, you can even save and load layouts for future use. You can:

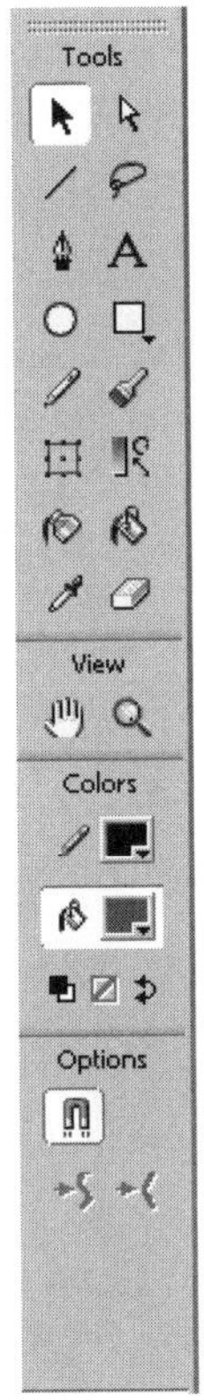

FIGURE 4.2 The Tool panel.

- Open panels by choosing the panel you want from the Window menu.
- Close panels by right-clicking the title bar and choosing Close Panel.
- Access a panel's options by clicking the Options Menu control button, shown in Figure 4.3.
- Resize a panel by dragging one of its borders.
- Expand or collapse a panel by clicking the Collapse Arrow button (Figure 4.3).
- Show or hide all panels by pressing the Tab key.
- Move a panel by dragging its Dragging Handle (Figure 4.3).
- Save a panel layout by choosing Save Panel Layout from the Window menu.
- Load a panel layout by choosing Panel Sets from the Window menu, and then choosing a custom layout.

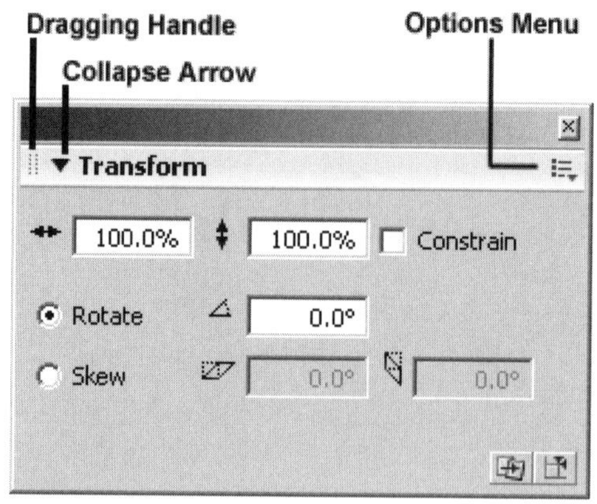

FIGURE 4.3 Panels.

You can also control which toolbars appear on the screen by choosing Toolbars from the Window menu and selecting or clearing the toolbars you want.

Scenes

Your timeline can be broken up into separate scenes for better organization. Your entire movie does not have to exist on a single timeline. For example, you can place an introduction in one scene that moves to the next scene that contains the main animation, followed by a final scene that contains the conclusion. The Scene panel, shown in Figure 4.4, contains all of the tools you need to work with scenes.

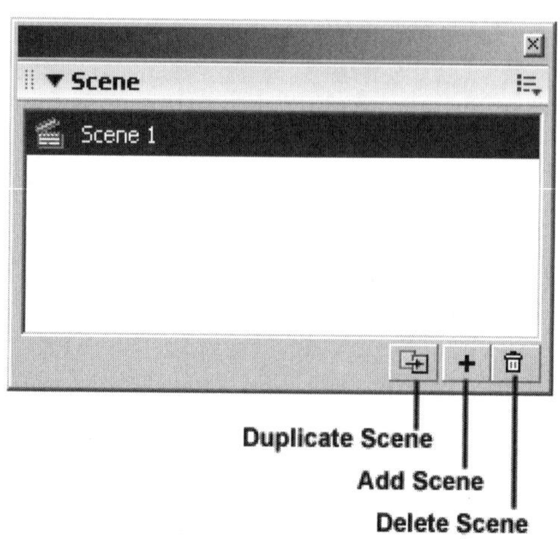

FIGURE 4.4 The Scene panel.

- To add a scene, click the Add Scene button in the Scene panel.
- To rename a scene, double-click the scene name in the Scene panel.
- To delete a scene, click the scene you want to delete and click the Delete Scene button.
- To duplicate a scene, click the scene you want to duplicate and click the Duplicate Scene button.
- To rearrange scenes, drag the scene to a higher or lower location.

Drawing

Flash MX has a host of drawing tools available at your fingertips. The most commonly used drawing tools are available right on the Tool panel. Let's get into which tool is right for different situations.

Colors

An integral part of creating anything of aesthetic value is choosing the right color combinations. Manipulating the color of your drawings can take your animations to a whole new level. There are several options when it comes to choosing colors. Two color pickers appear on the Tool panel—one is for the stroke color and the other is for the fill color, as shown in Figure 4.5. To set a color, click the Stroke Color or Fill Color button and click a color.

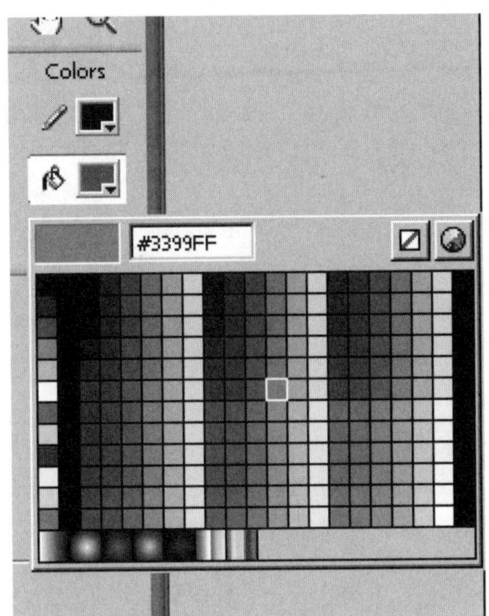

FIGURE 4.5 The Colors section of the Tool panel.

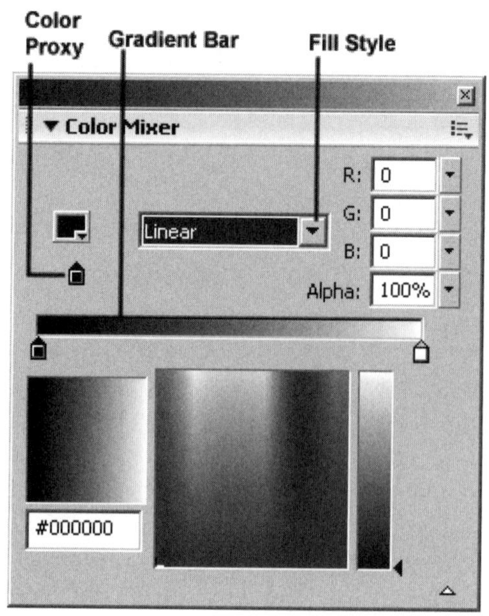

FIGURE 4.6 The Color Mixer panel.

When picking a color, often you will see a color on your Stage that you want to use, but may be unable to find an exact match. Such colors can be obtained in two ways: you can select the Eyedropper tool and click the color you want. Or, you can click a color picker and then click the color you want on the Stage.

Gradients

Rather that creating a solid fill, you have the option of creating gradients that shift from one color to another. To create a gradient, perform the following steps.

1. Open the Color Mixer panel.
2. Click the Fill Style arrow and choose Linear or Radial, as shown in Figure 4.6.
3. Click the gradient bar to place a color proxy.
4. Click a color proxy and choose a color from the color picker.
5. Drag a color proxy to achieve the desired gradient.

After a gradient has been created, it appears in the Fill Color box in the Tool panel and can be used on any shape. The gradient style and arrangement can be changed using the Fill Transform tool, shown in Figure 4.7. The Fill Transform tool allows you to rotate, stretch, and move the gradient to change its appearance.

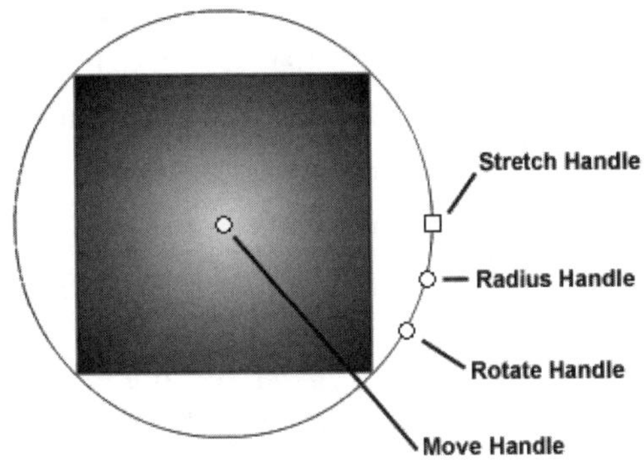

FIGURE 4.7 The Fill Transform tool.

- To rotate the gradient, drag the rotate handle.
- To move the gradient, drag the move handle.
- To stretch the gradient, drag the stretch handle.
- To change the radius of a radial gradient, drag the radius handle.

Simple Shapes

When drawing simple shapes, the Line tool, Oval tool, and Rectangle tool provide a great benefit. You simply click one of the tools and drag on the Stage to form your shape. If you hold down the Shift key as you drag, you get a diagonal, vertical, or horizontal line; a circle; or a square. Later in the chapter, you learn how to morph your drawings to create even more shapes.

Free-Form Drawing

If you need more than just the simple shapes provided, you can take advantage of some other tools. The Pencil tool and the Brush tool can be dragged on the Stage to create a line. The Pencil tool creates drawings that become lines or shape outlines, whereas the Brush tool creates drawings that are the same as a shape fill. To create free-form shapes, use the Pen tool to create an outline that becomes filled after completing a shape. The Pen tool works by creating a series of anchors that define the general shape.

- To draw straight lines, click on the Stage, and click again in another location.
- To draw curved lines, drag on the Stage, and drag again in another location.
- To end a line with an incomplete shape, double-click the mouse in another location.

- To create a complete shape, point at the starting anchor until a small circle appears next to the cursor and click.
- To erase a mistake, select the Eraser tool and drag over the mistake.

Morphing and Transforming Lines and Shapes

One of the greatest features of vector graphics is the ability to morph shapes after you have created them. Flash MX allows you to morph the shape of your drawings in a couple of different ways. You can select the Arrow tool, and drag the shape outline to a new location. Or, you can select the Subselection tool, click the shape you want to morph, and drag the white boxes and blue dots on the Stage.

Adjusting the scale, rotation, and skew of your drawings is also extremely handy. Again, due to the vector format, scaling drawings in Flash MX leaves your drawings looking just as crisp. The Free Transform tool, shown in Figure 4.8, allows you complete control over your drawing. To transform your image, you can choose from the following options.

- Select the Free Transform tool, click your drawing, and drag the black boxes to scale your drawing. If you hold down the Shift key as you drag, Flash MX maintains the same height-to-width ratio as you scale.
- Select the Free Transform tool, click your drawing, and drag the black lines to skew your drawing.
- Select the Free Transform tool, click your drawing, and drag the white circle to change the pivot point of your drawing.
- Select the Free Transform tool, click your drawing, point your mouse just outside of a corner so a partial circle with an arrow appears, and drag to rotate your drawing.

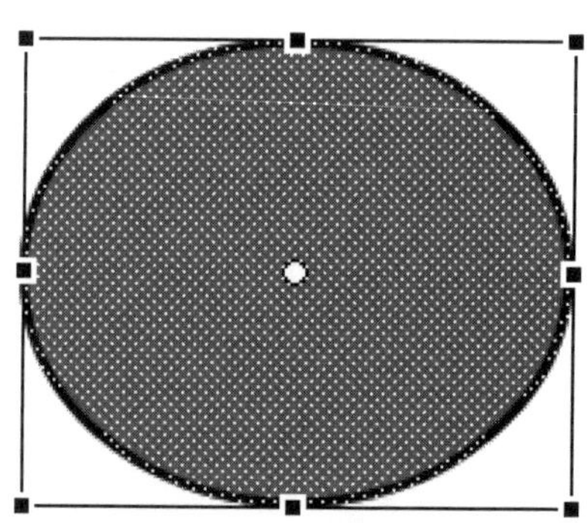

FIGURE 4.8 The Free Transform tool.

Symbols

As your movies become larger, organization becomes more important. An unorganized movie can quickly fall to pieces and leave you in a situation in which updates and incorporating interactive elements become impossible. The organization in your movie should move beyond using different layers, and should take advantage of symbols. Symbols can contain graphics, video, sound, and anything else that can exist on your main timeline. The main use of symbols is to contain assets that appear multiple times in your movie. Rather than having to redraw each asset every time it appears, Flash MX stores it once, and replicates it wherever you place it without increasing the file size. There are three different types of symbols.

Graphics: These symbols can contain drawings and imported pictures that need to be grouped or appear multiple times in your movie.

Buttons: These symbols are used for user interaction and can detect a variety of actions made with a mouse. They contain four frames that can have different appearances for the up, over, down, and hit states.

Movie clips: These symbols can be controlled with ActionScript and can contain any asset you want on its own individual timeline. When editing a movie clip, you have the same control as you would on the main timeline.

Creating Symbols

To create a symbol, perform the following steps.

1. Choose New Symbol from the Insert menu.
2. Select the behavior you want.
3. Select the registration point you want.
4. Click OK.

Converting a Currently Existing Asset to a Symbol

To convert a currently existing asset to a symbol, perform the following steps.

1. Select the assets you want to convert.
2. Choose Convert To Symbol from the Insert menu.
3. Select the behavior you want.
4. Select the registration point you want.
5. Click OK.

Modifying Symbols

Another great feature of symbols is that anytime you change the symbol, it updates all instances that exist in your movie. You have three options to edit your symbol: Edit, Edit in Place, and Edit in New Window. If you edit a symbol, a new tab appears and you edit it on its own Stage. If you use Edit in Place, the background becomes a faded color and you edit it right in context with everything else. If you use Edit in New Window, an entirely new window opens in which to edit the symbol. This is useful when you need to edit multiple symbols at the same time and arrange them around the screen. To edit your symbols, perform the following steps.

1. Right-click the symbol you want to edit and choose Edit, Edit In Place, or Edit In New Window.
2. Make the changes you want.
3. If editing in the same window, click your main movie. If editing in a different window, close the editing window.

The Library and Reusing Symbols

After creating a symbol, it is easy to place it in your movie multiple times. The Flash MX library organizes and stores all of the symbols in your movie. To open the library, if it's not already open, choose Library from the Window menu. To reuse your symbols, perform the following steps.

1. If it is not already open, open the library by selecting Library from the Window menu.
2. Drag the symbol you want from the library onto the Stage.

Animation

The popularity of Flash MX stems from its stunning animation abilities. Flash MX has a variety of ways to create animations that allow an animator full control over the movie.

Frame-by-Frame

Remember those drawings you made in the corner of your textbook to create small flipbook animations in math class? Well, frame-by-frame animation is just like that. It is the same technique used in the traditional 2D cell animation in animated films and cartoons. They involve a series of frames that appear one after another and create a movie that appears as fluid motion. The frame-by-frame style allows for more control over complex animations that don't involve simple motion. Although it does provide more precise control, it causes your movie to rapidly increase in file size because each frame is stored in the file.

Tweening

In traditional cell animation, the frames in-be*tween* the key frames are called "tweens." In Flash MX, tweened animation allows you to easily create movement and changes over time. They work by allowing you to specify the start point and end point of the animation, and choose whether you want a movement animation or a morphing animation. This form of animation allows for character and object motion that adds little to the file size because Flash MX only stores the first and last frames in the file. You can create two types of tweens in Flash MX—motion tweens and shape tweens. Motion tweens must be used between two frames that contain the same group or symbol (no ungrouped drawings or multiple objects allowed) to create simple movement. Shape tweens must occur between free-form drawings and create a morphing animation in which one drawing turns into another. You can control the speed of your tweens by increasing or decreasing the number of frames it takes to make the change or changing the ease setting. To create a tween, perform the following steps.

1. Create the first frame of your tween.
2. Create the last frame of your tween.
3. Click a frame between the first and last frame.
4. Click the Tween down arrow in the Properties panel and choose the tween you want.
5. Type the ease you want in the Ease field. A positive value slows the end of the animation, and a negative value slows the start of the animation.

Imported Video

Flash MX has made it easy to import video. When you bring video into Flash MX, it is immediately placed on the timeline so that you have complete control over the playhead. To import video, perform the following steps.

1. Choose Import from the File menu.
2. Browse to the file you want.
3. Click Open.
4. Type the values you want in the Quality, Keyframe Interval, and Scale fields.
5. Click the Number of Video Frames to Encode down arrow and choose how many frames of the video you want imported for each frame in Flash MX.
6. Click OK.

Sound

Adding sound can take your movie to the next level. Dynamic presentations and animations can be made more powerful and provide a stronger impact by adding background music and sound effects. When adding a sound, you first have to determine where you want it to appear and how long you want it to play. You have several options on how you want your sound to play:

Event: Plays when a frame is entered and plays for its entire duration.

Start: Works the same as an event sound, but cannot have multiple instances playing at the same time.

Stop: Stops the specified sound.

Stream: Starts a sound on the desired frame, but stops when the movie stops. It cannot play longer than the frames it occupies. It also keeps in sync with the movie, so if the animations cannot keep up with the sound, it begins to drop frames.

Implementing sounds can occur anywhere on a timeline or button. When importing a sound, it is best to place it on its own layer so it doesn't become mixed up and lost in other frames. To place a sound in a movie, perform the following steps.

1. Choose Import To Library from the File menu.
2. Click the keyframe on which you want the sound to appear.
3. In the Properties panel, click the Sound down arrow and choose the sound you want.
4. Click the Effect down arrow and choose the effect you want.
5. Click the Sync down arrow and choose the sync you want.
6. Type how many times you want the sound to loop in the Loop field.

Testing

You can preview what your movie looks like throughout the creation process. Although you are able to see the layout and animations you create, you still don't get a chance to see exactly how everything comes together. Movie clips, buttons, and ActionScript in particular are not seen completely in authoring mode. To preview your movie, choose Test Movie from the Window menu.

Publishing

After completing your movie, you must create it in a form that is accessible to users. While authoring your movie, you are working with .fla files, which contain information that is not needed for playback. Flash MX provides a variety of options to automatically convert a .fla file into different types of files, including images files, video files, and executable files. The most common output method for movies is to create a .swf (Shockwave Flash) file. A .swf file is optimized for presentation on the Internet and can be viewed from any browser with a Flash plug-in. To select the type of file you want generated, perform the following steps.

1. Choose Publish Settings from the File menu.
2. Select the file types you want. If you choose to create an .html file, you must create a .swf file, as well. Flash MX uses the .html file to embed a Flash MX movie for presentation.
3. Click the tabs across the top and specify the settings you want for each movie.
4. Click OK to return to your movie or Publish to generate the files.

If you have already specified all of your settings and simply want to publish your movie, choose Publish from the File menu.

LEARNING THE APPLICATION PROGRAMMING INTERFACE

Now that you have learned the basics about the visual interface you use in Flash MX, it is time to move into the scripting language that controls things behind the scenes. Although the program is powerful using the tools provided with the GUI, the application programming interface (API) is a powerful setup that allows you full control over almost everything in your movie. An API serves to provide interactive, dynamic, and real-time control over everything that occurs through a written language. It is the interface through which the visual elements and programmed elements interact. The API provides the application with instructions on how to act.

The Actions Panel

To unlock the API in Flash MX, you must have a method to input your code. All of your programming is done through the Actions panel. The Actions panel is a Flash MX programmer's favorite tool: it provides everything you need, including color-coded code, a function library, autoformatters, an ActionScript reference, and much more. Accessing all of its features is simple! The first step is to decide what mode in which you want to work. The Action panel allows you to create and modify code in two ways, Normal Mode and Expert Mode. Normal Mode allows you to select all of your ActionScript from a list with a simple fill-in-the-blank method for creating everything. Expert Mode allows you to directly type your ActionScript into the window. For this book, you are shown how to create applications and are provided with prewritten code that you place into the panel. For this reason, it is most beneficial to work in Expert Mode. To set your mode, click the Panel Options button and choose Normal Mode or Expert Mode.

How ActionScript Works

ActionScript is the scripting language within Flash MX that allows you to add interactivity to your movies. ActionScript is a very straightforward language that allows you to work with the parts that you need while not requiring you to learn the entire language. It provides you access to everything in your movie, including the timeline, symbols, variables, text fields, and properties. ActionScript is based on the ECMA-262 Specification, the standard method of scripting in JavaScript. Because of this, ActionScript bears a strong resemblance to the style and syntax of JavaScript.

Object-Oriented Programming

The advancement of computers caused a major revolution in programming many years ago. In older languages, code was written in a linear manner that was devoid of objects. Today, the languages used organize information into groups called classes. A *class* is a general description that is used to create instances of itself called *objects*. Each of these objects has a set of properties and behaviors just like objects do in the real world. A common example is a human being. A human contains a variety of properties (characteristics), such as hair color, gender, and weight, and behaviors, such as walking, talking, and breathing. In this example, a human is the class, whereas individual people are objects. Each individual person has specific values for all of the generic properties and behaviors of a human.

The most common use of this theory is found while working with objects in your movie. All of your symbols are objects that exist on your screen. Each object belongs to a class that you defined when you created the symbol—these are what you see in your library. When you create an object on your screen, it has its own set of properties that make it unique from other objects that come from the same class. The most basic property is the relative location of each object in the movie. All objects in your movie exist relative to the timeline. The main timeline of your movie is the root of everything else and, as such, can be referred to as the `_root`. Each of the objects that exist on the main timeline has an instance name that you specify in the Properties panel. These objects exist on the root of your movie, and are referenced as `_root.object`, where *object* is your object's instance name. This style of notation that refers to the specific location of an object is known as an absolute target path. See Figure 4.9 for a visual representation.

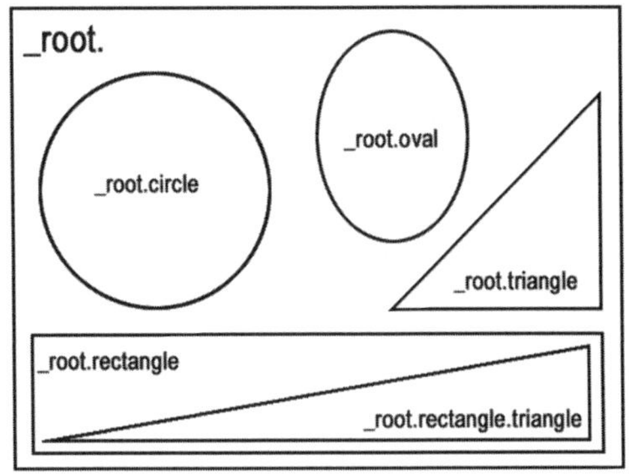

FIGURE 4.9 Absolute target paths.

Syntax

Just like any language, ActionScript has a set of rules that govern how it can be written. In English, we end sentences with periods and use commas to set apart phrases. In ActionScript, specific characters are also required to be placed in specific areas.

ActionScript uses dot syntax, which means a dot (`.`) is used to identify the properties and methods of objects and to reference the location of objects. For example, `_root.myVariable` refers to the variable `myVariable` on the main timeline. Likewise, `_root.myMovieClip` refers to the movie clip `myMovieClip` that exists on the timeline. You can also perform functions on specific symbols this way, by typing the path of an object, followed by a dot, and then the function—for example, `_root.myClip.play()`.

Curly brackets are used to group statements together. Anytime a series of statements exist under one thing, curly brackets identify where to start and end the group, as seen in the following example. The curly brackets tell Flash MX that everything between the brackets should occur on a release.

```
on (release) {
 name = "Jim";
 trace("Hello" + name);
}
```

Semicolons are used to identify the ends of lines. They identify where one complete statement ends so that it is not confused with the next one.

```
_root.barn.size = 500;
```

Parentheses are used to alter the order of operations in arithmetic and identify parameters that are being passed to a function. They serve to group together the information that is being passed around in ActionScript and allow you to pass multiple things at the same time. When passing multiple pieces of information with parentheses, commas (`,`) are used to separate each piece.

```
on (release) {
 total = 4 * (3 + 5);
 myFunction("Testing", 40, false);
}
```

Forward slashes are used to create comments in your code. Comments are statements that have no effect on the movie or actions it performs; they simply serve to help a programmer keep track of what is happening, and give information to other developers who may be working with your code. There are two forms of comments that are used in Flash MX. The first involves two forward slashes (`//`); the second uses a forward slash and asterisk (`/*`) to start a comment and an asterisk and forward slash (`*/`) to end a comment.

```
// This line of code will not be read by the program.
/* These lines of code.
 Will not be read.
 By the Program */
```

Keywords are words that are reserved by ActionScript for a specific purpose. For example, you may not use the words `if` or `else` because they are keywords used for conditional statements. Keywords are color-coded in the ActionScript editor when you complete them.

Constants are values that never change and have specific values. The most commonly used constants contain the numerical value associated with keys on the keyboard. For example, the constant `Key.ENTER` cannot be changed and contains the numerical value for the Enter key.

Event Handlers

Where you place your code determines exactly how Flash MX interprets it. You can place code on a timeline, button, or movie clip anywhere in your movie. If you place code on a timeline, no event handler is required—the code is executed when the playhead arrives at that frame. If you are placing the code on a button or movie clip, an event handler is required to tell the software when to execute the code.

When working with buttons, the on event handler detects mouse actions performed on the movie clip. For example, to have a piece of code execute whenever a button is pressed, you would type:

```
on (press) {
 // Execute this Code
}
```

The event handlers that are associated with movie clips operate in a different manner. They detect different events through the onClipEvent handler. The on handler may only be placed on buttons and the onClipEvent handler may only be placed on movie clips.

```
onClipEvent (enterFrame) {
 // Execute this Code
}
```

Variables

Variables store values that may be used in your scripts. They can contain any type of data, be it numbers, text, or arrays. In Flash MX, initializing and setting a variable is simple; you just type the variable name, followed by an equal (=) sign, followed by the value you want stored. If you want to create a variable without assigning a value to it, use var followed by the variable name.

```
var myVariable
myVariable = 90;
```

Variables can either be seen as global, timeline, or local variables. A global variable is one that exists everywhere in your movie. A timeline variable is one that just exists inside of an object and must be referenced with an absolute path. A local variable is one that just exists inside a piece of code, such as a loop or function. For example, you have a movie clip named ball on the main timeline. This movie clip contains a variable named speed and a loop that contains the variable count. On the main timeline, you have a global variable that has been defined as _global.totalScore. The variable totalScore is a global variable and can be referenced from any timeline as totalScore. The variable speed is a timeline variable that exists inside of the movie clip ball and is referenced with an absolute target as _root.ball.speed. The variable count only exists within its loop and doesn't exist after the loop is exited.

Flash MX automatically detects the type of variable you are creating based on the values you assign. For example, if you assign a number to it, it is a number data

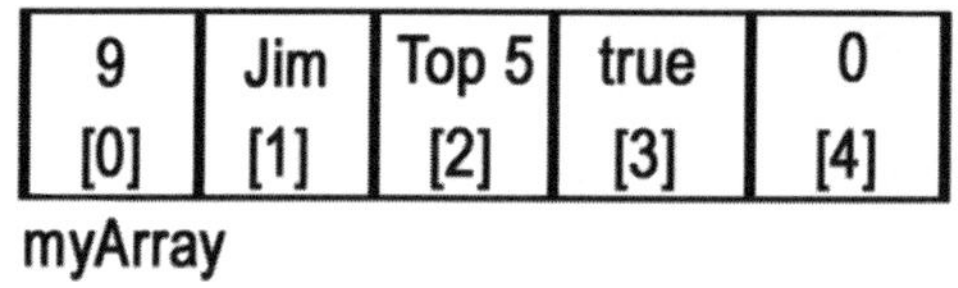

FIGURE 4.10 Contents of the array `myArray`.

type; if you assign a word to it, it is assigned a string data type; and if you assign an array to it, it is assigned an array data type.

Arrays are a series or list of data contained in one variable. Arrays can be used to store any form of data you want and are most useful when it would be beneficial to group a certain set of data together. As shown in Figure 4.10, an array is set up with slots that each have a unique number assigned that starts at 0 and counts up. There is no limit to how many variables an array can contain. Accessing an array is simple. To access the first slot in `myArray` shown in Figure 4.10, you type `myArray[0]`. `myArray[0]` is equal to `9` because that is the value contained in the first slot. Likewise, if you were to access `myArray[3]`, you would find that it contains the value `true`.

Data types are important because they dictate how operations may be performed on them. If you add two numbers, ActionScript returns the value of combining them arithmetically, whereas if you add two strings or a string and a number, ActionScript combines them into a string. For example, `4 + 4` returns `8`, but `My Number is + 4` returns `My Number is 4`. If a variable has been defined but has no value, it is a null value and contains no data. If a variable hasn't even been defined, it is known as undefined and does not exist.

Conditionals

Conditional statements answer the question `if`. They serve as a means to identify if a certain condition has been met, and then they execute code if such a condition has been met. It works by simply comparing the values you specify in your `if` statement and executing the following code should it be true. You can use an `else if` statement to compare another set of values should the initial `if` statement be false. Your final option is to use an `else` statement that executes a set of code, if none of the previous conditions were met. Curly brackets are used to contain all of the code you want executed, if your conditionals are true.

To compare values, you must be familiar with comparative operators. If you want your conditional to be true only if multiple conditions are met, you must use logic operators between each comparison. Table 4.1 outlines the various operators.

The values you are comparing must exist within parentheses following your `if` statement.

TABLE 4.1 Comparative and logical operators

Operator	*Function*
==	Test if equal
!=	Test if not equal
<	Test if less than
<=	Test if less than or equal to
>	Test if greater than
>=	Test if greater than or equal to
&&	And
||	Or
!	Not

```
if (myNumber == 4) {
 // Test to see if myNumber equals 4
} else if (myNumber < 4 || myNumber > 4) {
 // Test to see if myNumber is less than 4 or greater than 4
} else {
 // Execute when the "if" and "else if" are not true
}
```

Loops

Loops are similar to conditionals in that they repeatedly execute a set of code until a specific condition has been met. ActionScript has several types of loops. The main types are `for` loops, `while` loops, and `do...while` loops. `For` loops exist to help you count through cycles. They involve setting an iterator (counting variable), setting the condition upon which you want the loop to stop, and setting the increment you want to change every cycle. Each part is separated by semicolons (`;`) and the code you want to loop should be contained in curly brackets.

```
for (i = 0; i <= 5; i++) {
 // Loop And Increment i while it is less than or equal to 5
}
```

A `while` loop executes a set of code repeatedly until a condition is met. A variation on the `while` loop exists called the `do...while` loop. The `do...while` loop executes your code once before checking the conditional.

```
// While Loop
i = 4;
while (i > 0) {
    myVariable = 5 + i;
    i--;
}

// Do... while loop
i = 4;
do {
    i--;
} while (i > 0);
```

Functions

Whenever you have a set of code that is executed many times in various places, it may be a good idea to organize it into functions. Functions are sections of code that execute upon being called. You have the option of passing values into a function and having it use those values or simply calling it without sending it anything. To define and create a function constructor on the timeline, type `function`, then the name you want, followed by a list of the parameters you want passed into it. The variables you pass into it do not need to agree with the name you assign in the constructor; the variable names you provide in the constructor simply identify how the variable should be referenced inside the function without changing the original value. If you want your function to return a value, you must add a return statement by typing `return`, followed by the value you want returned. Access a function by typing its name followed by parentheses that contain the parameters that are to be passed into it. If there are no parameters to pass, leave them empty.

```
function myFunction (id) {
    // Creates a function named myFunction with a variable passed into
it.
}

function myReturnFunction () {
    return 5;
}

// Calls myFunction
myFunction(5);

// Calls myReturnFunction
myVariable = myReturnFunction();
```

Controlling Movie Playback

Another critical function of ActionScript is to control the timeline. Without ActionScript, your animations would play straight through with no pauses or breaks that allow for user input and interactivity. The following actions can be used to manipulate the playhead.

goto: Jumps to a frame or scene. One parameter sends it to a specific frame in the current scene; two parameters sends it to a specific frame in another scene.

```
gotoAndStop(1);
```

or

```
gotoAndPlay("Scene 1", 4);
```

stop() or play(): Stops or starts the movie.

getURL(): Goes to a different URL.

```
getURL("http://www.mysite.com", _blank);
```

When creating your movie, you can control specific aspects about how it plays back after being published. Using an `fscommand`, you can control if the movie scales when you resize it, if the movie has the standard Flash Player menu when you right-click, and if the movie plays full screen when running a projector file.

fullscreen: `True` plays the movie full screen; `false` plays it normally.

```
fscommand("fullscreen", true);
```

allowscale: `True` scales objects in the movie to the same proportions as the movie. `False` makes the movie always play at the same size.

```
fscommand("allowscale", false);
```

showmenu: `True` enables the full menu on right-click. `False` disables the menu.

```
fscommand("showmenu", false);
```

Debugging

Typically, when you are programming, things don't turn out exactly how you want them. When this happens, it can be difficult to track down the problem because it could exist in an infinite number of places. To help you identify bugs, Flash MX provides you with several tools.

The Trace Function

The `trace()` function is used in conjunction with the Output Panel that appears when you test your movie. Whenever you trace a value, it appears in the Output Panel. This function is most useful when trying to keep track of the values of a variable. You can trace anything, including variables, numbers, arrays, strings, and properties. To use the function, simply pass in the value you want to appear in the Output Panel.

```
trace("currentName = " + currentName);
```

Using the Debugger

As your movies get larger and larger, and more anomalies appear, you can use the debugger to watch objects and their properties to discover why things aren't working. To open the debugger, choose Debug Movie from the Window menu.

Viewing Properties and Variables

After your debugger is open, you can track anything you want. The debugger has a list of all objects in your movie, an area to watch your properties and variables, and an area to step through code, as shown in Figure 4.11. To keep track of the properties and variables in your movie, perform the following steps.

1. Click the movie clip you want to watch.
2. Click the Properties or Variables tab.

Watching Variables

If you need to keep track of a set of important variables, you can use the Watch tab to input specific variables and keep track of their values. To watch a variable, perform the following steps.

1. Click the Watch tab.
2. Right-click the Watch window and choose Add.
3. Double-click a cell in the Name column and type your variable.
4. Press the Enter key.

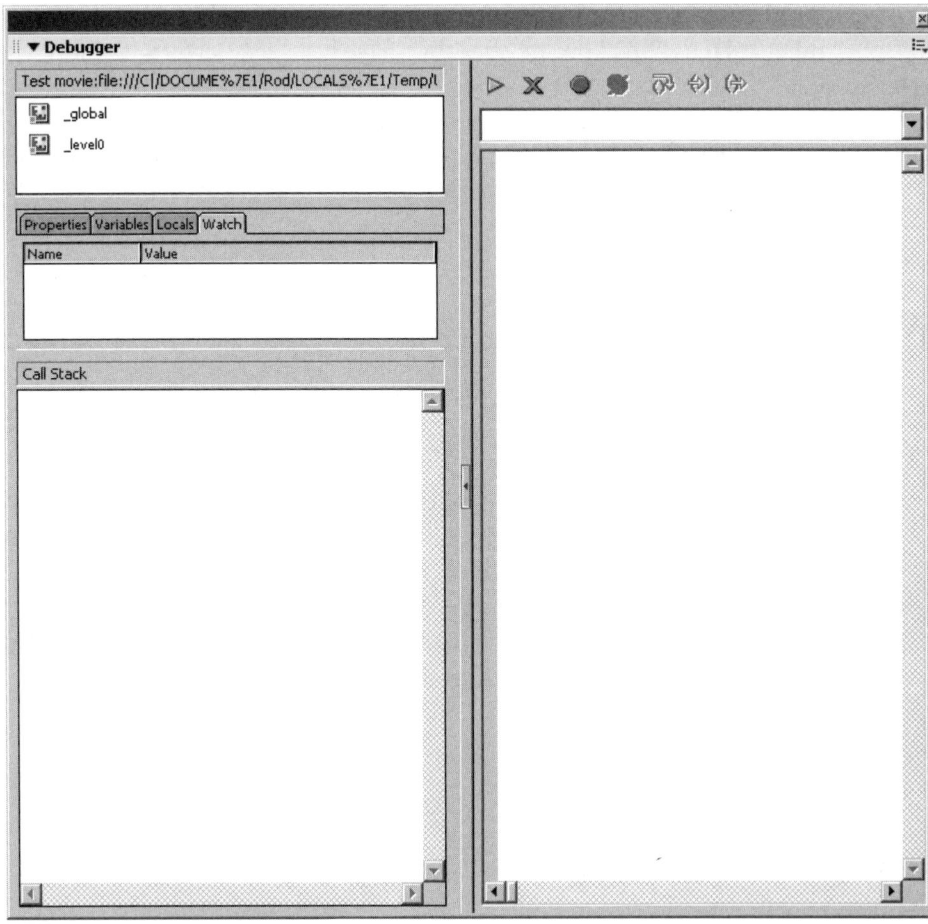

FIGURE 4.11 The Debug panel.

Breakpoints

If you have a piece of code that is being problematic and you want to carefully advance through it, you can set breakpoints in your code that pause the movie in Debug mode. To set or remove a breakpoint, perform the following steps.

1. In the Actions panel, click the line of code on which you want to set or remove a breakpoint.
2. Click the Debug Options button and choose Set Breakpoint or Remove Breakpoint.

After setting your breakpoints, you can debug your movie and watch what happens. To use breakpoints after they have been set, perform the following steps.

1. Click the Continue button to continue playing the movie.
2. Click the Toggle Breakpoint button to turn breakpoints on and off.
3. Click the Step Over, Step In, and Step Out buttons to advance the debugger into, out of, and over functions.

SUMMARY

A basic understanding of how Macromedia Flash MX 2004 works provides you with the means to delve deeper and discover much more about the program. This chapter is intended as a basic introduction, not a complete guide to Flash MX. By now, you should be familiar with both the GUI and API, know how to make drawings and symbols, and apply ActionScript to the timeline and onto your movie clips. This foundation has provided you with all the information you need to perform and, more importantly, understand the upcoming tutorials. Having a grasp on these topics lets you move beyond and begin creating your own Advergame masterpieces.

PART II

The Concepts

5 The Concept: Conceptualizing an Advergame from the Ground Up

It is great to know everything there is to know about branding, marketing, the history of gaming, and every genre of gaming, but when it comes down to it, you won't get anywhere until you can actually conceptualize your game program. At the beginning stages of development, you need to make sure you dive in with all of the background knowledge covered in the preceding two chapters. The goal of the this chapter and Chapter 6, The Creation: Building an Advergame, is to teach you how to mentally go through the process of creating a game. As with creating any program, a game must be organized and crafted in a logical order to function properly without bugs.

Although you may be eager to get started on the actual construction, most of your time is actually going to be spent in the steps that lead up to the final creation. We have broken down the process into two main sections, "The Concept" and "The Creation" (covered in this chapter and Chapter 6, respectively). "The Concept" never looks at what you're going to do, or even how you're going to do it; instead, it focuses on identifying your product and audience, and then designing a game and interface that appeal to the audience while accomplishing your product goals.

STEP 1: WHAT'S YOUR PRODUCT?

It is important to look at the brand as it relates to the company's underlying business strategy. A well-defined strategy helps everyone involved with the brand have a clear and consistent idea of what it is they are trying to achieve. The game should reflect the corporate strategy and be in concert with the brand image. While playing the game, the customer should have the feeling that he wants to be associated with the company and others who share similar interests and values. Because imagery is so important to branding, the look and feel of the game should reflect the visual elements used in the company's other marketing campaigns. The challenge is to blend the brand imageries with a game experience that makes sense and is enjoyable to play.

First, you need to identify the product. If you are marketing the brand itself, your strategy is different than if you were marketing a new product or a preexisting product. Next, you need to identify the objective. What exactly is your game trying to do? It is very important to know what exactly you're setting out to do with the Advergame; if it is created aimlessly, you could end up with a fun game that does little to promote your message. Advergames can serve to get the word out on a new product, create a brand image that is widely recognized, show off the features of an existing product in a fun way, or anything else you want. The last part of this step is to take the time to consider your target audience. At whom are you targeting the game? This should be a study in demographics; what age group, gender, level of education, and so on are you aiming to reach? Will the player need to have some specific knowledge to play the game? You need to make certain you know what your audience needs to be provided with. If you don't gauge your audience first, you'll end up providing a game that isn't entertaining to the people you are most hoping to influence. For example, if you're targeting young children, a flashy, rich interface with simple gameplay is needed. If you create a game that requires a great deal of reading, trivia knowledge, or is complex, adults may enjoy it, but most children will quickly move onto something else.

If you are developing an Advergame for a client, budgeting always becomes a key component in the mix. Although game developers would love unlimited budgets and few deadlines, the realities of the world must be confronted—time and money. Unless you are developing the game for "experience" (that is, for free), your client usually provides you with a budget range and timetable for completion. In the budget process, be certain to factor in a contingency factor of at least 10% for changes that almost always occur during development. Careful upfront planning helps you choose a suitable game that provides the client with the best bang for their buck, and allows you to make a fair profit for your work.

STEP 2: WHAT'S YOUR GAME? OUTLINING A GAME FOR YOUR PRODUCT OR SERVICE

After establishing your game application, listing your objectives, and defining your audience, you need to outline a game that satisfies these requirements. The process of choosing a game may seem daunting at first—there are so many possibilities that it can be hard to decide where to start. The process of conceptualizing an Advergame differs for developers creating a game for themselves or their company and for those who are creating Advergames for a client. Either way, you first need to pick a game genre that your target audience will find enjoyable. You must carefully take all three elements into account—the game application, the objective, and the audience. A good place to begin is to choose a game genre. Let's take a look at some of the options when you are trying to decide what genre is best for your Advergame.

The Genre

Genre is a fancy name for a type or category of game that is marked with a distinctive style, form, or content—for example, a puzzle game, a board game, or a shooter game. Genres act as a common vocabulary for game designers. Understanding game categories provides you with a variety of options so you can choose an appropriate model from which to work. It also helps you communicate your ideas to others—"This Advergame is a puzzle game in which the player uses the client's products to solve problems and overcome the obstacles he encounters." Sometimes, game designers do not use a specific genre, but instead create hybrids composed of features from different categories. Features unique to one genre may be blended; for example, you can create a board game with puzzle game elements. Let's take a look at several popular Advergame genres.

Board games: Many computer board games are modeled directly from their real-world brothers. *Monopoly*® on the small screen looks and feels much like the game you play at the kitchen table. Often, enhancements or special features are added to the digital versions that take advantage of the power of the computer. The addition of music, sounds, animation, and artificial intelligence can deliver a new level of enjoyment to an old classic. One advantage in modeling an Advergame on a popular board game is that many players are already familiar with the rules of the game. Just be careful that your game design does not infringe on the copyrights and trademarks of others.

Quiz games: The popularity and longevity of quiz shows on television has firmly implanted this genre as an important part of our culture. Advergame developers can look to game shows for inspiration and gaming concepts. *Jeopardy!*®, *Wheel of Fortune*®, and *Who Wants to Be a Millionaire*® are popular television games that can inspire you with elements you can incorporate into your own unique application. With these games, you can easily personalize the show by incorporating your company name into the title and having the prizes fit in with your client's product or service. Quiz games are a good option if you want to test or present factual information about your company. They leave lots of room for attractive graphics and animations and can become a very immersive experience when music is added. These games also possess the same quality that board games do—familiar gameplay that can be picked up quickly.

Puzzle games: Puzzle games are a favorite of many people. Puzzle games allow you to create a game that entertains the user while allowing you to add a lot of information supporting your company. Usually, people playing puzzle games are most interested in the puzzle being solved, so they likely won't be turned off by heavy ads, as long as they don't interfere with the game. These games are also extremely customizable because opportunities for product placement are infinite. Every object can carry a logo and every objective can involve saving or solving something related to the company.

Shooter games: These are classic, addictive games that people have loved for decades. They all revolve around the concept of trying to destroy one or more adversaries before the bad guys destroy you. The games are created with a variety of styles. An *Asteroids*-style game involves a ship that can move anywhere on the screen and destroy enemies moving about, whereas a *Space Invaders*-style game involves a ship at the very bottom of the screen shooting at enemies that scroll downward. These games lend themselves well to products that are created to eliminate something, such as virus software stopping viruses, medicine destroying diseases, bug spray killing bugs, or household cleaners cleaning up messes.

Racing games: Designed to quicken the pulse, racing games offer a player the challenge of moving around a track or through an obstacle course at breakneck speeds. Danger lurks everywhere, making the player's dexterity and hand-eye coordination key to success. Adrenaline junkies and those addicted to danger love the thrill of success that comes with navigating through the course. These games can be made with varying difficulty, with the addition of obstacles and higher speeds. There's plenty of room for ad placement everywhere; just think about real racing—the track is surrounded by ads at every turn!

Sports games: One of the largest selling segments of the video game industry are sports games. We love to watch our favorite teams and players, and video games allow us to immerse ourselves in a sport, controlling everything that happens. All types of sports have been made into games. Everything including football, skiing, golf, and pool games have been made. Sports games allow for a lot of ad space, just as racing games do. Part of the sports experience has always involved advertising. Baseball parks and football fields are named after their corporate sponsors, and when you go inside, ads are everywhere. These games tend to be one of the most entertaining types of games, but they are also more difficult due to the physics involved in the motion of the ball.

Deciding on a Game

After picking the genre that best suits your situation, it is time to narrow your options even more. You must now select a game that exists within that genre. Follow the same process you took for picking the genre; try to match your audience to a game that can meet your objectives while not making your product seem out of place. Each of the genres has a broad range of games that appeal to different audiences. Puzzle games can be directed toward young children or adults. Sports games can be directed at hardcore sports fans or people who barely know what soccer is. The possibilities are endless; it is just a matter of finding what works best. You need to be certain that you do not pick a game that forces your product to be the "bad guy." For instance, you do not want to create a game in which your product is the target in a shooter game; you want it to triumph, not be defeated.

Brainstorming for a Client

If you are working with a client and are creating an Advergame for them with a team, the process can be very different. After you have learned about their brand, established a budget and objectives, and helped them understand a variety of game genres, you next need to gather all of the key people together and conduct a brainstorming session. In a brainstorming session, you want to generate a number of ideas and solutions. As the facilitator, begin by writing the project objectives on a white board. The best way to describe a good brainstorming session is "ordered chaos." The goal is to come up with as many ideas as possible during the session. Withhold judgment on ideas; instead, build on the ideas put forth by others. As the group loosens up, encourage and embrace wild ideas, and make everyone feel valuable to the process. After about 15 minutes of idea generation, compare the project objectives with the ideas generated. See if there is a group consensus about any one idea or combination of ideas. Hopefully, one concept comes out on top. As you end the meeting, let the group know the next task is to formalize these concepts into a design specification.

STEP 3: WHAT'S IT GOING TO LOOK LIKE?

Just as a contractor would never set out to erect a building without a detailed set of plans and specifications, game developers need a similar set of documents from which to work. It is important to have a good understanding of the big picture of your project before ever getting started.

To begin planning everything, a specification for the Advergame needs to be created. Game designers call the master specification the "design document." Although there is a natural tendency to keep the design informal (some pencil sketches and some notes), you (and your client) will be better served with a more formal approach. A detailed design document builds upon the basic design and may include a storyboard, script, timelines, programming specifications, graphics, voice-talent, and sound assets needed. Will the game be used online, or will it run from a CD? Are any special plug-ins needed? This level of detail helps you think through the entire project and uncover any "black holes" before the production phase. It is so much easier to make changes in the design document than it is in the actual game.

Creating the Design Document

After having decided on a game, it is time to figure out how things will come together. The first step should be a series of potential layout designs that can be compared to select the best option. These designs can be hand drawn or created in any program, such as Macromedia Flash™, Adobe Photoshop®, Adobe Illustrator®, Macromedia FreeHand®, or Jasc Paint Shop Pro™. The initial designs are intended to be quick, crude layouts that serve as a starting point for further design and allow you to organize everything on the screen. At this point, you need to begin thinking about what events will be happening on-screen and provide space for each condition. For example, if you are creating a racing game, you need to draw a basic track, including a finish line and the various interface elements. The interface elements include a timer, visual controls, and a Help, Pause, and Quit button. Figures 5.1 and 5.2 show two examples of potential, basic designs.

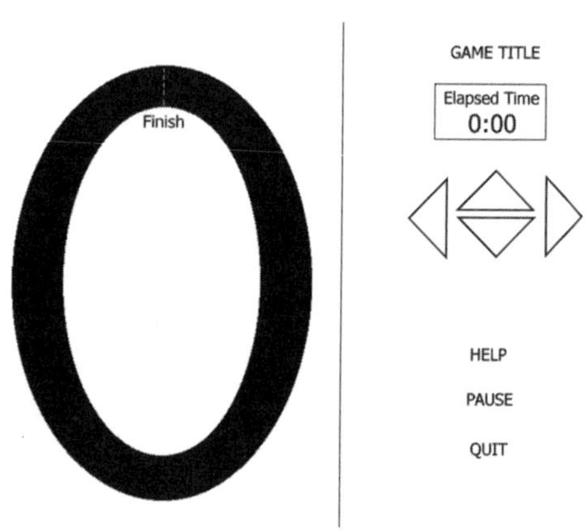

FIGURE 5.1 A sample layout.

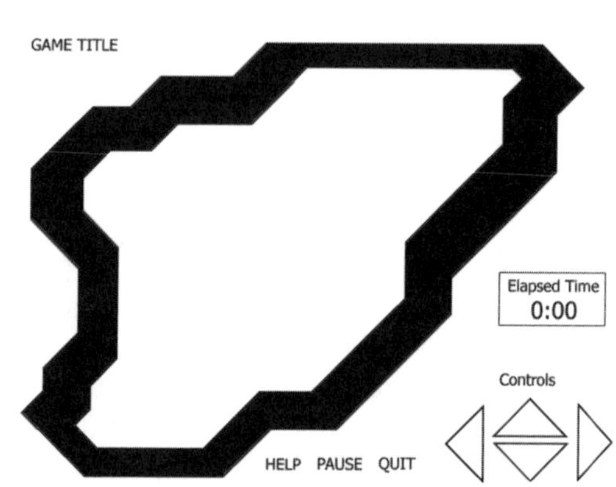

FIGURE 5.2 Another sample layout.

The best design is one that allows for the best placement of all necessary game elements while providing a feel that really draws the player into the game. It also needs to provide ample room for any extra advertising that needs to be included in the piece. For this reason, the layout in Figure 5.2 is much better for an Advergame because of the extra room in the center of the track.

In addition to the interface sketch, you also need to plan out all of the events that will occur in the movie. For example, in the racing game, you need to think about how a "You Won" or "You Lost" message would appear depending on how well the player performs. This part of the document can take several forms. You can create a storyboard with frames that illustrate the events occurring at different parts of the game, as shown in Figure 5.3, or you can map events out on a timeline, as illustrated in Figure 5.4. These formalized layouts help you follow the logical progression the game will take and are crucial for future steps in which you break down the interface and identify what causes the changes in your movie.

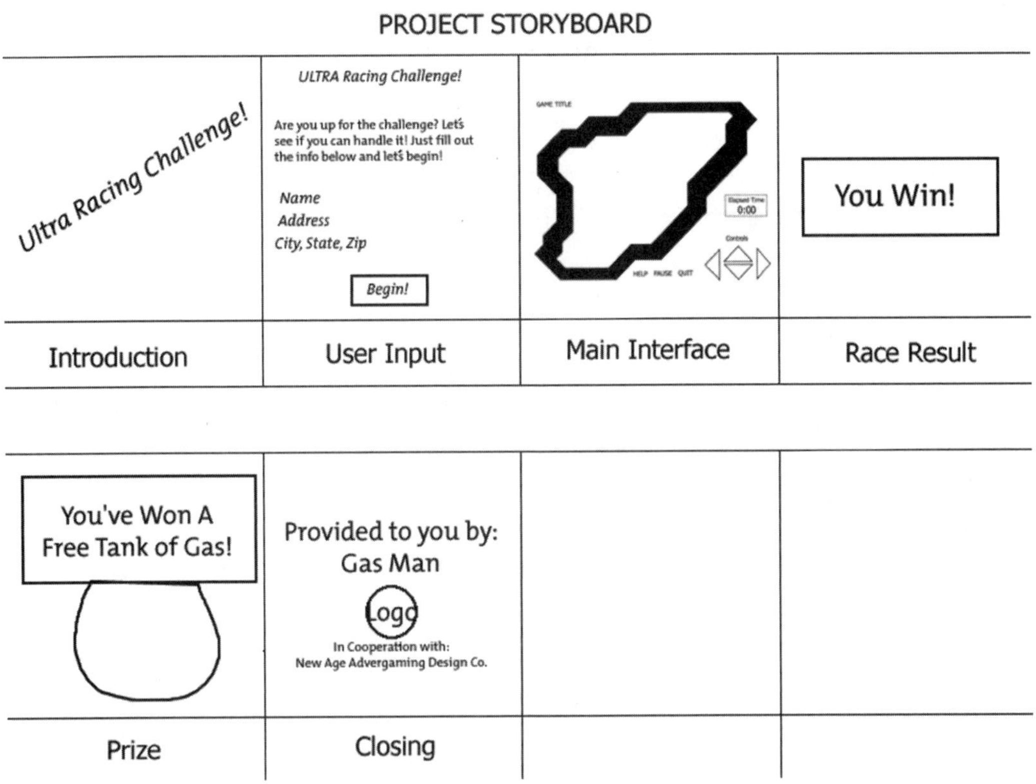

FIGURE 5.3 Sample storyboard.

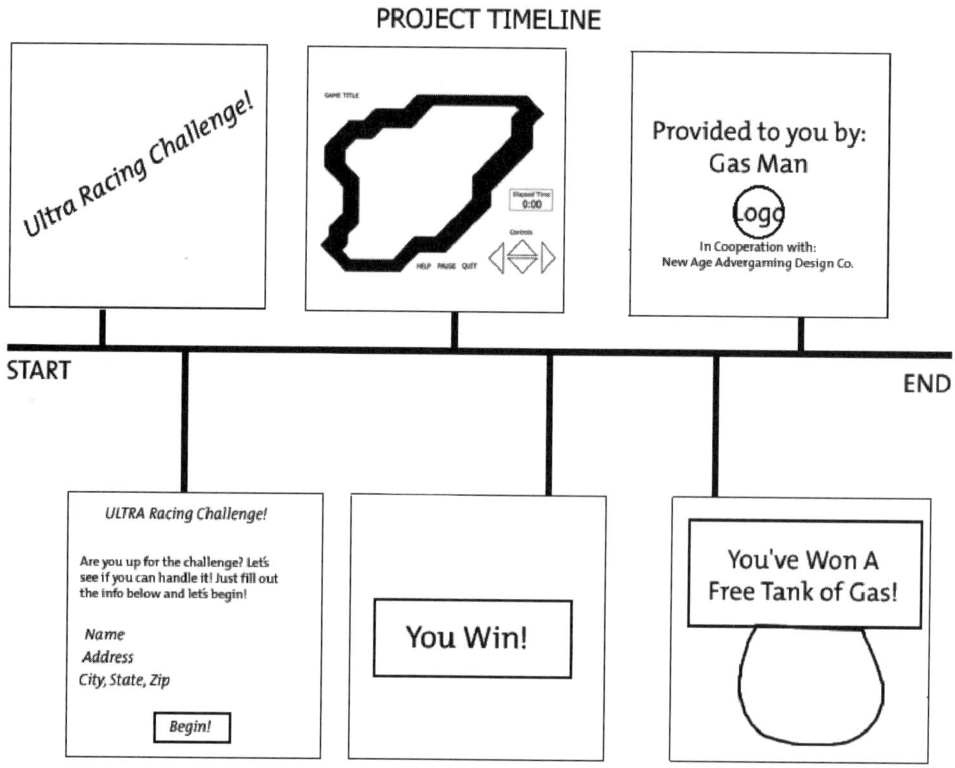

FIGURE 5.4 Sample timeline.

Next, you need to create a list of which assets you need to develop your game. These include sound effects, voice-overs, background music, special video, and anything else that needs to be incorporated.

Creating a Formal Interface

After settling on a basic design, the final interface needs to be fully drawn out. The formal interface design should contain the final graphics that will be incorporated into the game. Using the basic design as a loose guide, you can begin drawing. Each element needs to be placed in its proper location and specific styles need to become evident in the sketch. This is the step in which you begin to visualize exactly how your game is going to look. Instead of drawing generic shapes to represent your elements, they need to actually resemble their true form.

Design Changes

The design document also reduces "mission creep," a military term that describes the expansion of a mission beyond its original scope. Ideally, the design document contains the best ideas possible from the very beginning, but we all know that's not likely to happen. As the project gets underway and the creative juices start to flow, great new ideas may surface. Programmers and artists have a tendency to want to "improve" the initial design, and before you know it, a lizard becomes a fire-breathing dragon! If someone does have a good idea, and wants to incorporate it, a "change authorization form," as shown in Figure 5.5, can be sent to the client for approval. The supplemental form should outline exactly what the new change will be and detail the impact the change will have on deadlines, along with the costs associated with making the change. This process helps keep the project focused and on track without allowing the game to grow and grow to the point that it takes months to complete.

Changes to the design document can exist on several levels. Most often, the changes are a new idea that can easily be added without much hassle; however, sometimes they require integral parts of the game to be reworked with new graphics and programming. These more complicated changes need to be looked at carefully to see if the benefits outweigh the cost. These types of changes can be

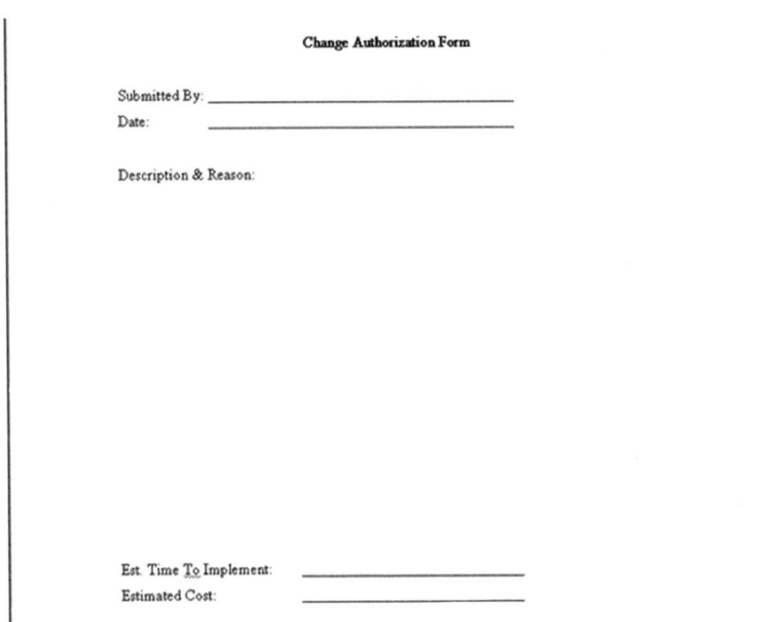

Change Authorization Form

Submitted By: ______________________

Date: ______________________

Description & Reason:

Est. Time To Implement: ______________________

Estimated Cost: ______________________

FIGURE 5.5 Sample change authorization form.

devastating to a project, pushing back the completion date and creating unforeseen pitfalls that did not exist in the original design document.

SUMMARY

The design document provides the information necessary to work efficiently and skillfully. The document should answer any questions about what objects need to look like and what is supposed to happen at various points in the game. With the document in hand, production on the game can finally commence. The design document outlines many aspects of the game that help you decide whether you will use Flash MX or Director MX to create the game. If you need help deciding which program you want to use, refer to Chapter 2, Tools of the Trade: Macromedia Flash MX 2004 and Director MX, in which each program's strengths and weaknesses are explained in detail.

A formal "kickoff" initiates the development of the game. If the game is being developed by a single person, this is simply deciding on project milestone dates and starting the game, but if a team is working together on the project, it means much more. In the latter case, the kickoff is a formal meeting in which each part of the project is assigned to a team member, and progress milestone dates are established. Regardless of the number of people working on the project, one last look should be made to the design document to ensure that there are no roadblocks. Start planning how to deal with the areas in the development process that pose the most difficult challenges. With some careful planning, attention to detail, and remaining focused, your Advergame can be completed on time and within budget.

6 The Creation: Building an Advergame

With the concept for our Advergame in place, we can begin the process of building our Advergame. The tools for our craft will be Macromedia Director MX or Macromedia Flash MX 2004, but before we can start using our tools to build our Advergame, we must set the foundation in place, for all pursuits must begin on a sturdy foundation. However, the process of developing an Advergame, or any video game, is not an easy one. This is an important fact that we must point out before we begin. This chapter does not show you a cookie-cutter method of writing games, a worksheet that you can follow from which magically an Advergame appears. In this chapter, we present strategies and a process that we follow throughout the rest of the book. These hone our vision and allow us to apply our creative energies in an organized and productive way. By imposing order on the chaos, we can build an Advergame.

STEP 4: IDENTIFYING THE ELEMENTS OF YOUR GAME

At this point, we have a clear idea of what the game looks like. We have ideas about how the user interacts with our game and how the game works. Now, we must take these ideas, categorize them, and put them into little, well-defined boxes. These boxes are the fundamental pieces of the game, the *elements* of the game. The elements that we discover shape the way in which our game is structured in its code; the better the classification, the simpler the code. But there is no magic way to come up with the ideal classification. This comes with experimentation and experience.

But let us develop a process that we can follow, which helps us find and categorize the elements. The first step of this process is deciding on a clear *specification*. This should be a written specification, not just something we come up with in our heads and then pluck ideas from our thoughts. Putting ideas down on paper allows us to be specific, allows us to look at our ideas as a whole, and allows us to more clearly see the relationships between the ideas. For example, let us write a specification for a *Pac-Man* game.

A Pac-Man character, shaped like a big mouth that moves around in a maze, eats pellets to collect points. He eats a pellet by passing over it. These pellets line the path throughout the maze. If he eats all the pellets, he moves on to the next level. However, in his way are ghosts that chase him, and they kill him if they catch him. A ghost catches Pac-Man if he runs into him, or if Pac-Man runs into the ghost. But, if Pac-Man eats a special power pellet, he can now eat the ghosts, and they run away from him. This vulnerability only lasts a short period of time. If he eats a ghost, the ghost returns to a pen in the center of the maze. When the period of vulnerability ends, the eaten ghosts leave the pen and reenter the maze to chase Pac-Man, and all ghosts that have not been eaten resume chasing Pac-Man. Our character has a limited number of chances, or lives, to collect all of the pellets in a level. When he runs out of lives, the game is over.

With our specification in hand, we can find the elements. From the specification we have written, we list the basic elements:

- Pac-Man
- Ghost
- Pellet
- Power Pellet
- Maze
- Level
- Game
- Points
- Lives
- Pen

The items in this list follow directly from the words of the specification, particularly the nouns. To reiterate the significance of this step, one of the most important things we can do to make the process of building an Advergame easier, is to develop a very clear specification. This allows us to come up with the essential elements much more efficiently.

STEP 5: RECOGNIZING HOW THE GAME'S ELEMENTS INTERACT

Having developed the list of elements, we can now begin the process of determining how these elements interact. This process helps us to see how the elements that we have defined relate to one another in a functional way—in essence, how they communicate with one another and how the user communicates with these elements to produce the gameplay. Again, having a clear specification tremendously helps in working this step, as some of the relationships become self-evident. In deciding the other relationships, the ones that must be inferred from the specification, our understanding of the game increases, and we can avoid many surprises. Of course, we should make clear that in the course of any complex task such as this, surprises are inevitable. We may find that a particular relationship needs fine-tuning, or implementing one relationship exposes yet other relationships. Or, we may find that a particular set of relationships is unworkable in practice, and needs to be completely rethought. In these cases, we end up right back in this step. That is the nature of the process of software development; we don't ever completely leave the drawing board. When you read the chapters in Part III of this book, The Creations, you might get the impression that we just came up with the ideas and the implementation in one linear, straight shot. Unfortunately, that's the limitation of presenting these ideas in a book form. But trust us; we go back and forth between these steps just like everybody else. It may seem frustrating at first, and it still is frustrating for seasoned developers, but it gets easier with experience. But, if it were easy, everybody would be doing it, right?

Let us use the specification to come up with the relationships between the different elements in the Pac-Man game. These relationships are more easily seen when represented in diagram form. This area is very well-documented; there are many different ways of doing this, and it can easily become very complicated. But, for our purposes, we keep it simple. The elements are in bubbles, and we connect the bubbles with arrows; the base of the arrow is on the element that is the doer of some relationship, and the point of the arrow points to the element that is the object of the relationship. To demonstrate how we do this, we pick apart the relationships in our sample Pac-Man game. The following are words and sentences, with the italics representing the relationship, the subject of the sentence being the doer, and the direct object being the object (well, grammar is a little more complicated than that, but it should be clear which is the doer and which is the recipient). This way, it should be fairly clear how we arrive at the diagrams in Figures 6.1 through 6.3. So, on with the relationships in sentence form:

Pac-Man moves around in a Maze.

Pac-Man moves when the user *presses down* on one of the arrow keys on the keyboard. This causes Pac-Man to move up, down, left, or right, depending on the key pressed at a certain distance. Moving this certain distance, Pac-Man could potentially *hit* a wall, in which case that move is *not allowed*. See Figure 6.1.

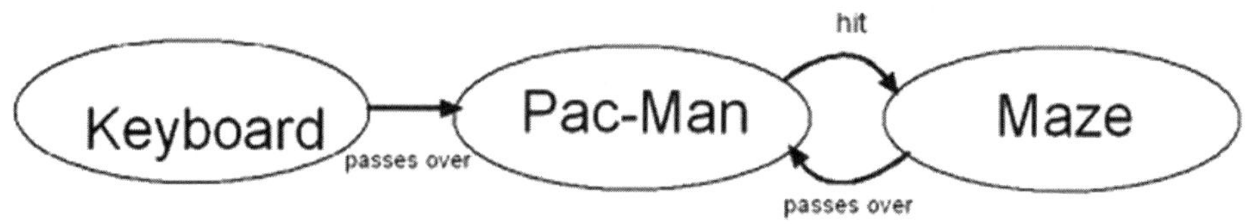

FIGURE 6.1 Pac-Man moves around in a Maze.

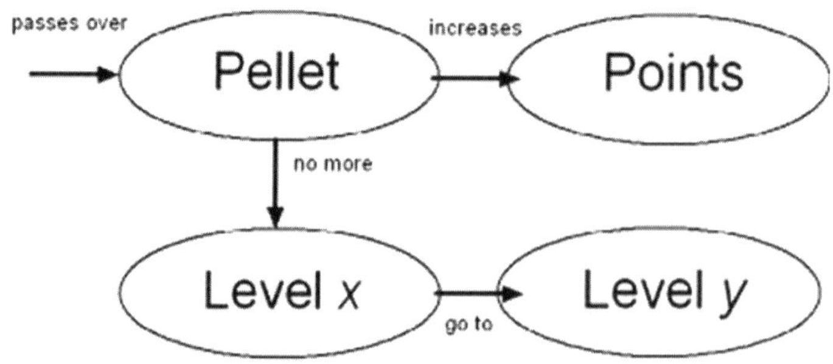

FIGURE 6.2 Pac-Man eats Pellets to collect Points.

Pac-Man eats Pellets to collect Points.

Pac-Man eats a Pellet by *passing over* it, and the action of eating the Pellet causes Points to *increase* the number displayed. When there are *no more* Pellets, the user *goes to* Level *y* from Level *x*. Otherwise, the user *stays in* Level *x*. See Figure 6.2.

Pac-Man runs into Ghost or Ghost runs into Pac-Man.

Pac-Man can *run into* a Ghost, or a Ghost can *run into* Pac-Man. If the Ghosts are chasing Pac-Man, then the Ghost that catches Pac-Man *kills* him. If Pac-Man *passes over* a Power Pellet, then the Ghosts must *flee*. And then, if Pac-Man *runs into* a Ghost, Pac-Man *kills* that Ghost. When Pac-Man *passes over* the Power Pellet, this *starts* a **Timer**. When the Timer reaches zero, the Ghosts may *chase* Pac-Man again. If a Ghost *kills* Pac-Man, the number of Lives *decreases*. When the number of Lives reaches zero, *go to* **Game Over**. Notice that in finding the relationships, we actually found another two elements, Timer and Game Over. See Figure 6.3.

Now that we have the relationships, we have a better idea of how the game works at a much more detailed level. This understanding makes things much easier when we actually write the code.

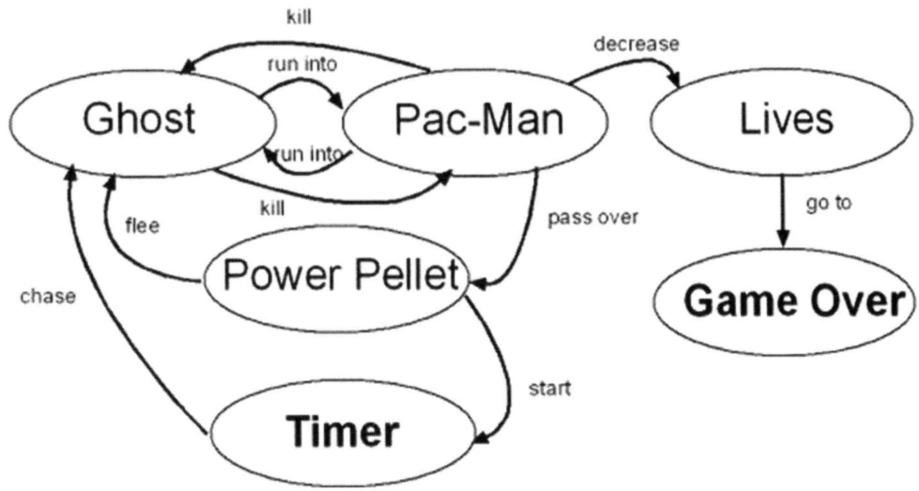

FIGURE 6.3 Pac-Man runs into Ghost or Ghost runs into Pac-Man.

STEP 6: IDENTIFYING THE FUNCTIONALITY OF YOUR GAME

With the relationships determined in diagrams, we can begin the process of translating this representation into one that Director MX or Flash MX understands. In this step, the relationships between ideas are transformed to *function calls* between *objects*. In Macromedia Director MX terminology, these are *messages* between *sprites*. In Macromedia Flash terminology, these are *actions* done on *symbols*. In this chapter, we speak generically, so that this material is universally applicable. In Part III of this book, we implement these ideas specifically for Macromedia Director MX or Macromedia Flash MX 2004.

The translation process is fairly straightforward. First, we must determine if the relationship is something that is already pretty much provided by Macromedia Director MX or Macromedia Flash MX 2004. That is, we don't have to write more than one or two lines of code to implement the relationship. If this is the case, we won't have to write a separate message handler or action. However, if implementing the relationship is more complex then that, then it is better to write a separate handler or action for it. This keeps the code from becoming too messy, and makes it easier to debug if something goes wrong. Also, keeping things separate makes things easier to change, in the event the relationship is correct but our implementation of the relationship is not. That way, we don't have to dissect the code from a lot of surrounding code. After we add something really complex, removing it might cut out other important code or change the code in ways that we cannot at first glance understand (or many, many glances). This leads to another good practice when we write our scripts. Always keep backups! It's possible to ruin a script in the course of tweaking. Figuring out exactly which functions to write is made much easier with the diagrams we make.

The functions are the relationships, and the functions belong to the object that is on the receiving end of the relationship. The doer of the relationship calls the function. In Director MX, these functions make up the *message handlers* of the *behavior*, and the doer sends a *message* to the receiver to make it do things. In Flash MX, similarly, these functions make up the *actions* belonging to a *symbol*, and the doer calls the action. In the games we develop in Part III, we show this in much greater detail. For now, let us go over the general idea of the functionality of the Pac-Man game, step-by-step, following the outline in Step 5.

Pac-Man moves around in a Maze.

presses down:

This can be implemented intrinsically, within the body of the script, or a frame script can send a message to Pac-Man. This should be implemented as a function in either case, sticking to the principle of code separation. We can simply call this function from the function called when we enter the frame, and pass it the numeric code of the key that is pressed. Because Pac-Man is on the receiving end of this action, we add the function `keyPress` to the Pac-Man object.

hit wall & not allowed:

Both Macromedia Flash MX 2004 and Macromedia Director MX provide good collision detection functions, so we implement this functionality without using custom functions.

Pac-Man eats Pellets to collect Points.

passing over:

Macromedia Flash MX 2004 and Macromedia Director MX both provide functions to do this. No custom function required. When a Pellet is passed over, we must reduce the number of Pellets by one. We can represent this as a *global variable* whose value we decrement.

increase:

When a Pellet is passed over, we must tell the `Points` object to increase its value. So, the Pellet calls the `increasePoints` function belonging to the `Points` object.

no more:

We can use the global variable described earlier to determine when we have reached this point. We now call the `go to` function.

go to & stay in:

We don't need a handler to do this; it's a built-in operation of both platforms.

Pac-Man runs into Ghost or Ghost runs into Pac-Man.

run into:

This is collision detection, which is a built-in operation.

kills:

Pac-Man can kill a Ghost and a Ghost can kill Pac-Man. Each must send a message to the other telling the object to die. Because the messages must be unique, so we do not confuse killing Pac-Man with killing a Ghost, we use two different function names: `killPacMan` and `killGhost`. The function `killPacMan` belongs to the `PacMan` object because he is the receiver of the kill relationship, and the function `killGhost` belongs to the `Ghost` object because it is the receiver of that kill relationship.

passes over:

This is collision detection, which is a built-in operation.

flee:

The Power Pellet tells each Ghost to flee. Because the Ghost is the recipient of the relationship, the function `flee` belongs to the `Ghost` object.

starts:

The Power Pellet starts a Timer, during which the Ghosts are vulnerable to being eaten. Now, there is no actual `Timer` object on the screen, so the responsibility for managing the Timer must go to the script controlling the frame. So, the Power Pellet calls the function `startTimer` belonging to the frame script.

chase:

When the Timer, which is managed by the frame script, reaches a count of zero, it tells each Ghost to chase Pac-Man again. Because the Ghost is the recipient of this relationship, the function `chase` belongs to the `Ghost` object.

decreases:

Here is an interesting case. Let's assume that there is a maximum of three lives. Each life is represented as a little Pac-Man image. Each one is a separate entity. To control all of them, we should implement this in a frame script because this script is not attached to any one sprite. In this way, the frame script can send a message to each life indicator when Pac-Man calls the function `decreases`. The life indicator disappears when this happens, and controlling the visibility of objects is built into both platforms. So, clearly, because the frame script is now the recipient of the action, the function `decreases` belongs to it.

go to:

We don't need a handler for this; it is a built-in operation.

So, now we have the list of the preliminary functions. It is preliminary because later we may find that the specification is incomplete, or that we want to add more features to the game. In these cases, we must return to Step 4 to redesign the insufficient parts or incorporate new functionality and proceed from there. Game development is definitely not a linear process. The next step is to develop these functions into a working game. All the previous steps give us the skeleton, the early parts of Step 6 give us the names of the muscles, and now we stick these muscles onto the skeleton to get our game going. There are no hard and fast rules for doing this. Like writing a story, the words come from your own mind, following a plot of your design. There are many techniques to do this, starting from the plot devices listed in Part I, The Tools. Learn these first. They are the building blocks of game development. With these techniques in mind, you can come up with the outline, the sequence of steps that make up each function. In computer terminology, this is called *pseudocode*. Pseudocode is not Lingo or ActionScript. It is English, structured in the form of a programming language, with each step precisely worded, the way we are using words in formulating the specification with each encompassing one basic action. To demonstrate how we do this, let's write the pseudocode for the function `keyPress`. The psuedocode we present here is very, very basic. In actual practice, this would involve many more steps, but for simplicity, we look at one function in isolation. Part III shows in much more detail how this would look in practice.

function keyPress (argument: keyCode - the code of the key that was pressed):

1. Save the (`x, y`) coordinate pair location of `PacMan`.
2. If the value of `keyCode` is `39` (the right arrow key):
   Increase the value of `PacMan`'s `x` coordinate by the amount of `PacMan`'s width.
3. If the value of `keyCode` is `37` (the left arrow key):
   Decrease the value of `PacMan`'s `x` coordinate by the amount of `PacMan`'s width.
4. If the value of `keyCode` is `40` (the down arrow key):
   Increase the value of `PacMan`'s `y` coordinate by the amount of `PacMan`'s height.

5. If the value of `keyCode` is `38` (the up arrow key):
   Decrease the value of `PacMan`'s `Y` coordinate by the amount of `PacMan`'s height.
6. If `PacMan` intersects the Maze, this move is invalid:
   Put `PacMan` in the location saved in Step 1.

Let's look at this in more detail. After the function name, we list the *arguments*. When you call a function, you must provide it with values corresponding to each of the *variables* in the *argument list*. A variable is a name that has a value associated with it. The value associated with a variable can be changed. So, in the preceding example, `keyCode` is a variable that has the value of the numeric code of the last key pressed associated with it. This value is associated with `keyCode` when this function is called. Notice that each step is very specific. We spell out *exactly* what happens to Pac-Man in each step. Notice also, that the hyphen in Pac-Man's name is gone. You cannot have hyphens in the names of variables or other names.

Pseudocode is useful for beginners and experts alike. However, experts don't write so much down in their pseudocode. For them, it is simply a tool to formulate the plot, and each line can represent several lines of Lingo or ActionScript. For the beginner, English (or some other *human* language) is a more natural medium in which to formulate ideas because he has not developed the fluency to think in Lingo or ActionScript. For the beginner, it is probably easier to write the script in fully developed pseudocode and then translate to Lingo or ActionScript. But in either case, remember that pseudocode is your friend!

SUMMARY

In this chapter, we present a process for developing an Advergame. This process begins by identifying the building blocks, the *elements*, of our game. The next step is to tie these elements together, to find the relationships between them that define the way in which they function in the game. Then, we must define precisely this functionality using diagrams and precisely worded sentences in a human language. With all the pieces in place, we can begin the process of putting them together, to create the code that drives our game. This process is not linear, even though we provide numbered steps. These numbers are not necessarily a sequence of steps, but a way of categorizing ideas. In the course of development, we may find ourselves going backward and revisiting steps many times. This is the natural state of affairs. After all, there is no magic cookie-cutter method to making an Advergame.

7 The Launch: Getting the Word Out on Your Game

The final goal of any Advergame is to actually get returns on your investment, but before that can ever happen, you must find a way to get your Advergame into the hands of your target audience. You can use a variety of methods to successfully deploy a game, and in this chapter, we take a closer look at some of those options. Factors such as the computer demographics of your target audience, the speed at which you want the game delivered, how it is packaged, and the budget you have to work with must all be considered. We begin by taking a look at some of the different aspects of game delivery and how these factors can impact the method of delivery you choose. After working through the process of choosing the delivery method, we talk about how to use Macromedia Flash MX 2004 and Macromedia Director MX publishing tools to optimize your project for the medium you have selected.

DECIDING ON A METHOD OF DELIVERY

Sometimes, it is best to start with the end result in mind. So let's start by looking at several of the final delivery methods and work backward to find out which kinds of game deployment situations fit best. Advergames may be distributed using one or more media choices; to keep things simple, we divide them into four main categories—Web, CD-ROM, kiosk, and cell phone distributions. In the next few sections, we look at each category in-depth.

Web Distribution

The Internet has caused the distribution of products, services, and advertising to reach new levels. Today, you can go online to buy everything from groceries to pizza to cars. You can obtain technical support on a broken appliance, check the latest news, or just have fun surfing. One thing is for certain when you are online—advertising is everywhere! Within minutes of logging on, you are exposed to dozens of enticing products and services, available 24/7, and usually just a keyclick away. With broadband Internet access becoming widespread, people are downloading more, watching richer multimedia content, and browsing more every day, which makes this an ideal landscape for the distribution of your Advergame. The Web, like all distribution options we look at, has its advantages and disadvantages. It allows for a large number of people to access your content, for a modest monetary investment, and entails little time or manpower to distribute. One shortcoming of the Internet is its size. Your Advergame can easily get lost in a sea of content. Other limitations revolve around the file size of the game. It takes a long time for gamers with slower connections to download large files, especially those involving video or heavy graphics and sound.

Advertising on the Web comes in many forms, many of which can be tapped as resources for getting the word out about your game. The three most popular methods of deployment are:

- Sending out an e-mail with the game to a mailing list
- Offering your Advergame on your company Web site or on a popular game portal (such as *www.kewlbox.com*)
- Providing a full standalone game for download that people can play on- or offline

Each of these methods has its own unique advantages and disadvantages that must be weighed carefully.

Advertising by E-Mail

With spam e-mails becoming so commonplace today, the idea of sending an e-mail advertising your game to an entire mailing list seems annoying to some, but it can still be a very effective method. The method that you should use doesn't involve underhanded tricks or sending mail to individuals who don't want it—instead, it relies on the address books and e-mail lists of interested clients and customers that your company has collected. Permission-based marketing relies on individuals who have requested information about your products or services and have disclosed their contact information willingly. You can prepare an e-mail for these situations in two ways—one involves including the game inside the body of the e-mail for people to play right in their inbox, and the other involves sending a link to your Web site that provides the game. Each method has its advantages and disadvantages. With the first method, the user is immediately shown the graphics and sounds in the game and quickly becomes interested in what exactly it's doing. On the other hand, it requires games to have small file sizes because large attachments can be bounced back by e-mail clients, alienates some clients because the game can be disrupting at work, and cannot be viewed by clients who disable or do not support ActiveX controls. The second method is distributed to the same people without any of the disadvantages of the other method, but is much easier to ignore and forget, which increases the potential number of users who never try the game.

Hosting on a Company Web Site

Hosting a game on your company's Web site has several benefits. First, it doesn't risk irritating customers who dislike blast e-mail, and second, it drives traffic through your Web site in order to reach the game. After people arrive at the Web site, the chances of them browsing other sections for information on your company increase, helping people become more familiar with your business. The disadvantage to simply launching it on your site is the need to expose it to more individuals. As Dan Ferguson, Creative Director for Blockdot told me, "Simply putting your Advergame on your own Web site is like Target putting a billboard inside one of their stores." The idea of the game is often to drive traffic to the site in the first place. So, making the game available on your Web site often is best when used in conjunction with a blast e-mail that directs people to the main site, where they can follow a link to the actual game or with a card that can be handed to customers or clients who come into the office.

Providing a Standalone Game for Download

The final method of providing a full download is useful for games that have large file sizes or have enough information to be able to accomplish its objectives by allowing someone to play it repeatedly. It's also beneficial for those who want to get the game now and try it later, or those who have dial-up Internet access and don't want to tie up a phone line while playing the game.

Advantages of Web Distribution

In summary, the advantages of Web distribution include the following.

- Is cost-effective
- Has a large potential audience
- Spreads well by word of mouth

Disadvantages of Web Distribution

In summary, the disadvantages of Web distribution include the following.

- Advertising on the Web has begun to irritate people—your message may get filtered out before it reaches its intended target.
- The Web is huge and your game can easily be overlooked.
- Slow download speeds limit file size.

CD-ROM Distribution

The CD-ROM has revolutionized the way media is exchanged today. Not only can large amounts of data be stored, but music can also be recorded with amazing clarity on a small disk. The high-capacity CD-ROMs available today, which store 700 MB of information, provide more than enough space for an Advergame or series of Advergames. In fact, so much space is available that extras, such as videos or a presentation, can be included on the same disc. CD-ROM duplication has become extremely cheap and the methods for duplication can be tailored to your situation. For large distributions, a copy of the CD-ROM can be sent to a company that presses large numbers of CD-ROMs in a short period of time. For smaller distributions, CD-Rs can now be found at 20 cents and lower, allowing you to burn the CD-Rs in-house on a standard CD burner. Technology has advanced to the point that even DVD-ROMs are available. DVD-ROMs can store up to 4.7 GB of information on one disc, but this is probably more than most people need.

CD-ROM distribution can utilize several venues, including mailings, handouts to clients and/or customers who come by the company, "giveaways" at trade shows or public areas, and even CD-ROM business cards. Each method has its own benefits that are discussed in the next sections, but CD-ROMs in general have benefits and drawbacks. CD-ROMs provide you with the ability to include large amounts of information on familiar and easy-to-handle media. Because people are actually receiving a product in these situations, they are more apt to try it out because they have something solid to look at. In addition, receiving a CD-ROM from a company tends to signify that the company felt it was worth investing money to produce products for customers and clients to view, making people feel more appreciated by the company. The disadvantages to CD-ROMs include the fact that they do cost more than other feasible alternatives, and once distributed, there is no chance to recall them in the event information needs to be updated and redistributed.

Distributing CD-ROMs through Mailings

Distributing a CD-ROM through mailings is an excellent way to distribute the game. Because they arrive in a package addressed to an individual, people are more inclined to open it and try it out. For example, Chrysler sent out a CD-ROM insert in *WIRED Magazine* that was packed full of information, with exclusive video and music from Celine Dion and a link to their Advergame that was hosted on their Web site. The CD-ROM's fancy packaging and labeling made it almost irresistible to try out, giving Chrysler a "foot-in-the-door" to showcase their cars. It's also a sure way to have people receive the game and know it got to them. With the filtering out of e-mail attachments and monitoring at the workplace, it's likely that some Web releases can get lost or accidentally filtered out as spam—a problem not experienced with a package sent to a person. The main downside is that the additional packaging and shipping increases the cost per CD-ROM. It is also difficult when a new company may not have developed mailing lists for distribution purposes.

Distributing CD-ROMs through Company Handouts

A company handout is a good way to get the game out, if your objective is to convince an interested client to try your products and services, convince a current customer to request more of your services, or even to remind them that your company is here when they need you. It's easy to hand out, doesn't require extra people to distribute, and doesn't need extra money invested in packaging. This method is not ideal for companies that need to introduce the game to new people who are not familiar with the company.

Distributing CD-ROMs through Giveaways

"Giveaways" are also an excellent way to distribute your CD-ROM because of the same benefits listed previously for a company handout, while allowing for a broader audience. Giveaways describe the process of handing out CD-ROMs at stands, trade shows, or public areas. Because people pass by who normally wouldn't visit your company, more people get their hands on your game, and exposure increases. The downside is that this method requires an employee to distribute the product, which increases costs.

Distributing CD-ROMs through CD-ROM Business Cards

A final method that has been appearing recently is CD-ROM business cards. CD-ROM business cards are business card-sized CD-ROMs that are either rectangular or circular shape, fit in the recessed section of your CD-ROM drive, and operate in the same way as a traditional CD-ROM. They are typically printed with a label on one side that contains standard contact information and are distributed through the company handout method. The only additional disadvantage these CD-ROM business cards have is their reduced size—typically around 30–50 MB of space. Although this is significantly smaller than a full CD-ROM, for most Advergames, it is still more than enough room for the game and to allow for additional material, if needed.

Advantages of CD-ROM Distribution

In summary, the advantages of CD-ROM distribution include the following.

- Makes people feel the game was created for them
- Has many distribution options
- Is low-cost duplication—great for handouts
- Is a physical reminder of your company

Disadvantages of CD-ROM Distribution

In summary, the disadvantages of CD-ROM distribution include the following.

- Is expensive and difficult to distribute to extremely large audiences due to extra costs, such as packaging and shipping
- Is not possible to change content after distribution

Kiosk Distribution

Kiosks can be found everywhere, including malls, department stores, supermarkets, and movie theaters. A kiosk is a booth that has been set up in an area that has people passing by. The purpose of the kiosk is to attract attention to a company and provide information on what it's offering. They are typically manned, although standalone varieties also exist. Kiosks can be used to provide information and to help attract people to your representatives in a couple ways, either through an oral or on-screen presentation followed by your Advergame, or by setting up the game on several computers and allowing people to come up and play them. Kiosks are typically the most expensive method that can be utilized because space must be rented, the kiosk needs to be designed, equipment needs to be purchased, and people must be paid to staff them. The advantages are great because they allow representatives to accompany the Advergames and provide additional information while the games are played. They are also placed in locations that can help increase exposure to the company and attract people who have not thought about using a company's products and services before.

Advantages of Kiosk Distribution

In summary, the advantages of kiosk distribution include the following.

- Has a strong presence
- Provides representatives who can talk with interested parties

Disadvantages of Kiosk Distribution

In summary, the disadvantages of kiosk distribution include the following.

- Is very costly
- Is limited by a small number of potential players compared to other methods such as Internet distribution

Cell Phone Distribution

As text messaging on cell phones has become extremely popular, it is only natural that Advergames have spread into that realm as well. Text messaging on cell phones has begun to replace pagers because people can type short messages back and forth to be read at any time. Currently, cell phone technology limits the potential Advergames to those that follow a quiz game style because they can only contain text. You can expect this to change quickly. These cell phone-style games are ideal for bars and restaurants in which people can play them while sitting and waiting for their food or drinks and win free prizes. A well-deployed cell phone Advergame was the *Free Heineken on Your Mobile* game, which was released in the UK and is shown in great detail in Chapter 22, Interview and Case Study—AGENCY.COM. Heineken set up a game in which bar patrons could send a text message to a phone number with a special code that would start up the game. Then, the players had to answer a number of trivia questions—and if they won, they received a free Heineken. The game could be replayed as many times as the person wanted until he finally won. The game was interesting, new, and had a great prize, which made people very interested in trying it.

The downsides to the cell phone Advergame are that it is very limited to the types of games that can be created, and many people don't have or must pay extra for messaging features and, therefore, would not want to or be able to play the game.

Advantages of Cell Phone Distribution

In summary, the advantages of cell phone distribution include the following.

- Is a new and innovative style that interests people
- Has great prize opportunities
- Helps entertain people while waiting on services

Disadvantages of Cell Phone Distribution

In summary, the disadvantages of cell phone distribution include the following.

- Requires special infrastructure—technology is currently limiting game possibilities
- Requires text messaging feature on cell phones (which is more popular in Europe and Japan versus North America)

PUBLISHING ADVERGAMES—GETTING YOUR GAME READY FOR DISTRIBUTION

With an understanding of some of the distribution methods you can use, let's now turn our attention to techniques to optimize your game to fully take advantage of the distribution method you have chosen. In this section of the chapter, we look at the issues surrounding file types and how both programs manage memory. We start with file types. Each application provides a mechanism to streamline and simplify your authoring files by allowing you to create symbols and sprites. These both work in the same way—the program stores the data that represents objects on your Stage rather than saving them multiple times. Keeping this in mind while authoring your movie helps to keep your file sizes compact.

After the application is complete, you must find a way to prepare it for distribution. Both Flash MX and Director MX have advanced publishing tools that allow you to control how the final game is saved. Your game can be created in a variety of formats, including HTML, QuickTime®, and executable formats. When publishing your Advergame, each individual file type has a number of settings that allow you to customize everything from image and video compression to what direction the game loads in.

The actual process of publishing a movie was explained in Chapter 3, Macromedia Director MX, and Chapter 4, Macromedia Flash MX 2004. Instead of reviewing those topics again, we delve into what the different options are, why you would use each one, and how to tweak them to best fit our medium—although you have many options to choose from, we only focus on the pertinent ones.

Macromedia Director MX

Director MX evolved in the opposite direction of Flash. Instead of being created for the Web and spreading to other uses, Director MX used to be used mainly for executable formats. Eventually, people began to create games and other applications for the Web, and Shockwave began to take hold. To work with your publishing settings, choose Publish Settings from the File menu. In Director MX, the Publish Settings dialog box is solely focused on creating Shockwave files from your authoring file.

The idea behind Shockwave is the same as that behind Flash files; an HTML and Shockwave file work together to display the game. An HTML page embeds a link to the Shockwave file and displays it in a Web browser using a plug-in. Publish Settings has a Compression tab that is devoted to optimizing your game for the Web. Two elements can be compressed—the images and the audio. Table 7.1 outlines the various compression methods and what they do.

If you are creating a game for download or CD-ROM distribution, a projector file is the most useful. The projector file works in the same way as a Macromedia Flash projector; therefore, no additional plug-ins or files are needed to run the game. To create a projector file, simply consult Chapter 3 for step-by-step instructions. If you need a projector for both Mac OS and Microsoft Windows, each projector file must be created on its own operating system.

Macromedia Flash MX 2004

Naturally, Flash MX lends itself to creating games for the Web, but the program also makes stunning executables that can be viewed anywhere. To work with your

TABLE 7.1 Compression settings and functions

Setting	***Function***
Image Compression: Standard	Displays the images in the movie without additional compression.
Image Compression: JPEG	Tells Director MX to compress all images via a JPEG compression algorithm. A slider is available to specify the image quality. A higher value means a larger file and better images.
Shockwave Audio: Compression Enabled	If selected, the proceeding settings are applied. If cleared, the sounds exist in the same format as they were imported.
kBits/second	Sets what format sound files stored within Macromedia Flash MX 2004 are converted into during publishing. Clicking Set provides you with options. A lower kBits/second setting provides a smaller file with lower quality sound.
Convert Stereo to Mono	Converting all stereo sound to mono also saves file space. This is a useful feature when both the left and right sound channels are identical.
Comments	Selecting this box includes all comments stored with cast members, if this checkbox is selected. This increases your file size and is not necessary unless you want them included for a specific reason.

publishing settings, choose Publish Settings from the File menu. In the Publish Settings dialog box, the different methods of distribution are displayed. The GIF, JPEG, PNG, and QuickTime formats are available for static animations that need to be presented in a series of images, an animated GIF, or streaming video. Because none of these formats allows for user interactivity, they are not useful for an Advergame. The ones that are useful are the Flash, HTML, Windows Projector, and Macintosh Projector formats.

When creating an Advergame for the Web, your publishing method is always Flash and HTML formats. These two formats work together to allow visitors to play the game through their Web browser. Selecting the HTML checkbox activates both a Flash and an HTML tab. The Flash tab contains all of the settings that allow you to customize the Flash files for the Web. Table 7.2 outlines the options you can set to optimize your game. When publishing your movie, a Flash and HTML file is generated. Both files are required for broadcasting your game to the Web—the HTML file links to and displays the Flash file. For a user to view the game, Flash

TABLE 7.2 Options to optimize your Advergame

Setting	*Function*
Load order	Determines whether the Flash Player loads the movie starting from the first frame or from the last frame.
JPEG quality	Sets how much Macromedia Flash MX 2004 compresses graphics that have been imported into Flash. A higher value means a larger file and better images.
Audio stream/audio event	Sets what format sound files stored within Flash are converted into during publishing. Clicking Set provides you with options. A lower bit rate or sample rate reduces sound quality and file size. Converting all stereo sound to mono also saves file space. This is a useful feature when both the left and right sound channels are identical.

Player must be installed—although currently most computers come with the Flash Player preinstalled.

If you are developing your Advergame for download or for CD-ROM distribution, a projector file is more appropriate. Projector files package the game into an executable format that can be viewed on any computer regardless of what programs or plug-ins they have installed. Because most people run one of two operating systems—Mac OS or Microsoft Windows—two types of projectors are available. Windows Projectors are created as .exe files and Macintosh Projectors can be extracted from a .hqx file that is created. Executables also have the added bonus of being able to execute several `fscommands` that are not available in Flash files.

SUMMARY

Packaging your game for delivery is the final step that needs to be taken. At this point, the Advergame can be distributed for use, and with a little luck, enjoyed by millions. The final steps of ensuring that the game is optimized for your method of distribution is crucial because the most enjoyable and effective game won't get you anywhere if it's not easy for people to view. Keeping elements such as file size and distribution methods in mind throughout the entire process is very important and guarantees an effective launch. The process can stop here, or you can take it to the next level and follow up by implementing a method to track user statistics, high scores, and collect information. The next chapter discusses services and programs that allow you to obtain feedback on your games.

8 The Results: Tracking Site Activity and Measuring Success

Completing and sending out your game may not necessarily be the last part of your Advergame creation process. If you decided to create your Advergame to utilize the Web, you can set up a tracking system to monitor how long people play your game, the high scores, user statistics, and much more. To implement site tracking, you must first understand the ideas behind it.

UNDERSTANDING WHY TRACKING IS DONE

Tracking methods are implemented for a variety of reasons. They allow you to discover the effectiveness of the project and can serve as a basis for future marketing decisions. In the business world, undertaking an expensive project must show results. Spending thousands or tens of thousands of dollars on advertising for most companies is not something that's done casually.

The idea of tracking advertising is no secret—it exists for all ad mediums. Whether it's through the TV, newspaper, or Internet, customer surveys and influxes in business after the release of an ad give insight into the ad's effectiveness. Whenever filling out an order form or application, companies normally ask how you heard of them—through one of their advertisements, word of mouth, and so on—to gauge if they should invest more money into a particular advertising technique.

The Web is a new frontier for advertising that has many benefits—some of which cannot be tracked by traditional advertising metrics. In some cases, unique methods are used to capture information on how many times a game has been downloaded, played, passed on, and even linked to buying activity.

As we covered in earlier chapters, Web advertising can be interactive and animated, presenting potential customers with a dynamic ad that is more engaging. In addition, a whole new kind of ad tracking is possible with online ads. Unlike advertising in other media, creating ads for the Web does not require the end user to manually fill out any forms or surveys to find out how effective an ad was—applications and scripts can do all the work for you. With Advergames, you can collect information from the user in several different ways. In the next two sections, we discover what types of information can be gathered and how it is relevant to determining the effectiveness of your Advergame.

Visits

The most obvious method of tracking is finding out how many people have visited the site. Today, many Web sites determine their effectiveness by how many "hits" they receive—and understandably so. A "hit" is tracked whenever someone arrives at a Web page—simply accessing it increments the number of hits a site has had. Although this doesn't let you know how long someone stayed, it does give you an opportunity to determine how many people at least stumbled across your site. Because every access increments the hit count, the number of hits from unique IP addresses can also be found. A user's IP address is a unique number that identifies a user on the Internet. When determining hits from unique IP addresses, if the same person accesses the page twice, it does not increment the hit count. This gives a more realistic count on the number of unique people who come by to visit, and also lets you determine how many "repeat hits" your site has received. Repeat hits are very desirable because it means people keep coming back to your Web site to see more. It is this count that Advergames aim to increase—part of their purpose is to keep people coming back through the Web site to view updates, promotions, and changes to company information.

Time Spent

Tracking visits is very important, but it doesn't let you know if the people who visited really spent time on your Web site. An advantage of Advergames is that they can track the total time someone spends playing the game and report it back to you. Tracking playtime gives you an idea of how engaging your content is—the longer people remain on your site, the more interested they are about what's happening. Branding impressions are built with frequency, duration, and from the context of where they appear. With Advergames, this is very important because it lets you know whether your game was enjoyable, and provides you with quantitative data on how long someone spent immersed in your advertising. It's at this point that many studies have found Advergames to be extremely effective because Advergames have the power to engage people to spend long periods of time immersed in a product and its image. Capturing this type of information in a database can help you build a dialogue with prospective customers and, in turn, strengthen their buying loyalty to your company.

Click-Throughs

Often, an Advergame acts as a pathway for potential customers to access other information about a company's products and services. Many Advergames provide players with links during the gameplay, or a link at the end, that points them to another portion of the Web site. Tracking users who "click-through" the Advergame into another portion of the site lets you determine if your game has prompted someone to learn more about your company and its products or services. A click-through can be tracked for each individual link that exists within the game to give insight into what portions of your advertising work best. If you are venturing into new territory with an Advergame, experimenting with different methods to achieve click-throughs in your game helps you discover which method works best for your audience.

In many other types of advertising, click-throughs are becoming a fairly useless metric. Click-through counts are dropping, and the click-through tends to only be a product of the "flashiness" of the ad rather than the actual content. A click-through typically doesn't translate into an interested customer, just someone who wanted to find out what an ad was about. Where your Advergames differ is that a user is playing it and can be convinced to click a link because of the information and image projected by the game. Suddenly, the click-through ratings become useful again because they rate the effectiveness of the game generating further interest.

More important than the number of click-throughs made is the click-through rate (CTR). The CTR is the number of click-throughs divided by the total number of times the ad is accessed multiplied by 100. A CTR provides you with a percentage that lets you know how often the game generates further interest.

User Information

A final form of tracking is similar to techniques employed today through traditional marketing surveys. An Advergame can provide fields for users to enter pertinent information so that your company can send them additional information or product offerings. Adding a form to your game allows you to ask users questions about the game, find out contact information, and if they are planning a purchase in the future. There is indeed an art to creating useful surveys, and it is worth taking the time to get it right because this data can often reveal trends and buying patterns that can provide your company with a competitive edge. If your company is trying to find a new way to deploy a survey, putting it in an Advergame may be an innovative way to accomplish that objective.

TRACKING TECHNOLOGIES

A wide variety of options are available when it comes to developing a system to collect tracking statistics. Two main options exist for an Advergame developer—to either create your own mechanism to collect data or to use a service provided by a third-party company to track and manage the data for you. Each method has its own strengths and weaknesses, so let's take a closer look before you make your deployment decision.

If you choose to create your own method, you need to use a Web programming language, such as PHP or ASP, to interact with a database, such as mySQL or MS SQL Server, that tracks and stores your data.

Tracking on Your Own

To create a system to track statistics from a Macromedia Flash MX 2004 movie on your own, you need to have a foundation in a Web programming language, such as PHP or ASP, and be familiar with programming for databases. Both technologies require the server on which you host your game to have the language and whatever database installed that you choose to use.

Both languages are focused on server-side scripting that allows you to have the server collect data, manipulate content, and much more. These features can be implemented through a variety of methods. They can be combined with HTML and can be used through a Web browser, or as independent scripts that reside on the server and perform actions when they are accessed and data is passed to them.

Using Ad Services

Ad services are ideal for large-scale deployments that are expected to have lots of traffic passing through them. They are commonly used by large businesses to ensure that a dependable and tested framework has been set up to process their data and find out the important statistics about their advertisements. Ad services are versatile and can track information on a variety of events that occur in your game. Each service is different and requires a different method for implementation—but those details are discussed between yourself and the company providing the service. The good news is that most Advergaming companies have developed their own unique tracking software, and it is often available for a nominal monthly fee.

Tracking Click-Throughs

A standard method that Macromedia is encouraging people to use involves incorporating a `clickTAG` into your games. The `clickTAG` method was designed to work with banner ads so that sites could track "click-throughs" that occurred. This same service works great in Advergames in which you want to determine if a player has actually "clicked-through." The `clickTAG` is a variable that is passed into the Macromedia Flash MX 2004 movie through the `EMBED` and `OBJECT` tags in an HTML file. The variable contains a special code and URL that connects to an ad tracking service, which can be passed through a `getURL` function to track user clicks on the site. To incorporate a `clickTAG` in your game, perform the following steps.

1. Edit your published HTML file in a plain text editor such as Notepad.
2. Insert the following code into the `EMBED` and `OBJECT` tags wherever your movie URL appears, replacing *mytracker.com/tracking* with your tracking service and *www.destinationURL.com* with a destination URL, if you are sending the user to a new site.

```
?clickTAG =http://mytracker.com/tracking?http://www.destinationURL.com
```

3. In Macromedia Flash MX 2004, open the Actions panel of the button you want to track and type the following code into the panel.

```
on (release) {
    getURL(clickTAG);
}
```

This mode of detection requires you to find an ad service that tracks and compiles the data sent by the click-throughs.

Ad Service Companies

There is no shortage of companies ready to help. A Google Directory search for "Web Tracking Services" revealed over 400 hits, with prices that range from free to thousands of dollars per month. A few companies that provide ad services are provided in the following list. You can contact them for more information on the services they offer and whether their solutions are right for you.

Bluestreak

www.bluestreak.com

Phone: 1-866-258-3787

E-mail: info@bluestreak.com

TRACK-STAR

www.vitabella.com

E-mail: sales@vitabella.com

MEI Roundhouse

www.maned.com/products/roundhouse/roundhouse.html

Phone: 1-800-638-1214

E-mail: webmaster@maned.com

SUMMARY

Tracking is an invaluable resource that gives real insight into the demographics of your audience, potentially helping you recognize untapped market potential. Even if an Advergame doesn't turn out as successful as you would like, often tracking helps you understand what your audience does not like. Whether it's something you take the time to learn yourself or utilize a third party, monitoring your game's success is definitely worthwhile.

PART III The Creations

9 epic Cosmetics

THE CONCEPT

Identifying Your Product: epic Cosmetics

epic Cosmetics is unveiling a new line of makeup that is supposed to take the industry by storm. They need to develop a game that showcases several of their new product lines with a fun and visually pleasing interface. The objective for this Advergame is to develop a game that introduces their new line and shows off its variety and ability to provide for women of all ages. The company is looking for a mostly visual design with brief descriptions of their products to develop a sense of identity. The new cosmetics line is targeted mainly toward young women and a good portion of the teen population. The prices are about midrange when compared to other brands. Most of the people in this demographic should be familiar enough with computers to perform simple tasks for which expert levels of coordination are not needed. Now that we know what the product is and what goals we aim to achieve, it is time to design a game around the cosmetics line.

Outlining a Game for epic Cosmetics

With the requirements of creating a simple and visual game, deciding which type shouldn't be difficult. Games with complicated user controls or games with heavy competition are immediately eliminated, making this one that should simply be enjoyable to play. A puzzle game, board game, or drag-and-drop game would serve well in this instance. They all allow for a player to quickly learn how everything works and quickly get started. The next factor to look at is what kind of genre would be good for a cosmetics line; although many genres can provide simple layouts, not all are suitable games for this product. Of these genres, a puzzle game or a drag-and-drop game would work. A puzzle game could be made that requires the player to outfit a model with a specific set of cosmetics to create a look shown on another model. On the other hand, a drag-and-drop game could allow a player to create her own looks on a model and customize it however she wants.

For this game, we have decided to go with the drag-and-drop style game that allows players to apply makeup to their own models. The inherent requirement for a line of makeup in the game allows for a seamless integration of the product into the game's interface without making the user feel swamped with ads. Every product in the game can resemble the actual packaging to help create an identity that people will recognize when they enter the stores.

The game's design itself doesn't need to be very complicated. All of the products should be easy to access and visible from the very beginning, because when players spend more time looking at the products, the identity becomes ingrained more and more into their minds. A good portion of the screen needs to be devoted to the model on whom the makeup will be applied. Because the game is focusing on cosmetics, the picture just needs to display the model from the shoulders up and showcase the products well. The other portion of the screen needs to display several products, such as lipstick, eyeliner, and blush. An area must be devoted to choosing the colors and styles that will be applied to the model. There also needs to be a Help button that provides the player with all the necessary information on how to play the game.

Before the game starts, there should be a brief splash screen that provides some basic information about the company and the new line of makeup. This can be mostly text with a Play, Help, and Exit button along the bottom. After the game is completed, an ending screen allows the users to input e-mail addresses of several friends to whom they want to have the game sent—this helps spread the word about the game.

Designing the Interface for epic Cosmetics

With a good idea of what you want in your Advergame, it is time to begin visualizing it graphically. For this design, we devoted the left third of the screen to display the model. The makeup can be displayed in the center of the screen, with oversized graphics to show off the packaging. The model also needs to have a variety of hair styles, lip colors, blush colors, and eye styles that can be changed. These options need a list of color and style choices that can be displayed beneath the makeup items. A Help button can be located in the bottom-right corner of the screen and an Exit button can be placed in the top-left corner, a familiar spot to find a Close button. Figure 9.1 shows a rough sketch of the interface.

Next, sounds need to be chosen for the game. Audible clicks should sound whenever new makeup is selected or applied. There should be a background music loop, upbeat and happy, to give the piece a warm and fun feel.

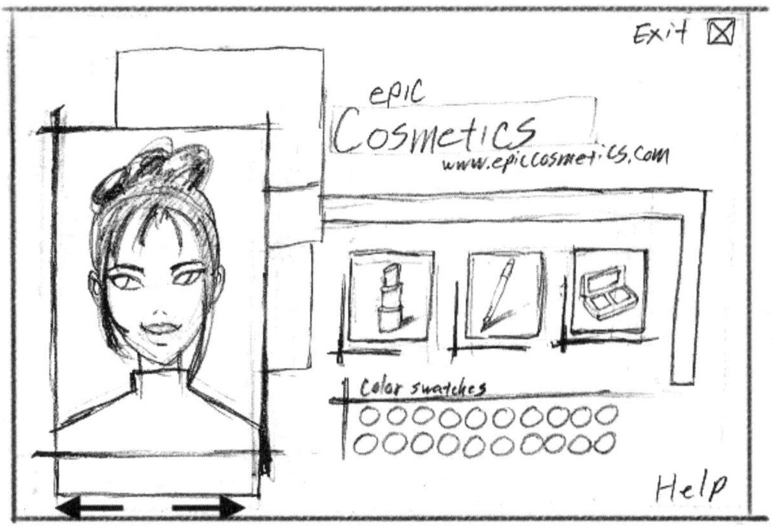

FIGURE 9.1 The interface for epic Cosmetics.

THE CREATION

Identifying the Elements of the epic Cosmetics Game

First, we start by compiling a list of every element that will be involved in the game. This takes the form of a simple, nested list that shows where everything needs to exist. The main introduction screen should include:

- Title
- Description
- Play button
- Exit button

The main game should include:

Model: Contains the base model picture and all of the model's parts

Hair: Includes a series of hair styles

Eyes: Includes a series of eyeliner styles and colors

Blush: Includes a series of blush colors

Lips: Includes a series of lip colors

Title: Displays the game title
Web site link: Takes you to the company's Web site
Exit button: Takes you to the ending screen
Help button: Displays the Help window
Help window: Guides a player through the game
Lipstick: Activates the lipstick
Eyeliner: Activates the eyeliner
Blush: Activates the blush
Hair style chooser: Cycles through the hair styles
Makeup options: Contains the makeup options
Blush color: Displays all the blush colors
Lipstick color: Displays all the lipstick colors
Eyeliner style: Displays all the eyeliner styles

The ending screen should include:

E-mail Address fields: Provides fields for the user to type addresses
Submit button: Sends a link to the game to the e-mail addresses
Goodbye text: Thanks the user for playing

Figure 9.2 shows the interface with all of the elements identified.

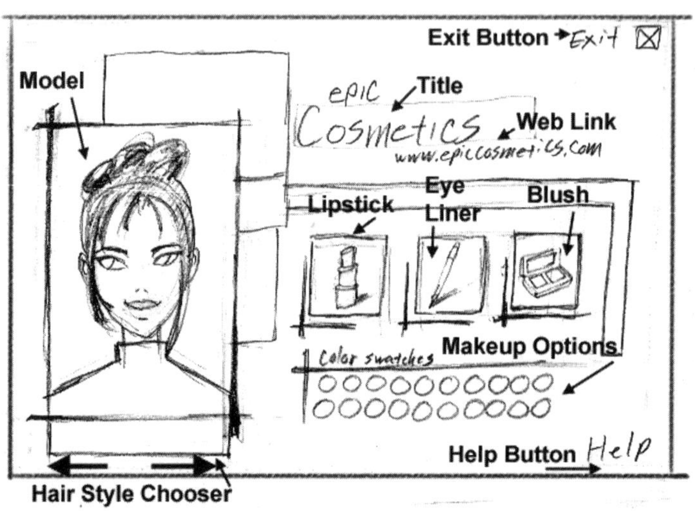

FIGURE 9.2 Interface elements.

Recognizing How the Game's Elements Interact

After establishing all of the elements that exist within the game, it is time to figure out the interactions that will occur between them. In the epic Cosmetics game, everything should be very straightforward. Most of the interactions involve determining what makeup is selected and where it is being applied.

Starting at the introduction screen, the Play button starts the main game and the Exit button closes the game.

After arriving at the main game screen, everything becomes user-driven. The player has a variety of options from which to choose. She can click the Help button to access the Help window or click the Exit button to end the game at any time. The three cosmetic products become active when the user selects one. When the active makeup changes, the options for that product should also change to match the product that was used. When the player drags a product option on top of the appropriate part of the model, it changes the style of the part to the one the user chooses. The hair style chooser buttons cycle through the available hair styles displayed on the model.

Upon ending the game, the ending screen appears. On the ending screen, the player can enter e-mail addresses into the E-mail Address fields. The Submit button sends an e-mail to all of the e-mail addresses entered.

A flowchart should be created to visually map out what happens, as shown in Figure 9.3. This ensures that everything in your movie is planned and occurs smoothly.

Identifying the Actions of the epic Cosmetics Game

Most of the actions in the epic Cosmetics game depend on the states of certain elements. For example, the options displayed and applied to the model all depend on which makeup is active. After recognizing each condition, you can set up code that executes upon the states of other elements and events that occur.

The Hair

The model's hair is controlled differently than the rest of the makeup. The hair style is chosen by clicking two arrows on the bottom of the screen that cycle through the options. This requires a variable to keep track of the current style that can be incremented or decremented by one, depending on which arrow is clicked.

The Makeup

Based on the flowchart, we find that everything else stems off of which product is active; therefore, we must set up code that activates each product. Because all of the products perform the exact same actions—that is they become active—we can set

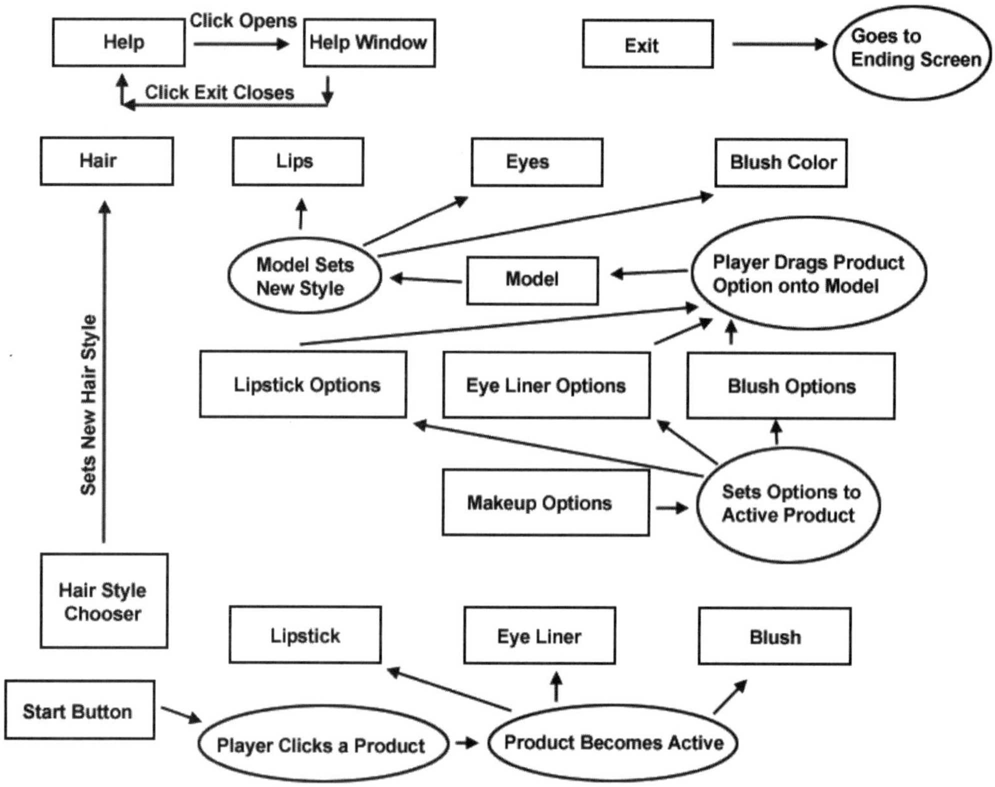

FIGURE 9.3 The epic Cosmetics flowchart.

up a function that executes the exact same set of code on each element, only with a different product specified for each.

First, let's take a look at how we are going to detect which product the user wants to be active. Because the mouse is the primary method of input, we detect mouseclicks to set the status.

There is only one event handler on each of the makeup products, the `onClipEvent(mouseDown)` handler. Anytime the left mouse button is pressed in the piece, the code contained within the handler executes. Because we are using a function to simplify the code, each element contains a call to the function held within the event handler. The function is responsible for setting a global variable that identifies which product is currently active and for advancing the active element to the frame containing the active appearance upon determining if the mouse was clicked on an element. The pseudocode for the function should look something like the following example.

1. If the mouse intersects a makeup item when the mouse is clicked: Proceed to Step 2. Else, do nothing.
2. Set a global variable that tracks what the current product is to the product that has been clicked.
3. Set the timeline of all elements to their inactive state.
4. Advance the timeline of the element that has been clicked to its active state.

The Makeup Options

The makeup options are responsible for displaying the makeup that the player actually drags onto the model to apply the makeup. Because the makeup options are dependent on the state of several makeup elements, the makeup options element is responsible for constantly checking to see which product is active and for setting its options to correspond appropriately. The best method to constantly monitor a value is to use the `onClipEvent(enterFrame)` handler to have your code executed every time the screen's frame is refreshed. Each set of options should be stored on a separate frame within the makeup options element. The pseudocode is as follows:

1. If the current product is not the same as it was the last check: Unload color circles and proceed to Step 2. Else, do nothing.
2. If the active makeup is lipstick: Go to the lipstick options frame.
3. If the active makeup is eyeliner: Go to the eyeliner options frame.
4. If the active makeup is blush: Go to the blush options frame.

After arriving at the options screen for the selected makeup, all of the colors need to be created. Rather than create separate symbols for each color, we can have one color circle duplicated and set to the appropriate color for each. Again, because every option screen requires the exact same color circles, a function can be created that passes in an array, which contains all the colors needed. The pseudocode for this step should appear as follows:

1. Duplicate the base movie clip and increment the number in its name by one.
2. Set the location of the new movie clip relative to the original clip.
3. Set the color of the new clip to the color in the array that corresponds to it.

After setting the proper options, the user needs to be able to apply the makeup. To do this, the individual options need to be dragged onto the model. These options can also be set up with a function that performs the same action on each one. The function needs to have an option and the makeup it belongs to passed into it as well, to tell the model what to apply. The following pseudocode shows what should happen when the `onClipEvent(mouseDown)` handler is activated.

1. If the mouse is pressed down:
   Proceed to Step 2. Else, do nothing.
2. If the mouse is located on the current option when pressed:
   Start dragging the item.
3. If the mouse is released:
   Proceed to Step 4. Else, continue dragging.
4. Return option back to its original location.
5. If the mouse is released on the model:
   Proceed to Step 6. Else, do nothing.
6. Advance the model's timeline to display the color or style that corresponds with the option.

The Remaining Elements

The Start button simply advances the movie to the actual game scene. Here, the Help button makes the Help window visible and inactivates all dragging—to make this work, all of the previous functions need to make certain that the Help window is closed before performing any actions. In the Help window, a Close button returns the player to the main screen and reactivates everything. The Exit button closes down the game.

Also, located in the game screen is the hair style chooser that is responsible for setting the model's hair style. The left and right arrows cycle through the available styles by moving the current frame of the hair element.

Putting It All Together

ON THE CD

Now that we have planned all aspects of the epic Cosmetics game, it is time to begin setting up the actual piece. Begin by opening the chapter09template.fla file in the \files\templates\ folder on the CD-ROM.

Setting Up the Stage

The following steps involve placing graphics that have already been created onto the Stage and positioning them properly, to create a visually pleasing interface. All of these symbols can be dropped on the same layers, but a wiser method is to place all of the symbols of a similar nature on the same layer. For instance, the lipstick, eyeliner, and blush can all be placed on a layer called Makeup.

1. Drag the Background symbol onto the Background layer from the library and set the X and Y coordinates to 11.8 and 15.5, respectively.
2. Drag the Game Title symbol onto the Buttons layer from the library and set the X and Y coordinates to 237.8 and 39.2, respectively.
3. Drag the Web Link symbol onto the Buttons layer from the library and set the X and Y coordinates to 303.1 and 110.3, respectively.
4. Drag the Hair Style Background symbol onto the Hair Style Buttons layer from the library and set the X and Y coordinates to 35.1 and 364.8, respectively.
5. Drag the Hair Style Arrow symbol onto the Hair Style Buttons layer from the library and set the X and Y coordinates to 163.7 and 372.3, respectively.
6. Drag the Hair Style Arrow symbol onto the Hair Style Buttons layer from the library, rotate it 180°, and set the X and Y coordinates to 14.2 and 372.3, respectively.
7. Drag the Makeup Options symbol onto the Makeup Options layer from the library and set the X and Y coordinates to 260.6 and 280.2, respectively.
8. Drag the Exit Button symbol in the Interface folder onto the Buttons layer from the library and set the X and Y coordinates to 488.3 and 4.3, respectively.
9. Drag the Help Button symbol onto the Buttons layer from the library and set the X and Y coordinates to 477.9 and 371.4, respectively.
10. Drag the Help Window symbol onto the Help Window layer from the library and set the X and Y coordinates to 250.6 and 124.1, respectively.
11. Drag the Lipstick symbol onto the Makeup layer from the library and set the X and Y coordinates to 260.6 and 180, respectively.
12. Drag the Eyeliner symbol onto the Makeup layer from the library and set the X and Y coordinates to 343 and 180, respectively.
13. Drag the Blush symbol onto the Makeup layer from the library and set the X and Y coordinates to 420.8 and 180, respectively.
14. Drag the Model symbol onto the Model layer from the library and set the X and Y coordinates to 26.9 and 93.2, respectively, as shown in Figure 9.4.

Understanding the Model Symbol

The graphics that you have placed on the screen have already been internally organized—that is within many of the symbols, other symbols and timelines exist that have been named and positioned for you.

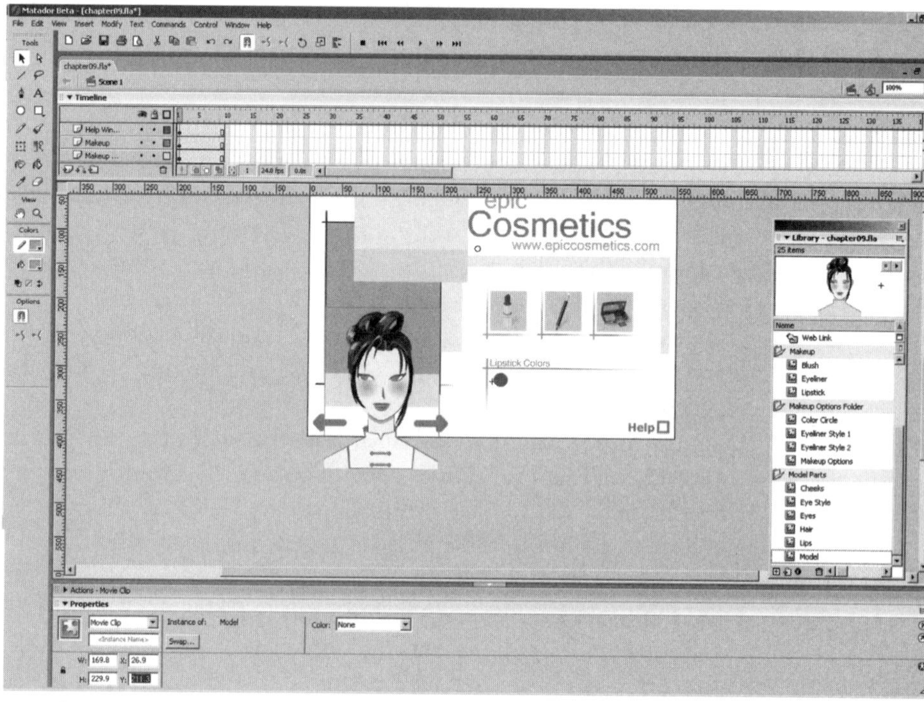

FIGURE 9.4 Positioning the Model symbol.

Start by double-clicking the model to view and edit the symbol. Inside, a set of layers contain the various body parts on the model, as shown in Figure 9.5. Except for the Body and the Eyes layer, they contain the various colors and styles for the elements. To see how each one is set up, double-click the Lips, Cheeks, or Hair symbols. In each of these sections, a layer contains a stop action every 10 frames with a label that serves as markers for the various options. These labels correspond to the instance names of the colors you will be applying.

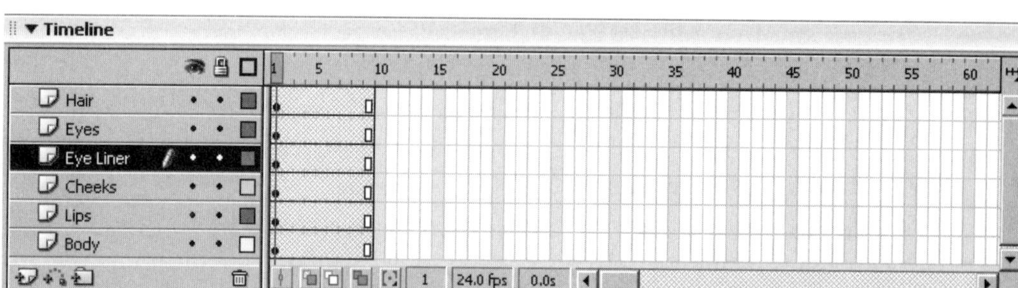

FIGURE 9.5 The Model symbol timeline.

Now, go back to the Model symbol and double-click the Eyes symbol that contains the eyeliner. Here, notice it is set up in the same manner as the other parts, except that there are three layers instead of two. This part contains the Eyeliner Style symbol that contains two different styles of eyeliner. These are set just like the various colors are, with each style having a unique label on the timeline. The colors are stored in the bottom Colors layer and are displayed through the mask layers. If you unlock the Eye Style layer, Figure 9.6 shows how you will see that the eyeliner itself is colored a bright green that never appears—the color that is actually displayed in the box underneath the mask. This arrangement allows you to have one set of styles that displays all the colors, rather than having a different set for each color.

Programming the Interface Elements

Now that you are familiar with how the model works, all that is left is programming. First, we need to take care of all the interface elements that act independent of the actual game. This ensures that we do not forget them later. We need to start by putting a stop action on frame 1 of the main timeline. This ensures that when the game arrives at this screen, it stops and lets the user play.

1. Add a new layer at the top of the timeline and name it Actions and Labels.
2. Label the first frame Game.
3. Type "stop();" in the Actions panel.

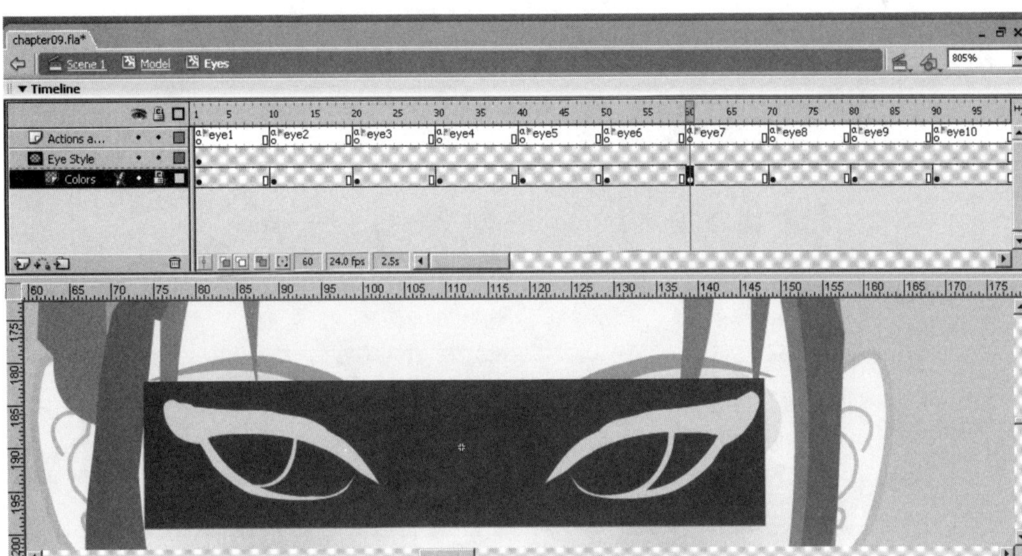

FIGURE 9.6 The Eye Style symbol's mask setup.

Next, we need to apply actions to the Web Link and Help buttons. The Web Link button simply opens a new Web browser window and takes you to the company's Web site when it is clicked. The Help button opens the Help window by advancing it to the Active frame label. Before we can have the button tell the Help window to go to the Active frame, we need to specify an instance name for the symbol.

1. Type the following code in the Actions panel for the Web Link button.

```
on (release) {
    getURL("http://www.epiccosmetics.com", "_blank");
}
```

2. Click the Help Window symbol on the stage and name it `helpWindow`, as shown in Figure 9.7.

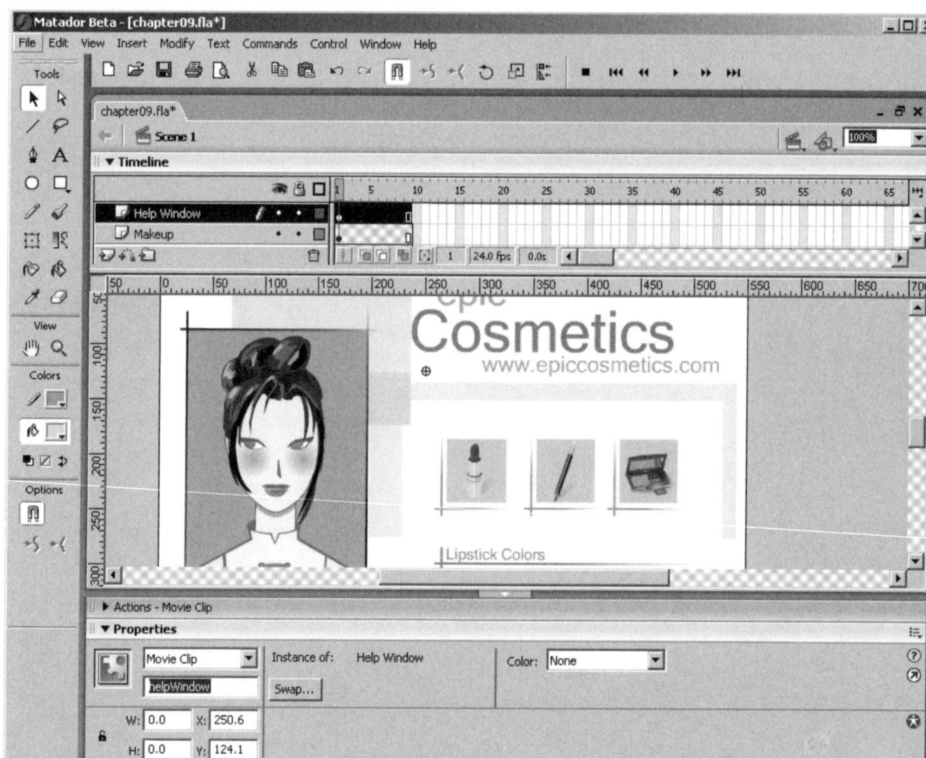

FIGURE 9.7 Naming the Help Window instance.

3. Type the following code in the Actions panel for the Help button.

```
on (release) {
    _root.helpWindow.gotoAndStop("Active");
}
```

After opening the Help window, two things need to happen. The program needs to set a variable that tells the entire movie that the window is open, and the Help window's Exit button needs to return you to the game and tell the movie that the window is closed.

1. Double-click the Help Window symbol.
2. On frame 1, type "_global.helpOpen = false;" before the stop action in the Actions panel.
3. On frame 10, type "_global.helpOpen = true;" before the stop action in the Actions panel.
4. Click the Help window's Exit button and type the following code in the Actions panel to close the window.

```
on (release) {
    this.gotoAndStop("Inactive");
}
```

   Next, the Exit button needs to be set up. First, we must set up an ending scene for the button to go to, then program the button to go to the scene.
5. In Scene 1, type the following code in the Actions panel for the Exit button.

```
on (release) {
    fscommand("quit");
}
```

Setting Up the Hair Style

Next, you need to set up code to cycle through the hair styles. There are two arrows that let the player cycle back and forth between the various options. Because we are now required to modify elements within the Model and Hair symbols, we need to assign them instance names, as well.

1. Click the Model symbol and assign it the instance name `model`.
2. Double-click the Model symbol.
3. Click the Hair symbol and assign it the instance name `hair`.

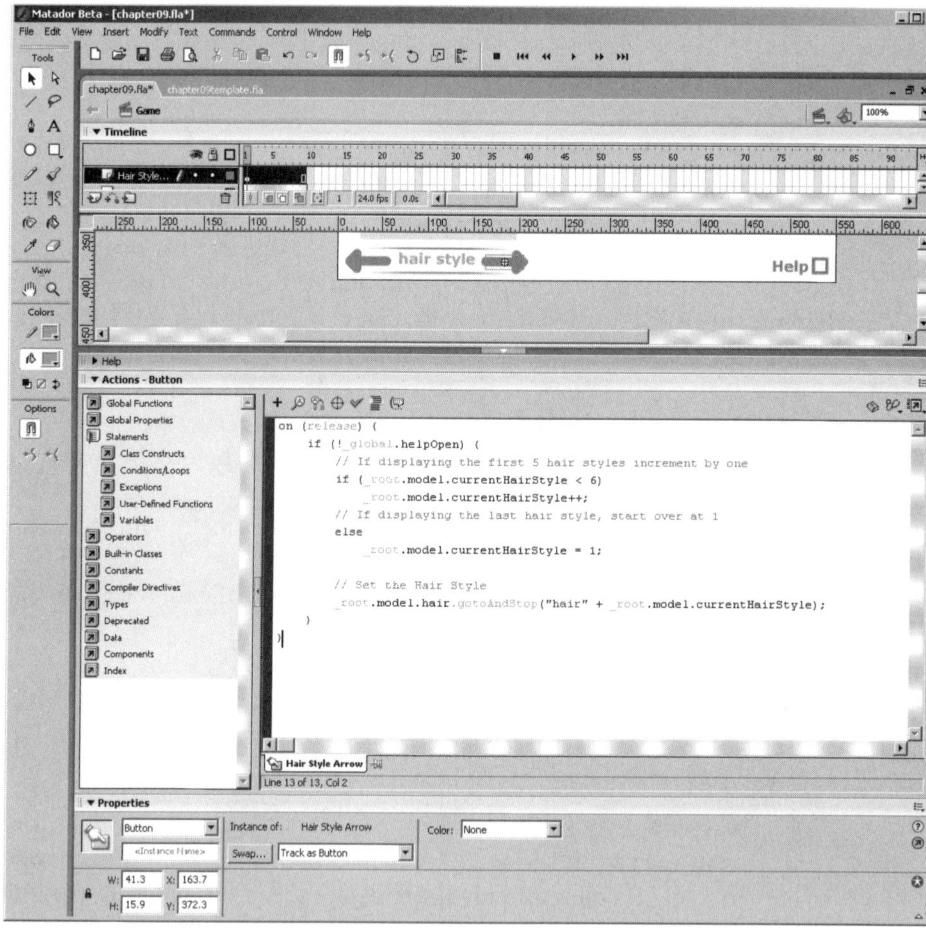

FIGURE 9.8 Applying code to the right arrow.

4. Return to the main timeline and type the following code on the Model symbol.

```
onClipEvent (load) {
    // Initializes the currentHairStyle variable
    currentHairStyle = 1;
}
```

5. On the right Hair Style Arrow, type the following code, as shown in Figure 9.8:

```
on (release) {
    if (!_global.helpOpen) {
```

```
        // If displaying the first 5 hair styles increment by one
        if (_root.model.currentHairStyle < 6)
            _root.model.currentHairStyle++;
        // If displaying the last hair style, start over at 1
        else
            _root.model.currentHairStyle = 1;

        // Set the Hair Style
        _root.model.hair.gotoAndStop("hair" +
_root.model.currentHairStyle);
    }
}
```

6. On the left Hair Style Arrow, type the following code:

```
on (release) {
    if (!_global.helpOpen) {
        // If displaying the last 5 hair styles, decrement by one
        if (_root.model.currentHairStyle > 1)
            _root.model.currentHairStyle--;
        // If displaying the first hair style, go to the last hair
style
        else
            _root.model.currentHairStyle = 6;

        // Set the Hair Style
        _root.model.hair.gotoAndStop("hair" +
_root.model.currentHairStyle);
    }
}
```

Setting Up the Makeup

After setting everything else up, it's time to go to the bulk of the game—the makeup. First, we need to start by labeling each product's instance name. To keep things consistent with the model parts, the names should correspond to the part to which they apply. Set the Lipstick, Eyeliner, and Blush instance names to lips, eyes, and cheeks, respectively.

After setting the instance names, we can create the function that is responsible for activating the makeup products. Because the function is accessed by all three products, the function needs to be placed on the main timeline and have a global scope, so that it may be accessed anywhere in the movie.

1. On frame 1 of the main timeline, type the following code before the stop action in the Actions panel.

```
_global.setMakeup = function(instanceName) {
    // Confirm that the mouse down occurred on a product
    if (!_global.helpOpen && instanceName.hitTest(_root._xmouse,
_root._ymouse, true)) {
        // Set the instance name to currentMakeup
        currentMakeup = instanceName._name;

        // Set All Products to Inactive
        _root.eyes.gotoAndStop("Inactive");
        _root.lips.gotoAndStop("Inactive");
        _root.cheeks.gotoAndStop("Inactive");

        // Set the Current Makeup to Active
        instanceName.gotoAndStop("Active");
    }
}
```

2. On each of the makeup products, type the following code in the Actions panel.

```
onClipEvent (mouseDown) {
    setMakeup(this);
}
```

Displaying Makeup Options

After setting up the code to select a product and set the `currentMakeup` variable, it is time to display the appropriate makeup options. The Makeup Options symbol is set up with three labels—lips, eyes, and cheeks. Each of these labels corresponds to the names that can be saved in the `currentMakeup` variable. The code to determine which options should be displayed resides on the Makeup Options symbol.

After creating the code to display the proper options, the game needs to generate all of the color options available for each product. Because each option is different, an array that stores all of the colors that will be used needs to be passed into the function that duplicates the color options.

1. On the Makeup Options symbol, type the following code in the Actions panel to create the color option duplicating function, as shown in Figure 9.9.

```
onClipEvent (load) {
    function colorDuplicator (colors) {
        // Determine how many options should be on each row
        horizontalCount = colors.length / 2;
```

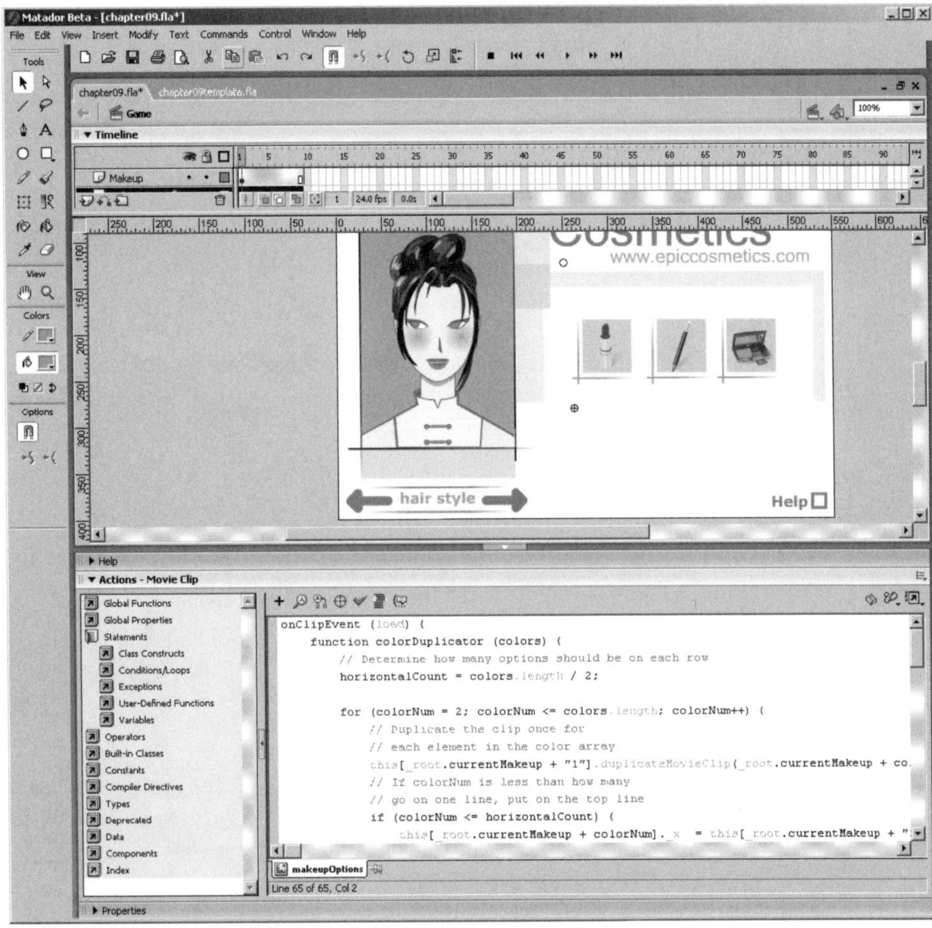

FIGURE 9.9 Applying code to the Makeup Options symbol.

```
        for (colorNum = 2; colorNum <= colors.length; colorNum++) {
            // Duplicate the clip once for
            // each element in the color array
            this[_root.currentMakeup +
"1"].duplicateMovieClip(_root.currentMakeup + colorNum, colorNum - 1);
            // If colorNum is less than how many
            // go on one line, put on the top line
            if (colorNum <= horizontalCount) {
                this[_root.currentMakeup + colorNum]._x  =
this[_root.currentMakeup + "1"]._x + 30 * (colorNum - 1);
                this[_root.currentMakeup + colorNum]._y  =
this[_root.currentMakeup + "1"]._y;
            // Else put on bottom line
```

```
            } else {
                this[_root.currentMakeup + colorNum]._x  =
this[_root.currentMakeup + "1"]._x + 30 * (colorNum - horizontalCount -
1);
                this[_root.currentMakeup + colorNum]._y  =
this[_root.currentMakeup + "1"]._y + 30;
            }

            // Set the option color based on the array
            makeupColor = new Color(this[_root.currentMakeup +
colorNum]);
            makeupColor.setRGB(colors[colorNum - 1]);
        }

    }
}
```

2. On the Makeup Options symbol, type the following code in the Actions panel to display the makeup options for the active product.

```
onClipEvent (enterFrame) {
    // Only change frames if makeup changes
    if (_root.currentMakeup != oldMakeup) {
        // Remove Previous Color Options
        for (colorNum = 2; colorNum <= colors.length; colorNum++)
            removeMovieClip(this[oldMakeup + colorNum]);
        // Advance to New Color Options
        this.gotoAndStop(_root.currentMakeup);
    }

    // Retain current makeup type
    oldMakeup = _root.currentMakeup;
}
```

After the options are presented properly, you can add the final functionality in the game—applying the colors and styles to the model. This is all done by dragging an option onto the model and having it display the proper lips, cheeks, or eyes. First, we need to set up the options to store the starting positions of each option. Then, you write the function that allows you to drag and apply the makeup, and, finally, you put the function calls on all of the options.

1. From the Library, edit the Color Circle symbol.
2. On frame 1, type the following code in the Actions window to retain the initial element positions, as shown in Figure 9.10.

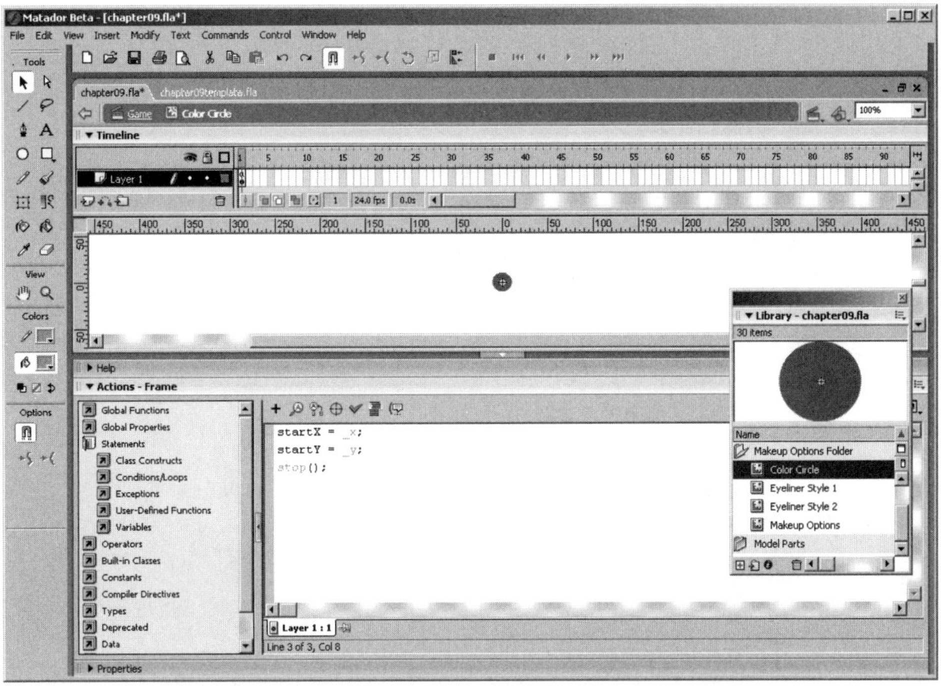

FIGURE 9.10 Editing and initializing variables for the Color Circle symbol.

```
startX = _x;
startY = _y;
stop();
```

3. Repeat Steps 1 and 2 for the Eyeliner Style 1 and Eyeliner Style 2 symbols.
4. In the Library, edit the Eyes symbol.
5. Unlock the Eye Style layer and set the Eye Style symbol's instance name to `style`. This is used to change the eyeliner style.
6. On the Makeup Options symbol, type the following code in the Actions panel below the `colorDuplicator` function to create the code that starts dragging the options:

```
function startDragging (instance) {
    if (instance.hitTest(_root._xmouse, _root._ymouse, false) &&
!_global.helpOpen)
        instance.startDrag();
}
```

7. Below the `startDragging` function, type the following code in the Actions panel to create the code that determines if an option was applied, and change the appropriate part to the new style.

```
function applyColor (instance) {
    // If Object is Placed on the Model
    if (instance.hitTest(_root.model)) {
        // If the object is an eyeliner style change the eyeliner
        style.
        if (instance.style == true)
            _root.model.eyes.style.gotoAndStop(instance._name);
        // Else, change the color of the appropriate part.
        else
            _root.model[_root.currentMakeup].gotoAndStop(instance._
            name);
    }

    // Stop dragging the option and return it
    // to its original position.
    stopDrag();
    instance._x = instance.startX;
    instance._y = instance.startY;
}
```

8. In the Library, double-click the Makeup Options symbol.
9. In the Lips, Eyes, and Cheeks sections, apply the following code to the color circles.

```
onClipEvent (mouseDown) {
    _parent.startDragging(this);
}

onClipEvent (mouseUp) {
    _parent.applyColor(this);
}
```

In the Eyes section, apply the following code to the two eyeliner styles.

```
onClipEvent (mouseDown) {
    // Identifies element as an eyeliner style
    this.style = true;
    _parent.startDragging(this);
}

onClipEvent (mouseUp) {
    _parent.applyColor(this);
}
```

With that, your game should be fully functional. All that remains now is setting up the starting scene.

Setting Up the Introduction Scene

The introduction scene contains basic information about the game and allows users to exit the game. Let's start setting it up. The introduction screen should end up as shown in Figure 9.11.

1. In the Scene panel, rename Scene 1 to Game.
2. In the Scene panel, add a new scene above Game and name it Introduction.
3. Choose Timeline form the Insert menu, and then choose layer.
4. Rename Layer 2 to *Elements* and Layer 1 to *Background.*
5. From the library, drag the Background symbol onto the Background layer and set the X and Y coordinates to 21.4 and 34.7, respectively.
6. From the library, drag the Introduction Text symbol onto the Elements layer and set the X and Y coordinates to 113.6 and 138.2, respectively.
7. From the library, drag the Start Button symbol onto the Elements layer and set the X and Y coordinates to 48.5 and 340.7, respectively.
8. From the library, drag the Exit Button symbol onto the Elements layer and set the X and Y coordinates to 442.6 and 340.7, respectively.
9. From the library, drag the Game Title symbol onto the Elements layer and set the X and Y coordinates to 208.6 and 3.1, respectively.

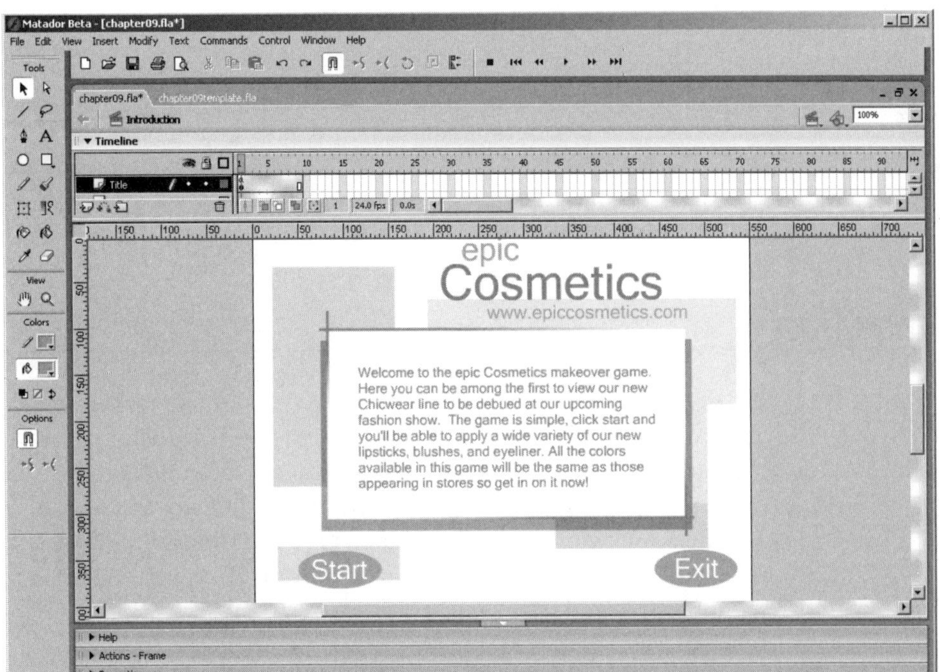

FIGURE 9.11 The introduction scene layout.

10. From the library, drag the Web Link symbol onto the Stage and set the X and Y coordinates to 259.3 and 76.5, respectively.
11. On frame 1, type the following code in the Actions panel.

```
stop();
```

After placing all of the elements, the code for each element needs to be applied. Only three of the elements actually need code—the Web Link, the Start button, and the Exit button. The Web Link code is identical to the code we set up in the Game scene. The Start button code is simply an action that advances the timeline to the Game scene, and the Exit button quits the game using an `fscommand`.

1. Type the following code in the Actions panel for the Web Link button.

```
on (release) {
    getURL("http://www.epiccosmetics.com", "_blank");
}
```

2. Type the following code in the Actions panel for the Start button.

```
on (release) {
    gotoAndStop("Game", 1);
}
```

3. Type the following code in the Actions panel for the Exit button.

```
on (release) {
    fscommand("quit");
}
```

SUMMARY

ON THE CD

With that, the epic Cosmetics game is complete and should work just like the completed game chapter09.fla that can be found in the same directory as the template. Were this game to be actually deployed, a variety of methods could be used. Actual copies of the game could be included in a CD-ROM that is available at all epic Cosmetics counters for people to pick up. If a more economical method is desired, a Web site release with an e-mail sent out to the company's mailing list would drive traffic right into the game.

10 epic Realtors' Strongest Link

THE CONCEPT

Identifying your Product: epic Realtors

Unlike the game in the previous chapter, this one focuses on a brand instead of a specific product. epic Realtors has requested that an Advergame be made to effectively present information about the company, in such a way that the player receives a prize at the end. As with any Advergame, the first thing we must focus on is what needs to be presented. The company wants information on its history, missions, goals, and services to be provided along with an interface that carries their logo to help create a sense of brand identity. They want a feel that is modern, yet traditional enough to appeal to the potential homeowner market.

Outlining a Game for epic Realtors

With the customer requesting an information-rich game, your options are fairly limited. First, a method of presenting a significant amount of textual information must be found. The most obvious method is to have the player read a block of text, which could be difficult because most people want to just play the game, not read a brochure. Other methods include presenting random facts and tips during the game or asking trivia questions about the company. The problem with facts and trivia is that they allow the player to complete the game without absorbing as much as reading would allow them. On the other hand, a trivia game allows the player to test his knowledge about the company, while being presented with the right answer after each question is completed.

The best approach in this situation is to find a method of presenting a large amount of information that the players can read, while simultaneously quizzing them about the information. With this in mind, a quiz game meets our needs.

Now that we have a general idea of what kind of game needs to be produced, it's time to focus and begin choosing a specific game to create. Quiz games exist in all sorts of forms, including board games, TV shows, card games, and Web sites. This game is not intended to be a difficult one that frustrates the player, but instead is intended to catch the player's attention and keep attention on the company. Because the customer wants a lot of information presented, the gameplay will not be as strong as it could be, so graphics become much more important. It needs a compelling design with fluid, eye-catching graphics. A TV-style game show would best lend itself to such a game because you can have the player answering questions while putting in any kind of a "hint" system you desire. For this game, you can have the player answering questions to the best of his ability. When the player is unable to answer a question, he can click the Hint button and the hint section provides him with the information he needs to answer the question. The hint section can contain an explanation of everything the company wants to present. The quiz itself serves to ensure that the player actually has learned something about the company. You also need some sort of point system that keeps track of how well the player is doing, so that the game can determine if he has earned a prize.

Now that you have an idea of everything you want in the game, you need to think about how the game is actually going to function. You can often make a great game by picking a popular TV show and creating a variation of it. In this case, we create a game called epic Realtors' Strongest Link. It contains a similar layout as its TV show, with a wise-cracking host and several other players to compete against. The game's scoring system operates by increasing the total score for each correct answer any player makes. As successive questions are answered correctly, the points awarded for each increases. If anyone gets a question wrong, the score is immediately reset to zero. To avoid losing all of the earned points, the player may "bank" the money and save it from any potential loss. Whether the player wins depends on how many points are earned by the end of the game.

Designing the epic Realtors' Strongest Link Interface

Now that you have a game idea, the next step is to design an interface. The interface needs to be clean, straightforward, and easy to navigate. First, we must begin by sketching the layout of all the major areas. With any quiz game, the center point of the game is the question and answer choices. With this in mind, reserve the majority of the space in the center of the screen to display them. Second, an important part of keeping the piece interesting is the animated host, so the area to the left of the questions contains the host animation. The host is able to both pull out a card at the beginning to start asking questions, and put it up at the end to announce the winner. When a question is answered correctly or incorrectly, the host has a caption bubble that appears to notify the player of what happened.

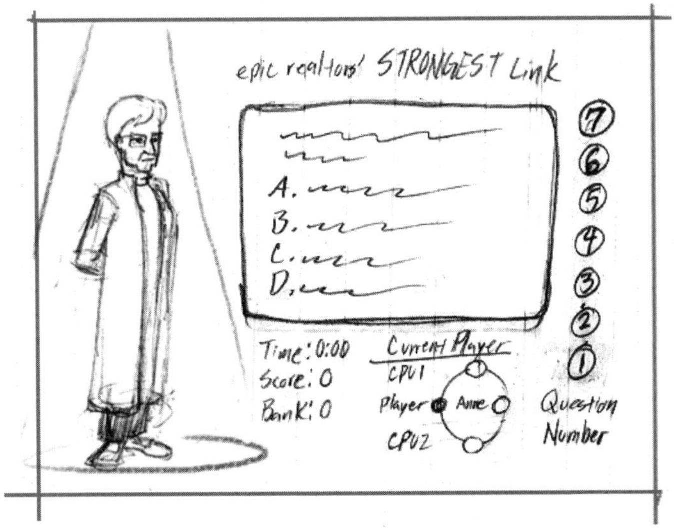

FIGURE 10.1 A rough sketch of the epic Realtors' Strongest Link interface.

You also need to have an area that keeps track of the time, score, and bank, along with a setup that keeps track of the current player. Buttons are needed to place points in the bank, start the game, and display the hint information, which can appear in place of questions. A rough sketch of the interface can be seen in Figure 10.1.

Next, the situations that trigger sounds need to be identified. You need to have background music, a sound for the start and end of the game, a voice that declares whether the player answers the question properly, and various "waiting" sounds for the host to make.

THE CREATION

Identifying the Elements of epic Realtors' Strongest Link

Start by compiling a list of every element in the interface you created. In your list, you need to nest elements that exist within other elements. For the Strongest Link game, the following elements exist.

Game title: Displays the title of the game

Current question bar: Shows the question number that is currently being displayed

Host: Has unique motions for each situation in the game; is an animated character

- **Start:** Begins the game when the host pulls out the question cards
- **Waiting for response:** Includes random movements, yawns, and wise-cracks
- **Correct answer:** Displays a caption bubble telling the player that he is correct
- **Incorrect answer:** Displays a caption bubble telling the player that he is incorrect
- **End:** Ends the game when the host announces the results

Main window: Contains all the information being presented

- **Question:** Displays the current question
- **Answers:** Displays the current answer choices
- **Hints:** Contains several paragraphs explaining the company
- **Final score:** Shows how each player performed and who won
- **Time:** Displays the time remaining in the game

Score area: Contains the score elements

- **Current score:** Displays the current score
- **Bank:** Displays the total points saved

Players: Contains the icons that represent each player; the current player's icon appears green

- **Host:** The one who asks questions
- **Computers:** The player's opponents
- **Player:** The person playing the game

Bank button: Saves current points

Hint button: Displays hint information

Start button: Starts the game

Figure 10.2 shows the interface with each element identified.

Recognizing How the Game's Elements Interact

Figuring out each individual element in the game is the most difficult part. After recognizing all the interactions that take place, creating the game becomes a simple process of typing out the necessary code, rather than blindly programming individual elements.

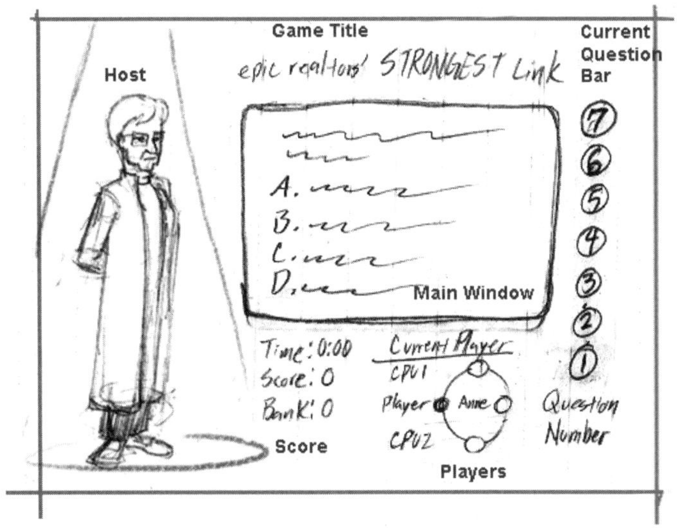

FIGURE 10.2 Interface elements.

The Start button sets the entire game into motion. After it is clicked, the main window selects a random question to display, and waits for a user response. When the player responds, it compares the selected answer to the correct one and sends the result to the host element. The host plays an animation based on the result, increments the question number, adjusts the player's score when necessary, and then allows the next player to answer a question.

Meanwhile, as the game is being played, we must keep track of the score. When a question is answered properly, the score increases; when a question is answered incorrectly, the score is reduced to zero. When the Bank button is clicked, it saves all of the current points in the bank and protects them from the wrong answer penalty.

At any point during the game, the Hint button can be clicked to display the hint information in the main window.

A timer keeps track of how much time is left and when it reaches zero, the game ends. Likewise, if all the questions have been asked, the game ends and final scores are displayed.

The best way to visualize the interactions is to create a flowchart, which contains arrows that describe which elements are acting upon another element and what is supposed to happen. Having a flowchart to identify all items ensures that everything flows smoothly! Figure 10.3 shows a flowchart that has been created for this game.

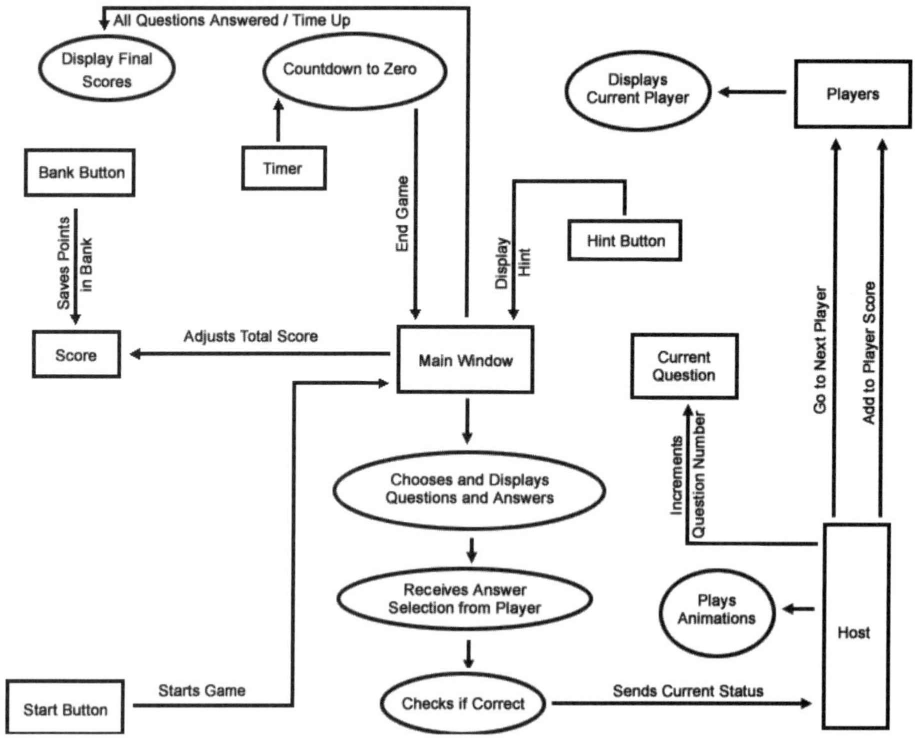

FIGURE 10.3 epic Realtors' Strongest Link flowchart.

Identifying the Actions of the epic Realtors' Strongest Link Game

The majority of the epic Realtors' Strongest Link game involves the simple navigational code outlined previously. Such areas do not have much complexity involved in incorporating them; they simply tell the timeline to go to another place when a certain event happens. Because all of the necessary functionality already exists within the game, there is no need to go further and specifically choose the line or two of code for each action.

The Main Window

The only element that requires involved programming is the main window because it must advance and display the question, select the computer's answer, and compare answers to the correct answer to see if the player and computers are answering questions correctly. The three actions can be broken up into individual functions because they are executed many times during the piece.

The `nextQuestion` *Function*

The `nextQuestion` function is executed every time a question is answered. First, it makes sure that there is another question to ask. If there is, it advances one question; if there isn't, it goes to the ending screen. After confirming the availability of the next question, a question needs to be picked, at random, from the set of questions included in the game. The function needs to include a method of comparing the current question to the previous questions that have been asked, to ensure the same question isn't asked multiple times. After a question is chosen, it is displayed in the window. Now for the pseudocode:

```
function nextQuestion ()
```

1. Increment the question number.
2. If the question number is greater than the total number of questions:
   Display scores.
3. Select a random question.
4. Compare question to array containing past questions. If it exists in the array:
   Start over at Step 3.
5. Add question to the array containing past questions.
6. Display the current question.

The `computer` *Function*

The `computer` function is responsible for having the computer select a question. Because the computer has access to the variables that contain the correct answer, it is easy to ensure that it guesses the correct answer every time. Although this would make for a very challenging game, our aim here is to have a computer that answers correctly, most of the time. The computer randomly selects one of the four answers, with an equal probability of picking any of the choices. This approach only results in a correct answer one in every four times, making it an awfully dumb computer. To compensate for this, a condition needs to be added that sets the computer's choice to the correct answer more often. After selecting an answer, it needs to be compared to the correct answer, to find if the computer has answered the question correctly. Now for the pseudocode:

```
function computer ()
```

1. Choose a random number between 0 and 3.
2. Set the computer's answer to a letter (A, B, C, D) based on the number.
3. Set the computer to a correct answer 33% of the time.

The `checkAnswer` *Function*

The `checkAnswer` function is performed after each player's turn to determine if a question was answered correctly. If the player's choice is the same as the correct answer, the "Correct" animation plays, and the player's score and total score are increased. If the player's choice does not equal the correct answer, the "Wrong" animation plays, the correct answer is announced, and the score is set to zero.

```
function checkAnswer (player's answer choice)
```

1. If the correct answer equals the player's answer:
   Play "Correct" animation, and increment player score and total score.
2. Else:
   Play "Wrong" animation, display the correct answer, and set score to zero.
3. Advance to the next question.

Putting It All Together

ON THE CD

Now that we have walked through the process of designing and planning the epic Realtors' Strongest Link game, it is time to actually construct the game itself. As with the other sections, we start by working with the main window area. Let's get started. Begin by opening the chapter10template.fla file in the \files\templates\ folder on the CD-ROM.

The Main Window

As discussed previously, the main section directs most of the action in the game. Because this is the portion that dictates all of the action, it is important that you go through and set up the code to see how it turns out. The rest of the sections involve simple navigational changes, and have already been included in the template file.

1. Underneath the comment `//Questions`, type the following code:

```
question1 = "When was epic founded?";
question1A = "1990";
question1B = "1992";
question1C = "1998";
question1D = "2000";
question1Correct = "A";
```

2. Repeat Step 1, incrementing the question number by 1 every time, until you have created nine unique questions and answers.
3. Underneath the comment `//Next Questions`, type the following code for the next question function:

```
_global.answered = false;
selectedQuestions = new Array();
questionNumber = 0;

_global.nextQuestion = function () {
    // Set Computer Status to Blank
    root.computer.gotoAndStop("Blank");
    // Increment the Question Number
    questionNumber++;
    // If All 9 Questions have been displayed
    // set ending scores and show ending screen.
    if (questionNumber > 9) {
        playerScore = _global.scores[0];
        com1score = _global.scores[1];
        com2score = _global.scores[2];
        stopAllSounds();
        _root.window.gotoAndPlay("End");
    }

     // Pick a Random Question

     // Set the Current Question

}
```

4. Underneath the comment `//Pick a Random Question`, type the following code:

```
while (!questionPicked && questionNumber <= 9) {
    // Randomly Select a Question
    currentQuestion = random(9) + 1;
    questionPicked = true;

    // Compare Question to Previous Questions.
    for (i = 0; i <= selectedQuestions.length; i++) {
        // If Question has been picked, pick
        // the question again.
        if (currentQuestion == selectedQuestions[i])
            questionPicked = false;
    }
}
questionPicked = false;

// Add Question to selectedQuestions array.
```

```
selectedQuestions[questionNumber - 1] = currentQuestion;
_root.questionNumber.gotoAndStop("q" + questionNumber);
```

5. Underneath the comment `//Set the Current Question`, type the following code:

```
question = eval("question" + currentQuestion);
A = eval("question" + currentQuestion + "A");
B = eval("question" + currentQuestion + "B");
C = eval("question" + currentQuestion + "C");
D = eval("question" + currentQuestion + "D");
correct = eval("question" + currentQuestion + "Correct");
```

6. Underneath the comment `//Computer Turn`, type the following code:

```
function computer() {
    // Randomly select a letter
    randomChoice = random(4);
    switch (randomChoice) {
        case 0:         choice = "A";
                        break;
        case 1:         choice = "B";
                        break;
        case 2:         choice = "C";
                        break;
        case 3:         choice = "D";
                        break;
    }

    // Have the computer choose correctly 1/3 of the time.
    if (random(3) == 1)
        choice = correct;
    // Have the Display Show the Computer's Answer.
    _root.computer.gotoAndStop("Answered")

    // Check the computer's Answer
    checkAnswer(choice);
}
```

7. Underneath the comment `//Check Answer`, type the following code:

```
function checkAnswer(choice) {
    if (!_global.answered)
        // Compare Answer to the original
```

```
        if (choice == correct) {
            _root.anne.gotoAndStop("Correct");
            // Increment Score
            _global.scores[_root.player.currentPlayer]++;
            _root.score.score += _root.score.score + 100;
        } else {
            // Decrement Score
            _root.anne.gotoAndStop("Wrong");
            _root.anne.caption.gotoAndStop(correct);
            _root.score.score = 0;
        }
}
```

8. Underneath the `checkAnswer` function, type the following code to advance to the first question:

```
nextQuestion();
```

9. Hold down the Ctrl key and press Enter to preview your game.

SUMMARY

You have now completed the Strongest Link game! Now, you have a game that will teach your visitors a bit more about your company and give them a chance to claim a prize for making it through the game.

11 Mutt Chow Match-Up

THE CONCEPT

Identifying your Product: epic Mutt Chow

epic, one of the country's leading producers of dog foods, feels that its competitors are getting more attention lately and capturing a younger class of dog owners. epic realizes that it must continue to attract new, young customers to keep its product selling for generations to come. In this situation, epic simply wants potential customers to remember its name and associate its Mutt Chow line with happy, fun-loving dogs. With this goal in mind, the game should show a variety of breeds to increase the odds that a player is reminded of his own pet. Also, there is a slight chance that seeing so many images of cute, lovable dogs will make the player want to go and buy another dog or two. That, of course, would be very good for epic.

Outlining a Game for epic Mutt Chow

We have already decided that the Mutt Chow Advergame should include pictures of several different dogs. No specific breed of dog should be given more attention than another. This could turn off a potential customer by implying that his preferred breed is not as appealing or important as another. This sounds silly, but you must consider such things when attempting to create an Advergame to please a variety of potential customers.

So far, we have decided that the game should involve several uniform pictures of different types of dogs. We need to work our epic Mutt Chow products into the game, but simply mixing them in with the dog images would seem forced and would possibly confuse the player. A matching game suits our needs well, because the player must pay attention to the image on each card. While trying to match up pictures of dogs, the player flips over a card containing one of four epic products. These cards require no match to be made and give the player a free turn. This should make the player happy, to see epic products as they randomly appear on the screen. When displaying your product in a game, you must always be certain that viewing the product does not upset the player by taking away points, delaying the game, or anything else that could prove frustrating or annoying. Even though the player may not realize it, subconscious, emotional ties to the product are forming. The longer one plays the game, the stronger these ties become. If your game leaves the player feeling upset in some way, it will probably not result in the sale of your product.

This is a classic memory-matching game like you may have played as a child. Because all cards must fit on the screen at once, each image must be fairly small. It makes the most sense to show cartoon drawings instead of photographs on the cards, both for clarity and to give the game a fun atmosphere. To make certain the player is able to see the dogs' faces and isn't bored by tiny, generic dog silhouettes, only the faces appear on the cards. (The Chihuahua is an exception because it is so small to begin with.) Different colored backgrounds on the dog images give the player a little help in trying to keep all the different images straight. The cards featuring epic products have multicolored backgrounds to make them stand out from the normal cards. Of course, this is not enough to tell the player exactly how these cards are special, so some explanation must be provided.

To keep the game nice and simple, we include only the elements that are essential for play. The game needs cards, of course, a place for the player's score to appear, and a Reset button in case he wants to play again. Always be certain to encourage repeat play in your Advergames. The more times a potential customer plays the game, the more likely the product is to stick in his head. The game starts out by visually mixing up the cards and allowing the player to start looking for matches. After all the cards have been turned over, it is obvious to the player that the game is finished, because no more matches can be made. In fact, the only thing that the player can do, after all the cards are flipped, is press the Reset button. This resets the player's score and mixes up the cards once again. Thus, all of the game's elements remain on the screen from beginning to end, and only one graphical interface must be designed.

Designing the Mutt Chow Match-Up Interface

The matching-card images make up the bulk of the visual interface. We first decide upon the number of cards to be used and the image size of each. These values more or less dictate the size of the interface as a whole. If we make the grid 6 cards wide and 4 cards tall, we have 24 cards. Excluding the four cards containing epic products, this leaves 20 cards—10 possible matches. If each card is 80 pixels wide and 80 pixels tall with 10 pixels of free space around it, then an area of 530 by 350 pixels is required just to hold them all, as shown in Figure 11.1.

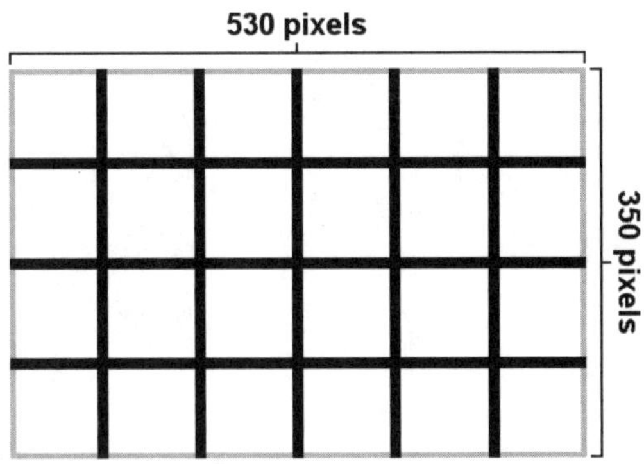

FIGURE 11.1 A grid illustrating the dimensions required by a particular card layout.

Of course, the entire interface cannot consist of just cards. We have to fit in a Reset button and a place for the player's score to appear. As mentioned earlier, this game also requires, at least, a very basic set of instructions. In addition, we must not forget to leave room for the game's title. If we arrange these additional elements so that they fit in an area the same size as a single row of cards (530 by 80 pixels), the game's dimensions become 530 by 440 pixels. With a border of 10 pixels, the final size of our game's interface is 550 pixels wide and 460 pixels tall, as shown in Figure 11.2. This should be compact enough to fit comfortably on most players' screens.

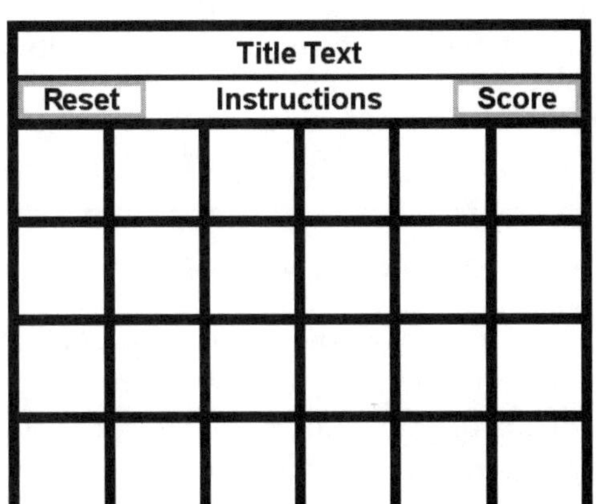

FIGURE 11.2 The final layout chosen for Mutt Chow Match-Up.

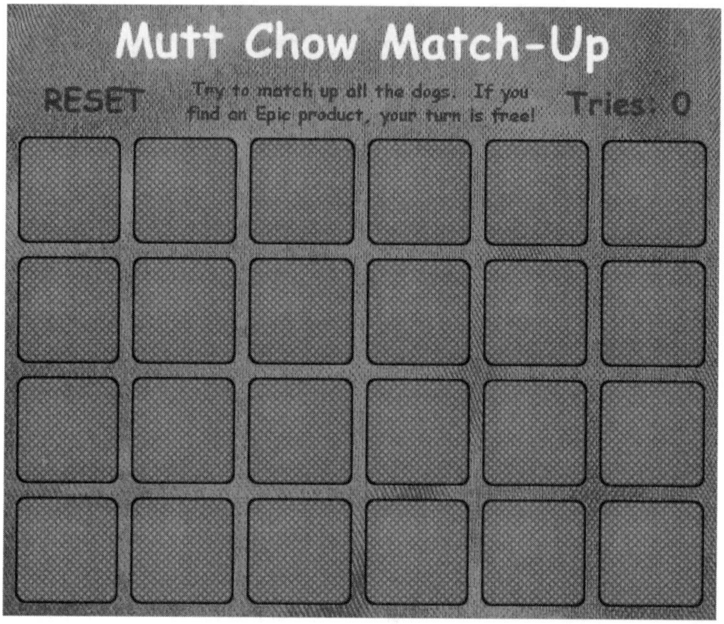

FIGURE 11.3 The Mutt Chow Match-Up interface complete with text and graphics.

For the image representing the back of each card, we use a generic reddish pattern. You may choose to put your company logo on the backs of the cards. Just be careful not to overwhelm the player with a sea of logos. The backs of the cards should appear very simple and subdued so the player can tell at a glance which cards are flipped over and which are not. When we fill in the images and text for our game's interface, it really starts to take shape, as shown in Figure 11.3.

THE CREATION

Identifying the Elements of Mutt Chow Match-Up

Start by compiling a list of all the major elements that your game requires. Whenever possible, wait to add special features, such as sounds and animations, until you have a basic version of your game up and running. Mutt Chow Match-Up is a very simple game and contains only the following major elements.

Game title: Displays "Mutt Chow Match-Up" on screen

Game instructions: Displays a short explanation of how to play the game

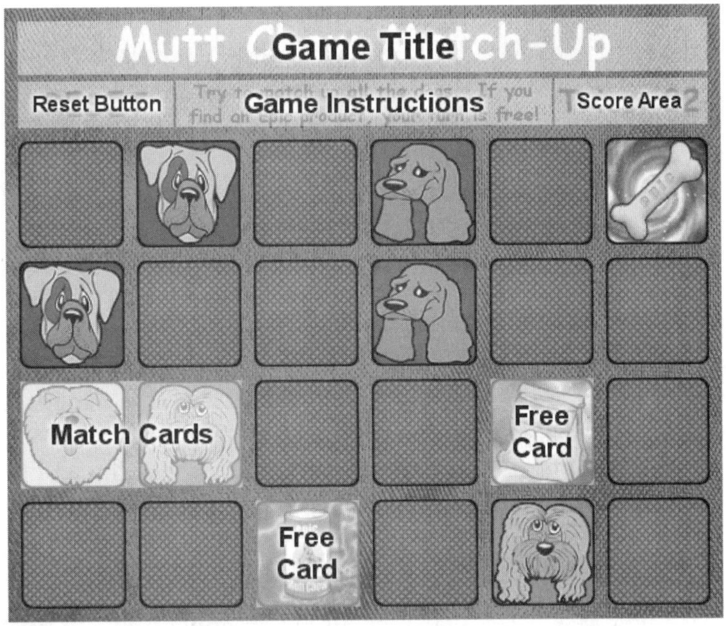

FIGURE 11.4 The Mutt Chow Match-Up interface with major elements identified.

Cards: Is represented by the Card Back member when not flipped over

- **Match cards:** Includes 10 pairs of dog images, which the player tries to match up
- **Free cards:** Includes four images of epic products, which stay flipped over and do not add to the player's score

Reset button: Resets the player's score and shuffles the cards for a new game

Score area: Displays the player's score labeled as "Tries"

For a clear view of how these elements appear in the game's interface, see Figure 11.4.

Recognizing How the Game's Elements Interact

As far as the programmer is concerned, Mutt Chow Match-Up is a game with no real *end*. This means that the game never has to check the player's progress to determine when to stop play or present some sort of results. When the player flips a card over (and its back image is no longer showing), it becomes inactive. *Free cards* (featuring epic products) stay inactive after they are flipped, but *match cards* (featuring pictures of dogs) require a match to be made or they revert to their original, *unflipped* state after a short delay. The game is over only when the player decides to click the Reset button or exit the program. Of course, after all the cards are inactive, this decision becomes quite easy to make.

When the player starts the game, the cards are shuffled, and the score is zero. Any of the cards whose backs are showing may be clicked on and flipped over. When this happens, the game must determine whether the chosen card is a match card or a free card. If a free card is flipped over, it stays that way, and normal play resumes. If a match card is flipped, then the player's score increases by one, and the card's face value is stored in a variable named `upCard`. When a second card is flipped, the process is essentially repeated. However, if a match card is chosen this time, it is compared to the face value of the first card. If there is a match, normal play resumes, but if there is not, both cards must unflip and become active once again. Figure 11.5 illustrates the game's logic using a flowchart.

Identifying the Scripts of Mutt Chow Match-Up

Mutt Chow Match-Up contains four Lingo scripts, only three of which are actually essential for play. The Slide into Place behavior is simply an animation effect to show the player that the cards are being mixed up. Because this script is not actually required for the game to function, we discuss it last.

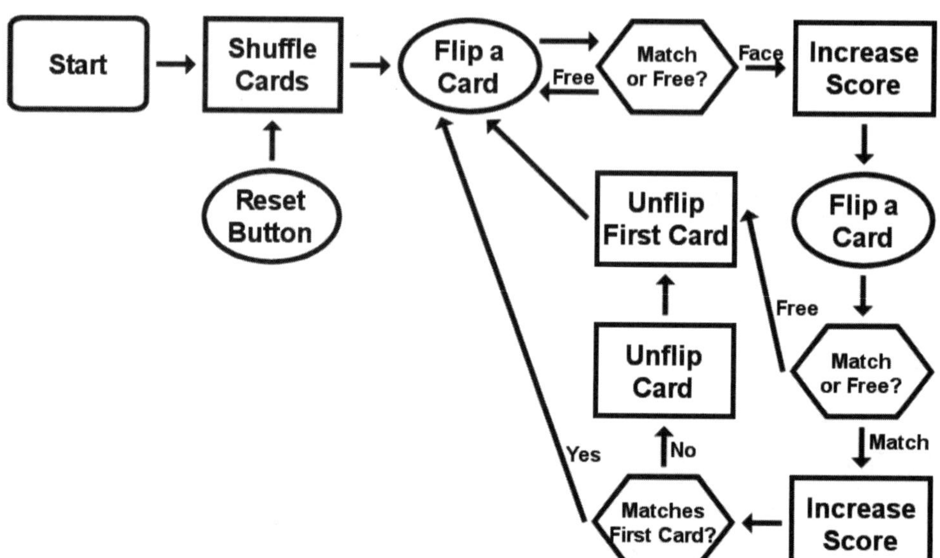

FIGURE 11.5 A flowchart for the Mutt Chow Match-Up Advergame.

When Mutt Chow Match-Up first begins to run, the game's Main movie script stores some values in global variables for later use: the game's dimensions (550 by 460 pixels), the text to precede the player's score ("Tries: "), and the channel number of the first card sprite (2). It makes the most sense to assign such constant values in the prepareMovie handler of a movie script. Soon after, the startMovie handler executes and calls the resetGame function. (The startMovie handler is used to call resetGame because resetGame deals with the card sprites and prepareMovie executes before these sprites are created.) This function starts by setting a few global variables to their default values, telling the Score Text member to display a score of zero, and calling the reset function of all sprites that have one. Next, temporary variables are used to shuffle the cards and set each card sprite's face property accordingly.

Each time the Director MX playback head exits a frame (after all other handlers for that frame have executed), the Main script's exitFrame handler checks to see if any cards need to be unflipped and reactivated. Another script (namely the Card behavior) determines which cards should be unflipped and adds them to the global unflipList. All sprites in this list are unflipped by Main after a specified delay of unflipTimer frames. If there were no delay, the player would not have a chance to see the second match card chosen when a match had been made. Without a match, the game would instantly unflip the cards. After the unflipping has been dealt with, Main's exitFrame handler replays the current frame and starts the cycle over again.

The Card behavior uses a face property to determine which image it should display when flipped and a flipped property to determine if that image is currently being displayed. By default, all cards are unflipped. If the player clicks on a particular card, its mouseDown handler executes. This calls the sprite's flip function, if the card is currently unflipped and the global unflipList is empty. The flip function sets the sprite's image based on its face property, checks upCard to see if a match has been made, and adjusts the player's score as discussed earlier.

The Reset Button behavior is the simplest in the game. It uses the mouseEnter and mouseLeave handlers to give the button a simple rollover color-change effect. The rgb function is used to specify color values within Lingo. It accepts values for red, green, and blue on a scale of 0 to 255. When the player clicks the Reset button, its behavior's mouseDown handler calls the global resetGame function of Main. This button is always active, but is really designed to be used when the player has flipped over all the cards and has nothing else to do.

As mentioned earlier, Slide into Place is applied to the card sprites to create a visual shuffling effect. However, it is written in such a way that it could theoretically work on any sprite. Whenever possible, it is best to write your scripts completely independent of one another. This helps keep your code clean and organized, and can be quite useful if you are able to reuse such scripts in future programs.

The Slide into Place behavior starts by storing its sprite's initial location in the `targetX` and `targetY` properties. Then, it calls its own `reset` function, which chooses a random spot offscreen to reposition the sprite and a random speed and direction to start it moving. The sprite's location is stored in the properties `x` and `y`, and its velocity is stored in `stepX` and `stepY`. The `x` and `y` properties must be used instead of working directly with the sprite's `locH` and `locV` properties because `locH` and `locV` can only hold integer values. This means that the smallest step value that would actually affect one of these properties is `1`. Therefore, the slowest a sprite is able to move (without standing still) is one pixel per frame. That's 30 pixels per second and not all that slow.

The script's `prepareFrame` handler deals with the actual movement of the sprite. Once during every frame, this handler checks to see how close the sprite is to its target (its original location on the Stage). If the sprite is close enough, then the handler snaps it into place and stops future motion by setting the `stepX` and `stepY` properties to zero. Next, the step properties are adjusted based on their current values, the target properties, and the distance between the sprite's current `x` and `y` values and its target values. This adjustment is what gives the sprite its shuffling movement and eventually brings it to its target coordinates. The step values are then used to increment `x` and `y`, and `x` and `y` are used to update the sprite's `locH` and `locV`.

Putting It All Together

We have walked through the development of the Mutt Chow Match-Up Advergame starting with the product and ideas, moving on to layout and interface design, and finally analyzing the game's elements, logic, and Lingo scripts. Now all that remains is for you to build the game yourself.

1. Open a copy of Director MX. It automatically creates a new, blank movie.
2. Choose Save from the File menu and save the movie to your hard disk.
3. Click the Stage. Director MX updates the Property Inspector.
4. Click the Movie tab of the Property Inspector.
5. Type "550" and "460" in the Stage Size fields.

Creating the Media Cast Members

To create the media cast members, perform the following steps.

1. Choose Import from the File menu.
2. Navigate to \files\templates\chapter11\ on the CD-ROM, select all the files in the directory, and click Import.

ON THE CD

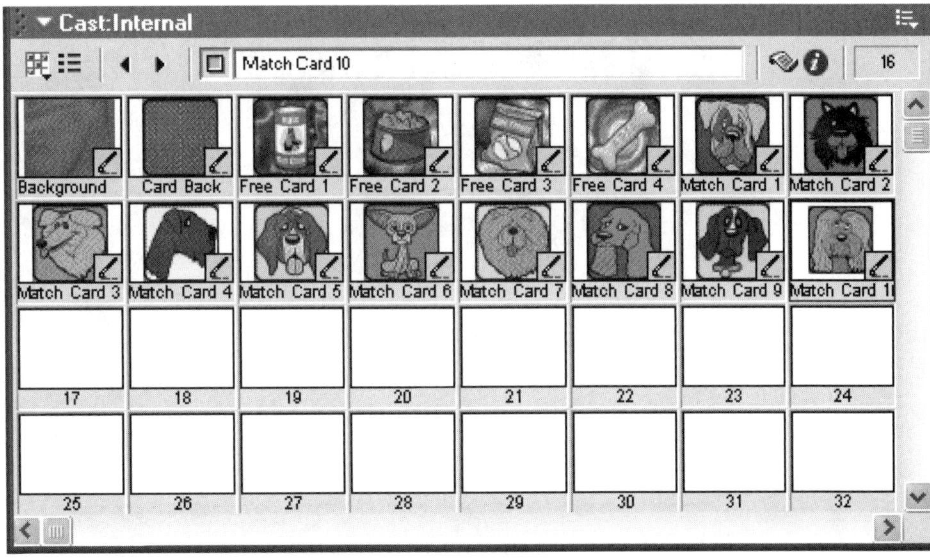

FIGURE 11.6 The imported cast members of Mutt Chow Match-Up.

3. Select the Same Settings for Remaining Images checkbox and click OK. Your movie's Internal cast should now contain the members shown in Figure 11.6.
4. Click the Text Window button on the Toolbar, as shown in Figure 11.7.
5. Type "Mutt Chow Match-Up" into the Text window and then select it.
6. Choose Comic Sans MS from the Font drop-down list.
7. Choose 36 from the Size drop-down list.
8. Type "40" in the Line Spacing field.
9. Click the Bold button, if it is not already depressed.
10. Click the Align Center button.

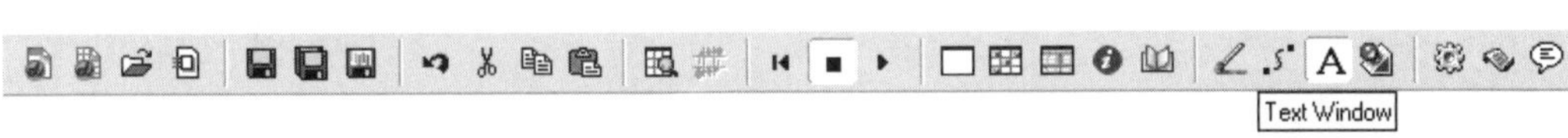

FIGURE 11.7 The Toolbar's Text Window button.

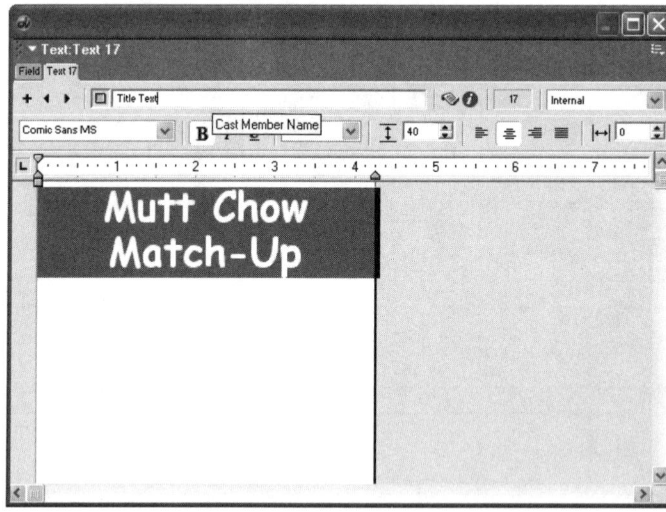

FIGURE 11.8 Naming the new Title Text cast member.

11. Type "Title Text" in the Cast Member Name field, as shown in Figure 11.8, and close the Text window.
12. Click an empty spot in the Cast window.
13. Click the Text Window button on the Toolbar.
14. Type the following text in the Text window and then select it: "Try to match up all the dogs. If you find an Epic product, your turn is free!"
15. Choose 14 from the Size drop-down list.
16. Type "18" in the Line Spacing field.
17. Type "Instructions Text" in the Cast Member Name field and close the Text window.
18. Click an empty spot in the Cast window.
19. Click the Text Window button on the Toolbar.
20. Type "RESET" in the Text window and then select it.
21. Choose 24 from the Size drop-down list.
22. Type "Reset Text" in the Cast Member Name field and close the Text window.
23. Click an empty spot in the Cast window.
24. Click the Text Window button on the Toolbar.
25. Type "Tries: 0" in the Text window.
26. Type "Score Text" in the Cast Member Name field and close the Text window.

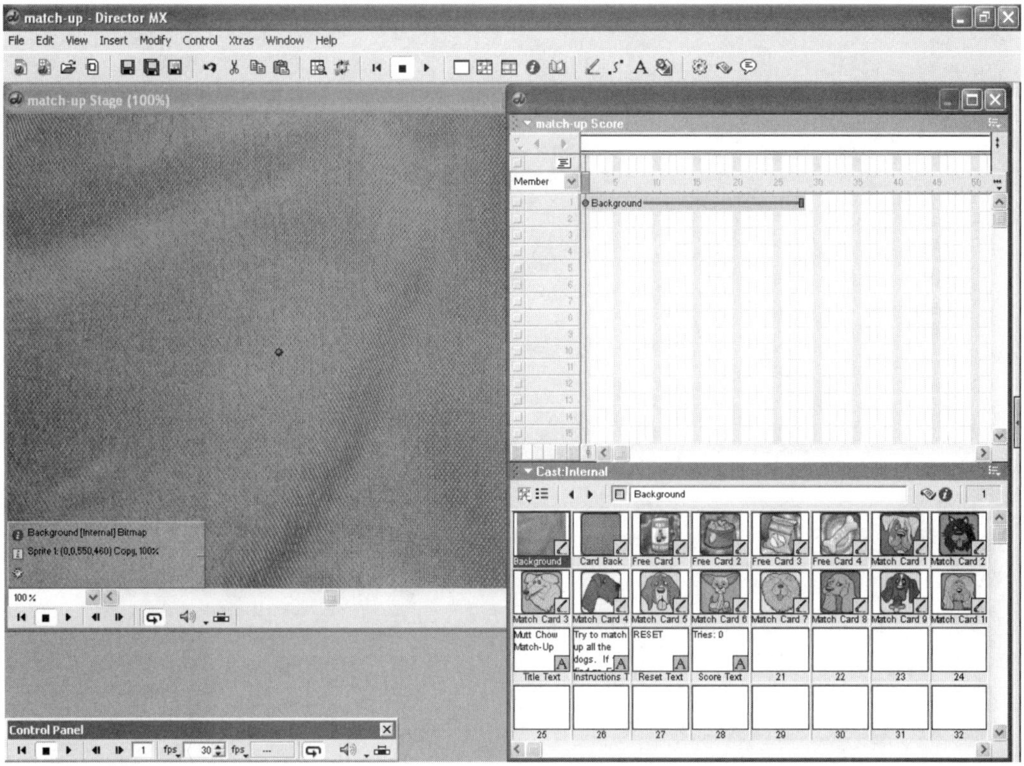

FIGURE 11.9 Creating a sprite from the Background cast member.

Setting Up Sprites on the Stage and in the Score

To set up the sprites on the Stage and in the Score, perform the following steps.

1. Drag the Background member from the Cast window into cell 1 of channel 1 of the Score, as shown in Figure 11.9.
2. Drag the Card Back member from the Cast window into cell 1 of channel 2 of the Score.
3. Click cell 2 of channel 2 of the Score. Director MX updates the Property Inspector.
4. Within the Property Inspector, type "50" in the X field and "140" in the Y field, as shown in Figure 11.10.
5. Choose Background Transparent from the Ink drop-down list.
6. Type "#A09080" in the Backcolor field.

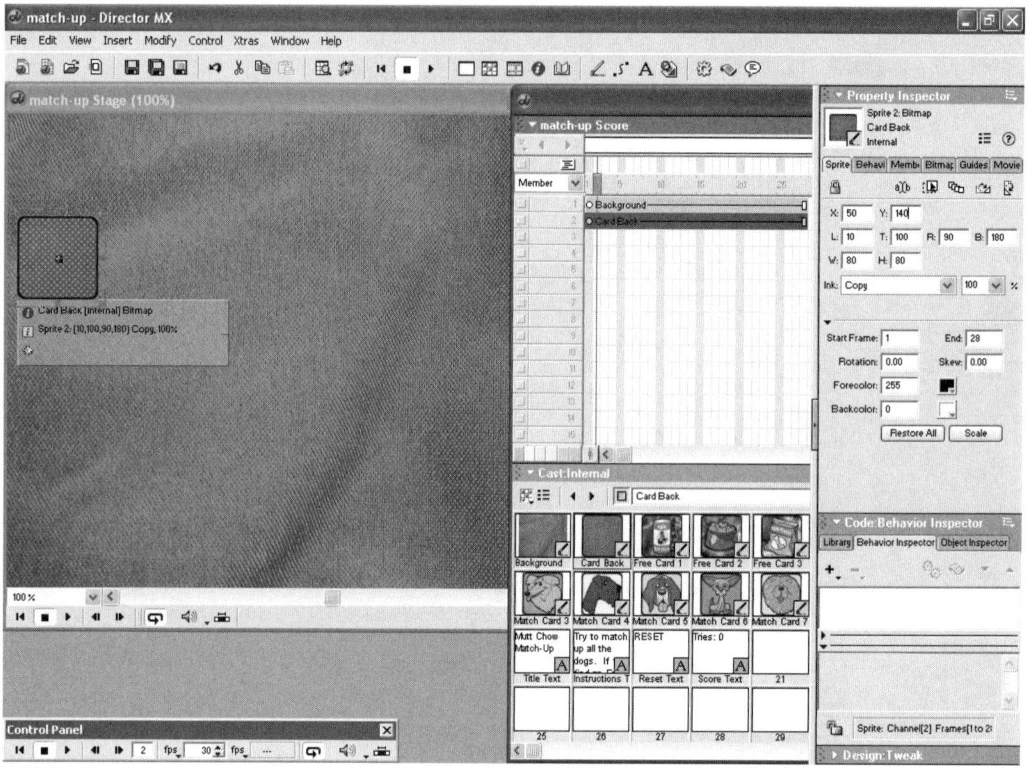

FIGURE 11.10 Positioning a Card Back sprite on the Stage.

7. Right-click cell 2 of channel 2 of the Score and select Copy Sprites, as shown in Figure 11.11.
8. Right-click cell 1 of channel 3 of the Score and select Paste Sprites.
9. Hold down the Shift key and press the down arrow nine times. This moves the new sprite 90 pixels down the Stage, as shown in Figure 11.12.
10. Click cell 2 of channel 2 of the Score, hold down the Shift key, and then click cell 2 of channel 3.
11. Right-click cell 2 of channel 2 of the Score and select Copy Sprites.
12. Right-click cell 1 of channel 4 of the Score and select Paste Sprites.
13. Hold down the Shift key and press the down arrow 18 times. This moves the new sprites 180 pixels down the Stage.
14. Click cell 2 of channel 2 of the Score, hold down the Shift key, and then click cell 2 of channel 5.
15. Right-click cell 2 of channel 2 of the Score and select Copy Sprites.

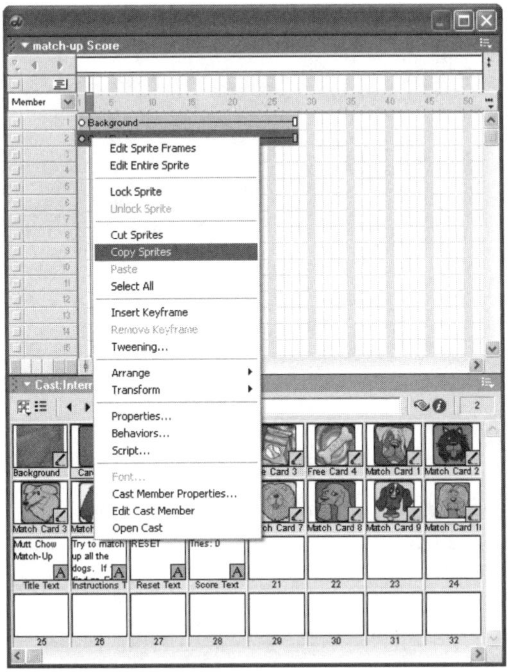

FIGURE 11.11 Copying the Card Back sprite of channel 2.

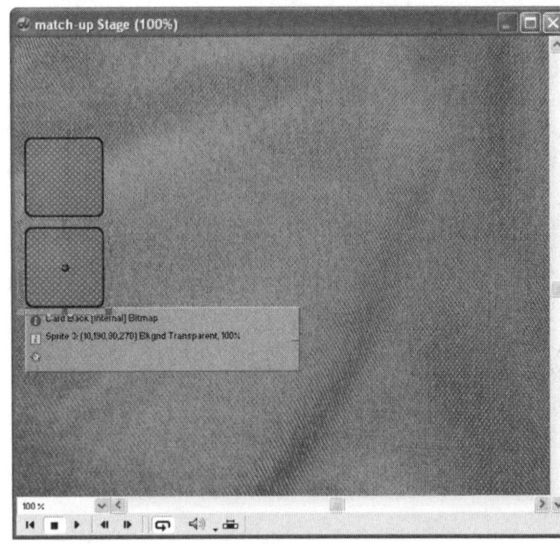

FIGURE 11.12 Positioning the new Card Back sprite on the Stage.

16. Right-click cell 1 of channel 6 of the Score and select Paste Sprites.
17. Hold down the Shift key and press the right arrow nine times. This moves the new sprites 90 pixels to the right on the Stage.
18. Click cell 2 of channel 2 of the Score, hold down the Shift key, and then click cell 2 of channel 9.
19. Right-click cell 2 of channel 2 of the Score and select Copy Sprites.
20. Right-click cell 1 of channel 10 of the Score and select Paste Sprites.
21. Hold down the Shift key and press the right arrow 18 times. This moves the new sprites 180 pixels to the right on the Stage.
22. Right-click cell 2 of channel 10 of the Score and select Copy Sprites.
23. Right-click cell 1 of channel 18 of the Score and select Paste Sprites.
24. Hold down the Shift key and press the right arrow 18 times. This moves the new sprites 180 pixels to the right on the Stage, as shown in Figure 11.13.
25. Drag the Title Text member from the Cast window into cell 1 of channel 26 of the Score.

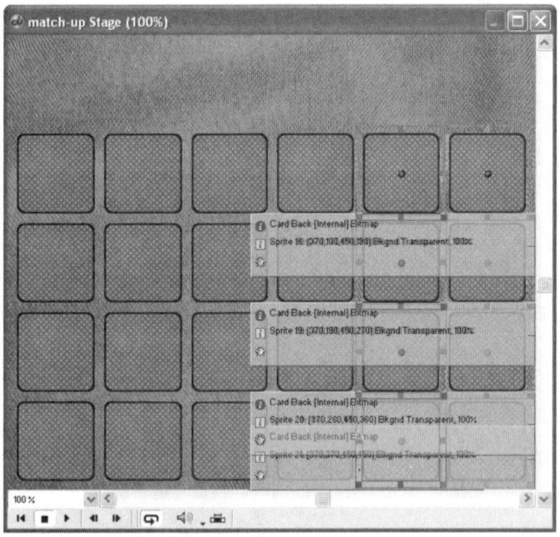

FIGURE 11.13 Positioning the final Card Back sprites on the Stage.

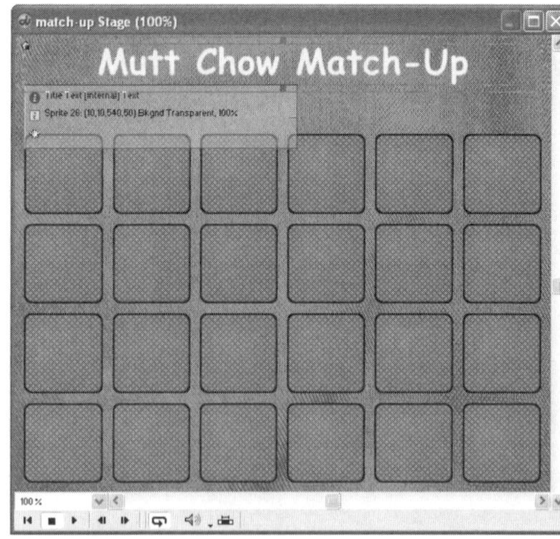

FIGURE 11.14 The Title Text sprite as it should appear on the Stage.

26. Click cell 2 of channel 26 of the Score. Director MX updates the Property Inspector.
27. Within the Property Inspector, type "10" in the X field and "10" in the Y field.
28. Type "530" in the W field.
29. Choose Background Transparent from the Ink drop-down list.
30. Type "#FFFF00" in the Forecolor field. The Stage should appear as it does in Figure 11.14.
31. Drag the Instructions Text member from the Cast window into cell 1 of channel 27 of the Score.
32. Click cell 2 of channel 27 of the Score. Director MX updates the Property Inspector.
33. Within the Property Inspector, type "130" in the X field and "55" in the Y field.
34. Type "290" in the W field.
35. Drag the Reset Text member from the Cast window into cell 1 of channel 28 of the Score.
36. Click cell 2 of channel 28 of the Score. Director MX updates the Property Inspector.
37. Within the Property Inspector, type "10" in the X field and "55" in the Y field.
38. Type "120" in the W field.

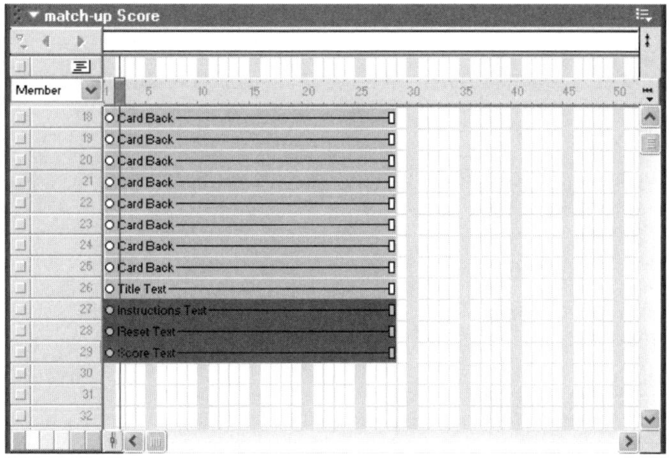

FIGURE 11.15 Selecting the text sprites of channels 27 through 29.

39. Drag the Score Text member from the Cast window into cell 1 of channel 29 of the Score.
40. Click cell 2 of channel 29 of the Score. Director MX updates the Property Inspector.
41. Within the Property Inspector, type "420" in the X field and "55" in the Y field.
42. Type "120" in the W field.
43. Click cell 2 of channel 27 of the Score, hold down the Shift key, and then click cell 2 of channel 29, as shown in Figure 11.15.
44. Within the Property Inspector, choose Background Transparent from the Ink drop-down list.
45. Type "#800000" in the Forecolor field.

Writing and Applying the Lingo Scripts

To write and apply the Lingo scripts, perform the following steps.

1. Click an empty spot in the Cast window.
2. Click the Script Window button on the Toolbar, as shown in Figure 11.16.

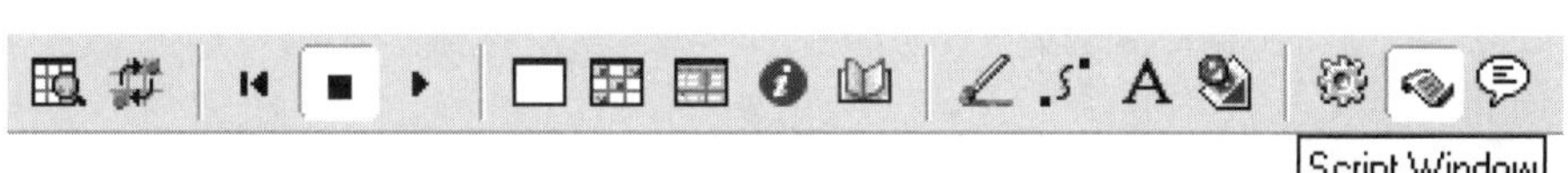

FIGURE 11.16 The Toolbar's Script Window button.

3. Type the following code in the Script window.

```
global stageW, stageH, cardOffset, scorePrefix, upCard, unflipTimer,
unflipList

on prepareMovie
    stageW = 550
    stageH = 460
    cardOffset = 1
    scorePrefix = member("Score Text").text.word[1]
end

on startMovie
    resetGame
end

on exitFrame
    -- Flip cards back over if necessary, but only after a delay.
    if unflipTimer > 0 then
        unflipTimer = unflipTimer-1
    else if unflipTimer = 0 then
        repeat with cardNum = 1 to unflipList.count
            unflipList[cardNum].unflip()
        end repeat
        unflipTimer = -1
        unflipList = []
    end if

    play the frame
end

on stopMovie
    -- This keeps the desired value of scorePrefix from being lost while
previewing in Director MX.
    member("Score Text").text = scorePrefix && "0"
end

on resetGame
    upCard = 0
    unflipTimer = -1
    unflipList = []
    member("Score Text").text = scorePrefix && "0"
    sendAllSprites(#reset)
```

```
    -- Assign and then mix up the cards.
    cardOrder = list(1, 1, 2, 2, 3, 3, 4, 4, 5, 5, 6, 6, 7, 7, 8, 8, 9, 9, 10,
10, 11, 12, 13, 14)
    repeat with cardNum = 1 to cardOrder.count
        swapCard = random(cardOrder.count)
        holder = cardOrder[cardNum]
        cardOrder[cardNum] = cardOrder[swapCard]
        cardOrder[swapCard] = holder
    end repeat

    -- Use the temporary cardOrder list to assign each card's face property.
    repeat with cardNum = 1 to cardOrder.count
        sprite(cardNum+cardOffset).face = cardOrder[cardNum]
    end repeat
end
```

4. Type "Main" in the Cast Member Name field, as shown in Figure 11.17, and close the Script window.
5. Click an empty spot in the Cast window.

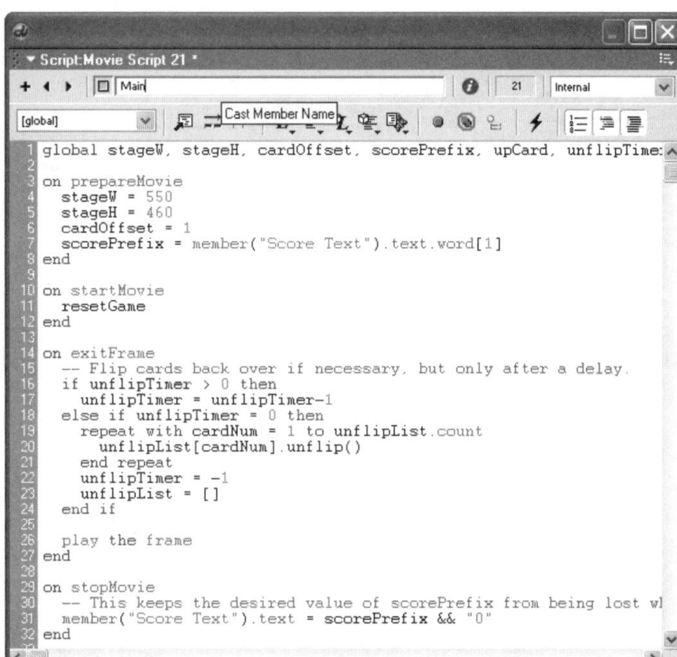

FIGURE 11.17 Naming the new Main movie script.

6. Click the Script Window button on the Toolbar.
7. Type the following code in the Script window.

```
global scorePrefix, upCard, unflipTimer, unflipList
property my, face, flipped

on beginSprite me
    my = sprite(me.spriteNum)
    reset
end

on mouseDown
    if flipped or unflipList.count > 0 then exit

    flip
end

on reset
    unflip
end

on flip
    -- Set the sprite to its appropriate "face-up" image.
    flipped = true
    if face <= 10 then
        cardName = "Match Card" && face
    else
        cardName = "Free Card" && (face-10)
    end if
    my.member = member(cardName)

    -- Check the upCard property to see if a match has been made or
not.
    if upCard = 0 then
        if face <= 10 then
            upCard = my
        end if
    else
        if upCard.face <> face then
            unflipTimer = 30
            unflipList.add(upCard)
            if face <= 10 then
                unflipList.add(my)
            end if
```

```
        end if
        upCard = 0
    end if

    -- Add one to the user's score unless a free card has been found.
    if face <= 10 then
        scoreNumber = integer(member("Score Text").text.word[2]+1)
        if scoreNumber < 100 then
            member("Score Text").text = scorePrefix && scoreNumber
        else
            member("Score Text").text = string(scoreNumber)
        end if
    end if
end

on unflip
    flipped = false
    my.member = member("Card Back")
end
```

8. Click the Script tab of the Property Inspector.
9. Choose Behavior from the Type drop-down list.
10. Within the Script window, type "Card" in the Cast Member Name field and close the window.
11. Click cell 2 of channel 2 of the Score, hold down the Shift key, and then click cell 2 of channel 25.
12. Drag the Card behavior from the Cast window onto the selected sprites of the Score, as shown in Figure 11.18.
13. Click an empty spot in the Cast window.
14. Click the Script Window button on the Toolbar.
15. Type the following code in the Script window.

```
property my

on beginSprite me
    my = sprite(me.spriteNum)
end

on mouseEnter
    my.color = rgb(255, 255, 0)
end

on mouseLeave
    my.color = rgb(128, 0, 0)
```

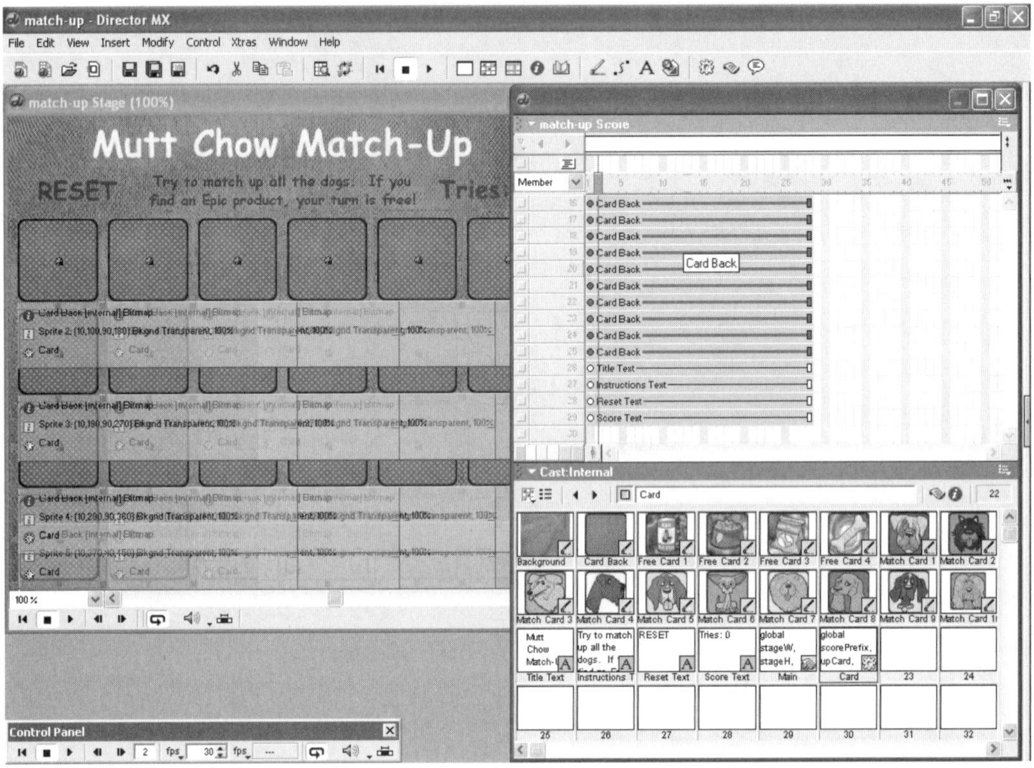

FIGURE 11.18 Applying the Card behavior to the Card Back sprites.

```
end

on mouseDown
    resetGame
end
```

16. Click the Script tab of the Property Inspector.
17. Choose Behavior from the Type drop-down list.
18. Within the Script window, type "Reset Button" in the Cast Member Name field and close the window.
19. Drag the Reset Button behavior from the Cast window onto the sprite in channel 28 of the Score.
20. Click an empty spot in the Cast window.
21. Click the Script Window button on the Toolbar.
22. Type the following code in the Script window.

```
global stageW, stageH
property my, x, y, stepX, stepY, targetX, targetY

on beginSprite me
    my = sprite(me.spriteNum)
    targetX = my.locH
    targetY = my.locV
    reset
end

on prepareFrame
    -- If the sprite is close enough to its target, snap it into place.
    if abs(targetX-x) < 2 and abs(targetY-y) < 2 then
        x = targetX
        y = targetY
        stepX = 0
        stepY = 0
    end if

    -- Adjust the step increments based on the target locations.
    if targetX <> x then stepX = (stepX+(targetX-x)/abs(targetX-x))*0.9
    if targetY <> y then stepY = (stepY+(targetY-y)/abs(targetY-y))*0.9

    x = x+stepX
    y = y+stepY

    my.locH = x
    my.locV = y
end

on reset
    -- Put the sprite in a random location offscreen, and start it
moving in a random direction.
    if random(2) = 1 then
        x = random(stageW+201)-101
        if random(2) = 1 then
            y = -100
        else
            y = stageH+100
        end if
    else
        if random(2) = 1 then
            x = -100
        else
```

```
            x = stageW+100
        end if
        y = random(stageH+201)-101
    end if
    stepX = random(101)-51
    stepY = random(101)-51

    -- Update the sprite's location and assign it to a random layer
from 101 to 200.
    my.locH = x
    my.locV = y
    my.locZ = 100+random(100)
end
```

23. Click the Script tab of the Property Inspector.
24. Choose Behavior from the Type drop-down list.
25. Within the Script window, type “Slide into Place” in the Cast Member Name field and close the window.
26. Click cell 2 of channel 2 of the Score, hold down the Shift key, and then click cell 2 of channel 25.
27. Drag the Slide into Place behavior from the Cast window onto the selected sprites of the Score.
28. Click frame 1 of the Score and then click the Play button on the Toolbar to play your game.

SUMMARY

You have now completed the Mutt Chow Match-Up game. From here, it is ready to be published and distributed! Soon, dog lovers everywhere will have a chance to pass time with a fun, new game.

12 The Spray-a-Bug Game

THE CONCEPT

Identifying Your Product: Bug Bee Gone

Bugs of all types are everywhere, annoying people to no end. epic Extermination has been in the pesticide business for many years and has been searching for a way to make people more familiar with their products. epic Extermination wants to showcase their number-one selling product with a game to help drive traffic through their site and increase awareness of their brand. Bug Bee Gone is a pesticide that is sold in aerosol cans for use on all types of insects found in the home. The company wants to show off its product's unique orange-colored packaging to help people identify Bug Bee Gone quickly and easily. The target audience for this game is people of all ages who could potentially be interested in buying the product. The game needs to be simple to play and based on a currently existing game with which most people are familiar. With this information in mind, it is time to start developing our game.

Outlining a Game for Bug Bee Gone

Now that it's time to decide what kind of game we want for this product, we need to start narrowing down our options. First, we can eliminate any game that has complex gameplay or requires people to learn a new game style. These requirements slim down our options pretty well, limiting us to just a couple of game genres that can be used. Quiz games and arcade games both lend themselves well to meeting this requirement. The next aspect that needs to be considered is the target audience we're targeting—people of all ages who are potential buyers of Bug Bee Gone. Quiz games tend to have a narrow range of audiences they can appeal to because they must be custom tailored for each group. In most situations, quiz games appeal to groups of people who are not very competitive, which leaves out younger audiences and some of the male audience. With quiz games eliminated, we are left with arcade games. Arcade games also have some issues with fitting the target audience, but certain ones work well for everyone. Arcade games can take many forms, ranging from a Quake-style, first-person shooter, to a fighter jet game—but what works best in this situation is one with which everyone is familiar.

After settling on a game genre, we need to decide how the actual game should work. Because using Bug Bee Gone involves spraying pests, it naturally lends itself to those games that involve eliminating targets. Two main categories come to mind with this kind of gameplay—the shooter games and the games that involving hitting objects with a mallet. A shooter game could be set up with the player wielding a spray can that he uses on pests moving about the screen. The other option is to create a *Whack-a-Mole* style game in which the player has a spray can instead of a mallet that he uses to exterminate bugs that pop up out of the game. In this case, the *Whack-a-Mole* style game would probably work best because it is enjoyed by people of all ages.

The game's design needs to revolve around the product's purpose, the extermination of pests. Therefore, instead of using a mallet to squash the objects that appear out of the game, a can of Bug Bee Gone can be used instead. The objects that appear out of the machine can be insects that must be sprayed with the can of Bug Bee Gone. The game needs to keep track of the player's score, the time remaining, and provide some sort of mechanism to start the game. The bugs need to be shaped so that they can extend out of the holes to a visible height that allows them to be sprayed.

The main interface should have two stages, one that displays introductory information, and one that allows users to play the game. The introductory screen needs to provide some information about the product and inform the player how the game is played. After the game has been completed, the program should advance to the final scene that displays the ending score and allows the player to e-mail a challenge to a friend—to help spread the game.

Designing the Spray-a-Bug Interface

Now that we know what we want in our Advergame, we need to begin laying it out visually. The majority of the screen is set aside for the actual gameplay. Because this style of game has become an arcade classic, we are going to have an actual machine drawn with holes that the insects pop out of. The starting mechanism is also designed in the same way, with a quarter that can be placed in a slot with a Start button that actually initiates the game. Each of the insects needs to have a normal and a hit state drawn. The can of Bug Bee Gone also needs a normal and a spraying state drawn. Figure 12.1 shows a rough sketch of the interface.

In addition to the various states for the insects and can, sounds need to be inserted that make the spraying and hit noises. A background loop can also be added to liven up the game.

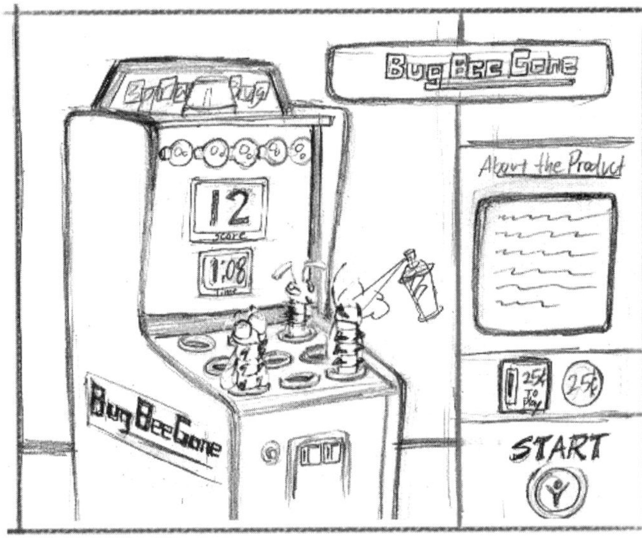

FIGURE 12.1 The Spray-a-Bug interface.

THE CREATION

Identifying the Elements of the Spray-a-Bug Game

First, we start by compiling a list of every element that is involved in the game. This takes the form of a simple, nested list that shows where everything needs to exist. The elements exist in three main sections: the start screen, the game screen, and the end screen.

The Start Screen

- Start background
- Quarter
- Coin slot
- Start button
- Product information
- Interface background
- Title
- Exit button

The Game Screen

- Interface background
- Exit button
- Score

- Time remaining
- Ant
- Roach
- Fly
- Bug Bee Gone
- Target
- Exit button

The End Screen

- E-mail fields
- Submit button
- Replay button
- Exit button
- Interface background
- E-mail title

Figure 12.2 shows the interface with all of the elements identified.

Recognizing How the Game's Elements Interact

After establishing all of the elements that exist within the game, it is time to figure out the interactions that occur between them. In this game, we follow it from beginning to end and track how one action leads to the next.

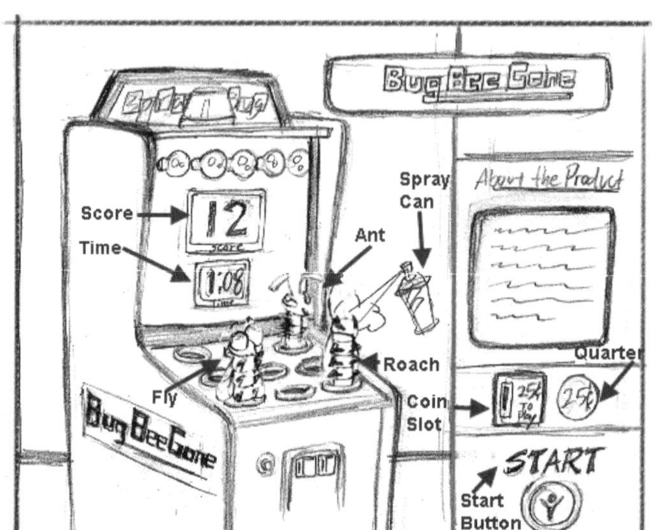

FIGURE 12.2 Interface elements.

The Start screen only serves to display information on the game. The player needs to drag the quarter onto the coin slot to activate the game, and then press the Start button to actually begin the game.

Upon arriving at the Game screen, the game should immediately begin. The machine has insects that pop out of and into the holes on top. If the mouse pointer is not on the interface elements, a spray can follows the mouse around the screen. When the mouse is clicked, the spray can shoots out a dose of Bug Bee Gone. If the spray hits one of the insects, the insect displays a hit state and moves back down. Whenever a bug is hit, the score counter increments. You also need a timer that counts down throughout the game. When the timer expires, the game needs to display the End screen. At any point throughout the game, the user may click the Exit button to quit.

Upon ending the game, the End screen appears. On the End screen, the player can enter e-mail addresses in E-mail fields. The Submit button sends an e-mail to all of the e-mail addresses entered.

A flowchart should be created to visually map out what happens, as shown in Figure 12.3. This ensures that everything in your movie is planned and occurs smoothly.

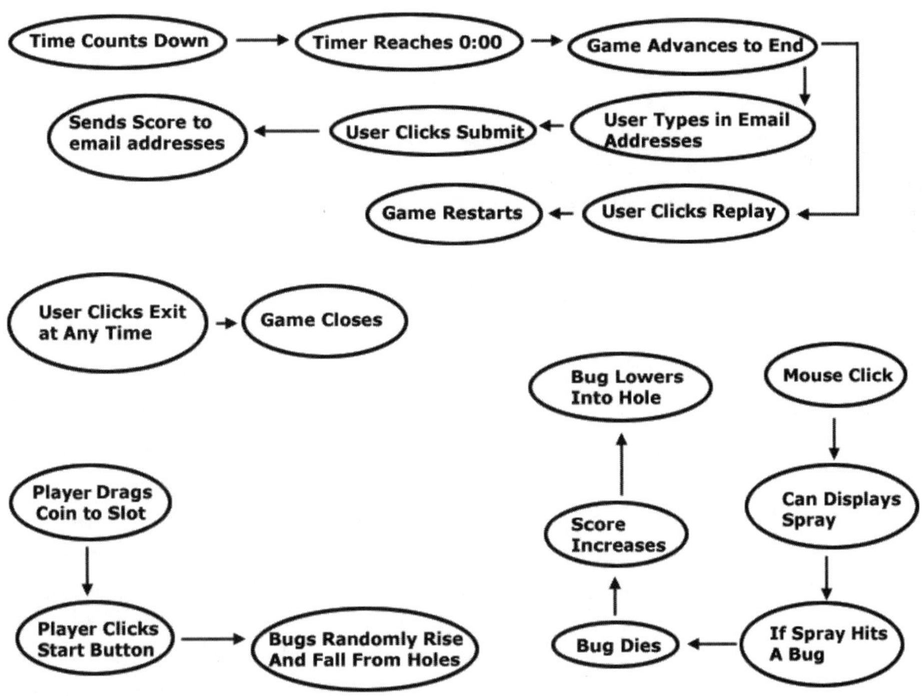

FIGURE 12.3 Spray-a-Bug flowchart.

Identifying the Actions of the Spray-a-Bug Game

In this game, there is no central element controlling what happens in various situations. The game has several independent series of events that occur—actions are performed when these series happen to collide.

The Bugs

Each of the bugs has its own animation that shows it rising up and down through the holes. Each animation also contains both a normal and a hit state. The insects should rise out of a random hole at a set interval of time. Because there are three different types of insects that can appear, they each need to be on their own cycle. Each cycle also needs to be offset from one another by several seconds so that all three don't appear and rise at the same time. To ensure that the insects rise and fall at scattered times, the code that tells a bug to rise out of a hole should be executed on the timeline of another bug. For example, the code to tell the roach to start rising is executed when the ant reaches its peak. When the roach reaches its peak, it tells the fly to start rising. The cycle continues until time is up. The code that places the bug in the proper location and initiates the rise can be contained in a function on the main timeline that is called within each individual bug animation.

When the bug is told that it has been hit, it displays its hit state until it moves back into the hole. After lowering back into the hole, the bug needs to return to its normal state. The pseudocode for the bug is shown in the following list.

1. Randomly select a hole.
2. If the selected hole is currently occupied:
   Go to Step 1. Else, proceed to Step 3.
3. Set the bug's coordinates to the proper hole.
4. Play the bug's animation.
5. Call the next bug's positioning and animation function.

The Spray Can

The can of Bug Bee Gone directs the action in the game. It is responsible for placing the mouse cursor and for moving around with the mouse whenever the mouse is in the game area. This requires the mouse pointer to be hidden whenever the can is following the mouse. An `onClipEvent(mouseDown)` handler needs to be set up on the can, to detect if the user presses the mouse button down to spray a bug. Before the spray is released, the can needs to confirm that the mouse is not out of the game area and on top of the interface. If the previous conditions have been met, the can needs to detect if it successfully sprayed a bug. This is done by doing a hit test to determine if the red target was located over a bug at the time the mouse was clicked. If so, the can should tell the bug that it has been hit and increment the score. Your pseudocode should appear similar to the following example.

1. If the cursor is to the left of the interface:
   Proceed to Step 2. Else, do nothing.
2. Hide the mouse cursor.
3. Follow the mouse position.
4. If the mouse is clicked:
   Proceed to Step 5.
5. If the spray hits a bug:
   Proceed to Step 6.
6. Tell the bug that it has been hit.
7. Increment score.

Putting It All Together

ON THE CD

Now that the game has been planned out, it is time to begin constructing the Spray-a-Bug game. Begin by opening the chapter12template.fla file in the \files\templates\ folder on the CD-ROM.

Understanding the Main Timeline

The main timeline is broken up into three sets of frames—Start, Game, and End. Each set of frames displays an entirely different screen with unique elements on each. Certain elements, such as the interface background and title, exist across all three sections and are placed on their own layer that extends across all of the frames. Each set of frames has a frame label that allows for easy navigation when the time comes to implement the navigational buttons.

The Start screen is set up with an inactive game machine with no interactive elements. There are four symbols on the right-hand side that need to be programmed to receive user input—the Start, Exit, Quarter, and Coin Slot elements. The Start screen can be seen in Figure 12.4.

When you move the playhead to the Game frames, the setup changes. Three bugs—the ant, roach, and fly animations—now appear on the screen, along with a can of Bug Bee Gone, and nine hot spots that are placed over the holes. On the interface side, another area displays the total bugs sprayed and total time remaining. The Start button from the previous set of frames has been replaced by an Exit button. The Game screen can be seen in Figure 12.5.

Moving to the End frames, most of the game is removed from the screen and replaced by a set of input fields followed by a Submit button. The right-hand side has several changes, as well. A dynamic text field has been added that displays the number of bugs the player exterminated in the blue box on the interface. Below the text is a new Replay button that takes the player back to the game for another round.

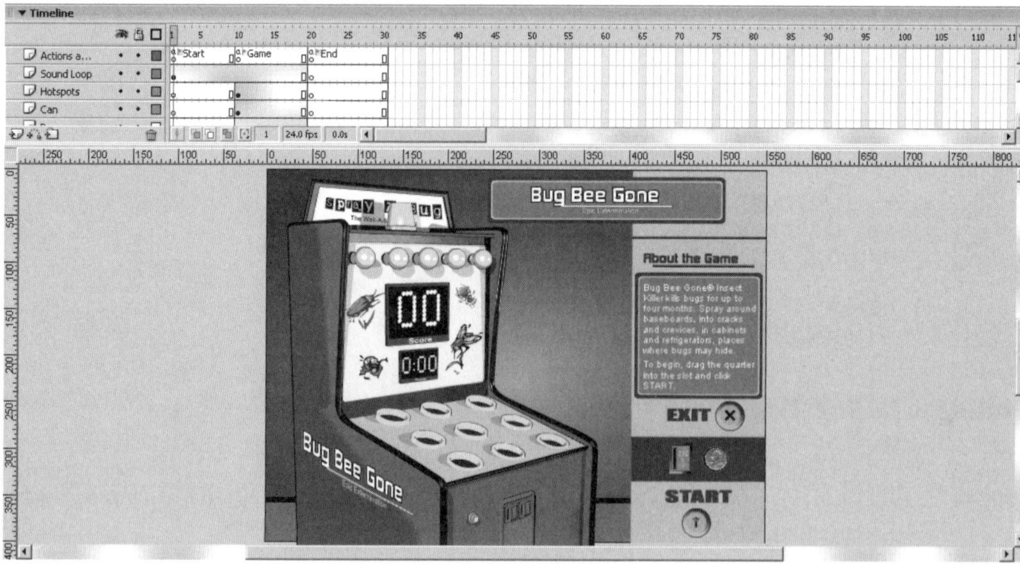

FIGURE 12.4 The Start screen. Copyright © 2003 epic software group, inc. and its licensors. All rights reserved.

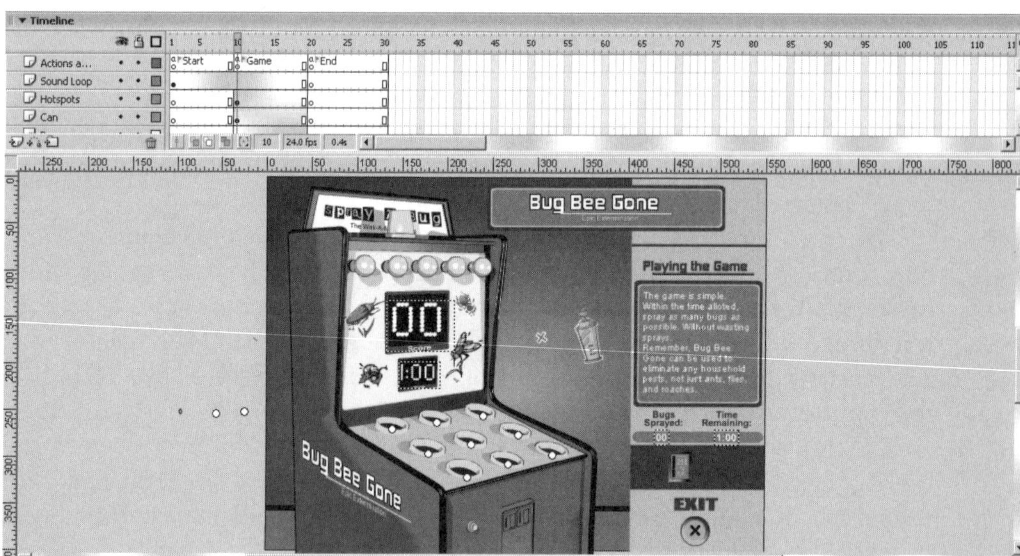

FIGURE 12.5 The Game screen. Copyright © 2003 epic software group, inc. and its licensors. All rights reserved.

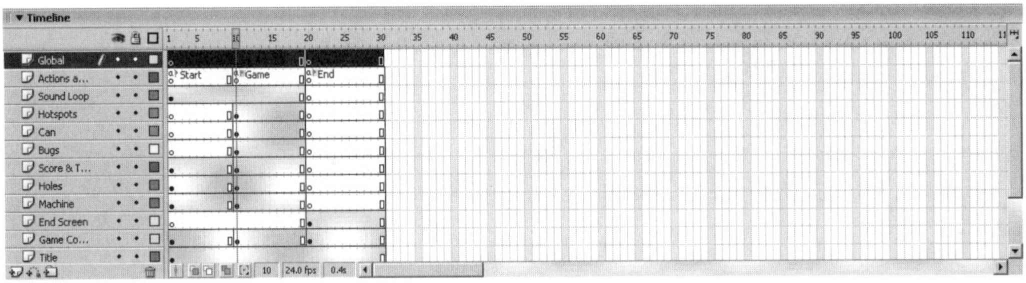

FIGURE 12.6 The Main timeline.

A global layer extends across the entire game to hold functions and variables that are accessed in various sections. The entire timeline can be seen in Figure 12.6.

The Start Screen

Now that you are familiar with how the elements are laid out, it is time to begin creating the game. First, we program the start of the game that kicks everything off. The Start screen is very simplistic and does not involve many objects. First, we write the code needed to exit the game. A function could be written to exit the game because multiple Exit buttons exist throughout the game, but because Macromedia Flash 2004 already has a built-in function for this, there is no need. To add the exit functionality, type the following code in the Actions panel of the Exit Button symbol:

```
on (release) {
    fscommand(quit);
}
```

The last step is to create the starting mechanism. As outlined in the previous section, the starting mechanism involves two steps—depositing the quarter in the coin slot and clicking the Start button. First, you need to apply the code to the coin to enable dragging, detect if it has been dropped on the coin slot, and move it back to its original location if it was dropped in the wrong spot. Then, you could activate the Start button and set the code that allows the player to move on to the game.

1. Set the Quarter symbol's instance name to `quarter`, as shown in Figure 12.7.
2. Set the Coin Slot symbol's instance name to `coinslot`.
3. Type the following code in the Actions panel of the Quarter symbol to initialize the variables that are used to return the quarter to its original location.

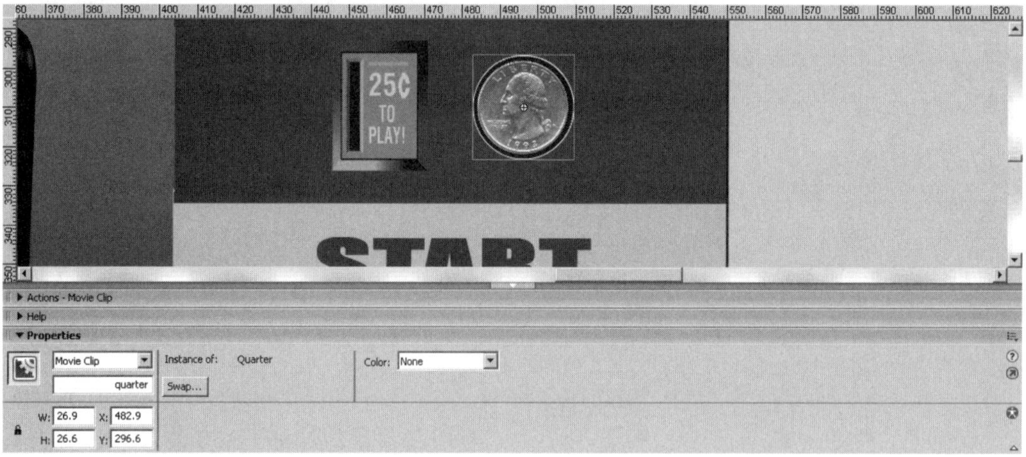

FIGURE 12.7 Naming the Quarter symbol.

```
onClipEvent (load) {
    startX = _x;
    startY = _y;
}
```

4. Type the following code in the Actions panel of the Quarter symbol, below the `onClipEvent(load)` handler.

```
onClipEvent (mouseDown) {
    if (this.hitTest(_root._xmouse, _root._ymouse, true))
        // Start Dragging the Quarter
        startDrag(this);
}

onClipEvent (mouseUp) {
    stopDrag();
    // If the coin is dropped on the coinslot
    // Play the Insert Coin Animation, set
    // the Start button to active, and hide
    // the quarter.
    if (this.hitTest(_root.coinslot)) {
        _root.startActive = true;
        _root.coinslot.gotoAndPlay("Insert Coin");
        this._visible = false;
    } else {
```

```
        // If the coin misses the coinslot
        // Return it to its starting position.
            this._x = startX;
            this._y = startY;
        }
    }
```

5. Type the following code in the Actions panel of the Start Button symbol.

```
on (release) {
    if (_root.startActive)
        gotoAndStop("Game");
}
```

The Game Screen

Up to this point, we have created all of the code needed to bring the player to the actual game—but more must be done before he can actually do anything. Let's start by setting up the interface elements on this screen—there is only the Exit Button symbol that uses the same code as the one in the previous section. Type the following code in the Actions panel of the Exit Button symbol:

```
on (release) {
    fscommand(quit);
}
```

The Bugs

Now that the entire interface has been created for the Game frames, we can now focus on the actual gameplay. We begin by creating the most complex portion of the code, which is responsible for randomly positioning the insects and playing the animations that show the bugs rising and falling. These bugs also need to be checking to see if they have been hit in order to alter their state, if necessary. The code needs to be created as a function that can be called from within any of the bugs, so it is best to create it as a global function on the main timeline. Because it only needs to apply in the Game section, we do not need to apply it to the global layer.

1. Type the following code in the Actions panel of frame 10 on the Actions And Labels layer below the stop action.

```
// Initialize Array to Track Occupied Holes
```

```
occupiedHoles = new Array(3);

_global.bugRise = function(bugName) {
    // Translate BugName into Numerical Location in
    // the Array
    switch(bugName) {
        case "ant":     bugLoc = 0;
                        break;
        case "roach":   bugLoc = 1;
                        break;
        case "fly":     bugLoc = 2;
                        break;
    }

    // Set the Occupied Hole for the current
    // Bug to 0 because it is waiting to be
    // assigned to one.
    occupiedHoles[bugLoc] = 0;

    // Randomly Select a Number between 0 and 9
    // Until A Number is Selected that Is Not
    // Being Currently Used
    do {
        hole = Math.floor(Math.random() * 10);
    } while (hole == occupiedHoles[0] || hole == occupiedHoles[1] ||
hole == occupiedHoles[2]);

    // Have the Bug Not Appear One in Every Five Times
    if (random(5) == 1)
        hole = 0;

    // Set the Bug's Hole in the occupiedHoles
    // Array to the Current Hole
    occupiedHoles[bugLoc] = hole;

    // Place the Bug at the Appropriate Hotspot
    _root[bugName]._x = _root["hole" + hole]._x;
    _root[bugName]._y = _root["hole" + hole]._y;

    // If the Bug is told not to display, Place it
    // Outside of the visible screen.
    if (hole == 0) {
        _root[bugName]._x = -50;
        _root[bugName]._y = -50;
```

```
    }

    // Play theRise and Fall Animation
    _root[bugName].gotoAndPlay("Down");
}

// Initiate the first Ant
bugRise("ant");
```

2. Type the following code in the Actions panel on the last frame of the Actions And Labels layer in the Ant Animation, Roach Animation, and Fly Animation timelines, as shown in Figure 12.8.

```
bugRise(this._name);
```

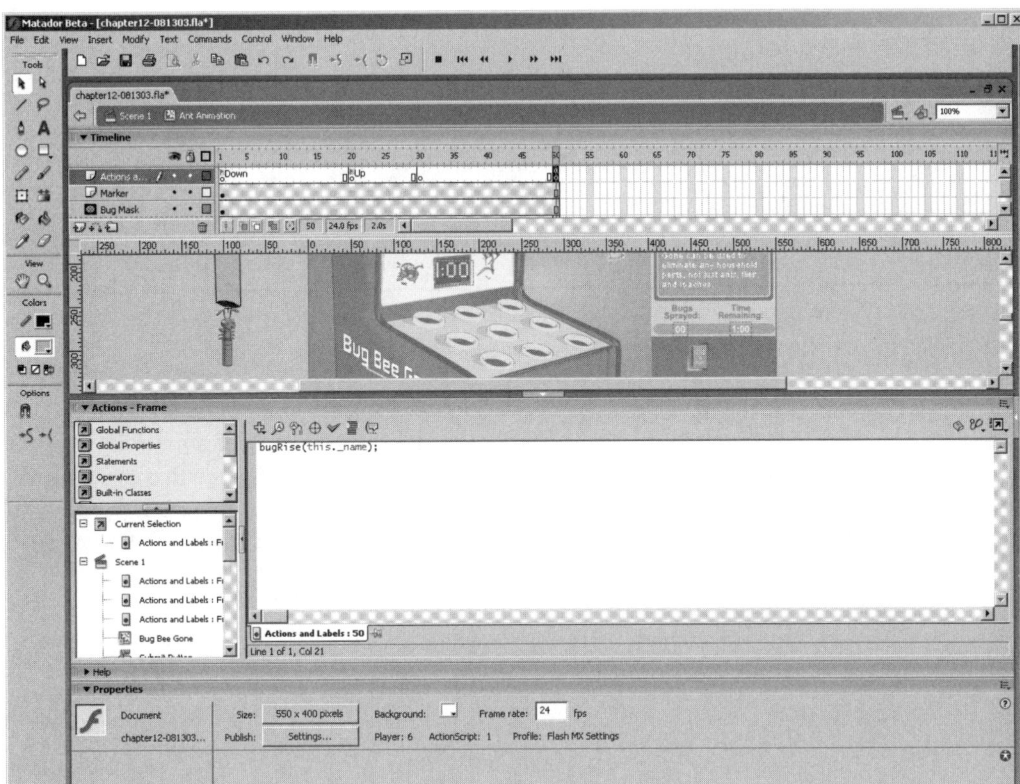

FIGURE 12.8 Inserting the call to the function `bugRise`.

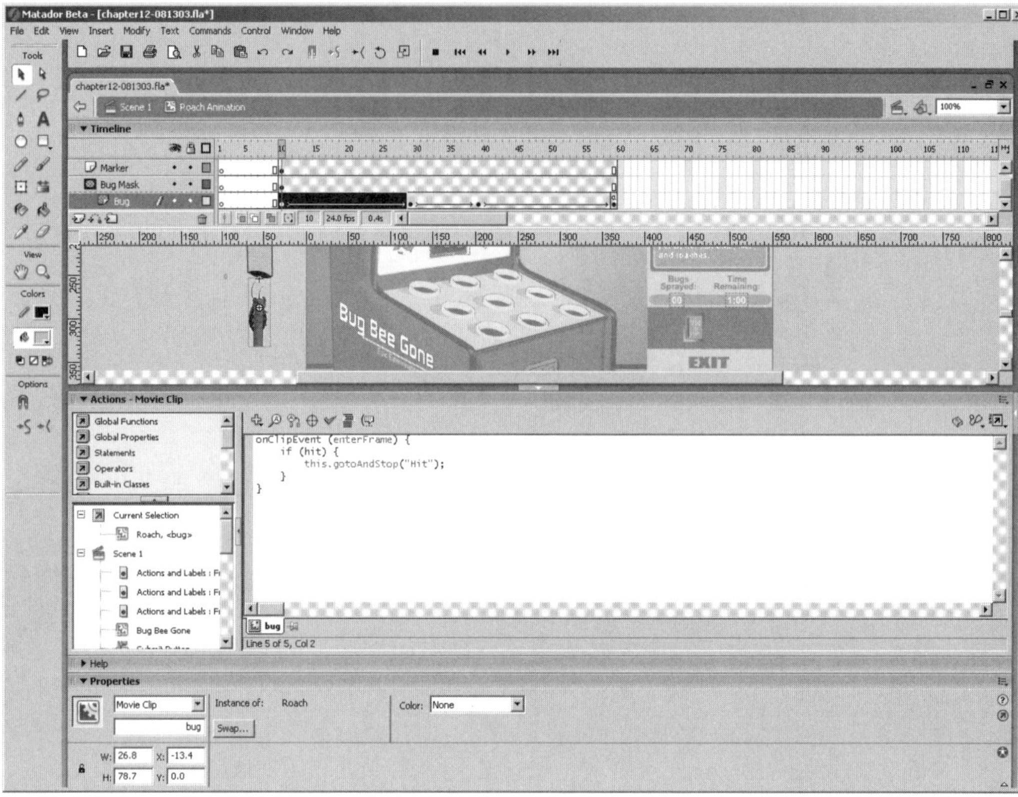

FIGURE 12.9 Inserting the code to display the bugs' hit states.

3. Except for the bug instances on the last frame of each animation, type the following code in the Actions panel of every bug instance that exists in the Ant Animation, Roach Animation, and Fly Animation timelines to have the bug's state reflect if it has been sprayed or not, as shown in Figure 12.9.

```
onClipEvent (enterFrame) {
    if (hit) {
        this.gotoAndStop("Hit");
    }
}
```

4. Type the following code in the Actions panel of the last frame of the Ant Animation, Roach Animation, and Fly Animation timelines to reset the bug to normal after the entire animation has played, as shown in Figure 12.10.

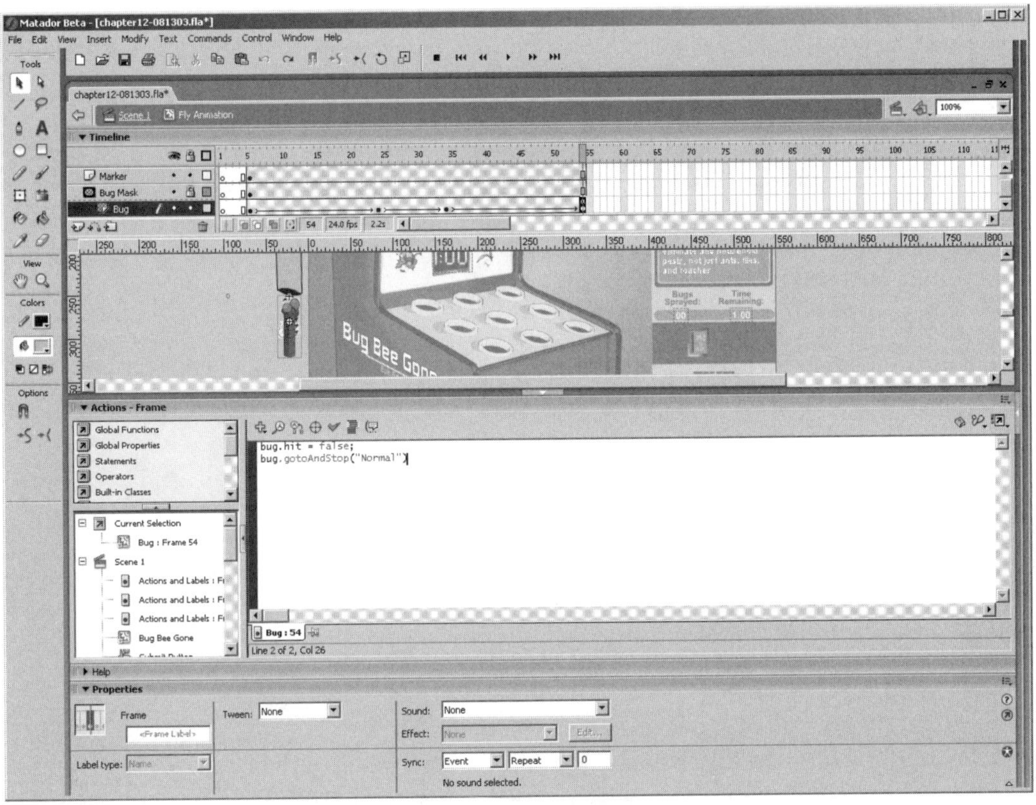

FIGURE 12.10 Inserting the code to return the bugs to their normal state.

```
bug.hit = false;
bug.gotoAndStop("Normal")
```

The Can

Now that the bugs have been created, one last element still needs to be added before the game can actually be played. Although this is not the final step of the game, it is the most important because it detects and decides what the user's input does. The code is only used on this spray can, so it can be placed directly on the symbol itself. The code is responsible for three things—following the mouse whenever it is moved, spraying the can when the mouse is clicked, and determining whether a bug has been sprayed. The code can be constructed in the following manner:

1. Type the following code in the Actions panel of the Bug Bee Gone symbol to set the starting score to 0.

```
onClipEvent (load) {
    _root.score = 0;
}
```

2. Type the following code below the `onClipEvent(load)` handler in the Actions panel of the Bug Bee Gone symbol to have the can follow the mouse position and hide the cursor when necessary.

```
onClipEvent (mouseMove) {
    // If the mouse is not over the interface
    if (_root._xmouse < 400) {
        // Set the Can's Coordinates to the Mouse's
        this._x = _root._xmouse;
        this._y = _root._ymouse;
        // Hide the Mouse Cursor
        Mouse.hide();
    } else {
        // Otherwise don't tell the can to follow the mouse
        // And show the mouse cursor
        Mouse.show();
    }
}
```

3. Type the following code in the Actions panel of the Bug Bee Gone symbol below the `onClipEvent(mouseMove)` handler to have the can spray and detect if a bug has been killed.

```
onClipEvent (mouseDown) {
    // If the mouse is clicked outside of the interface
    if (_root._xmouse < 400) {
        // Display the Spray Animation
        this.gotoAndPlay("Spray");

        // Detect if the Spray Hits a Bug that has
        // Not been hit before
        // If the condition turns out true, increment the
        // score and set the bug to hit.
        if (this.X.hitTest(_root.ant.bug) && !_root.ant.bug.hit) {
                _root.score++;
                _root.ant.bug.hit = true;
        } else if (this.X.hitTest(_root.roach.bug) &&
!_root.roach.bug.hit) {
                _root.score++;
```

```
                _root.roach.bug.hit = true;
        } else if (this.X.hitTest(_root.fly.bug) && !_root.fly.bug.hit)
{
                _root.score++;
                _root.fly.bug.hit = true;
        } else {
                // If the spray misses or the same bug
                // Is shot twice, deduct 1 point.
                if(_root.score>0)
                   _root.score--;
        }

    }
}
```

The Timer

The countdown timer is the final element that needs to be added to complete the actual game. The countdown timer allows the user to have one minute to spray as many bugs as possible. After the time is up, the game goes to the End screen and everything is over. Type the following code in the Actions panel on frame 10 of the Actions and Labels layer below the code that is already there.

```
// Initialize Timer Values
totalTime = 30;
startTime = getTimer();

onEnterFrame = function() {
    // Convert milliseconds to seconds
    totalSecondsElapsed = Math.Floor((getTimer() - startTime) / 1000);
    // Convert Time Elapsed to Time Remaining
    totalSecondsRemaining = totalTime - totalSecondsElapsed;
    // Break Total Seconds into Minutes and Seconds
    minutesRemaining = Math.floor(totalSecondsRemaining / 60);
    secondsRemaining = Math.floor(totalSecondsRemaining % 60);

    // If no minutes remain don't display a 0
    if (minutesRemaining == 0)
        minutesRemaining = "";

    // If less than 10 seconds remain display a 0
    // before the digit.
    if (secondsRemaining < 10)
        time = minutesRemaining + ":0" + secondsRemaining;
    else
```

```
            time = minutesRemaining + ":" + secondsRemaining;

            // If the time is up, hide the mouse and
            // go to the end
        if (totalSecondsRemaining <= 0) {
            Mouse.show();
            gotoAndPlay("End");
        }
}
```

The End Screen

The end screen is going to be the primary tool for distributing and spreading the game around. It contains the e-mail fields for people to send their score and a challenge to, displays the final score, and allows them to replay or exit the game. Let's begin by setting up the navigational buttons first.

1. Type the following code in the Actions panel of the Exit Button symbol:

```
on (release) {
    fscommand(quit);
}
```

2. Type the following code in the Actions panel of the Replay Button symbol:

```
on (release) {
    gotoAndStop("Game");
}
```

Next, the final score message needs to be created so that the player can know how many questions were answered correctly.

1. Type the following code in the Actions panel of frame 20 in the Actions and Labels layer below the stop command.

```
finalScore = "Congratulations! You exterminated " + _root.score + "
pests!";
```

After setting up the final message, the final task is to set up the e-mail code. These fields need to read the addresses that have been inserted and send out the e-mails to those individuals. This method simply uses a `getURL` function to open the user's default mail client and populate it with information to let the user send. To have Macromedia Flash 2004 automatically send the e-mail from within it, the files need to be hosted on a server and you need a custom script written in a language such as PHP or ASP. Type the following code in the Actions panel of the Submit Button symbol.

```
on (release) {
    email = "mailto:" + email1 + ";" + email2 + ";" + email3 + ";" +
email4 + ";" + email5 + "?subject=Your Friend Has Challenged You to A
Game of Spray a Bug!&body=I got a score of " + score + "! Just follow
this link to see if you can do better!
http://myepicwebdomain.com/sprayabug/\n-" + name;
 getURL(email);
}
```

SUMMARY

That completes the Spray-a-Bug game. Now Bug Bee Gone's message can be spread throughout the world as people begin to pass around the game. You can now publish the game and play it anytime you want. Figure 12.11 shows the game in action!

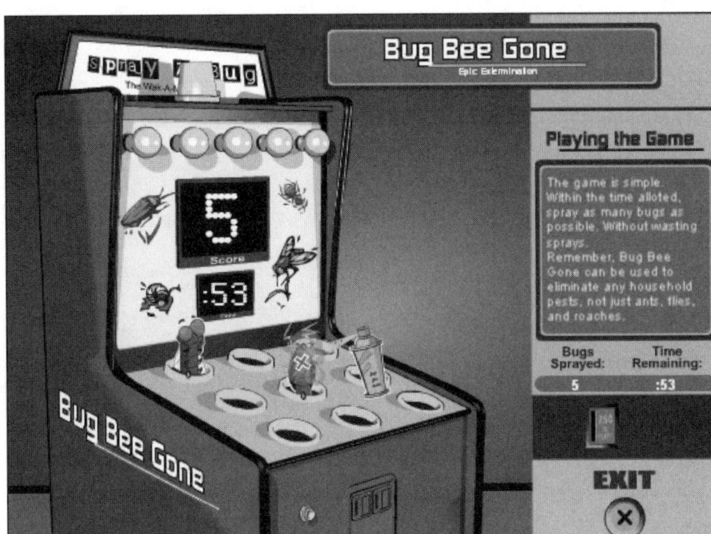

FIGURE 12.11 The completed Spray-a-Bug game.

13 Cellular Shuffle

THE CONCEPT

Identifying Your Product: epic Cellular Phones

epic Cellular Phones is a newcomer to the industry and wants to promote brand recognition for its line of cellular products and services. For this purpose, the company has chosen an advertising campaign based on pop-up ads delivered from a variety of popular Web sites. To make the ad more engaging and more likely to keep the Web surfer's attention, epic wants to incorporate a simple Advergame that delivers basic interactive content that can be downloaded quickly and grabs the surfer's attention. For this purpose, Macromedia Flash MX 2004 is ideal for the content due to the much smaller size of the vector-based graphics.

Outlining a Game for epic Cellular Phones

This application requires a very simple game that grabs the surfer's attention and is easy to play. This is a pop-up ad after all, so it cannot come with an instruction manual. It must be a game that most people are familiar with and must download quickly. This game cannot have any frills. The sole purpose is to draw the users into the ad so that they get the message and possibly even click through to the epic Cellular Phones Web site. A simple puzzle game that suits our purpose is the venerable tile slide game. Basically, the player is presented with an image broken up into tiles arranged in a grid with one tile missing. The player shuffles the pieces on the grid, slides the tiles around, and pushes a tile into the blank space, creating a new blank space where the tile was. Then, another tile can be moved, and so on, and so on, until the tiles are all moved to their proper positions. See Figures 13.1 and 13.2 to see how this works.

Designing the Cellular Shuffle Interface

The key to the design of the Cellular Shuffle interface is simplicity. All of the action occurs in a frame the size of a large pop-up banner. The game interface, the grid of tiles, dominates the central portion of the interface, giving a large area with which

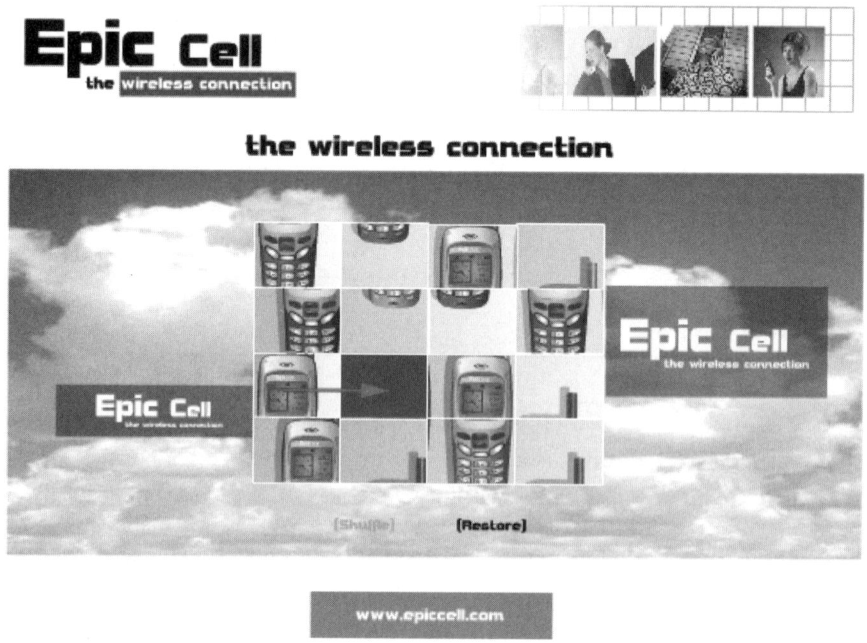

FIGURE 13.1 Sliding a tile right.

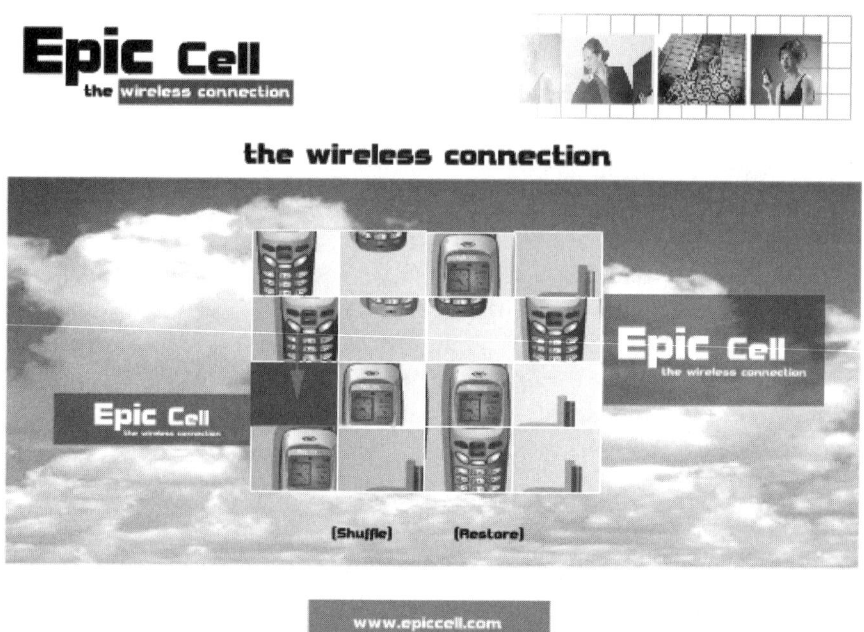

FIGURE 13.2 Sliding a tile down.

the player can interact. Surrounding the periphery are logos and a link to the epic Cellular Phones Web site. The two other user interface items are the Shuffle button, which randomly positions the tiles for the player to slide back into the correct position, and the Restore button, which replaces all the tiles to their original, correct positions.

THE CREATION

Identifying the Elements of Cellular Shuffle

The first step in identifying the elements of our Cellular Shuffle game is to come up with a clear specification. The game starts with all the tiles positioned in their correct places in the grid. One of these tiles is the blank tile. The player can click the Shuffle button to randomly position the tiles in the grid, or he can click the Restore button to place the tiles back into their starting positions. At any time, the player can click on a tile. However, the tile only slides when the blank tile is immediately above, below, left, or right of the tile.

From this specification, we arrive at the following elements:

- Grid
- Tile
- Blank tile
- Shuffle button
- Restore button

Recognizing How the Game's Elements Interact

Here are the interactions between the game's elements in sentence form, taken almost directly from the specification.

The game starts with all the tiles positioned in the correct places in the grid: The movie must position the tiles in the correct places in the grid. Here, tiles include the image tiles and the blank tile.

The player can click the Shuffle button to randomly position the tiles in the grid: When the mouse button is released over the Shuffle button, the grid randomly scrambles the tiles. The tiles do not randomly position themselves because that would be much harder to coordinate. The blank tile can be treated in the same way as the image tiles.

The player can click the Restore button to place the tiles back into their starting positions: When the mouse button is released over the Restore button, the grid restores the tiles back to their original positions. The blank tile can be treated the same way as the image tiles.

The player can click on a tile: The tile only slides when the blank tile is immediately above, below, left, or right of the tile. When the mouse button is released over a tile (even the blank tile), the tile slides only if there is a blank tile adjacent; that is, immediately above, below, left, or right.

Identifying the Scripts of Cellular Shuffle

Now, with the interactions between the elements specified at a fine level of detail, we can translate the relationships into specific ActionScript functions that make up the script of Cellular Shuffle.

The movie must position the tiles in the correct places in the grid: The movie positions the tiles by adding them to the grid. The function that does this is the `addTile` function of the `Grid` object.

When the mouse button is released over the Shuffle button, the grid scrambles the tiles randomly: When the mouse button is released over the Shuffle button, the `onRelease` handler of the `shuffle_button` object is called, which in turn calls the `scrambleTiles` function of the `Grid` object to shuffle the tiles. Scrambling the tiles is simply randomly swapping each of the tiles with some other random tile, by calling the `swapTiles` function of the `Grid` object.

When the mouse button is released over the Restore button, the grid restores the tiles back to their original positions: When the mouse button is released over the Restore button, the `onRelease` handler of the `restore_button` object is called, which in turn calls the `restoreTiles` function of the `Grid` object to restore the tiles back to their original position.

When the mouse button is released over a tile (even the blank tile), the tile slides only if there is a blank tile adjacent; that is, immediately above, below, left, or right: When the mouse button is released over a tile, the `onRelease` handler for that `Tile` object is called. The `onRelease` handler in this case refers to the `tileSlide` function of the `Tile` object. To determine if we should slide, we check all the adjacent tiles using the `tileAt` function of the `Grid` object and check if they are blank using the `isBlank` function also of the `Grid` object. If a blank tile is found, we simply swap the blank tile with the image tile using the `swapTiles` function of the `Grid` object to slide them. So, in sliding a tile, we consult the grid quite a bit. It knows things about other tiles and can do things to other tiles that the individual tile does not know or cannot do easily.

Putting It All Together

ON THE CD Now, we are ready to put the Cellular Shuffle game together. To begin, copy the movie chapter13-01.fla located at \files\templates\ on the CD-ROM to a working directory on the hard disk. This movie contains the graphics necessary to finish this movie, laid out in layers. There are no symbols. We build onto this movie step by step to create the full Cellular Shuffle game.

Preparing the Graphics

To prepare the graphics, perform the following steps.

1. Open the chapter13-01.fla movie that is located in the working directory.
2. Convert each tile into a movie clip, naming each tile by its position in the grid. For example, the tile at the first row and first column is tile1x1. However, name the blank tile simply "blank." See Figure 13.3 to see the basic idea of how the labeling should occur.
3. For each newly created Tile symbol, both image and blank, assign each tile an instance name that is the same as the symbol name.
   The rationale behind naming the symbols and tiles in this way is to increase the organization of the movie, which is a great aid to making the game easier to develop, and also to make it easier to deal with the instances programmatically using ActionScript, as we can now easily tell an image tile apart from a blank tile.
4. Save the movie.

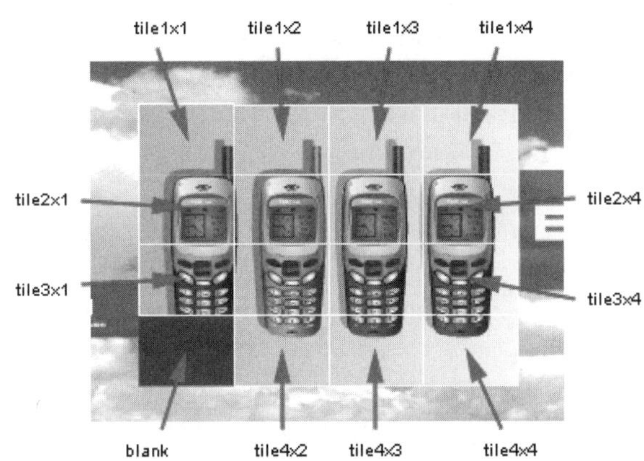

FIGURE 13.3 Labeling the Tile symbols.

Sliding the Tiles

To slide the tiles, perform the following steps.

1. Add a layer to Scene 1 and call it actions.
2. Create a blank keyframe in frame 1 of that layer.
3. Be certain that Expert Mode is enabled, and then add the code in Listing 13.1 into the Actions window.

The first function in the listing is the constructor for the `Grid` class. This function takes the size of the grid, in rows and columns, and creates a `Grid` object. It does this by assigning values to the properties of the `Grid` object, specified as the object in the script.

The next function is `addTile`. This function takes a row and column position in the grid and the tile to put in there. Then, it saves some important properties that we need later. Notice how we determine if the tile is blank. We convert the `Tile` into a `String` to get its name. Then, we can use `indexOf` to determine if the word "blank" is in the name. If so, the tile is the blank tile; otherwise, it is not.

Next is `tileSlide`. This function is called when the mouse button is released over the tile, and it checks the adjacent tiles using the `tileAt` function defined in the constructor. The columns of the tile grid are numbered starting with zero, and increase going from left to right, so we subtract one to specify the tile to the left (col – 1) and add one to specify the tile to the right (col + 1). Similarly, the rows of the tile grid are also numbered starting with zero, and increase going from top to bottom, with the tile above specified by subtracting one (row – 1) and the tile below specified by adding one (row + 1). If one of those tiles is the blank tile, determined by the `isBlank` function, we swap this tile with the blank tile. The `isBlank` function shown in Listing 13.1 is written in such a way that `tileSlide` can be made much simpler. The `isBlank` function actually checks if the row and column are inside the grid, returning `false` if it is not, and then checks if the tile is blank, returning `true` if so and `false` if not. This way, we can simply check each adjacent grid square to this tile, even if they do not exist.

Then, the `swapTiles` function simply swaps the `x` and `y` coordinates and the row and column of two tiles, and then actually moves them around in the grid.

Finally, the `onLoad` handler starts the game. It is attached to the scene via the `_root` object. The grid is created here and the tiles are positioned on the grid.

To start the movie, press Ctrl-Enter (on Microsoft Windows) or Command-Enter (on Macintosh). Try playing the game.

LISTING 13.1 Adding tiles to the grid and sliding them.

```
//
// Create a Grid object
//
function Grid(rows, cols) {
    // Save the dimensions
    this.rows = rows;
    this.cols = cols;
    // Create the array of tile rows
    this.gridArray = new Array(rows);
    for(row = 0; row < rows; row++)
        // Create array of tile columns for each row
        this.gridArray[row] = new Array(cols);

    // Create the methods
    this.addTile = addTile;
    this.swapTiles = swapTiles;
    this.tileAt = function(row, col) {
        // Return the tile at the specified row and column
        return this.gridArray[row][col];
    }
    this.isBlank = isBlank;
}

//
// Add a tile to the Grid
//
addTile = function(row, col, tile) {
    // Place the tile in the grid at the row and col
    this.gridArray[row][col] = tile;
    // Save the spot of the tile in the grid
    tile.row = row;
    tile.col = col;
    // Is this the blank tile?  The instance name will
    // have the word blank in it if it is
    tile.isBlank = String(tile).indexOf("blank") > 0;
    // Save the grid information in the tile so it can
    // refer back to it
    tile.grid = this;
    // When the mouse button is released over the tile,
    // call the tileSlide handler
    tile.onRelease = tileSlide;
```

```
}

//
// Slide a tile
//
tileSlide = function() {
    // Is the blank to the left?
    if(this.grid.isBlank(this.row, this.col - 1)) {
        // Slide left
        this.grid.swapTiles(this, this.grid.tileAt(
this.row, this.col - 1));
        return;
    }
    // Is the blank to the right?
    if(this.grid.isBlank(this.row, this.col + 1)) {
        // Slide right
        this.grid.swapTiles(this, this.grid.tileAt(
this.row, this.col + 1));
        return;
    }
    // Is the blank above?
    if(this.grid.isBlank(this.row - 1, this.col)) {
        // Slide up
        this.grid.swapTiles(this, this.grid.tileAt(
this.row - 1, this.col));
        return;
    }
    // Is the blank below?
    if(this.grid.isBlank(this.row + 1, this.col)) {
        // Slide down
        this.grid.swapTiles(this, this.grid.tileAt(
this.row + 1, this.col));
    }
}

//
// Is the tile blank?
//
isBlank = function(row, col) {
    // Is row and col in the grid?
    if((row >= 0 && row < this.rows) &&
       (col >= 0 && col < this.cols))
        // Does row and col in the grid refer to the blank
        // tile?
        return this.gridArray[row][col].isBlank;
```

```
        // If row and col is not in the grid, definitely not
        // blank.
        return false;
    }

    //
    // Swap two tiles in the grid
    //
    swapTiles = function(tile1, tile2) {
        // Save the position in the grid...
        orig_row = tile1.row;
        orig_col = tile1.col;
        // ...and the screen of the first tile
        orig_x = tile1._x;
        orig_y = tile1._y;
        // Move the first tile to where the second tile is
        tile1.row = tile2.row;
        tile1.col = tile2.col;
        tile1._x = tile2._x;
        tile1._y = tile2._y;
        // Move the second tile to where the first tile was
        tile2.row = orig_row;
        tile2.col = orig_col;
        tile2._x = orig_x;
        tile2._y = orig_y;
        // Make the changes to the grid
        this.gridArray[tile1.row][tile1.col] = tile1;
        this.gridArray[tile2.row][tile2.col] = tile2;
    }

    //
    // Initialize the movie
    //
    _root.onLoad = function() {
        // Create a grid
        grid = new Grid(4, 4);
        // Position the tiles on the grid
        with (grid) {
            addTile(0, 0, tile1x1);
            addTile(0, 1, tile1x2);
            addTile(0, 2, tile1x3);
            addTile(0, 3, tile1x4);
            addTile(1, 0, tile2x1);
            addTile(1, 1, tile2x2);
```

```
            addTile(1, 2, tile2x3);
            addTile(1, 3, tile2x4);
            addTile(2, 0, tile3x1);
            addTile(2, 1, tile3x2);
            addTile(2, 2, tile3x3);
            addTile(2, 3, tile3x4);
            addTile(3, 0, blank);
            addTile(3, 1, tile4x2);
            addTile(3, 2, tile4x3);
            addTile(3, 3, tile4x4);
    }
}
```

Activating the Buttons

To activate the buttons, perform the following steps.

1. On Scene 1, select the group with the text "(Shuffle)."
2. Convert the group into a symbol. Call it "Shuffle button" and select the Button behavior.
3. Double-click the newly created symbol to enter the timeline for the button.
4. Enter keyframes for Over and Down.
5. Select the Down keyframe and select the "(Shuffle)" group. Break it apart.
6. In the Properties panel, select a new color for the text. We use #00CCCC.
7. Now, select the Over keyframe. Select the group and convert it to a symbol. Call it "Shuffle button glow" and select the Movie Clip behavior.
8. Double-click the newly created symbol to enter the timeline for the movie clip.
9. In frame 1 of the movie clip, select the "(Shuffle)" group and break it apart.
10. Create a keyframe in frame 5 of the movie clip.
11. Select one of the frames between 1 and 5 and create a motion tween.
12. In the Properties panel, change the tween type to Shape.
13. Move the playback head from frame 1 to frame 5. The "(Shuffle)" text should fade from black to light blue.
14. Insert a layer called actions. Insert a keyframe at frame 5.
15. With frame 5 selected in the Actions layer, open the Actions panel.
16. Add the text "stop();". This stops the movie clip when the end has been reached, instead of moving the playback head to the beginning of the movie clip and starting over.
17. Click the Back Arrow button to return to the Shuffle button.

18. Insert a blank keyframe for Hit. Draw a box bigger than the "(Shuffle)" text and surround it with a big border. This gives a bigger target area for the mouse to land on.
19. Press Ctrl-Enter (on Microsoft Windows) or Command-Enter (on Macintosh) to start the movie. Try moving the mouse cursor over the button. It should fade into blue and stay blue as long as the mouse cursor is over the hit area of the button. Once the mouse cursor leaves the hit area, the button should turn black again.
20. Repeat these steps for the "(Restore)" button.

Shuffling the Tiles and Restoring Them

To shuffle the tiles and restore them, perform the following steps.

1. Return to Scene 1.
2. Select the "(Shuffle)" button.
3. Specify `shuffle_button` as the instance name.
4. Select the layer actions and select frame 1.
5. Open the Actions panel.
6. Modify the `_root.onLoad` function, as shown in Listing 13.2. The following code causes the function to actually shuffle the tiles to be called when the mouse is released over the Shuffle button.

LISTING 13.2 Arming the Shuffle button.

```
//
// Initialize the movie
//
_root.onLoad = function() {
    // Create a grid
    grid = new Grid(4, 4);
    // Position the tiles on the grid
    with (grid) {
        addTile(0, 0, tile1x1);
        addTile(0, 1, tile1x2);
        addTile(0, 2, tile1x3);
        addTile(0, 3, tile1x4);
        addTile(1, 0, tile2x1);
        addTile(1, 1, tile2x2);
        addTile(1, 2, tile2x3);
        addTile(1, 3, tile2x4);
        addTile(2, 0, tile3x1);
```

```
        addTile(2, 1, tile3x2);
        addTile(2, 2, tile3x3);
        addTile(2, 3, tile3x4);
        addTile(3, 0, blank);
        addTile(3, 1, tile4x2);
        addTile(3, 2, tile4x3);
        addTile(3, 3, tile4x4);
    }
    // Shuffle the tiles when the player
    // clicks on the shuffle button
    shuffle_button.onRelease = function() {
        grid.scrambleTiles();
    }
}
```

7. Add the code shown in Listing 13.3 to the Action.

This code is fairly straightforward. It simply goes through all the tiles, and for each tile, picks a random tile and swaps with the tile currently being looked at. The row number and column numbers used to locate a tile in the grid are zero-based; for example, with the rows, the first row is 0 and the last row is the number of rows minus one. This is why when we determine the random row and column, we multiply the random number we get by the number of rows or columns minus one. The range of numbers produced by `Math.random` is as low as 0 and as high as 1 with any number in between.

LISTING 13.3 Scrambling the tiles.

```
//
// Shuffle the tiles around
//
scrambleTiles = function() {
    for(row = 0; row < this.rows; row++)
        for(col = 0; col < this.cols; col++) {
            // Get a random row and column
            new_row = Math.round((this.rows - 1) * Math.random());
            new_col = Math.round((this.cols - 1) * Math.random());
            // and swap the tile at row and column with the
            // random row and column
            this.swapTiles(this.gridArray[row][col],
                this.gridArray[new_row][new_col]);
        }
}
```

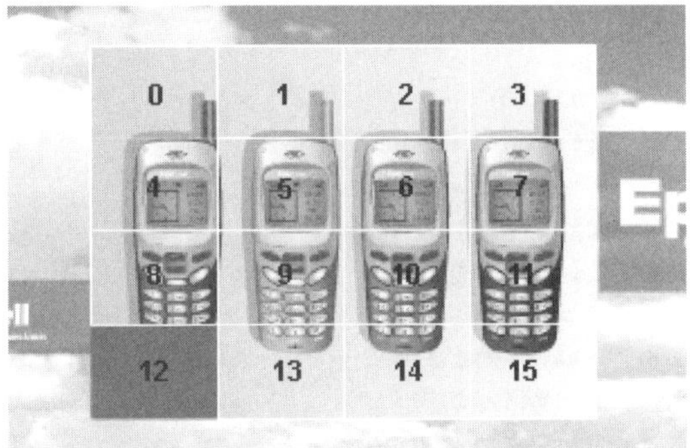

FIGURE 13.4 Counting tiles linearly.

8. Press Ctrl-Enter (on Microsoft Windows) or Command-Enter (on Macintosh) to start the movie. Click the Shuffle button. The tiles should assume random positions in the grid.
9. Repeat Steps 1 through 8 to restore the tiles to their original positions, but use `restore_button` as the instance name, modify the `_root.onLoad` handler, as shown in Listing 13.4, and add the code shown in Listing 13.5. In addition, make the changes in Listing 13.6, modifying the `addTile` function to store the original positions of the tiles in the grid.

The code in Listing 13.4 simply specifies the `onRelease` function of the Restore button, arming it to call the `restoreTiles` function when the mouse button is released over the "(Restore)" button.

The `restoreTiles` function is a little more complicated. Until this time, we have been accessing the array as row and columns. Here, to simplify the code, we think of the grid linearly, so that we can easily go to the next tile. See Figure 13.4 to see what linear addressing looks like on the grid. The idea behind this function is that we check the first tile to see if it is in the correct spot. If it is, we move on to the next tile. Otherwise, we check each tile following the current tile to find the one that goes in that spot. When we find the correct tile, we swap the two tiles. Then, we can move on to the next tile.

LISTING 13.4 Arming the Restore button.

```
//
// Initialize the movie
//
```

```
_root.onLoad = function() {
    // Create a grid
    grid = new Grid(4, 4);
    // Position the tiles on the grid
    with (grid) {
        addTile(0, 0, tile1x1);
        addTile(0, 1, tile1x2);
        addTile(0, 2, tile1x3);
        addTile(0, 3, tile1x4);
        addTile(1, 0, tile2x1);
        addTile(1, 1, tile2x2);
        addTile(1, 2, tile2x3);
        addTile(1, 3, tile2x4);
        addTile(2, 0, tile3x1);
        addTile(2, 1, tile3x2);
        addTile(2, 2, tile3x3);
        addTile(2, 3, tile3x4);
        addTile(3, 0, blank);
        addTile(3, 1, tile4x2);
        addTile(3, 2, tile4x3);
        addTile(3, 3, tile4x4);
    }
    // Shuffle the tiles when the player
    // clicks on the shuffle button
    shuffle_button.onRelease = function() {
        grid.scrambleTiles();
    }
    // Put the tiles back when the player
    // clicks on the restore button
    restore_button.onRelease = function() {
        grid.restoreTiles();
    }
}
```

LISTING 13.5 Putting the tiles back.

```
//
// Put the tiles back to their original positions
//
restoreTiles = function() {
    // get the total number of tiles
    totalTiles = this.rows * this.cols;
    // move each tile back to its original spot
```

```
    for(tile = 0; tile < totalTiles; tile++) {
        // figure out the row and column of the tile
        row = Math.floor(tile / this.cols);
        col = tile % this.cols;
        // and get the actual tile
        spotTile = this.tileAt(row, col);
        // is it already in the right spot?
        if (spotTile.origRow == row && spotTile.origCol == col)
            // already there, so don't move it
            continue;
        // search for the tile that goes in row and col from all
// the rest of the tiles
        for(searchTile = tile + 1; searchTile < totalTiles;
searchTile++) {
            // figure out the row and column of the tile
            searchRow = Math.floor(searchTile / this.cols);
            searchCol = searchTile % this.cols;
            // and get the actual tile
            otherTile = this.tileAt(searchRow, searchCol);
            // does the tile belong at row and col?
            if (otherTile.origRow == row &&
otherTile.origCol == col) {
                // yes, so swap
                this.swapTiles(spotTile, otherTile);
                // and move on
                break;
            }
        }
    }
}
```

LISTING 13.6 Keeping the original spots for later.

```
//
// Add a tile to the grid
//
addTile = function(row, col, tile) {
    // Place the tile in the grid at the row and col
    this.gridArray[row][col] = tile;
    // Save the original and current spot of the tile
    // in the grid
    tile.origRow = tile.row = row;
    tile.origCol = tile.col = col;
```

```
        // Is this the blank tile? The instance name will
        // have the word blank in it if it is
        tile.isBlank = String(tile).indexOf("blank") > 0;
        // Save the grid information in the tile so it can
        // refer back to it
        tile.grid = this;
        // When the mouse button is released over the tile,
        // call the tileSlide handler
        tile.onRelease = tileSlide;
}
```

10. Press Ctrl-Enter (on Microsoft Windows) or Command-Enter (on Macintosh) to start the movie. Click the Shuffle button. The tiles should assume random positions in the grid. Now click the Restore button. The tiles should all go back to their starting positions.
11. That's all there is to the Cellular Shuffle!

SUMMARY

This concludes the design and implementation of the Cellular Shuffle game, a simple tile slide game. The major concept in this game is the use of a 2D array to keep track of the tiles, along with linking this array to the actions available to ActionScript, such as mouseclicks, to keep the array and the tiles on the screen up to date. This game also demonstrates the use of increasing the effectiveness of pop-up advertising using "active" content.

14 Tasty Tic-Tac-Toe

THE CONCEPT

Identifying Your Product: epic E&E Candies

E&E candies, produced by the Olde Tyme epic Candy Co., have always been a staple on candy shelves across the nation. But over the past few years, sales have been consistently falling, as a new generation of kids grows up with an ever-widening selection of flashy new candies. As part of a larger campaign of new packaging, commercials, and contests, epic hopes to bring E&E candies back into the limelight with Advergames such as Tasty Tic-Tac-Toe. epic's goal is to attract younger consumers by offering an E&E-themed arcade Web site while, at the same time, appealing to its older customers' sense of nostalgia by pairing such classic games as *tic-tac-toe* with its classic candies. The games are featured free of charge on epic's Web site, but Tasty Tic-Tac-Toe has a catch. If you want to play with your friends, you have to buy a package of E&Es.

Outlining a Game for epic E&E Candies

Everyone you know has probably played a game of tic-tac-toe at one time or another. And there's a reason for that. It's just a fun way to waste some time. The rules are simple, the games are short, and the competition is fierce. The fact that tic-tac-toe is such a popular childhood game makes it perfect to suit epic's needs. Children appreciate the game's simplicity, whereas adults remember both tic-tac-toe and E&E candies as timeless symbols of youth. It is epic's intention that all these warm, fuzzy feelings will bring E&E sales back to what they once were.

If our goal was to create a two-player tic-tac-toe game, then this would be a very short chapter. What makes Tasty Tic-Tac-Toe more complex is the artificial intelligence of its computer player. Still, the very basic level of artificial intelligence required to create a good tic-tac-toe player is nothing you can't handle. The computer player simply checks for a spot that will win the game, checks for a spot to block its opponent, and then, if no such spot has been found, uses a bit of strategy to decide which free spot to choose. If you learn to follow the same steps as Tasty Tic-Tac-Toe's computer player, you'll become an unbeatable tic-tac-toe master.

Designing the Tasty Tic-Tac-Toe Interface

Tic-tac-toe's standard three-by-three grid doesn't leave much room for improvement. With its empty spots set to respond to the player's mouseclicks, it serves as the simplest and most intuitive interface possible for a basic game of tic-tac-toe. We use such a grid in our game, of course, but to make the Tasty Tic-Tac-Toe interface complete, we also need to add buttons to let the player adjust the game's difficulty level and a bit of text just to remind people to buy some E&Es.

When designing a graphical interface for an unknown audience (such as visitors to a Web site), you must keep in mind that many computers are set to display in resolutions as low as 640 by 480 pixels. Because computer screens are generally wider than they are tall, it makes sense to position the text and difficulty buttons on either the left or right side of the square, tic-tac-toe grid. This layout allows for the largest grid size, while taking full advantage of available screen area. Simply because we read from left to right, it looks the most natural to have the game's introductory material (the title, instructions, and so on) on the left side of the grid. In theory, this is where the user looks first. Figure 14.1 illustrates the layout we use for Tasty Tic-Tac-Toe.

The gimmick that makes Tasty Tic-Tac-Toe an actual Advergame is its use of E&E candies instead of Xs and Os. This displays the product in such a way that it is the focal point of the game without seeming too obtrusive. As an added bonus, the game of tic-tac-toe can actually be played using E&E candy pieces. By pointing this out and suggesting it as a means to accommodate multiple players, Tasty Tic-Tac-Toe extends itself into the real world, and the purchasing of E&E candies becomes essential for play. The final version of the game's interface is shown in Figure 14.2.

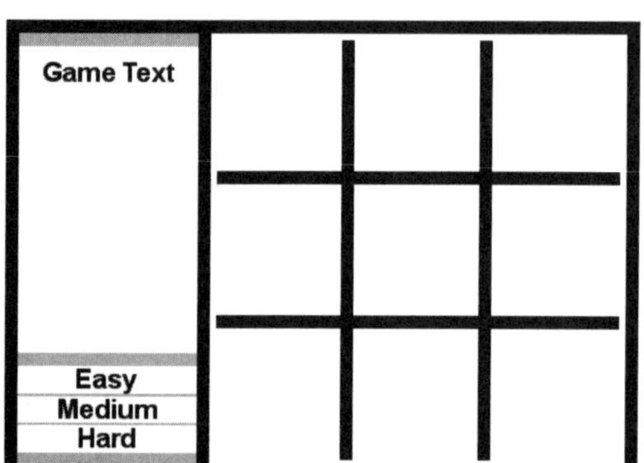

FIGURE 14.1 The basic layout of the Tasty Tic-Tac-Toe interface.

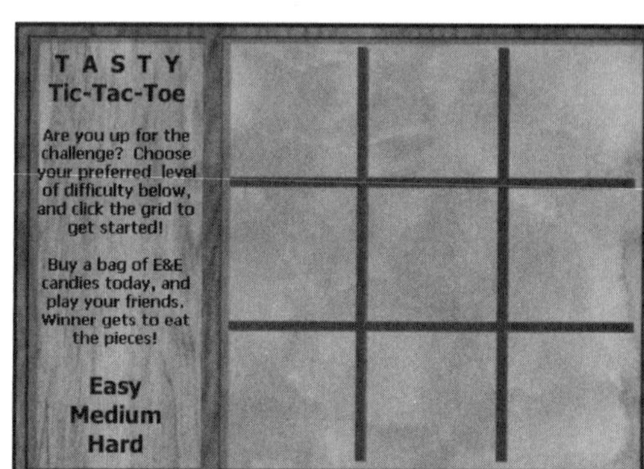

FIGURE 14.2 The Tasty Tic-Tac-Toe interface complete with text and graphics.

THE CREATION

Identifying the Elements of Tasty Tic-Tac-Toe

Start by compiling a list of all the major elements your game requires. Because tic-tac-toe is such a simple game, Tasty Tic-Tac-Toe requires very little user interaction. The player simply chooses spots on the grid until a winner is found or no more spots are available. The game consists of the following major elements:

Game text: Displays the game's title, basic instructions, and a plug for E&E candies

Grid spots: Display the game in terms of the randomly chosen E&E pieces and/or empty spaces

Empty spots: Fill with the player's E&E piece when clicked

Filled spots: Display either the player's or the computer opponent's E&E pieces

Easy button: Resets the game with a difficulty level of one

Medium button: Resets the game with a difficulty level of two

Hard button: Resets the game with a difficulty level of three

For a clear view of how these elements appear in the game's interface, see Figure 14.3.

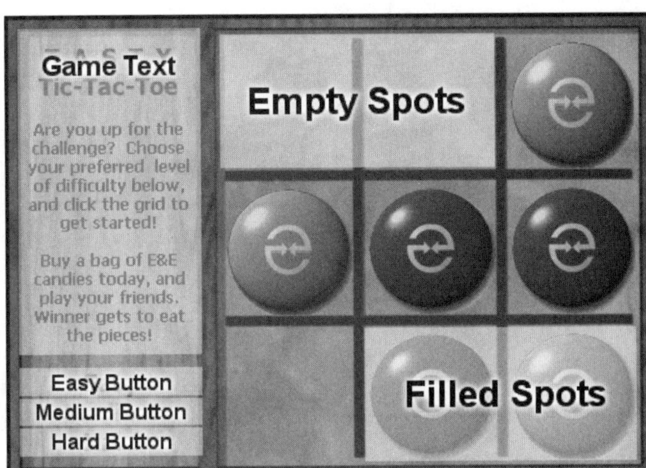

FIGURE 14.3 The Tasty Tic-Tac-Toe interface with major elements identified.

Recognizing How the Game's Elements Interact

The first thing a player of Tasty Tic-Tac-Toe should do is choose a difficulty level by clicking one of the buttons in the bottom-left corner of the interface. Each of these buttons has the effect of clearing the grid and starting a new game. The only difference between the buttons is the value assigned to a global variable named `skill`. This variable should range anywhere from `1` (easy) to `3` (hard). Its default value is `2`, so if a player goes straight to the grid without first selecting a difficulty level, the game is automatically set to medium difficulty.

Each time the player clicks an empty spot on the grid, his randomly selected E&E piece appears in the chosen spot, the grid is checked for a winner, and a timer is started to tell the computer opponent to make a move after a short delay. If a winner (or a full grid indicating a tie) is found at any time during play, neither player is allowed to make any further moves, and a sound plays based on the game's outcome. Figure 14.4 illustrates the logic of Tasty Tic-Tac-Toe using a flowchart.

Identifying the Scripts of Tasty Tic-Tac-Toe

Nearly all of Tasty Tic-Tac-Toe's Lingo code is in its `Main` movie script. The game's two behavior scripts really just call functions from `Main` based on detected mouseclicks. When the game first loads, the `Main` script's `prepareMovie` handler initializes a couple of global variables and calls `Main`'s `resetGame` function. This func-

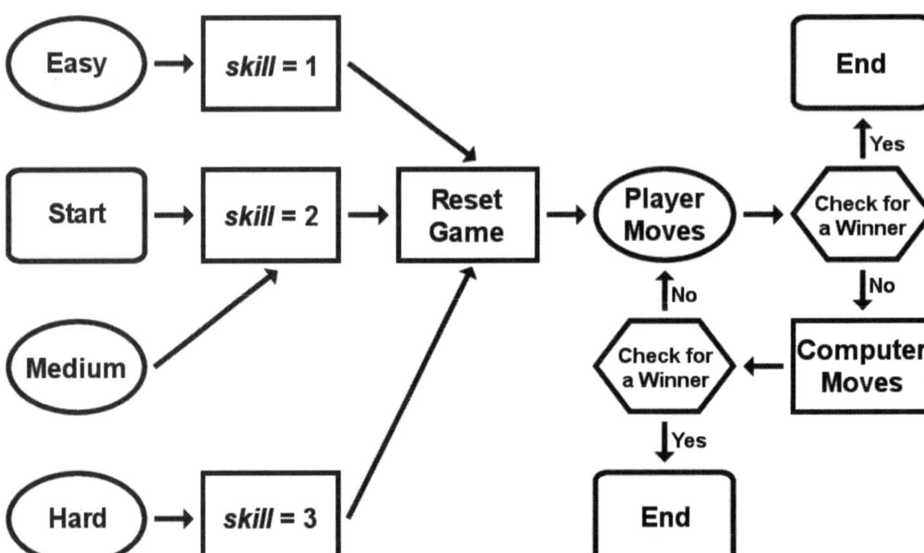

FIGURE 14.4 A flowchart for the Tasty Tic-Tac-Toe Advergame.

tion assigns random (but not matching) values from 1 to 5 to the variables playerPiece and computerPiece. These values indicate what colors of E&E candies the players will use in the following game. Next, resetGame sets the counter variable (used for delays) to 0, sets winner to false, fills the grid list with nine empty spaces, and calls the reset function of all sprites that have one.

The Piece behavior is designed to work with the E&E pieces that appear on the grid. Actually, the grid is always full of E&E pieces; sometimes, they are simply made transparent (with their blend properties set to zero). When the player clicks on any of these transparent sprites, the Piece behavior calls Main's movePlayer function and supplies the clicked sprite's channel number as an argument. The movePlayer function accepts this argument as a local variable named spotChosen. If the desired spot is available, the player's E&E candy appears, a sound plays, and the counter variable is set to 15. At this point, the Piece behavior calls Main's checkGrid function, but we won't discuss this until later.

Now that the counter variable has a value other than zero, the Main script's exitFrame handler has some work to do. Each time exitFrame is executed, it checks to see that counter has a value greater than zero. Because counter currently has a value of 15, exitFrame decreases this number by one, for each frame until counter reaches zero. Just before the counter variable reaches zero, roughly half a second has passed, and exitFrame is free to call the moveComputer function.

The Main script's moveComputer function begins by setting the local variables spotChosen to false and preferCorner to true. The spotChosen variable holds a value somewhere between one and nine before moveComputer is finished. This value represents the spot on the grid to which the computer player wants to move. The grid spots are numbered left to right and top to bottom, just as you would number the words on this page. The computer player uses preferCorner to keep from falling into a very simple trap set by the user. This is explained more fully as we continue to analyze the moveComputer function.

The grid list stores nine values, which represent the current game's grid in terms of Xs and Os. The computer player's pieces always appear as Os in this list, regardless of their color on the Stage. The computer player first uses this list to determine if a move can be made that will result in three Os in a row, either horizontally or vertically. If a spot is found, then spotChosen is used to hold its location, and the computer player looks no further. Otherwise, it checks diagonally for a winning spot. During this stage, the computer checks for a special situation in which an O is already in the center square and the user has placed Xs in opposing corners of the grid. If this were the case and the computer were to move into a free corner spot, the user might have a chance to take the remaining corner spot and effectively win the game, as shown in Figure 14.5. If this diagonal "XOX" arrangement is detected, the preferCorner variable is set to false to avoid such an outcome.

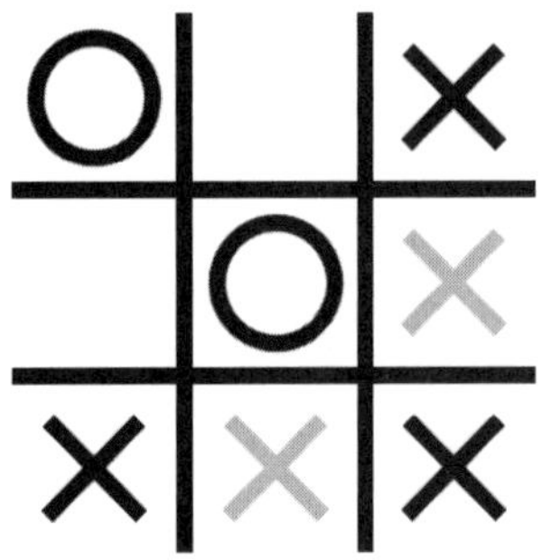

FIGURE 14.5 The reason for the `preferCorner` variable.

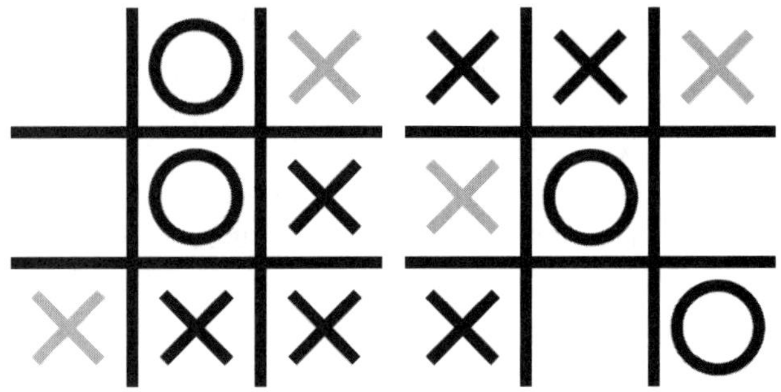

FIGURE 14.6 More grid arrangements that could result in the computer player losing to the user.

If the computer player finds no spot to win the game, it checks horizontally, vertically, and then diagonally for a spot that will block the user from winning. If no such spot is found and `spotChosen` still holds its original value of `false`, then the computer checks for a couple more special cases, which are illustrated in Figure 14.6.

If the computer hasn't found a good spot at this point, it first checks to see if the center square is still available and then uses the value of `preferCorner` to choose a free corner or side spot at random. If the user has set the difficulty level (and thereby the `skill` variable) to `3`, the computer player checks `spotChosen` one last time, and just chooses any open spot if the variable indicates nothing better has been found. If `skill` is `2`, however, there is a one in five chance that the computer player ignores the value of `spotChosen` and just chooses a free spot at random. If the `skill` variable has a value of `1`, then there is a 50% chance that the computer chooses a random spot. To finish the computer's turn, the `moveComputer` function adjusts the `grid` list, updates the screen, and plays a sound effect.

Once again, the grid has changed and the `Main` script's `checkGrid` function must be called. This function's sole purpose is to determine the outcome of the game and store it in the `winner` variable. If `winner` is set to anything other than its original value of `false`, then any calls to `movePlayer`, `moveComputer`, or `checkGrid` itself have no effect. If three Xs in a row are found using the `grid` list, then the user has won the game, and the `winner` variable is set to `1`. If three Os are found, then `winner` is `2`; if the grid is full with neither player making three in a row, the game is tied and `winner` is set to `3`. The `checkGrid` function ends by calling `endGame`, which plays one of three sounds to inform the user of the game's outcome.

Putting It All Together

We have walked through the development of the Tasty Tic-Tac-Toe Advergame starting with the product and ideas, moving on to layout and interface design, and finally analyzing the game's elements, logic, and Lingo scripts. Now all that remains is for you to build the game yourself.

1. Open Director MX; it automatically creates a new blank movie.
2. Choose Save from the File menu and save the movie to your hard disk.
3. Click the Stage. Director MX updates the Property Inspector.
4. Click the Movie tab of the Property Inspector.
5. Type "500" and "350" in the Stage Size fields.

Creating the Media Cast Members

To create the media cast members, perform the following steps.

ON THE CD

1. Choose Import from the File menu.
2. Navigate to \files\templates\chapter14\ folder on the CD-ROM, select all the files in the directory, and click Import.
3. Select the Same Settings for Remaining Images checkbox and click OK. Your movie's Internal cast should now contain the members shown in Figure 14.7.
4. Click the Text Window button on the Toolbar, as shown in Figure 14.8.
5. In the Text window, type "T A S T Y", press Enter, type "Tic-Tac-Toe", and then select the text.
6. Choose Tahoma from the Font drop-down list.
7. Choose 18 from the Size drop-down list.

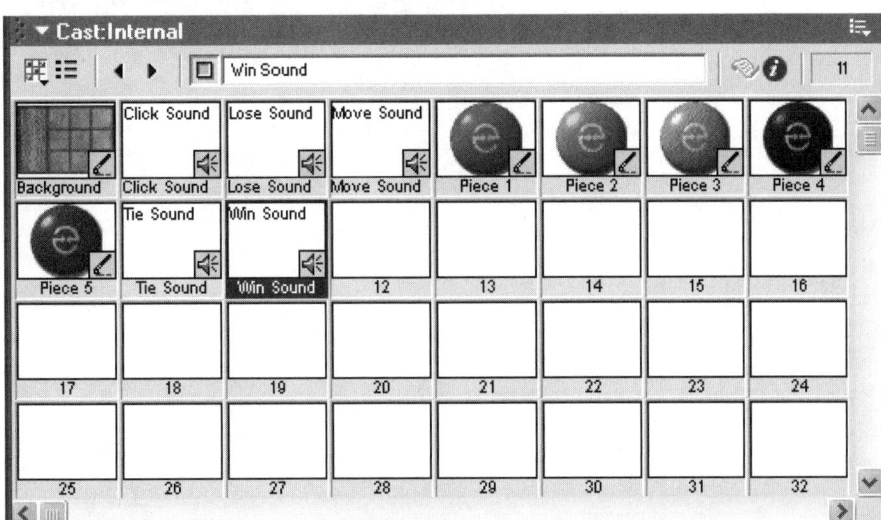

FIGURE 14.7 The imported cast members of Tasty Tic-Tac-Toe.

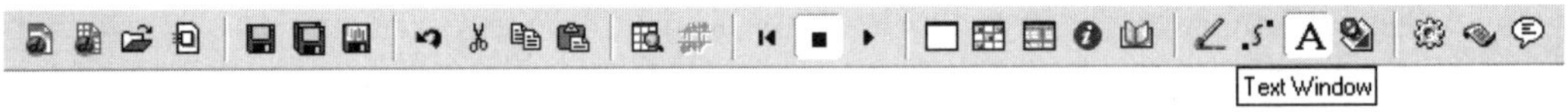

FIGURE 14.8 The Toolbar's Text Window button.

8. Click the Bold button if it is not already depressed.
9. Click the Align Center button.
10. Skip a line, type the following text into the Text window, and then select it. "Are you up for the challenge? Choose your preferred level of difficulty below, and click the grid to get started!
    Buy a bag of E&E candies today, and play your friends. Winner gets to eat the pieces!"
11. Choose 12 from the Size drop-down list.
12. Type "Game Text" into the Cast Member Name field, as shown in Figure 14.9, and close the Text window.
13. Click an empty spot in the Cast window.
14. Click the Text Window button on the Toolbar.
15. Type "EASY" in the Text window and then select it.
16. Choose 18 from the Size drop-down list.
17. Type "Easy Text" in the Cast Member Name field and close the Text window.
18. Click an empty spot in the Cast window.

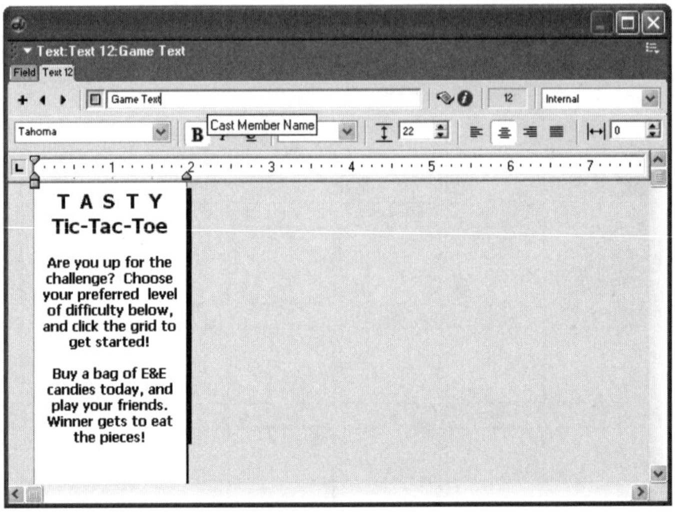

FIGURE 14.9 Naming the new Game Text cast member.

19. Click the Text Window button on the Toolbar.
20. Type "MEDIUM" in the Text window and then select it.
21. Type "Medium Text" in the Cast Member Name field and close the Text window.
22. Click an empty spot in the Cast window.
23. Click the Text Window button on the Toolbar.
24. Type "HARD" in the Text window and then select it.
25. Type "Hard Text" in the Cast Member Name field and close the Text window.

Setting Up Sprites on the Stage and in the Score

To set up sprites on the Stage and in the Score, perform the following steps.

1. Drag the Background member from the Cast window into cell 1 of channel 1 of the Score, as shown in Figure 14.10.

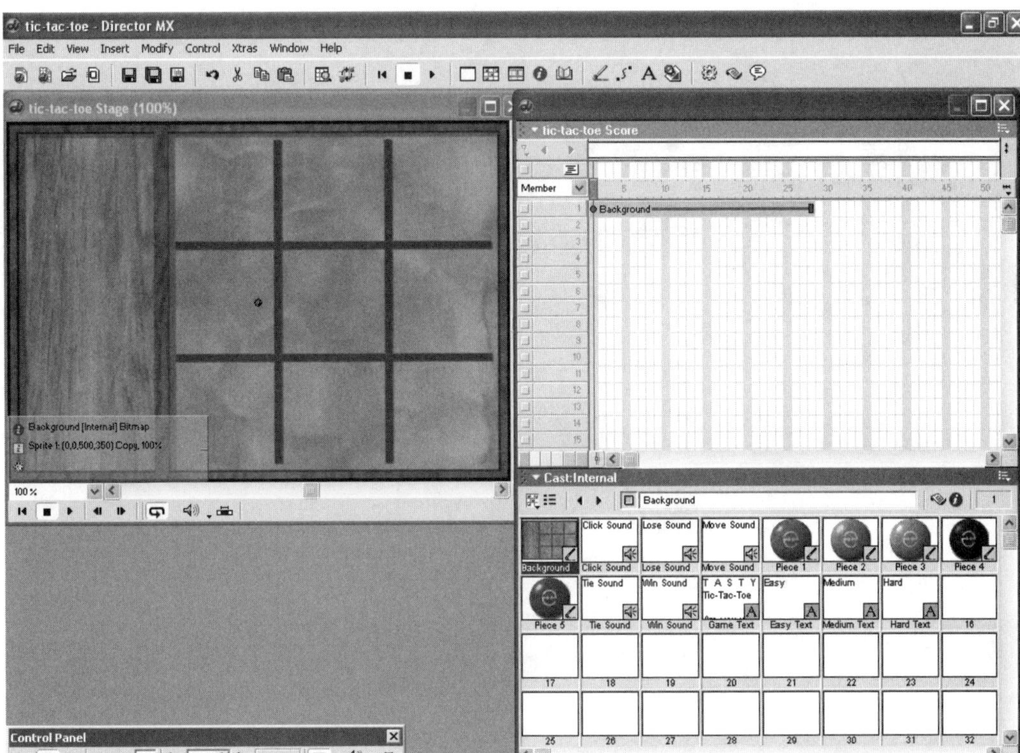

FIGURE 14.10 Creating a sprite from the Background cast member.

2. Drag the Piece 1 member from the Cast window into cell 1 of channel 2 of the Score.
3. Click cell 2 of channel 2 of the Score. Director MX updates the Property Inspector.
4. Within the Property Inspector, type "218" in the X field and "69" in the Y field, as shown in Figure 14.11.
5. Choose Background Transparent from the Ink drop-down list.
6. Choose 0 from the Blend drop-down list.
7. Right-click cell 2 of channel 2 of the Score and select Copy Sprites.
8. Right-click cell 1 of channel 3 of the Score and select Paste Sprites.
9. Within the Property Inspector, type "327" in the X field.
10. Right-click cell 1 of channel 4 of the Score and select Paste Sprites.
11. Within the Property Inspector, type "436" into the X field.
12. Click cell 2 of channel 2 of the Score, hold down the Shift key, and then click cell 2 of channel 4.

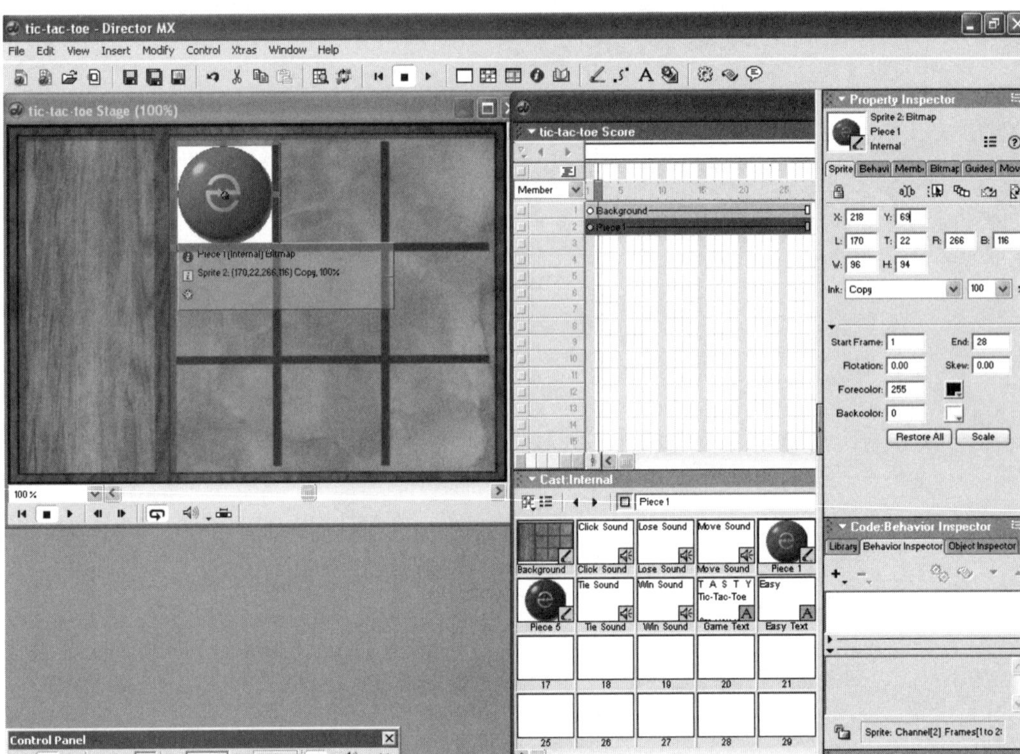

FIGURE 14.11 Positioning a Piece 1 sprite on the Stage.

13. Right-click cell 2 of channel 2 of the Score and select Copy Sprites, as shown in Figure 14.12.
14. Right-click cell 1 of channel 5 of the Score and select Paste Sprites.
15. Within the Property Inspector, type "178" in the Y field.
16. Right-click cell 1 of channel 8 of the Score and select Paste Sprites.
17. Within the Property Inspector, type "287" in the Y field, as shown in Figure 14.13.
18. Drag the Game Text member from the Cast window into cell 1 of channel 11 of the Score.
19. Click cell 2 of channel 11 of the Score. Director MX updates the Property Inspector.
20. Within the Property Inspector, type "10" in the X field and "20" in the Y field.

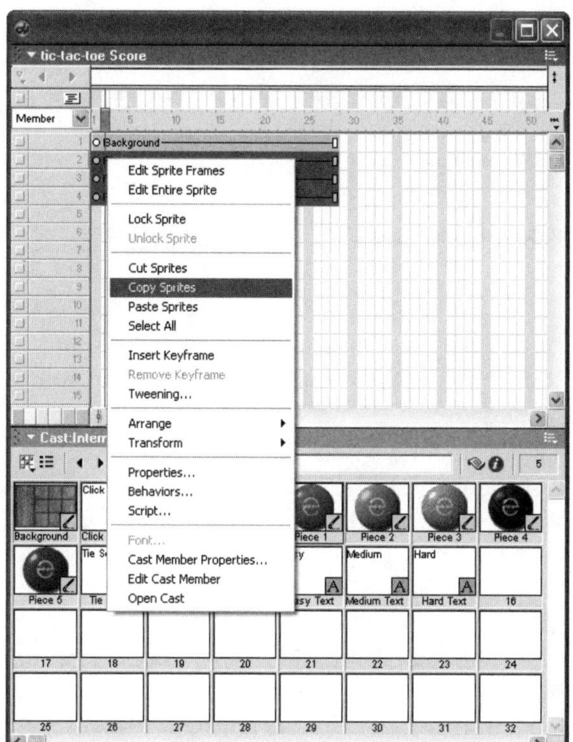

FIGURE 14.12 Copying the Piece 1 sprites of channels 2 through 4.

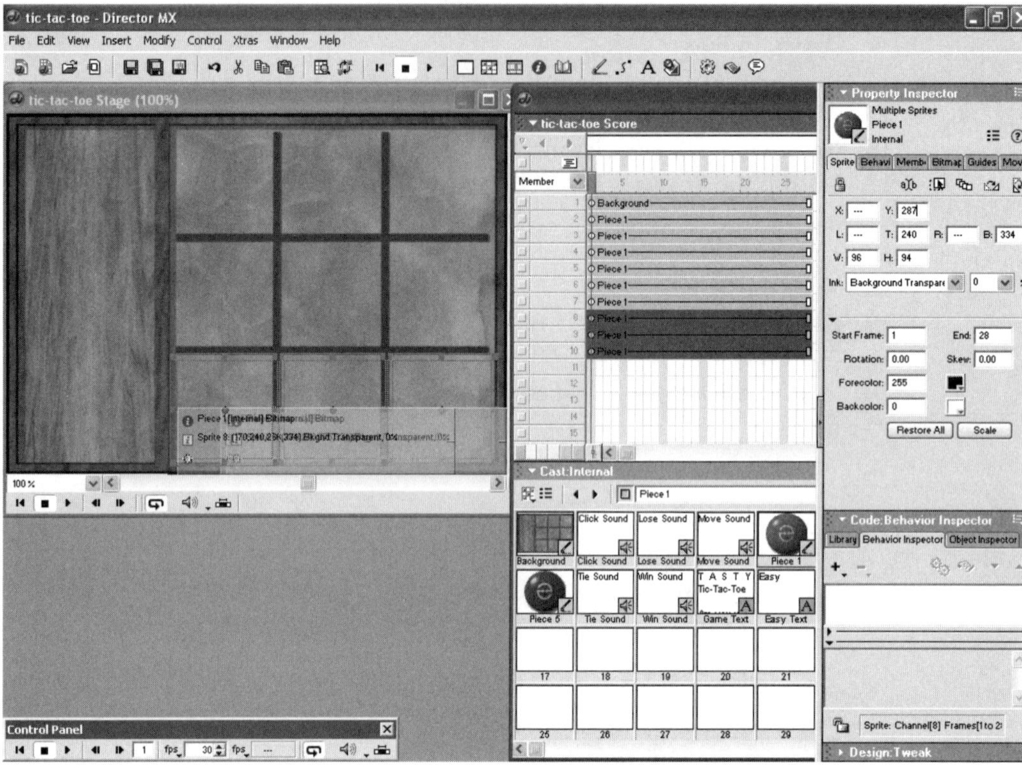

FIGURE 14.13 Positioning the final Piece 1 sprites on the Stage.

21. Drag the Easy Text member from the Cast window into cell 1 of channel 12 of the Score.
22. Click cell 2 of channel 12 of the Score. Director MX updates the Property Inspector.
23. Within the Property Inspector, type "10" in the X field and "264" in the Y field.
24. Drag the Medium Text member from the Cast window into cell 1 of channel 13 of the Score.
25. Click cell 2 of channel 13 of the Score. Director MX updates the Property Inspector.
26. Within the Property Inspector, type "10" in the X field and "286" in the Y field.

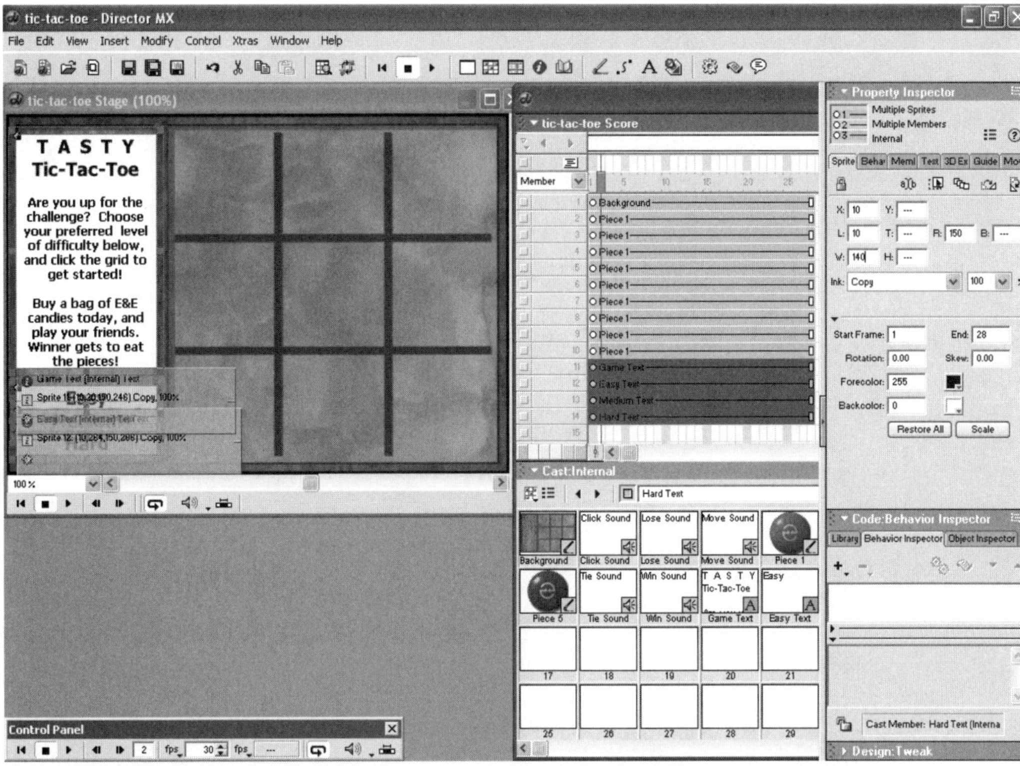

FIGURE 14.14 Positioning the text sprites of channels 11 through 14 on the Stage.

27. Drag the Hard Text member from the Cast window into cell 1 of channel 14 of the Score.
28. Click cell 2 of channel 14 of the Score. Director MX updates the Property Inspector.
29. Within the Property Inspector, type "10" in the X field and "308" in the Y field.
30. Click cell 2 of channel 11 of the Score, hold down the Shift key, and then click cell 2 of channel 14.
31. Within the Property Inspector, type "140" in the W field, as shown in Figure 14.14.
32. Choose Background Transparent from the Ink drop-down list.

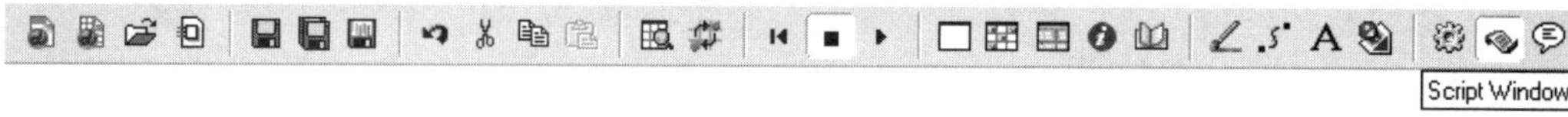

FIGURE 14.15 The Toolbar's Script Window button.

Writing and Applying the Lingo Scripts

To write and apply the Lingo scripts, perform the following steps.

1. Click an empty spot in the Cast window.
2. Click the Script Window button on the Toolbar, as shown in Figure 14.15.
3. Type the following code in the Script window.

```
global spotOffset, skill, playerPiece, computerPiece, counter, winner,
grid

on prepareMovie
    spotOffset = 1
    skill = 2
    resetGame
end

on exitFrame
    -- Let the computer opponent move when the counter is finished.
    if counter > 0 then
        if counter = 1 then
            moveComputer
            checkGrid
        end if

        counter = counter-1
    end if

    play the frame
end

on resetGame
    -- Choose random colors for the candy pieces.
    playerPiece = random(5)
    computerPiece = playerPiece
    repeat while computerPiece = playerPiece
        computerPiece = random(5)
    end repeat
```

```
    -- Reset the game with an empty grid.
    counter = 0
    winner = false
    grid = [" ", " ", " ", " ", " ", " ", " ", " ", " "]
    sendAllSprites(#reset)
end

on movePlayer spotChosen
    if winner then exit

    -- Finish the player's turn if the chosen spot is available.
    spotChosen = spotChosen-spotOffset
    if grid[spotChosen] = " " then
        grid[spotChosen] = "X"
        sprite(spotChosen+spotOffset).member = "Piece" && playerPiece
        sprite(spotChosen+spotOffset).blend = 100
        puppetSound(1, "Move Sound")
        counter = 15
    end if
end

on moveComputer
    if winner then exit

    spotChosen = false
    preferCorner = true

    -- Check horizontally and vertically for a spot to win.
    repeat with spot = 1 to 3
        gridString = grid[3*(spot-1)+1] & grid[3*(spot-1)+2] &
grid[3*(spot-1)+3]
        if gridString = " OO" then
            spotChosen = 3*(spot-1)+1
        else if gridString = "O O" then
            spotChosen = 3*(spot-1)+2
        else if gridString = "OO " then
            spotChosen = 3*(spot-1)+3
        end if

        gridString = grid[spot] & grid[spot+3] & grid[spot+6]
        if gridString = " OO" then
            spotChosen = spot
        else if gridString = "O O" then
            spotChosen = spot+3
```

```
        else if gridString = "OO " then
            spotChosen = spot+6
        end if
    end repeat

    -- Check diagonally for a spot to win.
    if not spotChosen then
        gridString = grid[1] & grid[5] & grid[9]
        if gridString = " OO" then
            spotChosen = 1
        else if gridString = "O O" then
            spotChosen = 5
        else if gridString = "OO " then
            spotChosen = 9
        else if gridString = "XOX" then
            preferCorner = false
        end if

        gridString = grid[3] & grid[5] & grid[7]
        if gridString = " OO" then
            spotChosen = 3
        else if gridString = "O O" then
            spotChosen = 5
        else if gridString = "OO " then
            spotChosen = 7
        else if gridString = "XOX" then
            preferCorner = false
        end if
    end if

    -- Check horizontally and vertically for a spot to block.
    if not spotChosen then
        repeat with spot = 1 to 3
            gridString = grid[3*(spot-1)+1] & grid[3*(spot-1)+2] &
grid[3*(spot-1)+3]
            if gridString = " XX" then
                spotChosen = 3*(spot-1)+1
            else if gridString = "X X" then
                spotChosen = 3*(spot-1)+2
            else if gridString = "XX " then
                spotChosen = 3*(spot-1)+3
            end if

            gridString = grid[spot] & grid[spot+3] & grid[spot+6]
            if gridString = " XX" then
```

```
                spotChosen = spot
            else if gridString = "X X" then
                spotChosen = spot+3
            else if gridString = "XX " then
                spotChosen = spot+6
            end if
        end repeat
    end if

    -- Check diagonally for a spot to block.
    if not spotChosen then
        gridString = grid[1] & grid[5] & grid[9]
        if gridString = " XX" then
            spotChosen = 1
        else if gridString = "X X" then
            spotChosen = 5
        else if gridString = "XX " then
            spotChosen = 9
        end if

        gridString = grid[3] & grid[5] & grid[7]
        if gridString = " XX" then
            spotChosen = 3
        else if gridString = "X X" then
            spotChosen = 5
        else if gridString = "XX " then
            spotChosen = 7
        end if
    end if

    -- Block the user's weak attempt at strategy.
    if not spotChosen then
        if grid[4] & grid[1] & grid[2] = "X X" then
            spotChosen = 1
        else if grid[2] & grid[3] & grid[6] = "X X" then
            spotChosen = 3
        else if grid[4] & grid[7] & grid[8] = "X X" then
            spotChosen = 7
        else if grid[8] & grid[9] & grid[6] = "X X" then
            spotChosen = 9
        end if

        if grid[7] & grid[1] & grid[2] = "X X" or grid[4] & grid[1] &
grid[3] = "X X" then
```

```
            spotChosen = 1
        else if grid[1] & grid[3] & grid[6] = "X X" or grid[2] & grid[3] &
grid[9] = "X X" then
            spotChosen = 3
        else if grid[1] & grid[7] & grid[8] = "X X" or grid[4] & grid[7] &
grid[9] = "X X" then
            spotChosen = 7
        else if grid[7] & grid[9] & grid[6] = "X X" or grid[8] & grid[9] &
grid[3] = "X X" then
            spotChosen = 9
        end if
    end if

    -- If a spot is not found, choose a reasonable spot.
    if not spotChosen then
        if preferCorner then
            if grid[1] = " " or grid[3] = " " or grid[7] = " " or grid[9]
= " " then
                spotChosen = 5
                repeat while grid[spotChosen] <> " "
                    spotChosen = random(4)
                    if spotChosen = 2 then
                        spotChosen = 7
                    else if spotChosen = 4 then
                        spotChosen = 9
                    end if
                end repeat
            end if
        else
            if grid[2] = " " or grid[4] = " " or grid[6] = " " or grid[8]
= " " then
                spotChosen = 5
                repeat while grid[spotChosen] <> " "
                    spotChosen = random(4)
                    if spotChosen = 1 then
                        spotChosen = 6
                    else if spotChosen = 3 then
                        spotChosen = 8
                    end if
                end repeat
            end if
        end if
    end if

    -- Weaken the computer opponent based on the chosen skill level.
```

```
    case skill of
        1: if random(2) = 1 then spotChosen = false
        2: if random(5) = 1 then spotChosen = false
    end case

    -- Choose a random open spot if a better choice has not been found.
    if not spotChosen then
        spotFound = false
        repeat with spot = 1 to 9
            if grid[spot] = " " then spotFound = true
        end repeat
        if spotFound then
            repeat while not spotChosen
                spotChosen = random(9)
                if grid[spotChosen] <> " " then spotChosen = false
            end repeat
        end if
    end if

    -- Finish the computer opponent's turn.
    if spotChosen then
        grid[spotChosen] = "O"
        sprite(spotChosen+spotOffset).member = "Piece" && computerPiece
        sprite(spotChosen+spotOffset).blend = 100
        puppetSound(2, "Move Sound")
    end if
end

on checkGrid
    if winner then exit

    -- Check horizontally and vertically for a winner.
    repeat with spot = 1 to 3
        gridString = grid[3*(spot-1)+1] & grid[3*(spot-1)+2] &
grid[3*(spot-1)+3]
        if gridString = "XXX" then
            winner = 1
        else if gridString = "OOO" then
            winner = 2
        end if

        gridString = grid[spot] & grid[spot+3] & grid[spot+6]
        if gridString = "XXX" then
             winner = 1
```

```
        else if gridString = "OOO" then
            winner = 2
        end if
    end repeat

    -- Check diagonally for a winner.
    gridString = grid[1] & grid[5] & grid[9]
    if gridString = "XXX" then
        winner = 1
    else if gridString = "OOO" then
        winner = 2
    end if
    gridString = grid[3] & grid[5] & grid[7]
    if gridString = "XXX" then
        winner = 1
    else if gridString = "OOO" then
        winner = 2
    end if

    -- Check for a tie game.
    if not winner then
        repeat with spot = 1 to 9
            if grid[spot] = " " then exit
        end repeat
        winner = 3
    end if

    if winner then endGame
end

on endGame
    case winner of:
        1: puppetSound(3, "Win Sound")
        2: puppetSound(3, "Lose Sound")
        3: puppetSound(3, "Tie Sound")
    end case
end
```

4. Type "Main" in the Cast Member Name field, as shown in Figure 14.16, and close the Script window.
5. Click an empty spot in the Cast window.
6. Click the Script Window button on the Toolbar.
7. Type the following code in the Script window.

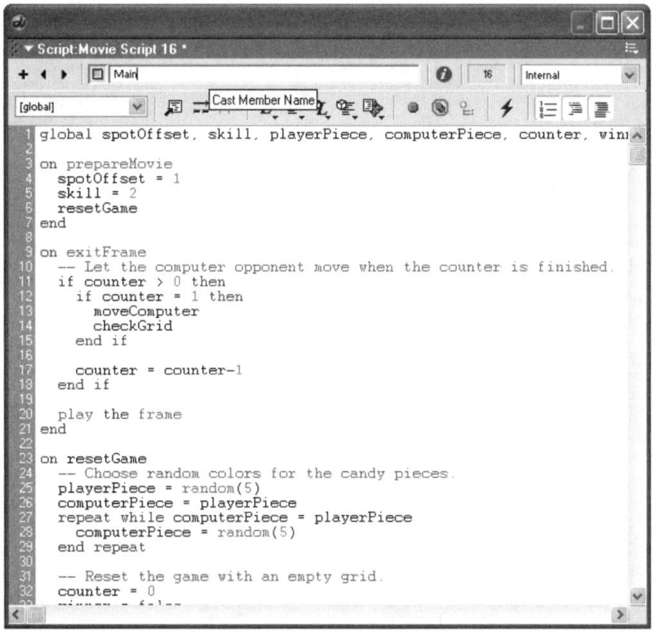

FIGURE 14.16 Naming the new `Main` movie script.

```
global counter
property my

on beginSprite me
    my = sprite(me.spriteNum)
end

on mouseDown
    if counter > 0 then exit

    movePlayer(my.spriteNum)
    checkGrid
end

on reset
    my.blend = 0
end
```

8. Click the Script tab of the Property Inspector.
9. Choose Behavior from the Type drop-down list.

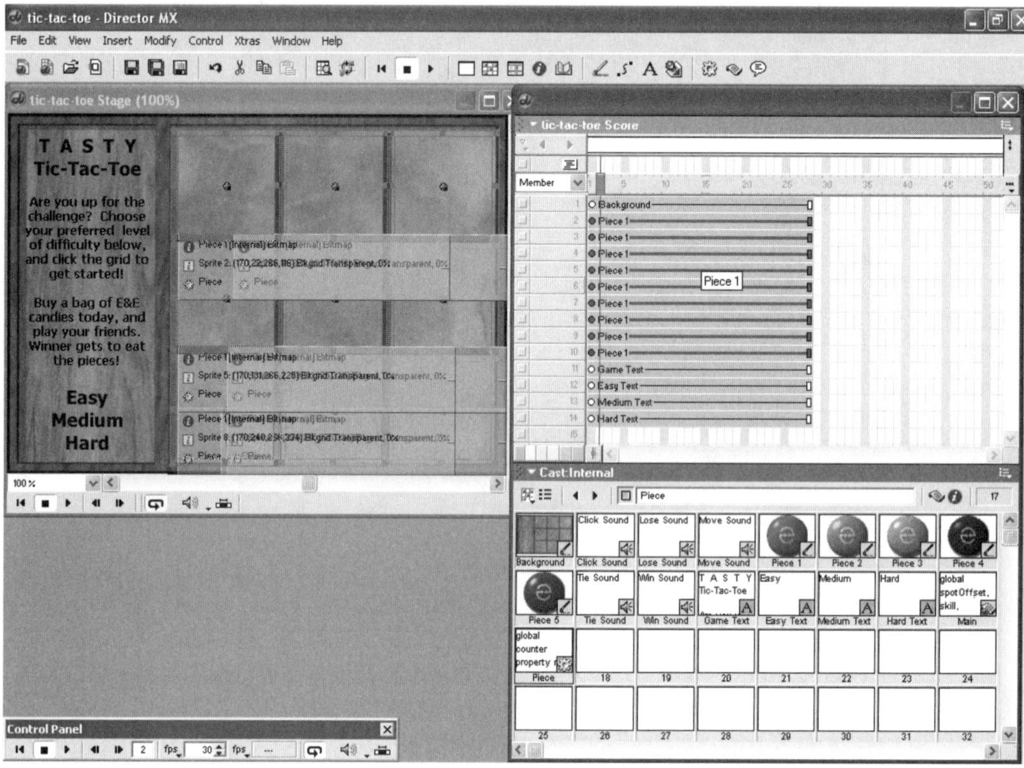

FIGURE 14.17 Applying the Piece behavior to the Piece 1 sprites.

10. Within the Script window, type "Piece" in the Cast Member Name field and close the window.
11. Click cell 2 of channel 2 of the Score, hold down the Shift key, and then click cell 2 of channel 10.
12. Drag the Piece behavior from the Cast window onto the selected sprites of the Score, as shown in Figure 14.17.
13. Click an empty spot in the Cast window.
14. Click the Script Window button on the Toolbar.
15. Type the following code in the Script window.

```
global skill
property my, setSkill

on beginSprite me
    my = sprite(me.spriteNum)
```

```
end

on mouseEnter
    my.color = rgb(255, 0, 0)
end

on mouseLeave
    my.color = rgb(0, 0, 0)
end

on mouseDown
    puppetSound(1, "Click Sound")

    skill = setSkill
    resetGame
end

on getPropertyDescriptionList
    return [#setSkill: [#comment:"Skill Level:", #format:#integer,
#default:2] ]
end
```

16. Click the Script tab of the Property Inspector.
17. Choose Behavior from the Type drop-down list.
18. Within the Script window, type "Reset Button" in the Cast Member Name field and close the window.
19. Drag the Reset Button behavior from the Cast window onto the sprite in channel 12 of the Score.
20. Type "1" in the Skill Level field and click OK, as shown in Figure 14.18.
21. Drag the Reset Button behavior from the Cast window onto the sprite in channel 13 of the Score.
22. Click OK.

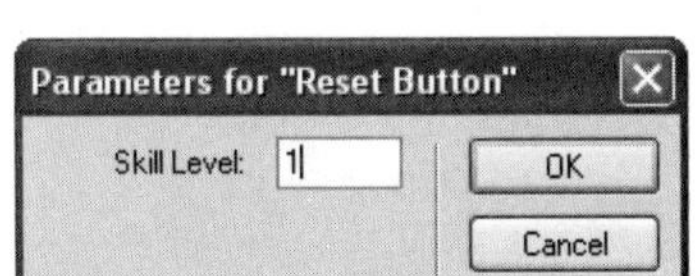

FIGURE 14.18 Supplying a value for the Skill Level parameter of the Reset Button behavior.

23. Drag the Reset Button behavior from the Cast window onto the sprite in channel 14 of the Score.
24. Type "3" in the Skill Level field and click OK.
25. Click frame 1 of the Score and then click the Play button on the Toolbar to play your game.

SUMMARY

With that, your Tasty Tic-Tac-Toe game is complete. It is now ready to be published and added to the E&E Web site's arcade. With the game's artificial intelligence that can be set to different difficulties, the game is sure to be a hit with a broad range of people.

15 epic Holiday Shoppe

THE CONCEPT

Identifying Your Product: epic Holiday Shoppe

epic Holiday Shoppe is opening at a local mall for the holiday season, to sell a variety of ornaments, trees, and a number of other products. They are only open for about a month, so they need to increase the community's awareness quickly before it's too late. So, they have decided to use a direct mail approach to attract customers to the store. To increase the odds of delivering the message, they are mailing CD-ROMs with a holiday game rather than taking the ordinary paper route. They need something that people will find enjoyable that provides an extra bonus—a coupon for 10% off at the end of the game. The game makes the player aware of the store and after completing the game, he is presented with a map, store location, and hours of operation.

Outlining a Game for the epic Holiday Shoppe

The epic Holiday Shoppe does not have the budget for a really complex game, so they want a simple, yet enjoyable game. For this, the puzzle game genre is ideal. Puzzles can be easily "themed" for the holidays which will fit the type of business in which epic Holiday Shoppe engages. The game we have chosen for this purpose is a variant of the "Simon Says" game, which is basically a memory-oriented game. The idea of this game is to repeat a sequence that the computer plays. With each successful repetition of the sequence, another item is added to the sequence, making the game harder and harder as play continues. For the holiday theme, we use a set of singing nutcrackers, to tie into the theme of the famous *Nutcracker* ballet. Each nutcracker sings a particular note. The nutcrackers sing a sequence of notes, and then the player clicks the nutcrackers in the correct sequence. If the player does successfully repeat the sequence, the game displays the map of the mall and the store's location, and gives the player the opportunity to claim the 10% off coupon as thanks for playing the game. This increases the exposure of the epic Holiday Shoppe brand, and hopefully entices the player to visit the store.

Designing the epic Holiday Shoppe Interface

Due to the simplicity of the game, there is not much to the interface. The interface is oriented around the five nutcrackers. Each is a different color to help the player remember which nutcracker played which note. The entire interface is centered on a traditional wooden bookshelf, projecting a warm, holiday feeling. To this, we integrate the interface elements—the buttons that make things happen in the game. The first button is the Play button, which starts the game. See Figure 15.1. The next button is the Instructions button, which displays the instructions in a panel that appears on top of the interface. To go back to the game and make the instructions go away, the player can click the "X" button. See Figure 15.2. And finally, when the player has finished the game, he can click the Exit button to return to the operating system. But, before we let the user go, we present him with an exit screen showing the map and an invitation to claim the 10% off coupon. See Figure 15.3. Clicking the "X" button exits the game. And finally, when the player makes a mistake in re-

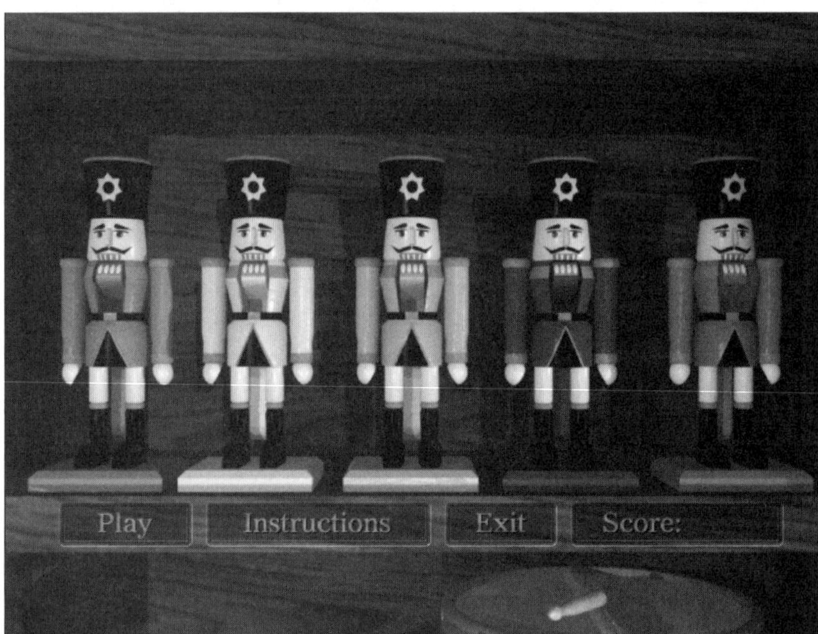

FIGURE 15.1 The epic Holiday Shoppe interface.

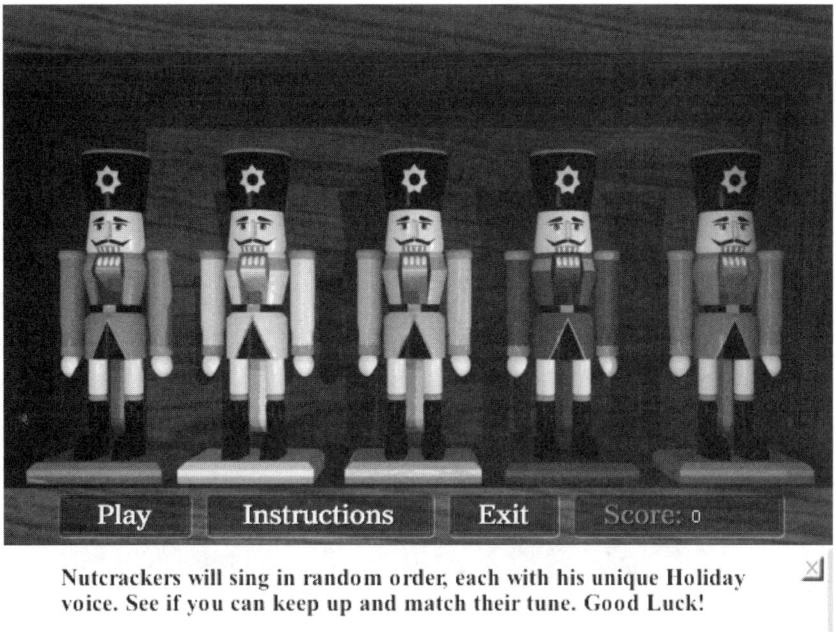

FIGURE 15.2 The instructions.

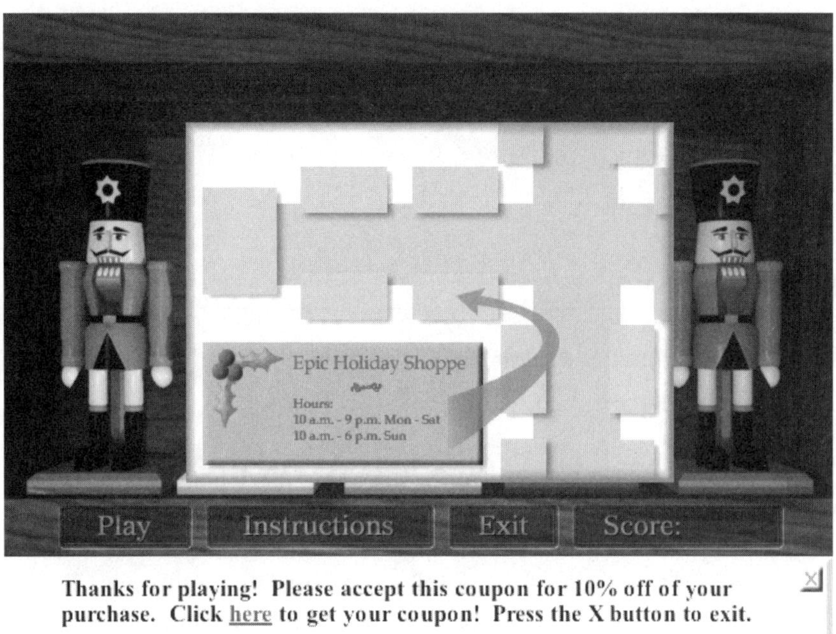

FIGURE 15.3 The Exit screen.

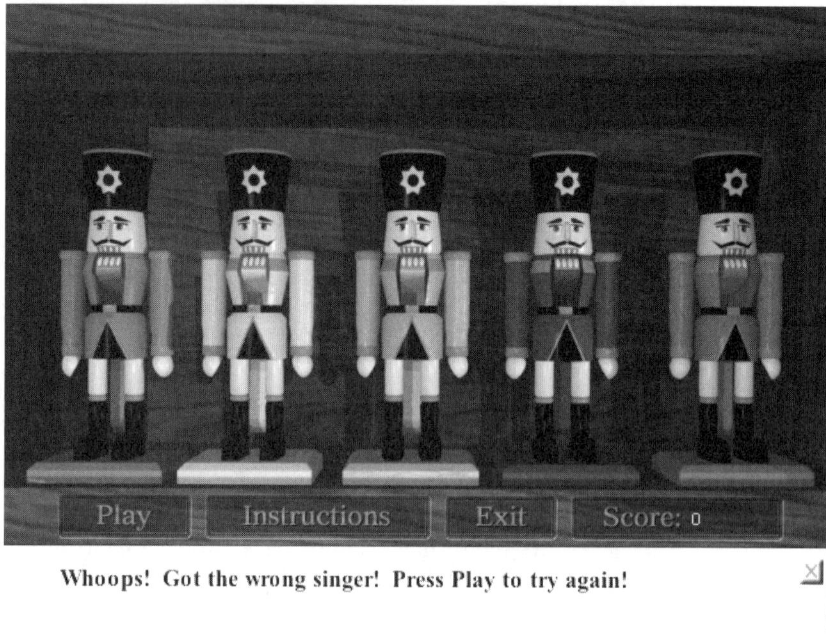

FIGURE 15.4 Try again!

peating the sequence, a note is displayed informing him of the mistake and providing instructions on how to play again. See Figure 15.4.

To let the player know when he has moved the mouse over an active element, or a hot spot, we change the cursor to the hand. The active elements include the buttons and regions surrounding the nutcracker figures.

THE CREATION

Identifying the Elements of epic Holiday Shoppe

We start by compiling a list of the elements of the game. To do this, we look at each screen of the game in depth. There are four in total. First, there is the Game screen. This is where the main action of the game takes place. The next screens have the same structure, but differ only on the message displayed. Each of these screens displays a message in a raised panel that resembles a dialog box. These screens are the Instructions screen, the "Wrong" screen, and the Exit screen. The Exit screen also displays the mall map. Clicking the "X" button on the Instructions screen and the Wrong screen simply returns the player to the game. Clicking the "X" button on the

Exit screen exits the projector and returns the player to the operating system. Now, for the list of elements:

- Game screen

  Singing Man: The nutcrackers that sing tones.

  Picker: The user interacts with the hot spot above the Singing Man, which communicates the choice to the game script.

  Controller: This element is the behind-the-scenes agent that determines when the Picker can pick and when the Singing Man can play the sequence that the player repeats. This is the brains behind the operation.

  Rollover button: These are the buttons on the game interface. They are called Rollover buttons because they become active when rolled over, and do not have any state change when clicked.
- Instructions screen

  Rollover button: This is the same as on the Game screen.

  Push button: This is the "X" button, which does not exhibit a state change when rolled over, but only when clicked.
- Wrong screen

  Rollover buttons: This is the same as on the Game screen.

  Push button: The "X" button behaves the same way as on the Instructions screen.
- Exit screen

  Rollover buttons: This is the same as on the Game screen.

  Push button: The "X" button behaves the same way as on the Instructions screen.

Recognizing How the Game's Elements Interact

The interactions between the elements in this game are fairly straightforward. First of all, the Rollover buttons and the Push button do not interact with any other element, leaving us with the three most important elements—the Picker, the Singing Man, and the Controller. The Picker is the hot spot over a particular Singing Man. When the player clicks the mouse button inside this hot spot, the Picker tells the Controller the choice that the player made. The Controller then decides whether the action of picking translates to the Singing Man singing. The Controller keeps track of when it is the player's turn to enter the sequence and when the computer is playing the sequence. When the computer is playing the sequence, the Picker's notifications are ignored. Only when it is the player's turn does the Controller tell the Singing Man to sing when the Picker notifies the Controller. However, the

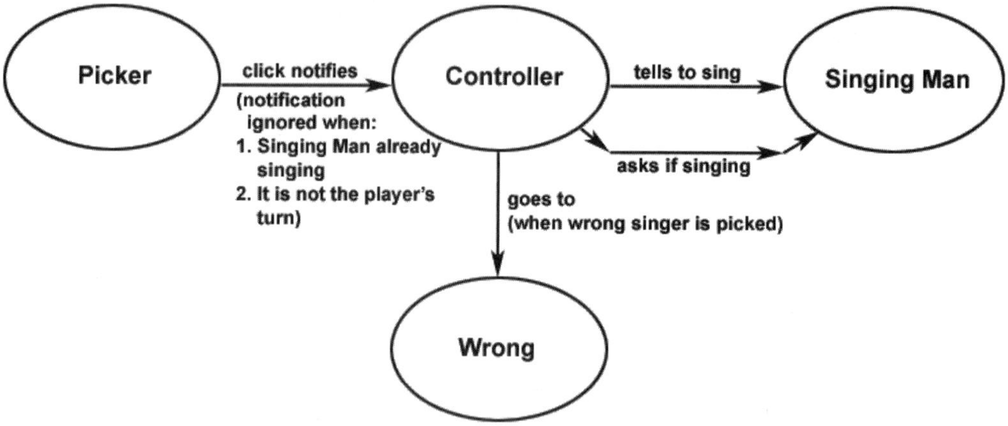

FIGURE 15.5 Diagram of the relationships between the elements.

Controller again ignores the Picker's notification if the Singing Man is already singing when he is picked. See Figure 15.5.

Identifying the Scripts of the epic Holiday Shoppe

The behaviors follow almost directly from the list of elements. Some additional behaviors are needed to handle the details, but these are in the periphery. The core of the game functionality is in the relationship between the Picker, the Singing Man, and the Controller.

The Picker

The behavior for the picker is straightforward. The most important action happens when the mouse is released over the hot spot, in the `on mouseUp` handler. Here, the Picker notifies the frame script (which is the Controller) that the Singing Man (to which the Picker belongs) has been picked. The Picker knows which Singer it belongs to simply by the organization of the Score. The Singing Man is in the Sprite channel immediately preceding the Picker. And, less importantly, for the benefit of the player, the mouse cursor changes to the hand cursor when the mouse enters the hot spot and then back to the normal arrow when the mouse leaves the hot spot.

The Singing Man

The behavior for the Singing Man is also fairly straightforward. Basically, the Singing Man only has to react to the Controller's requests. The Controller asks the Singing Man to sing and asks if the Singing Man is still singing. The Singing Man only knows that it has told Macromedia Director MX to start playing his voice.

When told to sing, the Singing Man notes the request in a variable. At the beginning of each frame, the Singing Man must check if Macromedia Director MX is still playing his voice, but this only needs to be done if the Singing Man was asked to sing, which he can determine by checking the variable. Another very important thing that the Singing Man must do is add his sprite to the global list of singers. This list is set to an empty list when the movie is prepared, and the singers themselves fill this list. The list is crucial to the Controller.

The Controller

Now, we look at the most complex behavior, the brains behind the operation. There are two fundamental phases of operation—the player's turn and the computer's turn. The Controller keeps track of the state and plays the sequence or allows the player to enter the sequence according to this state. However, initially, the game is not in progress. For this, we have a third state, the "not playing" state. Clicking the Play button moves the game from *not playing* to the *computer's turn*, so that the computer can take the first turn. From this analysis, we come up with a new behavior—the behavior for when the mouse button is released over the Play button, which we call Start Game. So, the action each time the game enters a new frame is described by the following pseudocode:

1. If the game state is the computer's turn:
   Tell the computer to take its turn; that is, play the sequence.
2. If the game state is the player's turn:
   Allow the player to take his turn.

This routine basically processes the result of taking his turn. The Controller is only notified when the player has taken his turn.

So, we have two courses of action that the Controller can take on each frame. It can process the player's turn or the computer's turn. Let's start with the computer's turn. In the beginning of the computer's turn, before it has played any notes, we add a note to the sequence, increasing the difficulty for this round. Initially, at the beginning of the game, we are adding the first note of the sequence. With each subsequent round, we increase the length of the sequence. After a singer is added to the list, let the first singer in the sequence sing, getting the ball rolling for the computer's turn. Next, for each step of the computer's turn, we play a subsequent note of the sequence. We check on each frame if the current singer has stopped singing before allowing the next singer to sing. After all singers have sung, the player's turn can start. The pseudocode for the computer's turn is as follows:

1. Is this the beginning of the computer's turn? This is true if the current position in the sequence is zero.

If no, proceed to Step 5.
2. Add a singer to the sequence.
3. The current position in the sequence is one.
4. Let the first singer sing.
5. Has the current singer stopped singing?
   If no, do nothing further.
6. Go to the next singer in the sequence by increasing the current position of the sequence by one.
7. Are there any more notes to sing?
   Yes, go to Step 10.
8. Start the player's turn.
9. Take no further actions—the computer's turn is done.
10. Tell the Singing Man next in the sequence (now at the current position of the sequence) to sing.

The player is allowed to take his turn when the computer has finished playing the sequence. The Picker notifies the Controller when the player picks a Singing Man. The request is received in a message handler of the Controller. If it is not the player's turn or a Singing Man is already singing, we leave the handler, thereby ignoring the message. The game's state tells us when it is the player's turn. We keep track of the Singing Man that the player picked in another variable, and we keep track of the singer so long as he is singing. Once the singer is not singing, the variable is set to `void`—that is, no value—so that we can pick another Singing Man. If the player selects the wrong Singing Man, we play the "wrong" sound, so we need to keep track of the sound channel so that we can go to the "wrong" frame once the "wrong" sound is finished playing. We have yet another variable to keep track of this. To get the ball rolling on the player's turn, we call a handler to start the player's turn, with the following pseudocode:

1. Reset the current position in the sequence to zero to indicate the beginning of the player's turn.
2. Set the game's state to the player's turn.
3. No singer is picked yet, so set our picked singer to `void`.
4. The player is not wrong yet, so the "wrong" sound is not playing. Set this variable to `false`.

The player's turn starts with the notification. If it is the player's turn and there is no Singing Man singing, we do not ignore the notification of the player's choice. We move the current position in the sequence to the next position, mark the Singing Man for the next phase, and let the Singing Man sing. The psuedocode follows:

1. Is it the player's turn and is no Singing Man singing?
   If wrong on both counts, do nothing. We ignore the notification.
2. The player has picked the next Singing Man, so we move the current position in the sequence.
3. Record this Singing Man for the next phase.
4. And let this Singing Man sing.

Now, we can look at the next phase of the player's turn—the fundamental steps. This phase occurs for each frame, but is only acted upon when a notification has occurred. After the picked Singing Man has stopped singing, we can check the sequence to see if the Singing Man is the correct one. If this is true, we reset the variable holding our Singing Man to `void` so that we can pick another. If the Singing Man is the last one, reset the current position in the sequence to zero, update the score, and start the computer's turn. Otherwise, if the player picked the wrong Singing Man, wait until the sound channel is available before issuing the "wrong" sound. Mark that we have started playing the sound. Now, while we still have the Singing Man, if the player is wrong, we wait until the channel is free again before we stop playing and go to the "wrong" screen. The pseudocode follows:

1. Has a Singing Man been picked (do we have a Singing Man in our variable)?
   If not, do nothing more.
2. Is our Singing Man singing?
   If not, do nothing more until he is done singing.
3. Did the player pick the right singing man?
   If not, go to Step 10.
4. Set our Singing Man variable to `void` so the player can pick another Singing Man.
5. Is this the last Singing Man?
   If not, go to Step 9.
6. Reset the current position in the sequence back to zero for the computer to start its turn.
7. Set the score to the current length of the sequence; that is, an extra point for repeating a sequence correctly.
8. Set the state of the game to the computer's turn.
9. The player's turn is over. We do not proceed any further.
10. Is the player wrong, and if so, is the sound channel still playing the "wrong" sound?
    If wrong on both counts, we do nothing further. Either the player is not wrong or the "wrong" sound is still playing. After the "wrong" sound is done playing, proceed to Step 11.

11. The wrong sound is done playing. The game is officially over, so set the game state to "not playing."
12. Go to the "wrong" frame.

That is all there is to the player's turn, and all there is to the Controller. This covers the core of the game. What follows next are the behaviors for the remaining parts of the game—the behaviors for the items in the periphery.

First, we cover the behaviors corresponding to the elements in our list—Rollover button and Push button. In the Score, two sprites are associated with each type of button—the highlighted state for the Rollover button and the push state for the Push button, along with the hot spot where mouseclicks are registered and acted upon the appropriate button. These are straightforward. When the player enters the hot spot, for both types of buttons, the mouse turns into the hand cursor. For the Rollover button, the associated highlighted image also becomes visible, indicating the button is active. When the mouse cursor leaves the hot spot, the mouse cursor turns back into the normal arrow cursor. And for the Rollover button, the highlighted sprite disappears, indicating that the button is now inactive. The Push button behavior responds to button presses and releases while the mouse is in the hot spot. On a button press, the behavior makes the pushed-in sprite visible. On a button release, the behavior makes the pushed-in sprite invisible again, completing the effect of pushing and then releasing the button. In both cases, for the Rollover button and the Push button, the behavior is applied to the hot spot, as that is the sensitive region.

Now, we must come up with behaviors for the other, more periphery functionality of the game. First of all, Push button and Rollover button are generic, and represent the button's visual behavior. However, the actual behavior of the buttons when the mouse button is released requires further behaviors that are added on top of the hot spot sprite, where the generic behaviors are applied. We need a behavior to go to the Game screen, a behavior to go to the Exit screen, and a behavior to go to the Instructions screen. Also, when the "X" button is clicked on the Exit screen, we need to assign a behavior to that hot spot to actually exit the game. We call these behaviors Start Game, Go to Exit, Go to Instructions, and Quit Game. Further, we need a behavior to launch the Web site wherein the player can get the 10% off coupon. For this, we have the behavior Go to Web Site. And finally, for each of the Instructions, "Wrong," and Exit screens, we need to keep the playback head in the frame so that the player can interact with the buttons. For this, we have the behavior Stay Put.

Putting It All Together

ON THE CD

Now that we have the groundwork laid for the game, we can put this thing together. To follow along, open the chapter15template.dir file in the \files\templates\ folder on the CD-ROM. This movie contains only the necessary graphics to put the game together. The Score is completely empty. We implement this game screen by screen, starting with the Game screen and proceed through the Introduction, Wrong, and Exit screens.

The Game Screen

1. Place a marker in the marker channel for frame 1. Label this marker "Game."
2. Drag the Background cast member onto sprite channel 1 at frame 1.
3. Drag the Play cast member onto sprite channel 2 at frame 1.
4. Drag the Hot Spot cast member onto sprite channel 3 at frame 1. Open the Property Inspector for the sprite, and set X to 44, Y to 368, W to 99, and H to 30.
5. Click the Behavior tab of the Property Inspector, click the Plus button, and select New Behavior. Name the new behavior "Rollover Button." Enter the code from Listing 15.1 in the Script window. Close the Script window.

LISTING 15.1 The Rollover Button behavior.

```
property myHiLightSprite

on beginSprite me

    -- the highlight sprite is in the preceding sprite channel
    myHiLightSprite = sprite(me.spriteNum - 1)

    -- make the hilight invisible initially
    myHiLightSprite.blend = 0

end

on mouseEnter me

    -- the mouse has rolled over the hot spot

    -- make the hilight visible
    myHiLightSprite.blend = 100
    -- set the cursor and the cursor mask
    cursor [ member "hand", member "handMask" ]

end

on mouseLeave me
```

```
    -- the mouse has rolled out of the hot spot

    -- make the hilight invisible again
    myHiLightSprite.blend = 0
    -- back to the arrow cursor
    cursor -1
end
```

6. Return to the Property Inspector and click the Behavior tab. Again, click the Plus button and select New Behavior. Name the behavior "Start Game." Enter the code in Listing 15.2 in the Script window. Close the Script window.

LISTING 15.2 The Start Game behavior.

```
global gSequence        -- the sequence of singers
global gSequenceItem    -- the current singer in the sequence
global gGameState       -- the current state of the game

on mouseUp me

    -- the game starts with the computer playing
    -- the first sequence
    gGameState = #computerTurn
    -- the computer fills the sequence
    gSequence = []
    -- the sequence is empty
    gSequenceItem = 0
    -- the player has earned no points
    member("score").text = "0"
    -- go to the Game screen
    go to frame "Game"

end
```

7. Drag the Instructions cast member onto sprite channel 4 at frame 1.
8. Drag the Hot Spot cast member onto sprite channel 5 at frame 1. Open the Property Inspector and set X to 158, Y to 370, W to 171, and H to 30.
9. Click the Behavior tab of the Property Inspector. Click the Plus button and select the Rollover Button behavior.
10. Drag the Exit cast member onto sprite channel 6 at frame 1.
11. Drag the Hot Spot cast member onto sprite channel 7 at frame 1. Open the Property Inspector and set X to 344, Y to 371, W to 80, and H to 29.

12. Click the Behavior tab of the Property Inspector. Click the Plus button and select the Rollover Button behavior.
13. Drag the Score cast member onto sprite channel 8 at frame 1. Open the Property Inspector and set X to 529 and Y to 377. Set the Ink to Background Transparent.
14. Drag the Red Man cast member onto sprite channel 9 at frame 1.
15. Open the Behavior tab of the Property Inspector. Click the Plus button and select New Behavior. Name the new behavior "Singing Man." Enter the code in Listing 15.3. Close the Script window.

LISTING 15.3 The Singing Man behavior.

```
global gSingingMen          -- the list of singers

property mySinger           -- the singer
property mySingingVoice     -- the singer's voice
property myAmSinging        -- the singer is singing

on beginSprite me

    -- get the singer's sprite
    mySinger = sprite(me.spriteNum)

    -- look for the singer in the singer list
    -- add the singer to the list
    gSingingMen.append(mySinger)

    -- the singer's voice is the chord with the singer's number.
-- because the singers are arranged in order in the score, the
-- length of the list of singers is the same as the singer's
-- number in the score.
    mySingingVoice = member ("Chord" & gSingingMen.count)

    -- the singer is not singing right now
    myAmSinging = false

    -- so the singer sprite with the mouth open is not visible
    mySinger.blend = 0

end

on enterFrame me
```

```
    -- check if the singer has started singing
    if myAmSinging then
      -- the singer has started singing.  see if the singer has
      -- finished singing
      if not soundBusy(1) then
        -- the singer has finished singing, so mark the singer as
        -- not singing
        myAmSinging = false
        -- and make the mouth open sprite invisible again
        mySinger.blend = 0
      end if
    end if

end

on sing me

    -- check if the channel is currently playing another tune
    if not SoundBusy(1) then
      -- the channel is free, let the singer sing
      PuppetSound 1, mySingingVoice
      -- make the singer's mouth open sprite visible
      mySinger.blend = 100
      -- and mark the singer as singing
      myAmSinging = true
    end if

end

on amSinging me

    -- return the singer's singing state
    return myAmSinging

end
```

16. Drag the Hot Spot cast member onto sprite channel 10 at frame 1. Open the Property Inspector and set X to 28, Y to 100, W to 107, and H to 242.
17. Open the Behavior tab of the Property Inspector. Click the Plus button and select New Behavior. Name the new behavior “Picker.” Enter the code in Listing 15.4. Close the Script window.

LISTING 15.4 The Picker behavior.

```
property mySinger               -- the singer that is picked
--                              -- when the picker is clicked


on beginSprite me

    -- the score is laid out such that the hot spot is on the
    -- next channel after the singer
    mySinger = sprite(me.spriteNum - 1)

end

on mouseUp me

    -- inform the frame script that singer has been picked
    sendAllSprites(#pick, mySinger)

end

on mouseEnter me

    -- the mouse has entered the hot spot

    -- set the cursor to the hand
    cursor [ member("hand"), member("handMask") ]

end

on mouseLeave me

    -- the mouse has left the hot spot

    -- set the cursor back to the arrow
    cursor -1

end
```

18. Drag the Yellow Man cast member onto sprite channel 11 at frame 1.
19. Open the Behavior tab of the Property Inspector. Click the Plus button and select Singing Man.
20. Drag the Hot Spot cast member onto sprite channel 12 at frame 1. Open the Property Inspector and set X to 145, Y to 100, W to 107, and H to 242.

21. Open the Behavior tab of the Property Inspector. Click the Plus button and select Picker.
22. Drag the Orange Man cast member onto sprite channel 13 at frame 1.
23. Open the Behavior tab of the Property Inspector. Click the Plus button and select Singing Man.
24. Drag the Hot Spot cast member onto sprite channel 14 at frame 1. Open the Property Inspector and set X to 261, Y to 100, W to 107, and H to 242.
25. Open the Behavior tab of the Property Inspector. Click the Plus button and select Picker.
26. Drag the Blue Man cast member onto sprite channel 15 at frame 1.
27. Open the Behavior tab of the Property Inspector. Click the Plus button and select Singing Man.
28. Drag the Hot Spot cast member onto sprite channel 16 at frame 1. Open the Property Inspector and set X to 378, Y to 100, W to 107, and H to 242.
29. Open the Behavior tab of the Property Inspector. Click the Plus button and select Picker.
30. Drag the Green Man cast member onto sprite channel 17 at frame 1.
31. Open the Behavior tab of the Property Inspector. Click the Plus button and select Singing Man.
32. Drag the Hot Spot cast member onto sprite channel 18 at frame 1. Open the Property Inspector and set X to 504, Y to 100, W to 107, and H to 242.
33. Open the Behavior tab of the Property Inspector. Click the Plus button and select Picker.
34. Double-click on the frame script channel for frame 1, remove the existing code, and enter the code in Listing 15.5 in the Script window. Name the behavior "Controller." Close the Script window.

LISTING 15.5 The Controller behavior.

```
global gGameState           -- the state of the game
global gSingingMen          -- the list of singers
global gSequence            -- the sequence in which they sing
global gSequenceItem        -- the current singer in the sequence

property myWrong            -- the player made a mistake
property myPickedSinger     -- the player picked a singer

on enterFrame me

    -- check the state of the game
    case gGameState of
      #computerTurn:
```

```
        -- computer's turn; let the computer play the sequence
        me.computerTurn()
      #playerTurn:
        -- player's turn; let the player enter the sequence
        me.playerTurn()
    end case

end

on computerTurn me

    -- check if this is the start of the computer's turn
    if gSequenceItem = 0 then
      -- at the beginning of the computer's turn, add a random
      -- singer to the sequence
      gSequence.append(gSingingMen[random(gSingingMen.count)])
      -- start playing the sequence with the first singer
      gSequenceItem = 1
      -- let the first singer sing
      gSequence[gSequenceItem].sing()
    end if

    -- check if the current singer is still singing
    if not gSequence[gSequenceItem].amSinging() then
      -- the current singer has finished singing, so go to the
      -- next singer
      gSequenceItem = gSequenceItem + 1
      -- check if there are any singers left
      if gSequenceItem > gSequence.count then
        -- start the player's turn
        me.startPlayerTurn()
        -- and the computer's turn is done
        return
      end if
      -- let the next singer sing
      gSequence[gSequenceItem].sing()
    end if

end

on startPlayerTurn me

    -- no singers left, so start over from the beginning
    gSequenceItem = 0
```

```
    -- and let the player play back the sequence
    gGameState = #playerTurn
    -- no singers have been picked
    myPickedSinger = void
    -- and the player has not picked a wrong singer
    myWrong = false

end

on playerTurn me

    -- check if the player has picked a singer
    if myPickedSinger <> void then
      -- check if the picked singer is not singing and is not the wrong
      -- singer
      if not myPickedSinger.amSinging() then
        -- check if the singer is the correct singer
        if gSequence[gSequenceItem] = myPickedSinger then
          -- since the correct singer has been picked, allow the
 -- player
          -- to pick another singer
          myPickedSinger = void
          -- check if there are any other singers to pick
          if gSequenceItem = gSequence.count then
            -- there are no other singers to pick, so start over
         -- from the beginning
            gSequenceItem = 0
            -- update the score to the current length of the
         -- sequence
            member("score").text = string(gSequence.count)
            -- and let the computer play
            gGameState = #computerTurn
          end if
        else
          -- the player has picked the wrong singer
          -- check if the sound channel is available
          if not soundBusy(1) then
            -- the sound channel is available. check if the player
         -- is already wrong.
            if not myWrong then
              -- the player is not already wrong, so mark that the
           -- player is wrong
              myWrong = true
              -- play the wrong singer sound
              puppetSound 1, member("wrong")
```

```
          end if
        end if
      end if
    end if
    -- check if the wrong singer sound has finshed if the player
  -- is wrong
    if myWrong and not soundBusy(1) then
      -- stop playing
      gGameState = #notPlaying
      -- and go to the instructions screen
      go to frame "Wrong"
    end if
  end if

end

on exitFrame

  -- stay in this frame
  go to the frame

end

on pick me, whichSinger

  -- check if it is the player's turn and that the player can
  -- pick another singer
  if gGameState = #playerTurn and not myPickedSinger then
    -- the player has picked a singer, so we move up in the
    -- sequence of singers
    gSequenceItem = gSequenceItem + 1
    -- save the picked singer for later
    myPickedSinger = whichSinger
    -- and let the picked singer sing
    myPickedSinger.sing()
  end if

end
```

35. Open the Script window and click the Plus button. Name the new script "Global." Enter the code in Listing 15.6.
36. Open the Property Inspector and click the Script tab. Set the type of movie to Movie Script.

LISTING 15.6 The global movie script.

```
global gGameState          -- the state of the game
global gSingingMen         -- the list of singers

on prepareMovie

    -- initially not playing; waiting for player to
    -- click the Play button
    gGameState = #notPlaying
    -- let the Singers themselves fill the list of singers
    gSingingMen = []
    -- clear the score
    member("score").text = ""

end
```

37. Rewind the movie and play it. Clicking the Play button begins the game. The other buttons highlight when rolled over, but don't do anything when clicked. Just be certain not to get any wrong! There is no Wrong screen yet, so after the wrong sound, an error occurs. See Figure 15.6 for what the Score should look like and Figure 15.7 for the Stage.

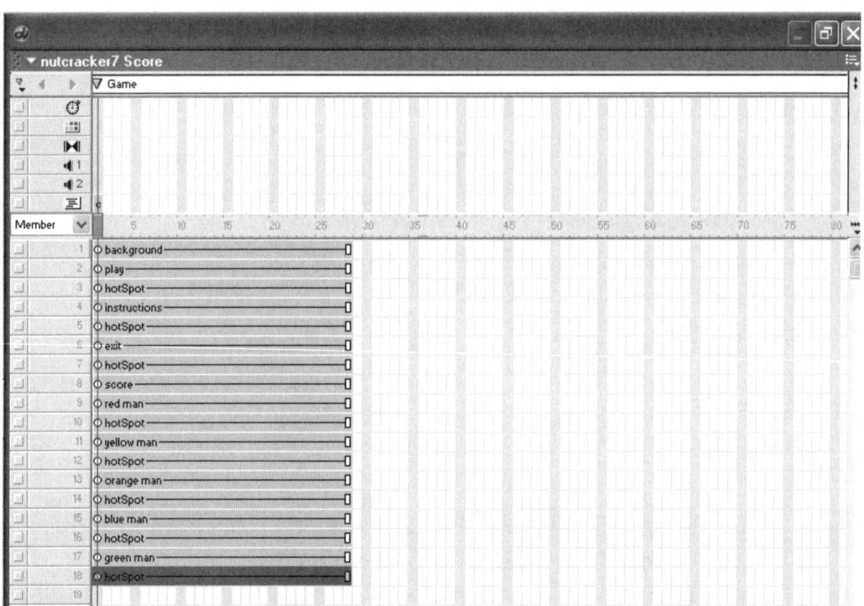

FIGURE 15.6 The Score after finishing the Game screen.

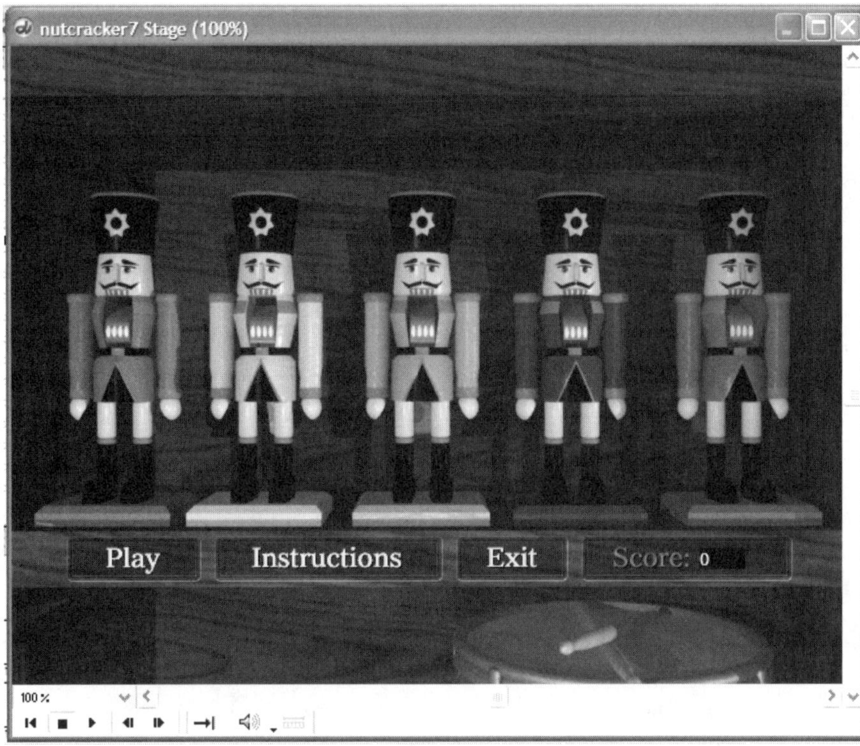

FIGURE 15.7 The Stage after finishing the Game screen.

The Instruction Screen

Now that we have created the primary game functionality, we can focus on the additional details. We start with the Instruction screen, which is activated by clicking the Instructions button in the user interface.

1. Drag the Panel cast member onto sprite channel 19 at frame 7.
2. Drag the Instruction Text cast member onto sprite channel 20 at frame 7. Open the Property Inspector and set X to 44 and Y to 423. Set the Ink to Background Transparent.
3. Drag the Exit Down cast member onto sprite channel 21 at frame 7.
4. Drag the Hot Spot cast member onto sprite channel 22 at frame 7.
5. Open the Property Inspector and set X to 610, Y to 413, W to 22, and H to 22 for the Hot Spot sprite.

6. Click the Behavior tab of the Property Inspector. Click the Plus button and pick New Behavior. Name the new behavior "Push Button." Enter the code in Listing 15.7. Close the Script window.

LISTING 15.7 The Push Button behavior.

```
property myPushSprite

on beginSprite me

    -- the pushed in sprite is in the preceding sprite channel
    myPushSprite = sprite(me.spriteNum - 1)

    -- make the hilight invisible initially
    myPushSprite.blend = 0

end

on mouseEnter me

    -- the mouse has rolled over the hot spot

    -- set the cursor and the cursor mask
    cursor [ member "hand", member "handMask" ]

end

on mouseLeave me

    -- the mouse has rolled out of the hot spot

    -- back to the arrow cursor
    cursor -1

end

on mouseDown me

    -- the mouse button pushed

    -- make the push image visible
    myPushSprite.blend = 100

end
```

```
on mouseUp me

    -- the mouse button released

    -- make the push image invisible again
    myPushSprite.blend = 0
end
```

7. Back in the Behavior tab, click the Plus button and select New Behavior. Name the new behavior "Go to Game." Enter the following code.

```
on mouseUp me

    -- go to the Game screen
    go to frame "Game"

end
```

8. Select the Hot Spot sprite in sprite channel 5.
9. Open the Behavior tab of the Property Inspector. Click the Plus button and select New Behavior. Name the new behavior "Go to Instructions." Enter the following code. Close the Script window.

```
on mouseUp me

    -- go to the Instructions screen
    go to frame "Instructions"

end
```

10. In the marker channel, create a new marker for frame 7 and name it "Instructions."
11. Double-click the frame script channel for frame 7, remove the existing code, and enter the following code in the Script window. Name the behavior "Stay Put." Close the Script window.

```
    on exitFrame me

    -- stay in the current frame
    go to the frame

end
```

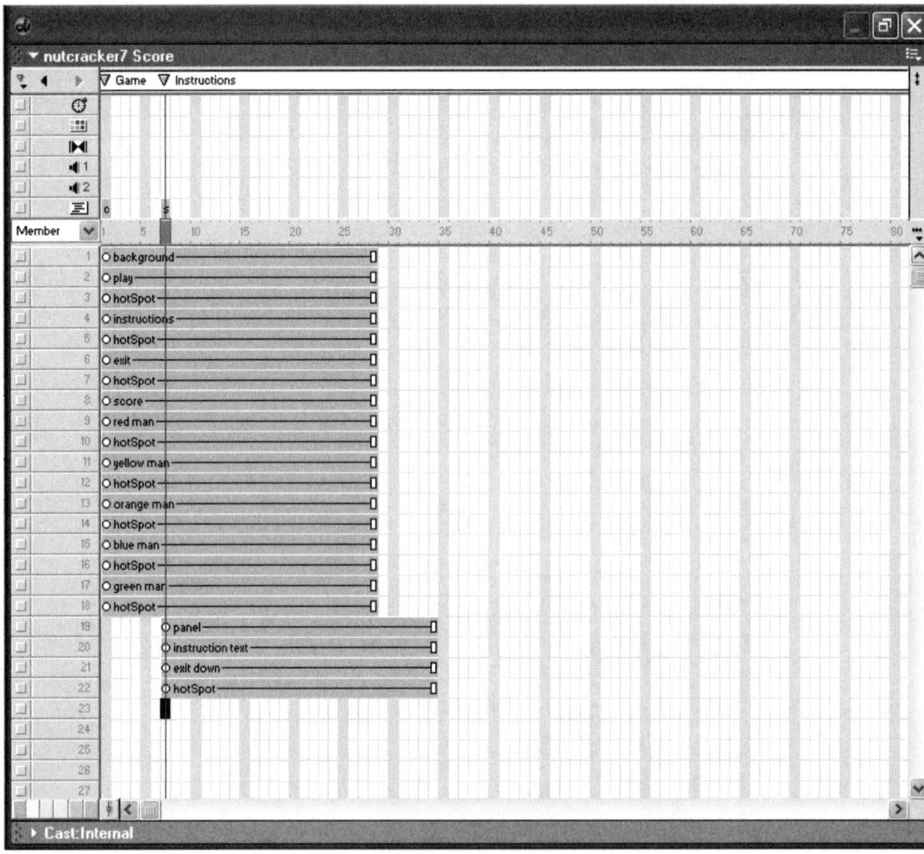

FIGURE 15.8 The Score after finishing the Instructions screen.

12. Rewind the movie and click Play. Now, click the Instructions button. This should take you to the Instructions screen. Clicking the "X" button returns you to the Game screen. See Figure 15.8 for what the Score should look like at this point. See Figure 15.9 for what the Stage looks like at frame 7, the Instructions screen.

The Wrong Screen

Next, we create the screen that informs the player that the sequence of Singing Men he selected is incorrect.

1. Split the Instruction Text sprite at sprite channel 20 at frame 15.
2. Select the Instruction Text sprite at frame 15. Exchange cast members with the Wrong Text cast member.

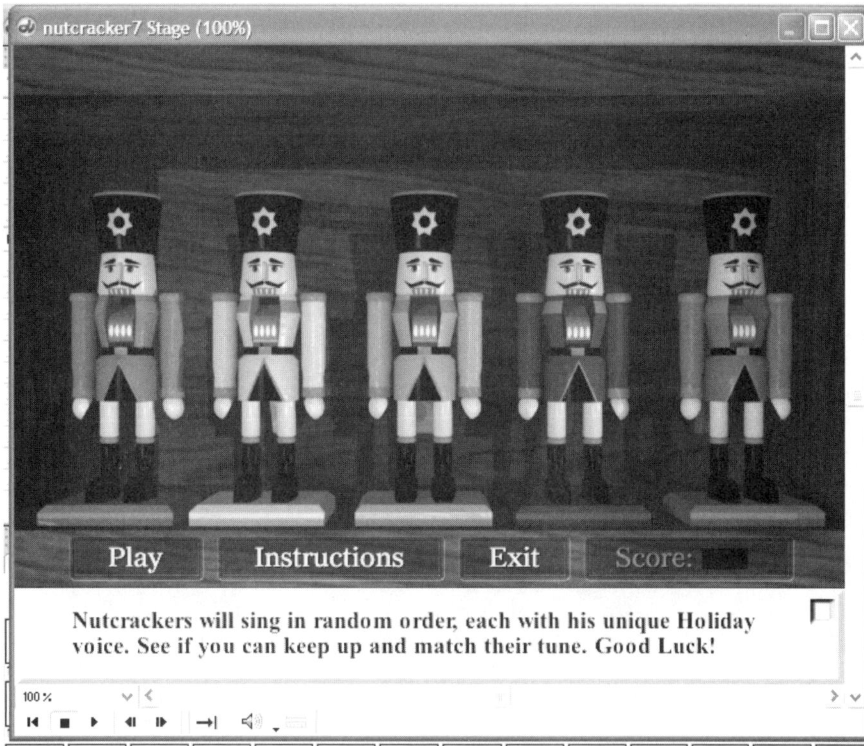

FIGURE 15.9 The Stage after finishing the Instructions screen.

3. Drag the Stay Put behavior onto the frame script channel at frame 15.
4. Add a marker in the marker channel at frame 15. Name it "Wrong."
5. Rewind and play the movie. Click Play and get the sequence wrong. This time, you get a dialog box telling you that you did not repeat the sequence properly. See Figure 15.10 for what the score should look like, and Figure 15.11 for what the stage should look like at frame 15, the Wrong screen.

The Exit Screen

Finally, we create the screen that is displayed when the player clicks the Exit button.

1. Drag the Mall Map cast member onto sprite channel 23 at frame 20. Open the Property Inspector and set X to 328 and Y to 217.
2. Split the Wrong Text sprite at sprite channel 20 at frame 20.
3. Select the Wrong Text sprite at frame 20. Exchange cast members with the Coupon Exit cast member.

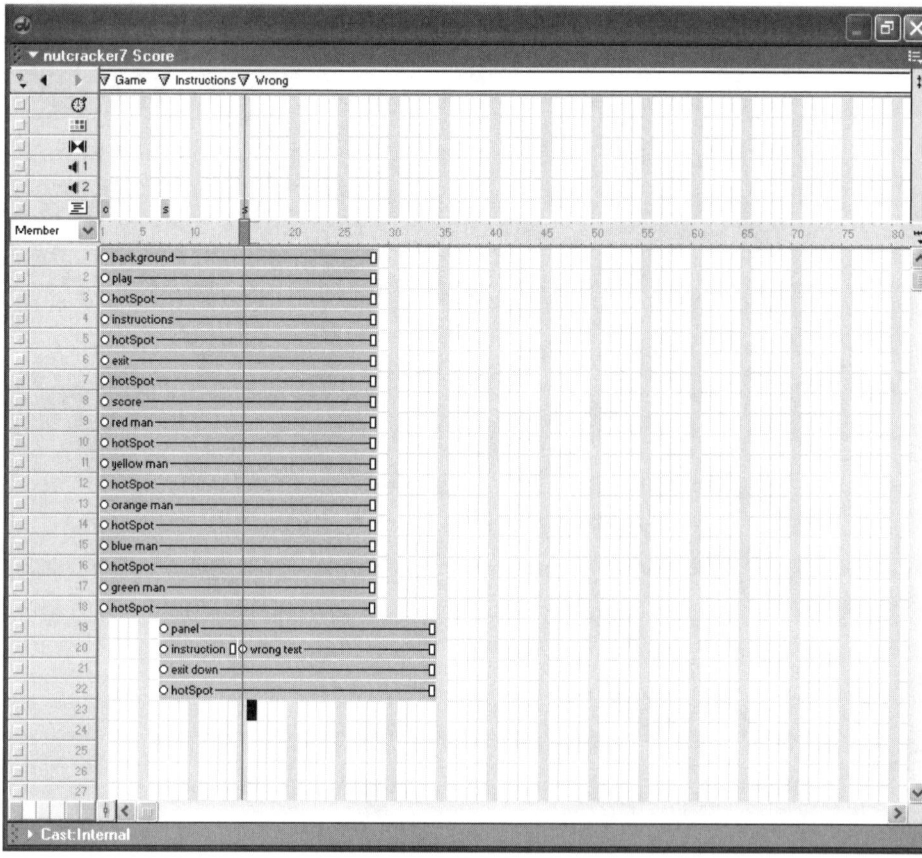

FIGURE 15.10 The Score after finishing the Wrong screen.

4. Open the Behavior tab of the Property Inspector. Click the Plus button and select New Behavior. Name the behavior "Go to Web Site." Enter the following code in the Script window. Close the Script window.

```
on hyperlinkClicked me, data

    goToNetPage(data)

end
```

5. Split the Hot Spot sprite at sprite channel 22 at sprite 20.
6. Click the Behavior tab of the Property Inspector. Remove the Go to Game behavior.

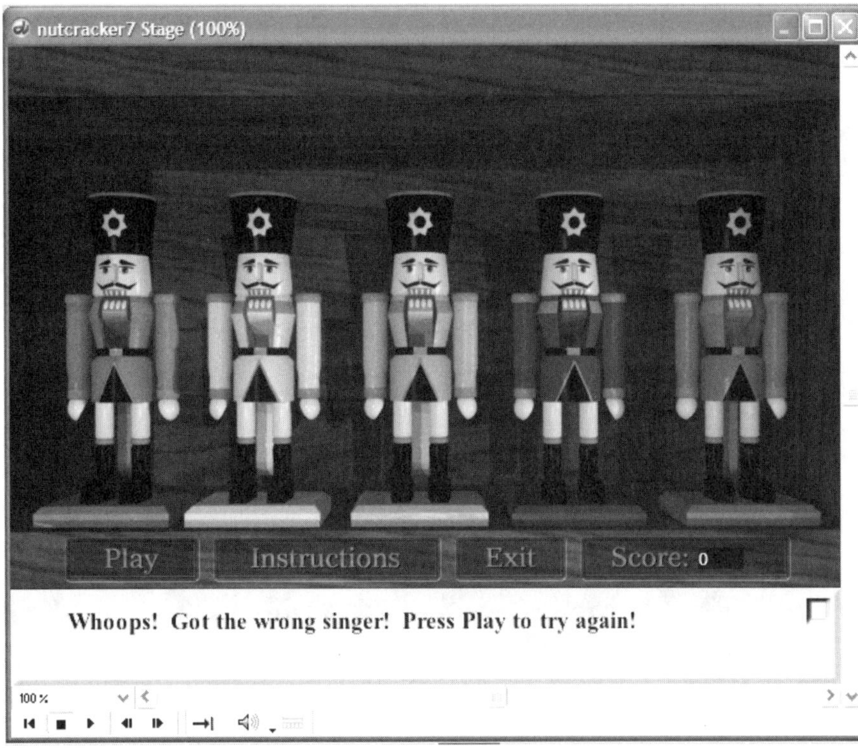

FIGURE 15.11 The Stage after finishing the Wrong screen.

7. Click the Plus button and select New Behavior. Name the behavior Quit Game. Enter the following code in the Script window. Close the Script window.

```
on mouseUp me

    -- exit the projector
    quit

end
```

8. Drag the Stay Put behavior onto the frame script channel at frame 20.
9. Select the Hot Spot sprite at sprite channel 6. Open the Behavior tab of the Property Inspector. Click the Plus button and select New Behavior. Name the behavior "Go to Exit." Enter the following code in the Script window. Close the Script window.

```
on mouseUp me

    -- mouse released over exit game button

    -- go to the Exit screen
    go to frame "Exit"

end
```

10. Add a marker in the marker channel at frame 20. Name it "Exit."
11. Rewind the movie and play it. Now, click the Exit button. The game should now take you to the Exit screen with the mall map. Clicking the Exit button here causes Director MX to exit (which causes the projector to exit). See Figure 15.12 for what the Score should look like, and Figure 15.13 for what the Stage should look like at frame 20, the Exit screen.

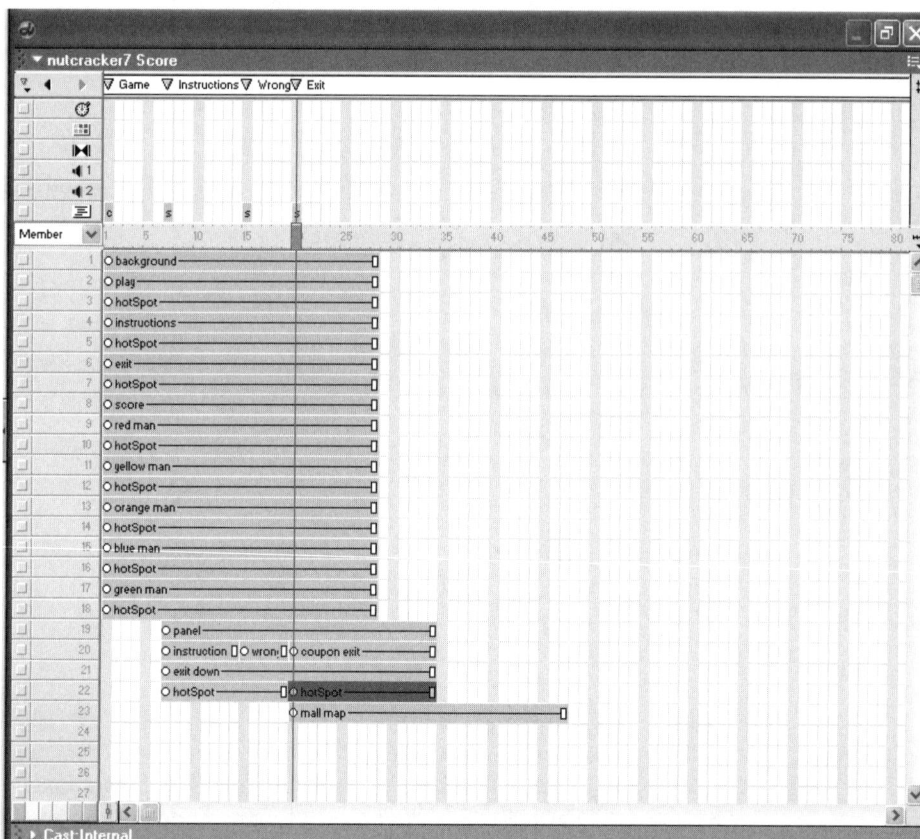

FIGURE 15.12 The Score after finishing the Exit screen.

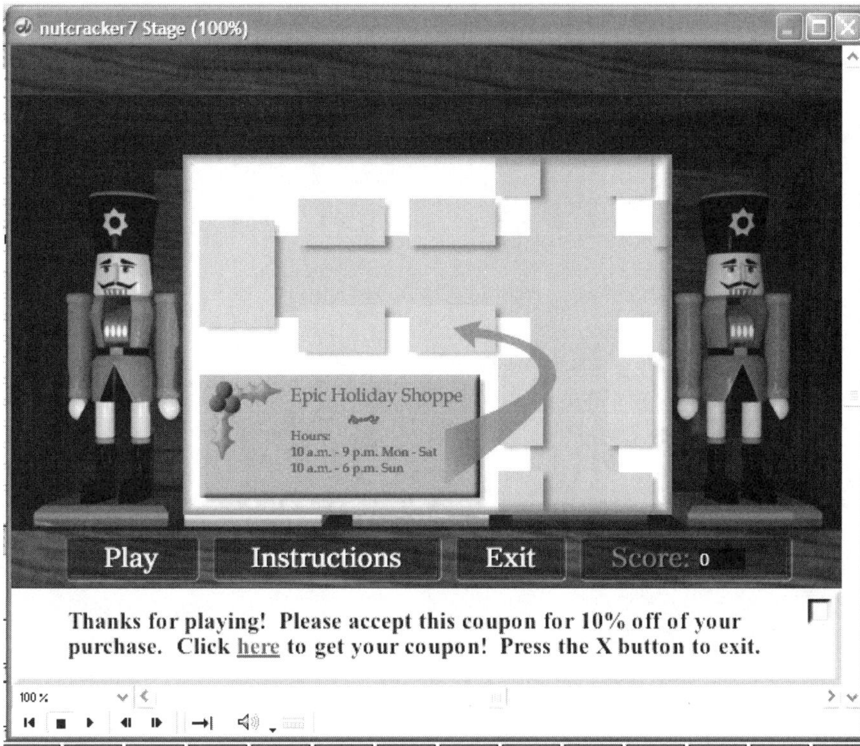

FIGURE 15.13 The Stage after finishing the Exit screen.

SUMMARY

This concludes the design and implementation of the epic Holiday Shoppe game, a simple "Simon Says" game. The major concept in this game is the management of a group of sprites with lists. The first list is the list of singers and the second sequence of singers, with each member of this sequence being the singer number in the list. This mechanism makes it very easy to have each singer sing in turn, for instance, as the movie goes forward while the computer is generating the sequence for the player to reproduce. This game also demonstrates the use of mass-market mailing combined with the attractive power of an Advergame to quickly generate brand recognition when time is of the essence.

16 High Voltage Pinball

THE CONCEPT

Identifying Your Product: epic Batteries

For as long as anyone can remember, epic Batteries have sold fairly well, but never well enough to outshine the country's two leading brands of batteries. In sales, epic has always come in a distant third. Certainly, third place in nationwide sales is not bad, but epic wants to be number one! And with the acquisition of some new technological advances and recent product-line expansion, the company just might have a shot. All epic needs now are a few well-placed billboards, some good TV and radio spots, and maybe an Advergame or two.

Outlining a Game for epic Batteries

When you think of batteries, chances are that you picture CD players, remote control cars, little toy robots, and other such gadgetry. Or, maybe you think of more basic concepts, such as electricity and magnetism. With High Voltage Pinball, the idea is to combine the low-tech fun of a classic pinball game with such high-tech features as electromagnetic attraction and repulsion. The game itself tells potential epic battery users that there is always room for a good thing to be made better through technology.

As with any computer pinball game, High Voltage Pinball has a few basic requirements. There must be a ball, a plunger (the thing that launches the ball onto the table), two flippers (to allow the user to have some control over the ball), barriers to guide the path of the ball, and, of course, a few obstacles to make the game fun to play. What makes High Voltage Pinball different from other pinball games (other than its appearance of course) is the type of obstacles that appear on the table. In addition to the basics (things that light up, give points, and/or bounce the ball in a given direction), we should be certain to include some special obstacles that relate to the product in some way.

The table should include a few obstacles with intermittent electromagnetic charges (designed to attract or repulse the ball) and a separate obstacle or two that trigger these charges. One of these triggers looks like a large epic battery and displays either a plus or a minus sign depending on the magnetism mode. The other trigger sets off a very short but extreme "power surge" when the ball rolls over it.

Designing the High Voltage Pinball Interface

When creating any pinball game, special attention to the layout of the table is essential. There must be adequate spacing between obstacles and barriers to allow the ball to move freely. After the ball is launched, it must be able to bounce around the top of the table for a while rather than consistently falling straight down to the flippers. Even after you think you have designed a good table layout, you may run into problems when you begin testing and debugging your game. It is important to stay flexible and not spend too much time on graphics until you are fairly certain that your layout will work properly.

Of course, your game's interface consists of more than just the layout of its pinball table. The player must have some instructions for play and be able to start and stop as he chooses. Therefore, the game's graphical interface should include a fair amount of text and a button to allow the user to switch between the Introduction, the Play, and the Pause modes. And throughout play, the title of the game, the number of balls remaining, and the player's score should appear quite prominent and obvious. Figure 16.1 shows a very basic form of the layout chosen for High Voltage Pinball.

Notice the differences in font size and spacing between the different text fields in Figure 16.2. When designing your own games with instructions that must fit in a particular area, feel free to play with font size and line spacing until you have

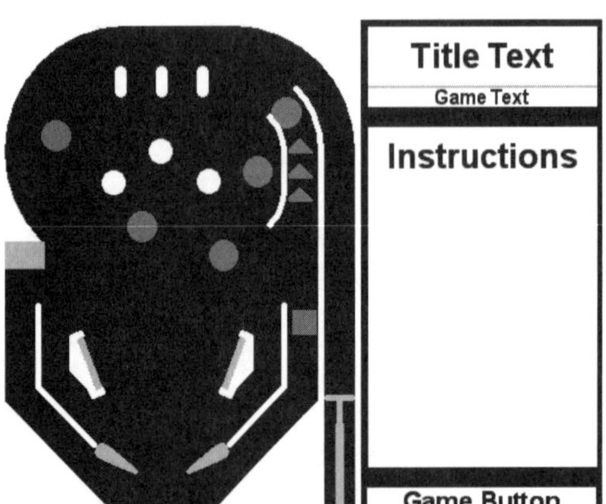

FIGURE 16.1 The basic layout of the High Voltage Pinball interface.

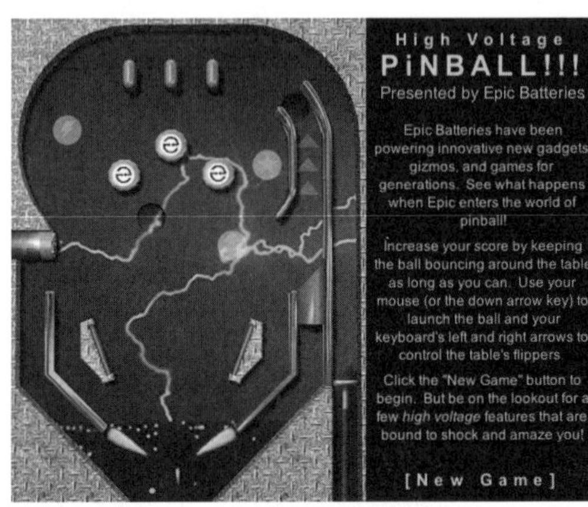

FIGURE 16.2 The High Voltage Pinball interface complete with text and graphics.

things looking just right. The game's interface really starts to take shape once text and graphics are applied, as shown in Figure 16.2.

THE CREATION

Identifying the Elements of High Voltage Pinball

Start by compiling a list of all the major elements your game requires. Even a game as complex as pinball can be broken down into just a few basic components. This is achieved by grouping similar components and possibly ignoring unimportant or minor elements of the game. High Voltage Pinball consists of the following major elements:

Title text: Displays "High Voltage PiNBALL!!!" in a large font

Game text: Displays the number of balls remaining and the player's current score

Instruction text: Displays a plug for epic Batteries and a short explanation of how to play the game

Table: Contains all the graphical elements of the game's pinball table

Ball: Is indirectly controlled by the player to gain points

Plunger: Is directly controlled by the player to launch the ball

Flippers: Are directly controlled by the player to keep the ball from being lost

Border: Keeps the ball from leaving the table in an inappropriate manner

Walls: Direct the path of the ball by blocking its passage

Obstacles: Affect the player's score and/or the path of the ball in various ways

Game button: Pauses, resumes, or starts a new game depending on the current game's status

Recognizing How the Game's Elements Interact

When High Voltage Pinball first begins, its New Game button is the only part of the interface that is active. This helps to ensure that the player actually reads the introductory instruction text rather than simply figuring out the game by trial and error. This is important because the introductory text also mentions epic Batteries. And after all, High Voltage Pinball is first and foremost an advertisement.

After the player discovers the New Game button, the pinball table becomes active, and the plunger fetches a new ball. By using either the mouse or the keyboard, the player then launches the pinball onto the table. The ball's sprite is stored in a global variable to allow the rest of the game's elements to easily test for collisions and other forms of interaction. The player only has direct control over the plunger and the two flippers. These items are, of course, used to keep the pinball bouncing around as long as possible. When the ball finally does fall off the bottom edge of the table, the cycle starts over with the plunger again fetching the offscreen ball. Figure 16.3 uses a flowchart to illustrate the logic of this process.

Identifying the Scripts of High Voltage Pinball

If you've looked at the High Voltage Pinball game from within Director MX, then you've probably noticed that it uses quite a few different Lingo scripts. Certainly, the design of the game could be more centralized by using fewer behavior scripts and a much larger movie script, but this sort of design would ignore the main part of programming in Director MX that makes it so convenient and fun—encapsulation. This is the idea that each element in a Director MX movie (effectively each sprite) should, for the most part, be in control of itself. Some central control is necessary of course, but, in general, the elements of High Voltage Pinball are fairly well encapsulated.

The game's `Main` movie script is used to initialize certain variables as the movie begins, but its main function is to store global functions to be called by the various behavior scripts when needed. Game is actually a behavior, but because it is applied

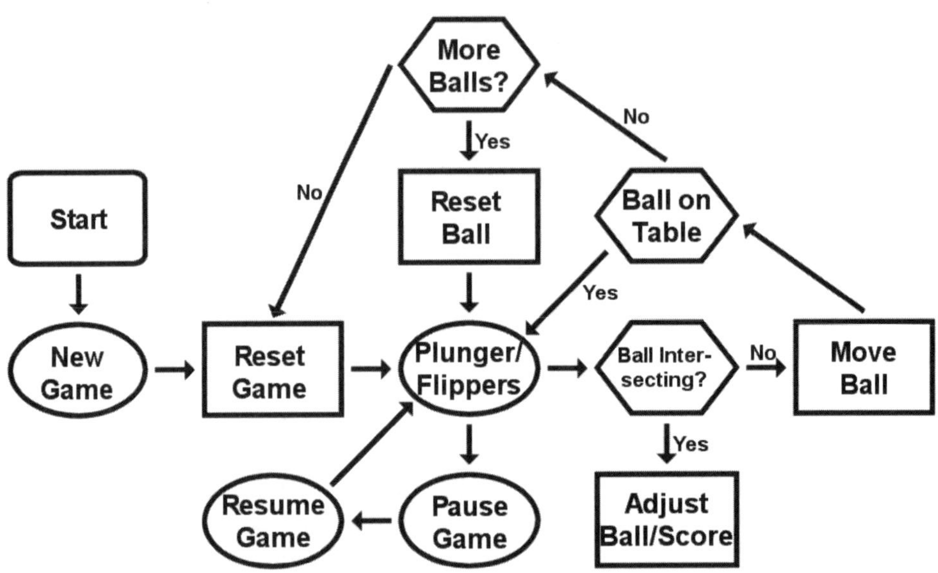

FIGURE 16.3 A flowchart for the High Voltage Pinball Advergame.

to a frame instead of a sprite, it works more like a global movie script. Upon entering its associated frame, Game calls the functions `preRefresh`, `refresh`, and `postRefresh` from any and all behaviors containing such functions. Then, it decrements the `timer` property of a global game list variable. This property is used to keep temporary magnetism modes going for a set amount of time and then to stop them. When the behavior's `exitFrame` handler is triggered, Game simply plays the current frame over again, effectively calling its own `enterFrame` handler and beginning the cycle anew.

You might think that because the pinball's sprite is so essential to play, its associated behavior would require a large amount of code. Actually, the Ball script is quite simple. All the code dealing with interaction between the ball and other sprites is handled within the behaviors of those sprites. Ball deals solely with internal issues such as keeping its trail and mask sprites updated. The entire behavior can be summarized in the following pseudocode.

```
The global variables are ball and game.
The property variables are trail, mask, x, y, oldX, oldY, stepY, and
stepY.

Begin the beginSprite handler with me as a parameter.
    Set ball to the sprite in the channel indicated by the spriteNum
property of me.
    Set trail to a list containing the sprites in the three channels
preceding ball.
    Set mask to a list containing the sprites in the two channels
preceding trail.
    Call the reset function.
End the handler.

Begin the reset function.
    Set x to 283.
    Set y to 600.
    Set oldX and oldY to x and y.
    Set stepX and stepY to 0.
End the function.

Begin the postRefresh function.
    Move ball to the spot indicated by x and y.
    Spread out the trail sprites evenly between the new location of
ball and the spot indicated by oldX and oldY.

    If the y property of ball is less than 550...
        Increment stepY by the gravity property of game.
```

```
            Multiply stepX by the friction property of game.
            Multiply stepY by the friction property of game.
            Make sure that stepX is no less than -30 and no larger than 30.
            Make sure that stepY is no less than -30 and no larger than 30.
        Otherwise, if the y property of ball is less than 600...
            Call the reset function.
            Decrement the ball's property of game by 1.

        Set oldX and oldY to x and y.
        Increment x and y by stepX and stepY.
        Call the global setBallMask function with x and y supplied as
    arguments.
    End the function.
```

The Plunger behavior consists of two small event handlers (`beginSprite` for variable initialization and `mouseDown` for mouse interaction) and a large `preRefresh` function. The bulk of this `preRefresh` function deals with the movement of the plunger itself, but there is a small section dealing with the Ball sprite. It states that if the Plunger and Ball sprites are intersecting, the ball should rest on top of the plunger and Ball's `stepY` property should be set to mimic that of Plunger (provided that the ball is not already moving upward more quickly than the plunger). The Flipper behavior is very similar to Plunger. However, its movement deals with the rotation property instead of `locV`, and its interaction with the Ball sprite is a bit more complex.

The only job of the Border and Wall behaviors is to deal with ball intersection. If the ball is intersecting with one of these behaviors' associated sprites, the script must move the ball so that it no longer intersects with any barriers, and then it must adjust the ball's velocity appropriately. The difficult part is figuring out how to adjust the ball's velocity. This can be achieved more or less through trial and error. The Obstacle behavior also deals with ball intersection, but it does so in a variety of possible ways depending on the values supplied for its script parameters (found in the `getPropertyDescriptionList` handler). Also, Obstacle is different than the Border and Wall scripts because it uses a `refresh` function instead of `preRefresh`. If you think back to the Game behavior, recall that the `preRefresh` functions are always called prior to `refresh`. This means that all ball–obstacle interaction occurs after interaction between the ball and barriers, such as borders and walls.

Putting It All Together

We have walked through the development of the High Voltage Pinball Advergame starting with the product and ideas, moving on to layout and interface design, and finally analyzing the game's elements, logic, and Lingo scripts. Now all that remains is for you to build the game yourself.

1. Open a copy of Macromedia Director MX. Director MX automatically creates a new blank movie.
2. Choose Save from the File menu and save the movie to your hard disk.
3. Click the Stage. Director MX updates the Property Inspector.
4. Click the Movie tab of the Property Inspector.
5. Type "500" and "400" in the Stage Size fields.
6. Type "#000000" in the Color field.

Creating the Media Cast Members

To create the media cast members, perform the following steps.

1. Click the Cast window. Director MX updates the Property Inspector.
2. Type "Media" in the Name field, as shown in Figure 16.4.
3. Click the Import button on the Toolbar.
4. Navigate to \files\templates\chapter16\ folder on the CD-ROM, select all the files in the directory, and click Import.

ON THE CD

5. Select the Same Settings for Remaining Images checkbox and click OK. Your movie's Media cast should now contain the members shown in Figure 16.5.

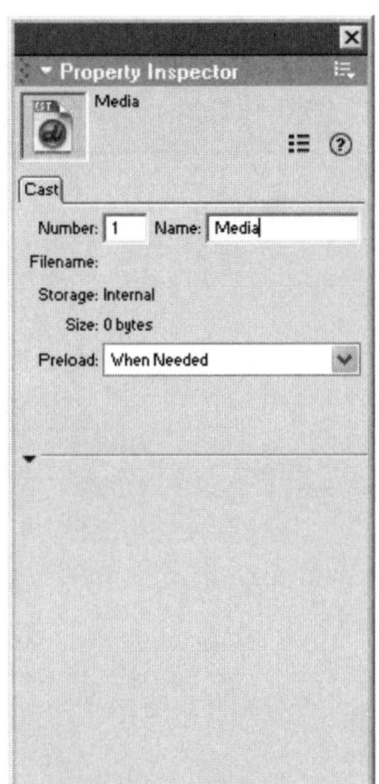

FIGURE 16.4 Renaming the movie's Internal cast.

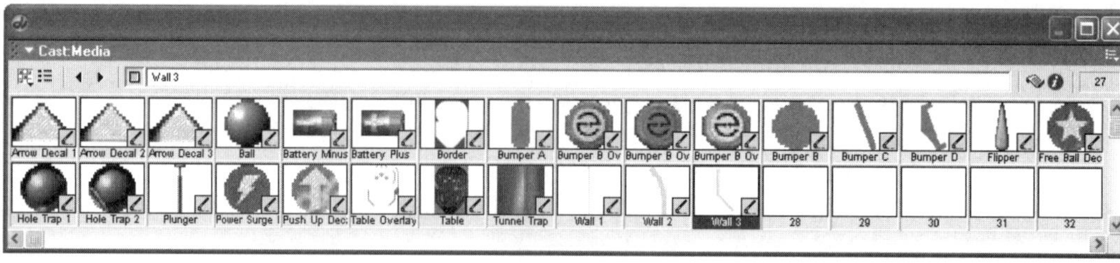

FIGURE 16.5 The imported cast members of High Voltage Pinball.

6. Within the Cast window, double-click the Plunger member.
7. Within the Paint window, select the Registration Point tool, adjust the crosshairs to line up with the top edge of the Plunger bitmap, as shown in Figure 16.6, and close the Paint window.
8. Within the Cast window, double-click the Flipper member.
9. Within the Paint window, select the Registration Point tool, adjust the crosshairs to line up five pixels from the bottom edge of the Flipper bitmap, and close the Paint window.
10. Within the Cast window, double-click the Hole Trap 2 member.

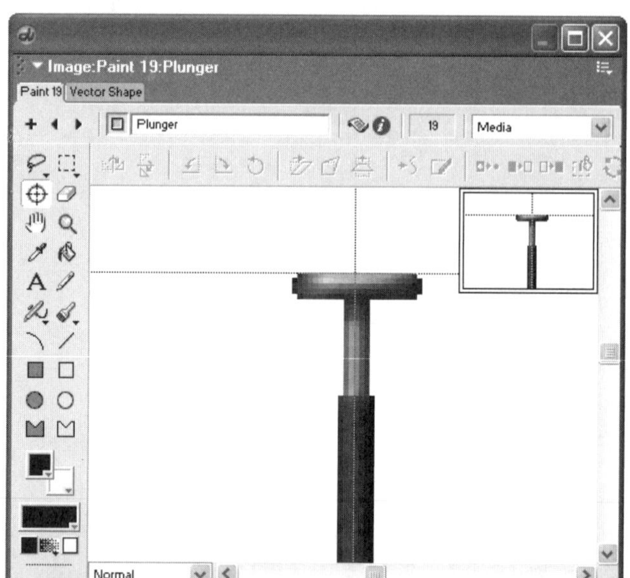

FIGURE 16.6 Adjusting the registration point of the Plunger member.

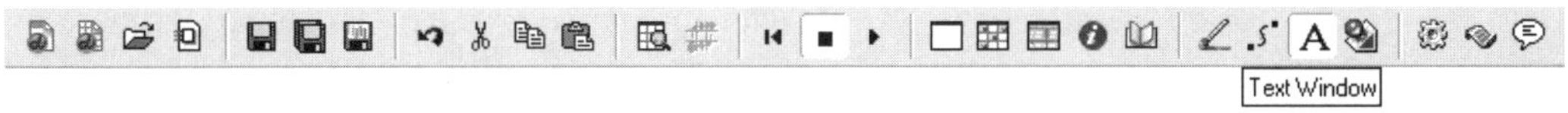

FIGURE 16.7 The Toolbar's Text Window button.

11. Within the Paint window, select the Registration Point tool, move the crosshairs one pixel up and to the right, and close the Paint window.
12. Click the Text Window button on the Toolbar, as shown in Figure 16.7.
13. Type "Presented by epic Batteries" in the Text window and then select it.
14. Choose Arial from the Font drop-down list.
15. Choose 14 from the Size drop-down list.
16. Click the Align Center button.
17. Check to make sure that the Bold, Italic, and Underline buttons are not depressed and the Kerning field is set to 0.
18. Type "Epic Text" in the Cast Member Name field and close the Text window, as shown in Figure 16.8.
19. Click an empty spot in the Cast window.
20. Click the Text Window button on the Toolbar.
21. Type "Balls: 3 / Score: 0" in the Text window.
22. Type "Game Text" in the Cast Member Name field and close the Text window.
23. Click an empty spot in the Cast window.
24. Click the Text Window button on the Toolbar.
25. Type the following text in the Text window and then select it.

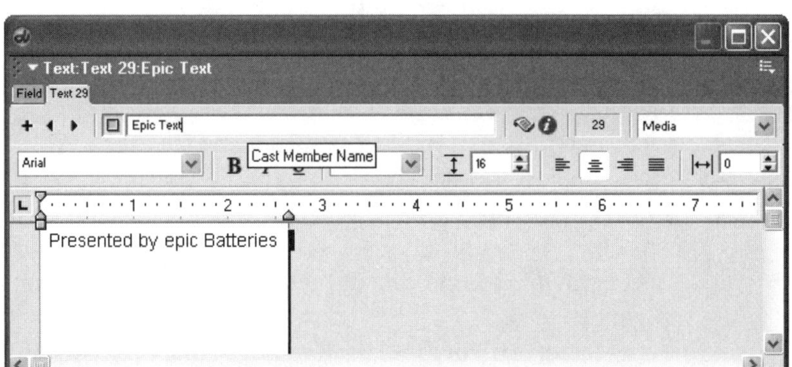

FIGURE 16.8 Naming the new epic Text cast member.

"epic Batteries have been powering innovative new gadgets, gizmos, and games for generations. See what happens when epic enters the world of pinball!" Press Enter, and then type, "Increase your score by keeping the ball bouncing around the table as long as you can. Use your mouse (or the down arrow key) to launch the ball and your keyboard's left and right arrows to control the table's flippers." Press Enter, and then type, "Click the New Game button to begin. But be on the lookout for a few high-voltage features that are bound to shock and amaze you!"

26. Choose 12 from the Size drop-down list.
27. Double-click the blank line after the first paragraph to select it and then type "6" in the Size drop-down list. Repeat for the blank line after the second paragraph.
28. Type "Instruction Text" in the Cast Member Name field and close the Text window.
29. Click an empty spot in the Cast window.
30. Click the Text Window button on the Toolbar.
31. Type "[New Game]" in the Text window and then select it.
32. Choose 14 from the Size drop-down list.
33. Click the Bold button.
34. Type "5" in the Kerning field.
35. Type "New Game Button" in the Cast Member Name field and close the Text window.
36. Click an empty spot in the Cast window.
37. Click the Text Window button on the Toolbar.
38. Type "[Pause Game]" in the Text window.
39. Type "Pause Game Button" in the Cast Member Name field and close the Text window.
40. Click an empty spot in the Cast window.
41. Click the Text Window button on the Toolbar.
42. Type "[Resume Game]" in the Text window.
43. Type "Resume Game Button" in the Cast Member Name field and close the Text window.
44. Click an empty spot in the Cast window.
45. Click the Text Window button on the Toolbar.
46. Type "High Voltage" in the Text window, press Enter, and then type "PiNBALL!!!".
47. Select only the second line of the text, and choose 24 from the Size drop-down list.
48. Type "Title Text" in the Cast Member Name field and close the Text window.

Setting Up Sprites on the Stage and in the Score

To set up sprites on the Stage and in the Score, perform the following steps.

1. Drag the Table member from the Cast window into cell 1 of channel 1 of the Score, as shown in Figure 16.9.
2. Drag the Border member from the Cast window into cell 1 of channel 2 of the Score.
3. Click cell 2 of channel 1 of the Score, hold down the Ctrl key, and then click cell 2 of channel 2.
4. Within the Property Inspector, type "150" in the X field, as shown in Figure 16.10.
5. Drag the Power Surge Decal member from the Cast window into cell 1 of channel 3 of the Score.
6. Click cell 2 of channel 3 of the Score. Director MX updates the Property Inspector.
7. Within the Property Inspector, type "47" in the X field and "92" in the Y field.

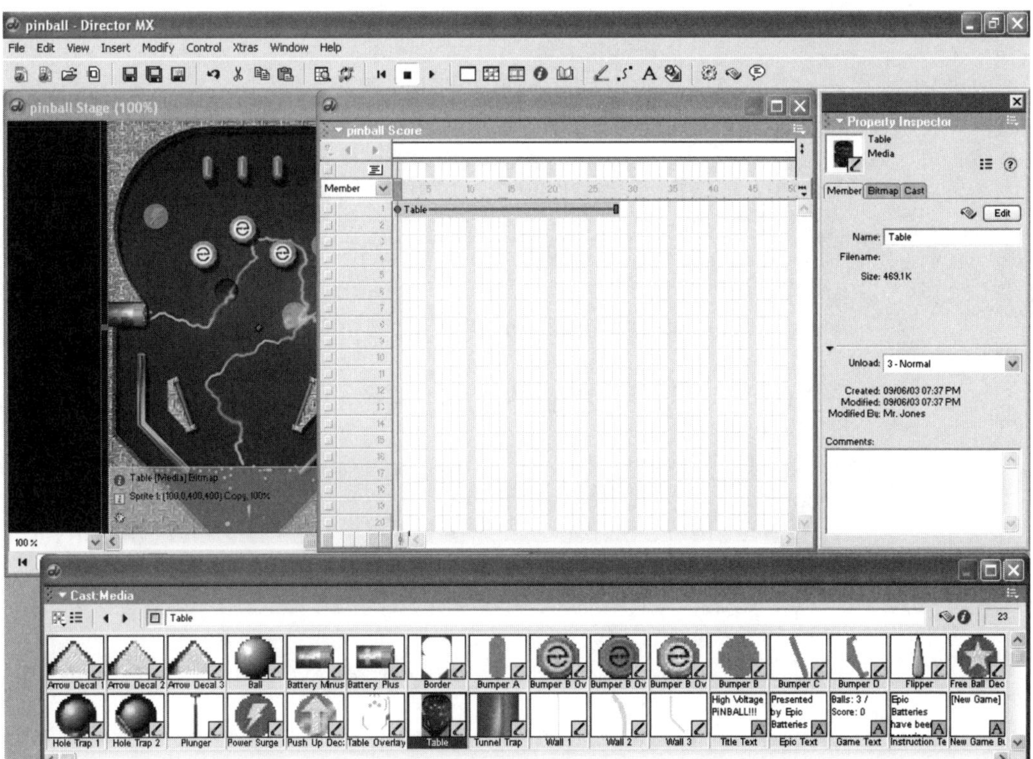

FIGURE 16.9 Creating a sprite from the Table cast member.

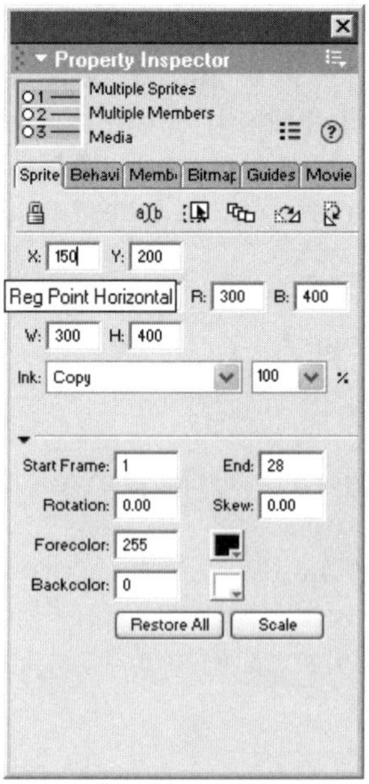

FIGURE 16.10 Positioning a Table sprite and a Border sprite on the Stage.

8. Drag the Free Ball Decal member from the Cast window into cell 1 of channel 4 of the Score.
9. Click cell 2 of channel 4 of the Score. Director MX updates the Property Inspector.
10. Within the Property Inspector, type "215" in the X field and "121" in the Y field.
11. Drag the Push Up Decal member from the Cast window into cell 1 of channel 5 of the Score.
12. Click cell 2 of channel 5 of the Score. Director MX updates the Property Inspector.
13. Within the Property Inspector, type "186" in the X field and "188" in the Y field.
14. Drag the Arrow Decal 1 member from the Cast window into cell 1 of channel 6 of the Score.
15. Click cell 2 of channel 6 of the Score. Director MX updates the Property Inspector.
16. Within the Property Inspector, type "101" in the Y field.
17. Drag the Arrow Decal 2 member from the Cast window into cell 1 of channel 7 of the Score.

18. Click cell 2 of channel 7 of the Score. Director MX updates the Property Inspector.
19. Within the Property Inspector, type "121" in the Y field.
20. Drag the Arrow Decal 3 member from the Cast window into cell 1 of channel 8 of the Score.
21. Click cell 2 of channel 8 of the Score. Director MX updates the Property Inspector.
22. Within the Property Inspector, type "140" in the Y field.
23. Click cell 2 of channel 6 of the Score, hold down the Shift key, and then click cell 2 of channel 8.
24. Within the Property Inspector, type "251" in the X field.
25. Drag the Ball member from the Cast window into cell 1 of channel 9 of the Score.
26. Click cell 2 of channel 9 of the Score. Director MX updates the Property Inspector.
27. Within the Property Inspector, type "283" in the X field and "600" in the Y field.
28. Right-click cell 2 of channel 9 of the Score and select Copy Sprites, as shown in Figure 16.11.

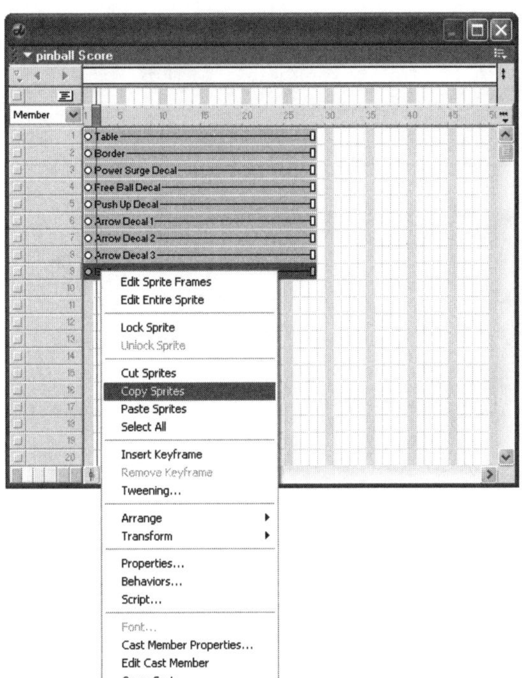

FIGURE 16.11 Copying the sprite in channel 9 of the Score.

29. Right-click cell 1 of channel 10 of the Score and select Paste Sprites. Repeat for channels 11 through 14.
30. Drag the Plunger member from the Cast window into cell 1 of channel 15 of the Score.
31. Click cell 2 of channel 15 of the Score. Director MX updates the Property Inspector.
32. Within the Property Inspector, type "282" in the X field and "300" in the Y field.
33. Choose Background Transparent from the Ink drop-down list.
34. Drag the Flipper member from the Cast window into cell 1 of channel 16 of the Score.
35. Click cell 2 of channel 16 of the Score. Director MX updates the Property Inspector.
36. Within the Property Inspector, type "85" in the X field and "344" in the Y field.
37. Type "120" in the Rotation field, as shown in Figure 16.12.
38. Right-click cell 2 of channel 16 of the Score and select Copy Sprites.
39. Right-click cell 1 of channel 17 of the Score and select Paste Sprites. Repeat for channels 18 through 20.

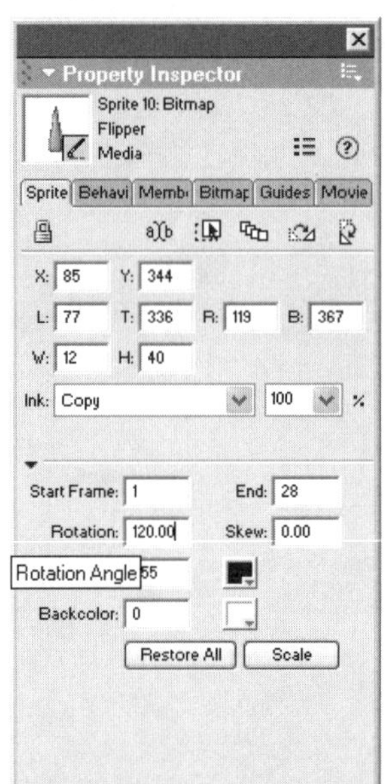

FIGURE 16.12 Rotating the first Flipper sprite 120 degrees to the right.

40. Click cell 2 of channel 20 of the Score. Director MX updates the Property Inspector.
41. Within the Property Inspector, type "185" in the X field.
42. Type "-120" in the Rotation field. Click the Flip Horizontal Button.
43. Right-click cell 2 of channel 20 of the Score and select Copy Sprites.
44. Right-click cell 1 of channel 21 of the Score and select Paste Sprites. Repeat for channels 22 and 23.
45. Drag the Table Overlay member from the Cast window into cell 1 of channel 24 of the Score.
46. Click cell 2 of channel 24 of the Score. Director MX updates the Property Inspector.
47. Within the Property Inspector, type "150" in the X field and "217" in the Y field.
48. Drag the Wall 1 member from the Cast window into cell 1 of channel 25 of the Score.
49. Click cell 2 of channel 25 of the Score. Director MX updates the Property Inspector.
50. Within the Property Inspector, type "257" in the X field and "226" in the Y field.
51. Drag the Wall 2 member from the Cast window into cell 1 of channel 26 of the Score.
52. Click cell 2 of channel 26 of the Score. Director MX updates the Property Inspector.
53. Within the Property Inspector, type "231" in the X field and "98" in the Y field.
54. Right-click cell 2 of channel 26 of the Score and select Copy Sprites.
55. Right-click cell 1 of channel 27 of the Score and select Paste Sprites.
56. Within the Property Inspector, type "144" in the Y field.
57. Click the Flip Vertical button, as shown in Figure 16.13.
58. Drag the Wall 3 member from the Cast window into cell 1 of channel 28 of the Score.
59. Click cell 2 of channel 28 of the Score. Director MX updates the Property Inspector.
60. Within the Property Inspector, type "55" in the X field and "284" in the Y field.
61. Right-click cell 2 of channel 28 of the Score and select Copy Sprites.
62. Right-click cell 1 of channel 29 of the Score and select Paste Sprites.
63. Within the Property Inspector, type "215" in the X field.
64. Click the Flip Horizontal button.
65. Drag the Bumper A member from the Cast window into cell 1 of channel 30 of the Score.

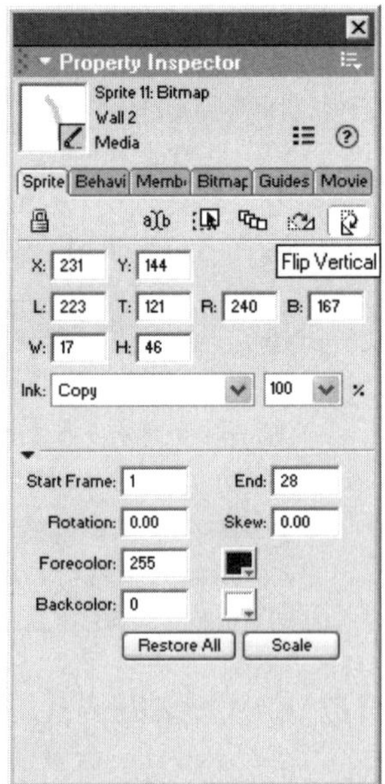

FIGURE 16.13 Flipping the new Wall 2 sprite vertically.

66. Click cell 2 of channel 30 of the Score. Director MX updates the Property Inspector.
67. Within the Property Inspector, type "101" in the X field and "49" in the Y field.
68. Right-click cell 2 of channel 30 of the Score and select Copy Sprites.
69. Right-click cell 1 of channel 31 of the Score and select Paste Sprites.
70. Click cell 2 of channel 31 of the Score. Director MX updates the Property Inspector.
71. Within the Property Inspector, type "135" in the X field.
72. Right-click cell 1 of channel 32 of the Score and select Paste Sprites.
73. Click cell 2 of channel 32 of the Score. Director MX updates the Property Inspector.
74. Within the Property Inspector, type "169" in the X field.
75. Drag the Bumper B member from the Cast window into cell 1 of channel 33 of the Score.
76. Drag the Bumper B Overlay 1 member from the Cast window into cell 1 of channel 34 of the Score.
77. Click cell 2 of channel 33 of the Score, hold down the Ctrl key, and then click cell 2 of channel 34.

78. Within the Property Inspector, type "95" in the X field and "130" in the Y field.
79. Drag the Bumper B member from the Cast window into cell 1 of channel 35 of the Score.
80. Drag the Bumper B Overlay 2 member from the Cast window into cell 1 of channel 36 of the Score.
81. Click cell 2 of channel 35 of the Score, hold down the Ctrl key, and then click cell 2 of channel 36.
82. Within the Property Inspector, type "134" in the X field and "105" in the Y field.
83. Drag the Bumper B member from the Cast window into cell 1 of channel 37 of the Score.
84. Drag the Bumper B Overlay 3 member from the Cast window into cell 1 of channel 38 of the Score.
85. Click cell 2 of channel 37 of the Score, hold down the Ctrl key, and then click cell 2 of channel 38.
86. Within the Property Inspector, type "174" in the X field and "129" in the Y field.
87. Drag the Bumper C member from the Cast window into cell 1 of channel 39 of the Score.
88. Click cell 2 of channel 39 of the Score. Director MX updates the Property Inspector.
89. Within the Property Inspector, type "75" in the X field and "274" in the Y field.
90. Right-click cell 2 of channel 39 of the Score and select Copy Sprites.
91. Right-click cell 1 of channel 40 of the Score and select Paste Sprites.
92. Within the Property Inspector, type "195" in the X field.
93. Click the Flip Horizontal button.
94. Drag the Bumper D member from the Cast window into cell 1 of channel 41 of the Score.
95. Click cell 2 of channel 41 of the Score. Director MX updates the Property Inspector.
96. Within the Property Inspector, type "73" in the X field and "275" in the Y field.
97. Right-click cell 2 of channel 41 of the Score and select Copy Sprites.
98. Right-click cell 1 of channel 42 of the Score and select Paste Sprites.
99. Within the Property Inspector, type "197" in the X field.
100. Click the Flip Horizontal button.
101. Drag the Hole Trap 1 member from the Cast window into cell 1 of channel 43 of the Score.

102. Click cell 2 of channel 43 of the Score. Director MX updates the Property Inspector.
103. Within the Property Inspector, type "118" in the X field and "165" in the Y field.
104. Drag the Hole Trap 2 member from the Cast window into cell 1 of channel 44 of the Score.
105. Click cell 2 of channel 44 of the Score. Director MX updates the Property Inspector.
106. Within the Property Inspector, type "240" in the X field and "73" in the Y field.
107. Drag the Tunnel Trap member from the Cast window into cell 1 of channel 45 of the Score.
108. Click cell 2 of channel 45 of the Score. Director MX updates the Property Inspector.
109. Within the Property Inspector, type "254" in the X field and "242" in the Y field.
110. Drag the Battery Plus member from the Cast window into cell 1 of channel 46 of the Score.
111. Click cell 2 of channel 46 of the Score. Director MX updates the Property Inspector.
112. Within the Property Inspector, type "19" in the X field and "188" in the Y field.
113. Click cell 2 of channel 2 of the Score, hold down the Shift key, and then click cell 2 of channel 46.
114. Hold down the Ctrl key and click cell 2 of channel 15.
115. Choose Matte from the Ink drop-down list.
116. Hold down the Ctrl key and click cell 2 of channel 11 of the Score. Repeat for channels 12 through 14 and 16 through 24.
117. Choose 0 from the Blend drop-down list.
118. Click cell 2 of channel 11 of the Score, hold down the Ctrl key, and then click cell 2 of channels 16 and 20.
119. Within the Property Inspector, choose 10 from the Blend drop-down list.
120. Click cell 2 of channel 12 of the Score, hold down the Ctrl key, and then click cell 2 of channels 17 and 21.
121. Within the Property Inspector, choose 20 from the Blend drop-down list.
122. Click cell 2 of channel 13 of the Score, hold down the Ctrl key, and then click cell 2 of channels 18 and 22.
123. Within the Property Inspector, choose 40 from the Blend drop-down list.
124. Drag the Title Text member from the Cast window into cell 1 of channel 47 of the Score.

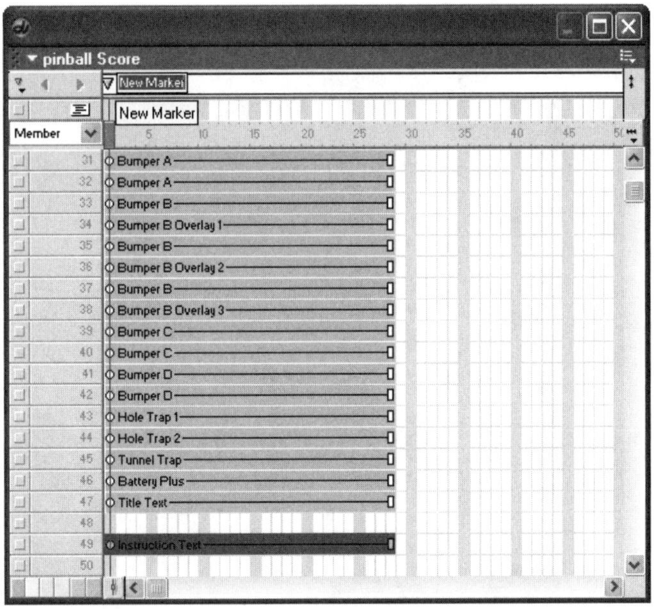

FIGURE 16.14 Creating a new marker within the Score.

125. Click cell 2 of channel 47 of the Score. Director MX updates the Property Inspector.
126. Within the Property Inspector, type "10" in the Y field.
127. Drag the Instruction Text member from the Cast window into cell 1 of channel 49 of the Score.
128. Click cell 2 of channel 49 of the Score. Director MX updates the Property Inspector.
129. Within the Property Inspector, type "86" in the Y field.
130. Click frame 1 of the Markers section of the Score window, as shown in Figure 16.14, type "Intro", and then press the Enter key.
131. Click frame 10 of the Markers section of the Score window, type "Game", and then press the Enter key.
132. Click frame 20 of the Markers section of the Score window, type "Pause", and then press the Enter key, as shown in Figure 16.15.
133. Drag the Epic Text member from the Cast window into cell 1 of channel 48 of the Score.
134. Drag the Game Text member from the Cast window into cell 10 of channel 48 of the Score.
135. Drag cell 19 of channel 48 of the Score to frame 28, as shown in Figure 16.16.

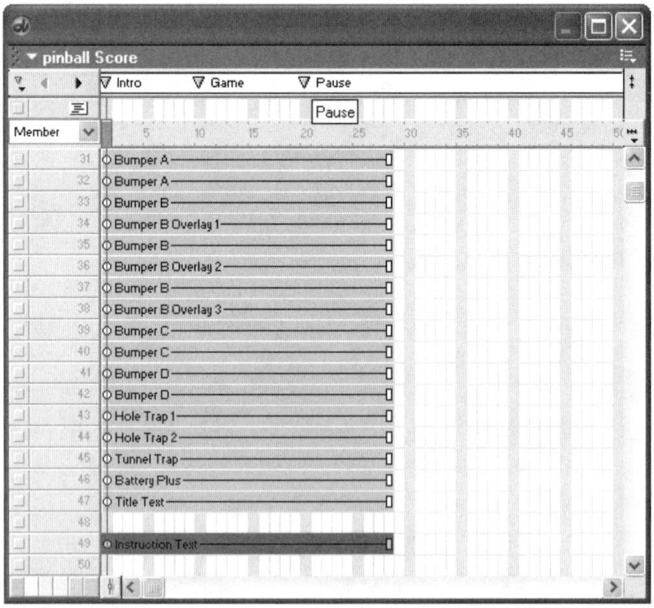

FIGURE 16.15 Naming the new Pause marker.

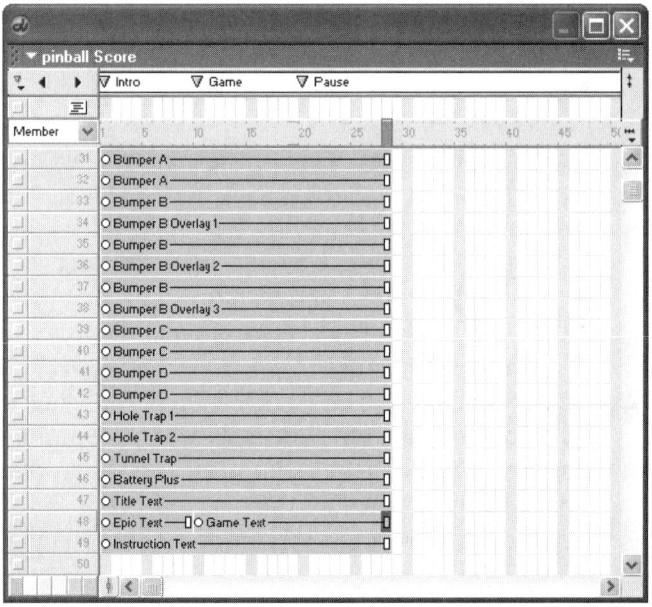

FIGURE 16.16 Extending the Game Text sprite to frame 28.

136. Click cell 1 of channel 48 of the Score, hold down the Shift key, and then click cell 28 of channel 48.
137. Within the Property Inspector, type "54" in the Y field.
138. Drag the New Game Button member from the Cast window into cell 1 of channel 50 of the Score.
139. Drag the Pause Game Button member from the Cast window into cell 10 of channel 50 of the Score.
140. Drag the Resume Game Button member from the Cast window into cell 20 of channel 50 of the Score.
141. Drag cell 47 of channel 50 of the Score to frame 28.
142. Click cell 1 of channel 50 of the Score, hold down the Shift key, and then click cell 28 of channel 50.
143. Within the Property Inspector, type "374" in the Y field.
144. Click cell 1 of channel 47 of the Score, hold down the Shift key, and then click cell 28 of channel 50.
145. Within the Property Inspector, type "305" in the X field.
146. Choose Background Transparent from the Ink drop-down list.
147. Type "#C0C0F0" in the Forecolor field.
148. Click cell 9 of channel 48 of the Score, hold down the Ctrl key, and then click cells 9, 19, and 28 of channel 50.
149. Right-click the Score's active cells and choose Insert Keyframe.
150. Within the Property Inspector, choose 0 from the Blend drop-down list.

Writing and Applying the Lingo Scripts

To write and apply the Lingo scripts, perform the following steps.

1. Within the Cast window, click the Choose Cast button and choose New Cast.
2. Type "Scripts" in the Name field and click Create.
3. Click the Script Window button on the Toolbar.
4. Type the following code into the Script window.

```
global game, ball, plunger, flipper, border

on prepareMovie
    resetGame
    flipper = [0, 0]
end

on resetGame
    game = [#balls:3, #score:0, #text:"", #mode:"", #timer:0,
#gravity:0.8, #friction:0.99]
```

```
end

on dirOf num
    if num < 0 then
        return -1
    else
        return 1
    end if
end

on lighter a, b
    if abs(a) < abs(b) then
        return a
    else
        return b
    end if
end

on heavier a, b
    if abs(a) > abs(b) then
        return a
    else
        return b
    end if
end

on ballSpeed
    return sqrt(power(ball.stepX, 2)+power(ball.stepY, 2))
end

on ballDist thing
    return sqrt(power(ball.x-thing.locH, 2)+power(ball.y-thing.locV,
2))
end

on ballTouching thing
    return (ball.mask[1].intersects(thing.spriteNum) or
ball.mask[2].intersects(thing.spriteNum))
end

on ballTouchDistX thing
    dist = 0
    repeat while not ballTouching(thing) and dist < 10
        dist = dist+1
        setBallMask(ball.x+dist, ball.y)
```

```
    end repeat
    setBallMask(ball.x, ball.y)

    temp = dist
    dist = 0
    repeat while not ballTouching(thing) and dist > -10
        dist = dist-1
        setBallMask(ball.x+dist, ball.y)
    end repeat
    dist = lighter(dist, temp)
    setBallMask(ball.x, ball.y)

    return dist
end

on ballTouchDistY thing
    dist = 0
    repeat while not ballTouching(thing) and dist < 10
        dist = dist+1
        setBallMask(ball.x, ball.y+dist)
    end repeat
    setBallMask(ball.x, ball.y)

    temp = dist
    dist = 0
    repeat while not ballTouching(thing) and dist > -10
        dist = dist-1
        setBallMask(ball.x, ball.y+dist)
    end repeat
    dist = lighter(dist, temp)
    setBallMask(ball.x, ball.y)

    return dist
end

on setBallMask newX, newY
    ball.mask[1].loc = point(newX, newY)
    ball.mask[2].loc = point((newX+ball.oldX)/2, (newY+ball.oldY)/2)
    updateStage
end

on stepBallBack thing
    tempX = ball.x
    tempY = ball.y
```

```
    distX = float(ball.x-ball.oldX)
    distY = float(ball.y-ball.oldY)
    denom = max(ballDist(ball.trail[3]), 1)
    repeat while ballTouching(thing)
        tempX = tempX-distX/denom
        tempY = tempY-distY/denom
        setBallMask(tempX, tempY)
    end repeat

    ball.x = tempX
    ball.y = tempY
end
```

5. Type "Main" in the Cast Member Name field, as shown in Figure 16.17, and close the Script window.
6. Click an empty spot in the Cast window.
7. Click the Script Window button on the Toolbar.

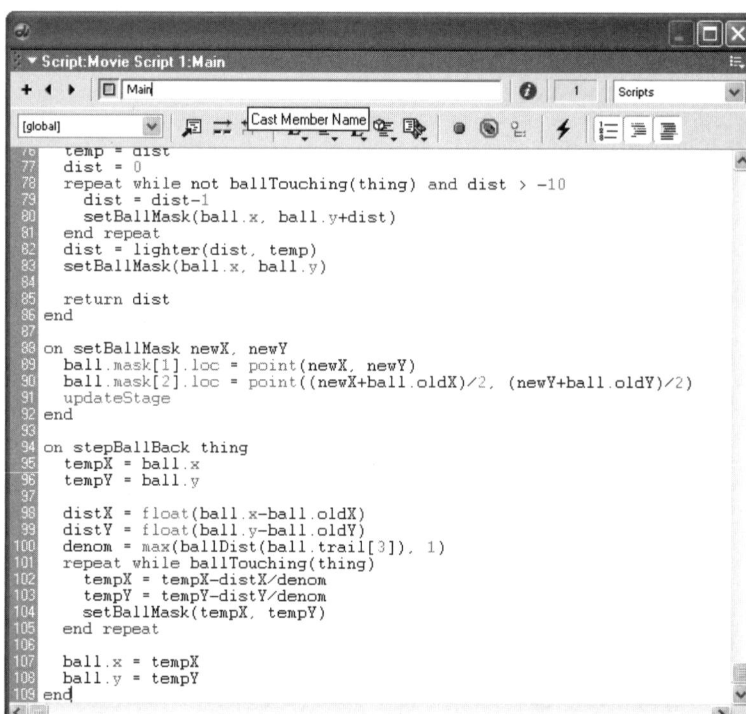

FIGURE 16.17 Naming the new Main movie script.

8. Type the following code in the Script window.

```
property playFrame

on exitFrame
    playNum = max(integer(playFrame), 0)
    if playFrame = "" then
        adjustNum = 0
    else if playFrame.char.count >= 2 then
        adjustNum = integer(playFrame.char[2..playFrame.char.count])
    end if

    if playNum > 0 then
        play playNum
    else if playFrame = "" or playFrame starts "+" then
        play the frame+adjustNum
    else if playFrame starts "-" then
        play the frame-adjustNum
    else
        play playFrame
    end if
end

on getPropertyDescriptionList
    return [#playFrame: [#comment:"Frame to Play:", #format:#string,
#default:""]]
end
```

9. Click the Script tab of the Property Inspector.
10. Choose Behavior from the Type drop-down list.
11. Within the Script window, type "Play Frame" in the Cast Member Name field and close the window.
12. Click cell 2 of channel 2 of the Score, hold down the Shift key, and then click cell 2 of channel 10.
13. Drag the Play Frame behavior from the Cast window into cell 1 of the Script channel of the Score, as shown in Figure 16.18.
14. Click OK.
15. Drag the Play Frame behavior from the Cast window into cell 20 of the Script channel of the Score.
16. Click OK.
17. Drag the Play Frame behavior from the Cast window into cell 28 of the Script channel of the Score.
18. Type "Game" in the Frame to Play field and click OK.

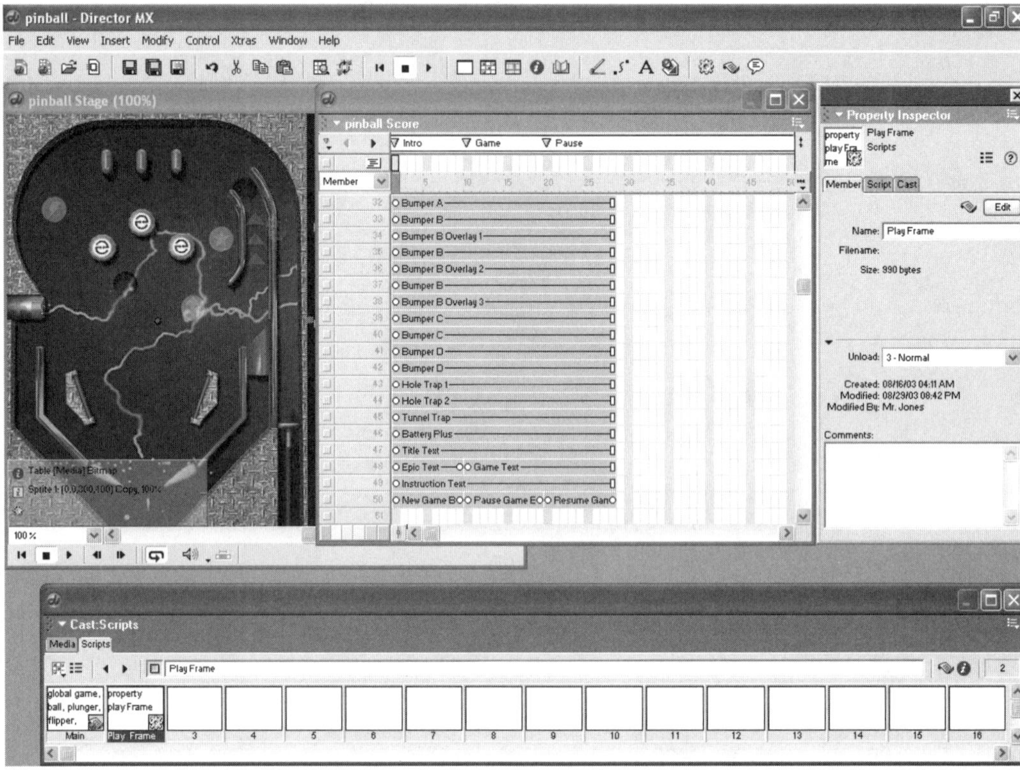

FIGURE 16.18 Applying the Play Frame behavior to frame 1 of the movie.

19. Click an empty spot in the Cast window.
20. Click the Script Window button on the Toolbar.
21. Type the following code in the Script window.

```
global game

on enterFrame
    sendAllSprites(#preRefresh)
    sendAllSprites(#refresh)
    sendAllSprites(#postRefresh)

    --Count down the game's timer while a special mode is active.
    if game.timer > 0 then
        game.timer = game.timer-1
    else
        game.mode = ""
    end if
end
```

```
on exitFrame
    play the frame
end
```

22. Click the Script tab of the Property Inspector.
23. Choose Behavior from the Type drop-down list.
24. Within the Script window, type “Game” in the Cast Member Name field and close the window.
25. Drag the Game behavior from the Cast window into cell 10 of the Script channel of the Score.
26. Click an empty spot in the Cast window.
27. Click the Script Window button on the Toolbar.
28. Type the following code in the Script window.

```
property my, normColor, lightColor

on beginSprite me
    my = sprite(me.spriteNum)
    normColor = rgb(192, 192, 240)
    lightColor = rgb(255, 255, 255)
end

on mouseEnter
    my.color = lightColor
end

on mouseLeave
    my.color = normColor
end

on mouseDown
    my.color = normColor
end

on mouseUp
    my.color = lightColor
    play the frame+1
end
```

29. Click the Script tab of the Property Inspector.
30. Choose Behavior from the Type drop-down list.
31. Within the Script window, type “Button” in the Cast Member Name field and close the window.

32. Click cell 1 of channel 50 of the Score, hold down the Shift key, and then click cell 28 of channel 50.
33. Drag the Button behavior from the Cast window onto the selected sprites of the Score, as shown in Figure 16.19.
34. Click an empty spot in the Cast window.
35. Click the Script Window button on the Toolbar.
36. Type the following code in the Script window.

```
global ball, game
property trail, mask, x, y, oldX, oldY, stepX, stepY

on beginSprite me
    ball = sprite(me.spriteNum)
    trail = [sprite(me.spriteNum-1), sprite(me.spriteNum-2),
sprite(me.spriteNum-3)]
    mask = [sprite(me.spriteNum-4), sprite(me.spriteNum-5)]
```

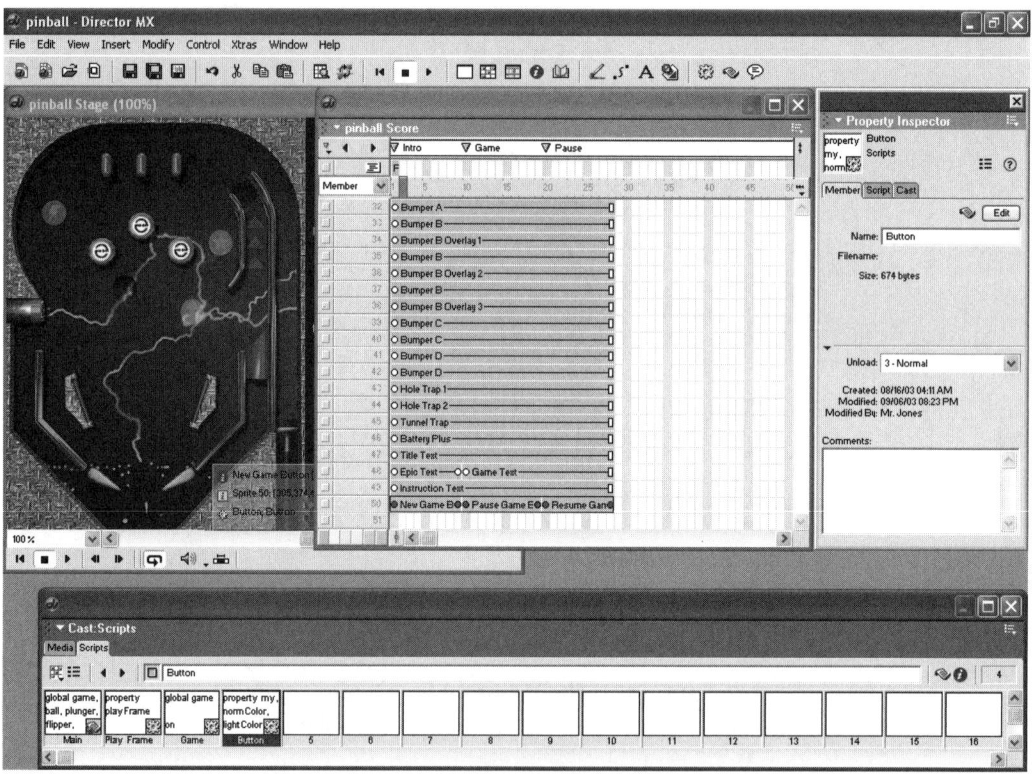

FIGURE 16.19 Applying the Button behavior to the selected sprites.

```
    reset
end

on reset
    x = 283
    y = 600
    oldX = x
    oldY = y
    stepX = 0
    stepY = 0
end

on postRefresh
    ball.loc = point(x, y)
    trail[1].loc = point((x*2+oldX)/3, (y*2+oldY)/3)
    trail[2].loc = point((x+oldX*2)/3, (y+oldY*2)/3)
    trail[3].loc = point(oldX, oldY)

    if ball.y < 550 then --Adjust the ball's velocity while it is in
play.
        stepY = stepY+game.gravity
        stepX = stepX*game.friction
        stepY = stepY*game.friction
        stepX = max(min(stepX, 30), -30)
        stepY = max(min(stepY, 30), -30)
    else if ball.y < 600 then --Set the ball offscreen to await the
plunger.
        reset
        game.balls = game.balls-1
    end if

    oldX = x
    oldY = y
    x = x+stepX
    y = y+stepY
    setBallMask(x, y)
end
```

37. Click the Script tab of the Property Inspector.
38. Choose Behavior from the Type drop-down list.
39. Within the Script window, type "Ball" in the Cast Member Name field and close the window.
40. Drag the Ball behavior from the Cast window onto the sprite in channel 14 of the Score.

41. Click an empty spot in the Cast window.
42. Click the Script Window button on the Toolbar.
43. Type the following code in the Script window.

```
global plunger, game, ball, border
property y, stepY, minY, maxY, mode

on beginSprite me
    plunger = sprite(me.spriteNum)
    minY = (the stage).rect.height-plunger.height
    maxY = (the stage).rect.height
    y = minY
    stepY = 0
    mode = ""
end

on mouseDown
    if mode = "diving" then exit

    mode = "dragging"
    y = max(min(the mouseV, maxY), minY)
    stepY = 0
end

on preRefresh
    if ball.y = 600 and game.balls >= 0 then --Go to fetch the ball
from its hiding spot.
        mode = "diving"
        stepY = 10
    else if mode = "surfacing" then --Return from offscreen with the
ball.
        if y+stepY < minY+1 then
            mode = ""
            y = minY
            stepY = 0
        else
            stepY = (minY-y)*0.1
        end if
    else if mode = "dragging" then --Allow the user to drag and release
the plunger.
        if the mouseDown then
            stepY = max(min(the mouseV, maxY), minY)-y
        else
            mode = "plunging"
        end if
```

```
    else if keyPressed(125) then --The down arrow is an alternate
method of using the plunger.
        if mode <> "diving" then
            mode = "pressing"
            stepY = 10
            if y+stepY > maxY then
                y = maxY
                stepY = 0
            end if
        end if
    else if mode = "pressing" then --The user has released the down
arrow.
        mode = "plunging"
    end if

    --Move the plunger at the speed desired to launch the ball.
    if mode = "plunging" then stepY = -power(plunger.locV-minY, 0.2)*12

    --If the ball is in contact with the plunger, let it sit on top and
move at the same speed.
    if ballTouching(plunger) then
        ball.y = y+stepY-10
        if ball.stepY > stepY then ball.stepY = stepY
        if mode = "diving" then mode = "surfacing"
    end if

    --Stop the plunger's movement at its minimum Y value.
    if y+stepY < minY then
        if mode = "plunging" then mode = ""
        y = minY
        stepY = 0
    end if

    y = y+stepY
    plunger.locV = y
end
```

44. Click the Script tab of the Property Inspector.
45. Choose Behavior from the Type drop-down list.
46. Within the Script window, type “Plunger” in the Cast Member Name field and close the window.
47. Drag the Plunger behavior from the Cast window onto the sprite in channel 15 of the Score.
48. Click an empty spot in the Cast window.
49. Click the Script Window button on the Toolbar.

50. Type the following code in the Script window.

```
global flipper, game, ball, border
property my, trail, adjuster

on beginSprite me
    my = sprite(me.spriteNum)
    flipper[integer(my.flipH)+1] = my
    trail = [sprite(me.spriteNum-1), sprite(me.spriteNum-2),
sprite(me.spriteNum-3)]

    --Used to mirror everything for the right flipper.
    if my.flipH then
        adjuster = -1
    else
        adjuster = 1
    end if
end

on preRefresh
    --React to designated key by "flipping."
    oldR = my.rotation
    if keyPressed(123+integer(my.flipH)) then
        if abs(my.rotation) > 60 then
            my.rotation = my.rotation-30*adjuster
            if abs(my.rotation) < 60 then
                my.rotation = 60*adjuster
            end if
        end if
    else if abs(my.rotation) < 120 then
        my.rotation = my.rotation+10*adjuster
    end if
    trail[1].rotation = (my.rotation*2+oldR)/3
    trail[2].rotation = (my.rotation+oldR*2)/3
    trail[3].rotation = oldR

    --Detect and handle a collision with the ball.
    if ballTouching(my) then
        tempY = ball.y

        --Adjust the ball so that it does not intersect with the
flipper.
        slant = float(abs(my.rotation)-90)/30*adjuster
        dist = max((ball.x-my.locH)*adjuster, 0)
```

```
        repeat while ballTouching(my)
            tempY = tempY-1
            setBallMask(ball.x, tempY)
        end repeat

        --Adjust the ball's velocity appropriately.
        if abs(my.rotation) < abs(oldR) then
            ball.stepX = ball.stepX+dist*0.3*adjuster
            ball.stepY = -dist*0.8
        else if ball.stepY > 0 then
            ball.stepX = ball.stepX+slant
            ball.stepY = 0
        end if

        ball.y = tempY
    end if
end
```

51. Click the Script tab of the Property Inspector.
52. Choose Behavior from the Type drop-down list.
53. Within the Script window, type “Flipper” in the Cast Member Name field and close the window.
54. Click cell 2 of channel 19 of the Score, hold down the Ctrl key, and then click cell 2 of channel 23.
55. Drag the Flipper behavior from the Cast window onto the selected sprites of the Score.
56. Click an empty spot in the Cast window.
57. Click the Script Window button on the Toolbar.
58. Type the following code in the Script window.

```
global border, ball

on beginSprite me
    border = sprite(me.spriteNum)
end

on preRefresh
    --Detect and handle a collision with the ball.
    if ballTouching(border) then
        tempX = ball.x
        tempY = ball.y

        --Adjust the ball so that it does not intersect with the
border.
```

```
        repeat while ballTouching(border)
            weightX = max(abs(border.locH-tempX)-abs(ball.stepY), 0)
            tempX = (tempX*weightX+border.locH)/(weightX+1)
            weightY = max(abs(border.locV-tempY)-abs(ball.stepX), 0)
            tempY = (tempY*weightY+border.locV)/(weightY+1)
            setBallMask(tempX, tempY)
        end repeat

        --Adjust the ball's velocity appropriately.
        distX = float(tempX-ball.x)
        if abs(distX) < 1 then distX = dirOf(distX)
        distY = float(tempY-ball.y)
        if abs(distY) < 1 then distY = dirOf(distY)
        denom = sqrt(power(distX, 2)+power(distY, 2))
        ball.stepX = ball.stepX+distX/denom*ballSpeed()*abs(tempX-
border.locH)/border.width
        ball.stepY = ball.stepY+distY/denom*ballSpeed()*abs(tempY-
border.locV)/border.height

        ball.x = tempX
        ball.y = tempY
    end if
end
```

59. Click the Script tab of the Property Inspector.
60. Choose Behavior from the Type drop-down list.
61. Within the Script window, type "Border" in the Cast Member Name field and close the window.
62. Drag the Border behavior from the Cast window onto the sprite in channel 2 of the Score.
63. Click an empty spot in the Cast window.
64. Click the Script Window button on the Toolbar.
65. Type the following code in the Script window.

```
global game, ball
property my, downSlope, adjuster

on beginSprite me
    my = sprite(me.spriteNum)

    --Used to mirror everything for "upward sloping" walls.
    if downSlope then
        adjuster = 1
    else
```

```
        adjuster = -1
    end if
end

on preRefresh
    --Detect and handle a collision with the ball.
    if ballTouching(my) then
        tempX = ball.x
        tempY = ball.y

        stepBallBack(my)
        bounceStep = abs(ball.stepX)/5*dirOf(-ballTouchDistX(my))
        rollStep = ball.stepY/30*dirOf(ballTouchDistY(my))*adjuster
        if bounceStep*rollStep < 0 then
            newStep = bounceStep
        else
            newStep = heavier(bounceStep, rollStep)
        end if
        newStep = heavier(newStep, dirOf(newStep))

        ball.x = tempX
        ball.y = tempY

        setBallMask(tempX, ball.y)
        repeat while ballTouching(my)
            tempX = tempX+dirOf(newStep)
            setBallMask(tempX, ball.y)
        end repeat
        distX = float(tempX-ball.x)
        denom = max(abs(distX), 1)
        ball.stepX = heavier(distX/denom*ball.stepY/30*adjuster,
newStep)

        ball.x = tempX
    end if
end

on getPropertyDescriptionList
    return [#downSlope: [#comment:"Downward Slope?", #format:#boolean,
#default:true]]
end
```

66. Click the Script tab of the Property Inspector.
67. Choose Behavior from the Type drop-down list.

68. Within the Script window, type "Wall" in the Cast Member Name field and close the window.
69. Click cell 2 of channel 25 of the Score, hold down the Ctrl key, and then click cell 2 of channels 26 and 28.
70. Drag the Wall behavior from the Cast window onto the selected sprites of the Score.
71. Click OK.
72. Click cell 2 of channel 27 of the Score, hold down the Ctrl key, and then click cell 2 of channel 29.
73. Drag the Wall behavior from the Cast window onto the selected sprites of the Score.
74. Clear the Downward Slope checkbox and click OK.
75. Click an empty spot in the Cast window.
76. Click the Script Window button on the Toolbar.
77. Type the following code in the Script window.

```
global game, ball
property my, timer, points, lightUp, bounceBall, bounciness, trapBall,
magnetic, boostX, boostY, randomness

on beginSprite me
    my = sprite(me.spriteNum)
    timer = 0
    boostX = [boostX, 0]
    boostY = [boostY, 0]
end

on refresh
    --Apply magnetic attraction or repulsion to the ball if necessary.
    if magnetic and game.mode <> "" then
        magnetism = 0
        if game.mode = "surge" then
            my.blend = random(100)
            magnetism = max(100-ballDist(my), 0)*0.00005*my.blend
        else if game.timer/30 mod 2 = 1 then
            my.blend = 100
            magnetism = max(200-ballDist(my), 0)*0.000001*random(100)
            if game.mode = "repulsion" then magnetism = -magnetism/10
        end if
        ball.stepX = ball.stepX+(my.locH-ball.x)*magnetism
        ball.stepY = ball.stepY+(my.locV-ball.y)*magnetism
    end if

    --Detect and handle a collision with the ball.
```

```
    if ballTouching(my) then
        if lightUp then my.blend = 100
        if not trapBall then game.score = game.score+points

        if bounceBall then
            stepBallBack(my)
            distX = float(ball.x-my.locH)
            distY = float(ball.y-my.locV)
            denom = max(ballDist(my), 1)
            ball.stepX = ball.stepX+distX/denom*bounciness
            ball.stepY = ball.stepY+distY/denom*bounciness
        end if

        if trapBall then
            if timer = 0 then
                timer = 30+random(30)
                setRandomBoost
            else if timer > 1 then
                ball.x = my.locH
                ball.y = my.locV
                ball.stepX = 0
                ball.stepY = -game.gravity

                my.blend = min(my.blend+10, 100)
                game.score = game.score+points

                timer = timer-1
            else if timer = 1 then
                ball.stepX = ball.stepX+boostX[1]+boostX[2]
                ball.stepY = ball.stepY+boostY[1]+boostY[2]

                my.blend = 0
            end if
        else
            setRandomBoost
            ball.stepX = ball.stepX+boostX[1]+boostX[2]
            ball.stepY = ball.stepY+boostY[1]+boostY[2]
        end if
    else
        if lightUp then my.blend = max(my.blend-5, 0)
        if trapBall then timer = 0
    end if
end

on getPropertyDescriptionList
```

```
    return [#points: [#comment:"Point Value:", #format:#integer,
#default:0], \
        #lightUp: [#comment:"Light Up?", #format:#boolean,
#default:false], \
        #bounceBall: [#comment:"Bounce Ball?", #format:#boolean,
#default:false], \
        #bounciness: [#comment:">>Bounciness:", #format:#float,
#default:0], \
        #trapBall: [#comment:"Trap Ball?", #format:#boolean,
#default:false], \
        #magnetic: [#comment:"Magnetic?", #format:#boolean,
#default:false], \
        #boostX: [#comment:"X Boost:", #format:#float, #default:0], \
        #boostY: [#comment:"Y Boost:", #format:#float, #default:0], \
        #randomness: [#comment:">>Randomness:", #format:#float,
#default:0]]
end

on setRandomBoost
    boostX[2] = float(51-random(101))/50*randomness
    boostY[2] = float(51-random(101))/50*randomness
end
```

78. Click the Script tab of the Property Inspector.
79. Choose Behavior from the Type drop-down list.
80. Within the Script window, type "Obstacle" in the Cast Member Name field and close the window.
81. Click cell 2 of channel 5 of the Score, hold down the Shift key, and then click cell 2 of channel 8.
82. Drag the Obstacle behavior from the Cast window onto the selected sprites of the Score.
83. Select the Light Up checkbox, type "-1" in the Y Boost field and "0.1" in the Randomness field, and click OK.
84. Click cell 2 of channel 30 of the Score, hold down the Shift key, and then click cell 2 of channel 32.
85. Drag the Obstacle behavior from the Cast window onto the selected sprites of the Score.
86. Select the Bounce Ball checkbox, type "1" in the Point Value field and "7" in the Bounciness field, and click OK.
87. Click cell 2 of channel 33 of the Score, hold down the Ctrl key, and then click cell 2 of channels 35 and 37.
88. Drag the Obstacle behavior from the Cast window onto the selected sprites of the Score.

89. Select the Bounce Ball checkbox, type "12" in the Bounciness field, and click OK.
90. Click cell 2 of channel 34 of the Score, hold down the Ctrl key, and then click cell 2 of channels 36 and 38.
91. Drag the Obstacle behavior from the Cast window onto the selected sprites of the Score.
92. Select the Light Up and Magnetic checkboxes, type "25" in the Point Value field, and click OK.
93. Drag the Obstacle behavior from the Cast window onto the sprite in channel 39 of the Score.
94. Select the Bounce ball checkbox, type "10" in the Point Value field, "8" in the Bounciness field, "10" in the X Boost field, and "-5" in the Y Boost field, and click OK.
95. Drag the Obstacle behavior from the Cast window onto the sprite in channel 40 of the Score.
96. Select the Bounce ball checkbox, type "10" in the Point Value field, "8" in the Bounciness field, "-10" in the X Boost field, and "-5" in the Y Boost field, and click OK.
97. Click cell 2 of channel 41 of the Score, hold down the Ctrl key, and then click cell 2 of channel 42.
98. Drag the Obstacle behavior from the Cast window onto the selected sprites of the Score.
99. Select the Bounce Ball checkbox, type "6" in the Bounciness field, and click OK.
100. Drag the Obstacle behavior from the Cast window onto the sprite in channel 43 of the Score.
101. Select the Trap Ball checkbox, type "1" in the Point Value field and "5" in the Randomness field, and click OK.
102. Drag the Obstacle behavior from the Cast window onto the sprite in channel 44 of the Score.
103. Select the Trap Ball checkbox, type "1" in the Point Value field, "-2" in the X Boost field, "-2" in the Y Boost field, "1" in the Randomness field, and click OK.
104. Drag the Obstacle behavior from the Cast window onto the sprite in channel 45 of the Score.
105. Select the Trap Ball checkbox, type "2" in the Point Value field, "-6" in the X Boost field, "-3" in the Y Boost field, "1" in the Randomness field, and click OK.
106. Click an empty spot in the Cast window.
107. Click the Script Window button on the Toolbar.
108. Type the following code in the Script window.

```
global game

on beginSprite
    preRefresh
end

on preRefresh
    --Update the player's number of balls and current score.
    if game.balls < 0 then
        resetGame
        play "Pause"
    end if
    if game.score > 9999999999 then game.score = 9999999999
    newText = "Balls:"&&game.balls&&"/ Score:"&& game.score
    if game.text <> newText then
        game.text = newText
        member("Game Text").text = game.text
    end if
end
```

109. Click the Script tab of the Property Inspector.
110. Choose Behavior from the Type drop-down list.
111. Within the Script window, type "Game Text" in the Cast Member Name field and close the window.
112. Drag the Game Text behavior from the Cast window onto the sprite starting in cell 10 of channel 48 of the Score.
113. Click an empty spot in the Cast window.
114. Click the Script Window button on the Toolbar.
115. Type the following code in the Script window.

```
global game, ball
property my

on beginSprite me
    my = sprite(me.spriteNum)
end

on refresh
    if ballTouching(my) and my.blend = 0 then
        game.mode = "surge"
        game.timer = 30
    end if
end
```

116. Click the Script tab of the Property Inspector.
117. Choose Behavior from the Type drop-down list.
118. Within the Script window, type "Power Surge" in the Cast Member Name field and close the window.
119. Drag the Power Surge behavior from the Cast window onto the sprite in channel 3 of the Score.
120. Drag the Obstacle behavior from the Cast window onto the sprite in channel 3 of the Score.
121. Select the Light Up checkbox and click OK.
122. Click an empty spot in the Cast window.
123. Click the Script Window button on the Toolbar.
124. Type the following code in the Script window.

```
global game, ball
property my

on beginSprite me
    my = sprite(me.spriteNum)
end

on refresh
    if ballTouching(my) and my.blend = 0 then game.balls =
min(game.balls+1, 3)
end
```

125. Click the Script tab of the Property Inspector.
126. Choose Behavior from the Type drop-down list.
127. Within the Script window, type "Free Ball" in the Cast Member Name field and close the window.
128. Drag the Free Ball behavior from the Cast window onto the sprite in channel 4 of the Score.
129. Drag the Obstacle behavior from the Cast window onto the sprite in channel 4 of the Score.
130. Select the Light Up checkbox and click OK.
131. Click an empty spot in the Cast window.
132. Click the Script Window button on the Toolbar.
133. Type the following code in the Script window.

```
global game, ball
property my

on beginSprite me
    my = sprite(me.spriteNum)
```

```
end

on refresh
    if ballTouching(my) then
        if random(2) = 1 then
            game.mode = "attraction"
            my.member = "Battery Plus"
        else
            game.mode = "repulsion"
            my.member = "Battery Minus"
        end if
        game.timer = 90+random(180)
    end if

    if game.mode = "attraction" or game.mode = "repulsion" then
        my.blend = min(my.blend+10, 100)
    else
        my.blend = max(my.blend-10, 0)
    end if
end
```

134. Click the Script tab of the Property Inspector.
135. Choose Behavior from the Type drop-down list.
136. Within the Script window, type "Battery" in the Cast Member Name field and close the window.
137. Drag the Battery behavior from the Cast window onto the sprite in channel 46 of the Score.
138. Drag the Obstacle behavior from the Cast window onto the sprite in channel 46 of the Score.
139. Select the Bounce Ball checkbox, type "5" in the Bounciness field and "7" in the X Boost field, and click OK.
140. Click frame 1 of the Score and then click the Play button on the Toolbar to play your game.

SUMMARY

With that, the High Voltage Pinball game is complete! This classic version of pinball, with a few modifications, is sure to attract people's attention. Incorporating new concepts such as magnetism that couldn't be done in classic pinball machines help to distinguish your game from the rest. Now, it's time to get the game published and sent out!

17 Blasteroids

THE CONCEPT

Identifying Your Product: epic Drill Bits

The epic Drill Bits Company has decided to create an interactive catalog for their line of drill bits. The line of oil field drilling bits has earned a reputation to drill through the hardest rock formations. To make their CD catalog more interesting, they have decided to include an Advergame that is small and addictive. They are hoping that the game will peak the customer's curiosity and get them to pop the CD into the computer for a look. Their new CD catalog is awesome and they are hoping the game helps them build a buzz about it at the trade show where it will be distributed. Their competition has nothing like it.

A warning to the reader: the game developed in this chapter, Blasteroids, although small and simple (for example, compared to id Software's *Quake*), is still a significant programming effort. For the sake of space, the process described in this chapter is not as exhaustive as the previous chapters. We strongly suggest you read the earlier chapters and become very familiar with the development process. Furthermore, this game requires advanced mathematical concepts, such as vectors and the operations on them. For the sake of space, we assume you know what these are and how to use them. A good algebra or physics book will come in handy if your math skills need refreshing.

Outlining a Game for epic Drill Bits

The obvious choice for a game that meets our criteria is an arcade game. Something as simple as a shooter game, such as *Asteroids*, is both simple and, if done right, very addictive. *Asteroids* is a game in which a ship flies around space destroying asteroids that move through one of several levels, while at the same time trying to avoid running into them. Because epic Drill Bits' products crush rocks, this is the perfect fit. To increase the relevance of the game, instead of using ordinary missiles, we use

Drill Bit Missiles. This further ties the game to the product and draws the player further into the product. If the action were not enough, to further increase the incentive to play, we offer prizes of nominal value for different, increasing point levels earned while playing the game.

Designing the Blasteroids Interface

The Blasteroids interface must match the design theme of the interactive catalog. This is to give the user a sense of continuity, such that he or she doesn't forget that the game is part of the catalog. Navigation through the catalog is achieved through large, beveled buttons, which are riveted to a metal floor plate for an industrial look. Consequently, we are using these large, beveled buttons to display information, such as the score and the number of lives, on a panel occupying the left side of the screen. Also, there is a button to allow the user to return to the catalog and a big button with the company name and its tagline. The rest of the screen is devoted to the playing area. As a backdrop, we use an image of the Ring Nebula, which is available on the NASA Web site. There's a lot of cool stuff there!

To communicate with the player, we use a stylized dialog box. Sticking to the industrial design theme, this dialog box has the same metal floor plate as the panel and riveted, beveled buttons for user interaction. For an enhanced visual effect, the dialog box slides onto the screen from underneath the panel.

The game starts with a dialog box containing the game instructions and the prize information sliding onto the screen, as shown in Figure 17.1. The user clicks a button to start the game. Then, depending on the player's results, one of several types of dialog boxes indicating Game Over can be displayed:

Better Luck Next Time: The player did not score enough points to win anything.

5,000 Points: The player scored enough points to win a yo-yo.

10,000 Points: The player scored enough points to win a calendar.

15,000 Points: The player scored enough points to win a coffee mug.

Grand Prize: The player beat all 20 levels, earning him a tote bag.

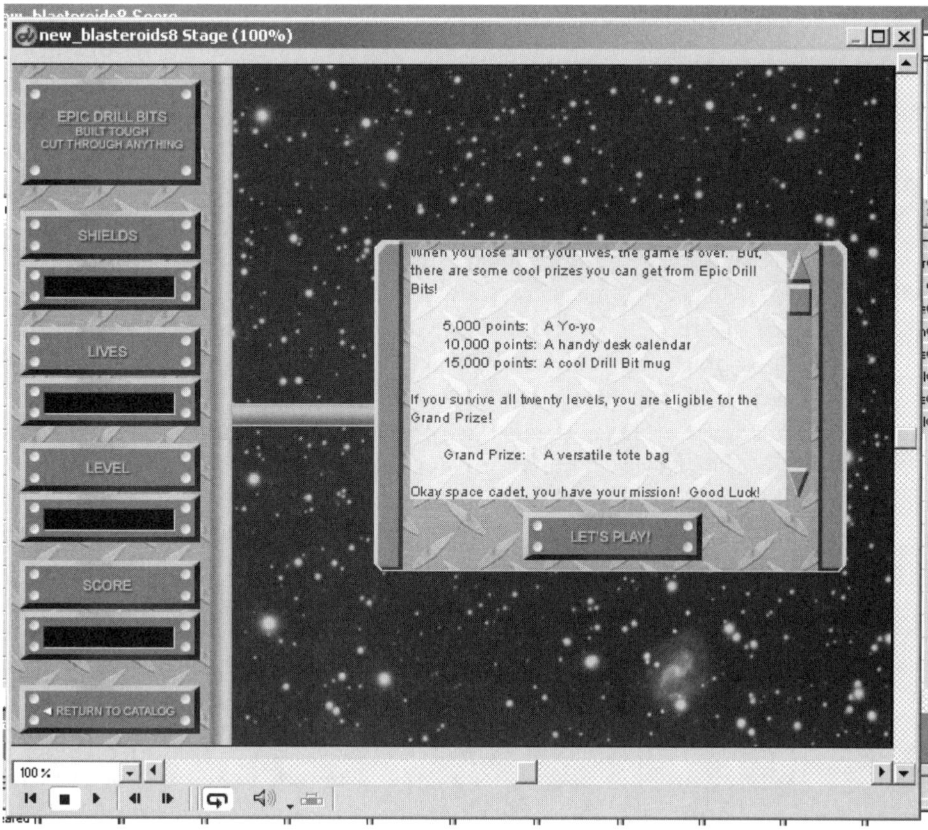

FIGURE 17.1 The interface.

THE CREATION

Identifying the Elements of Blasteroids

Specification

The game starts with the player's ship entering the playing area. The playing area is bounded so that when the ship leaves one side, it reenters on another side. The ship is controlled with several action keys. The left and right arrow keys control the rotation of the ship, with the left arrow key rotating the ship counterclockwise and the right arrow key rotating the ship clockwise. The down arrow key controls the thrusters. When it is pressed, the thrusters are engaged and the ship's speed increases in the direction it is pointing. To keep the game playable, the speed stops increasing at a specified speed limit. The spacebar fires the drill bit missiles. The missile is alive as long as it is inside the playing area. While alive, the missile cannot be fired again. This is important, as there are only a limited number of missiles. After the missile is outside the playing area, the missile is dead, and can be fired again.

Sharing the playing area with the ship are the asteroids, as shown in Figure 17.2. There are a certain number of asteroids launched at the beginning of each level and the asteroids move at a certain speed, both values based on the current level of the game. The asteroids move in straight lines, and just like the ship, when they leave the playing area, they reenter on the other side. If an asteroid is hit with a drill bit missile, it breaks up into smaller pieces. One of these pieces can be a prize, which we describe shortly. If a missile hits one of these smaller pieces, it simply disappears. After all the asteroids in a level have been cleared, the game can go to the next level.

The asteroid can come into contact with the ship, as shown in Figure 17.3. Before this happens, though, the shields deflect the asteroid away. Each hit by an asteroid lowers the shield strength and the shield strength continues to fall while the contact persists. The shields are normally down, but are raised during this period of contact. Eventually, the shields run out. If an asteroid now hits the ship, the ship explodes and another enters the playing area to take its place, as long the player has lives left. The player starts with three lives, and when the player has run out of lives, the game is over. The player scores 50 points for each large asteroid destroyed and 100 points for each small asteroid destroyed.

When a drill bit missile hits a larger asteroid, a prize can be launched in the form of a heart or a shield, as shown in Figure 17.4. The heart represents another life and the shield represents an increase in shield strength. The prize has a maxi-

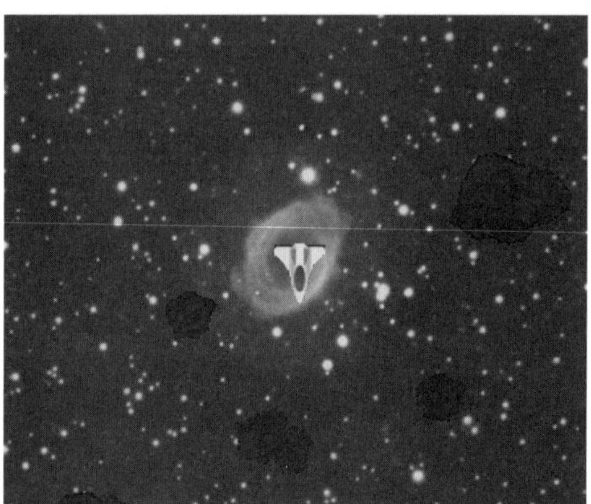

FIGURE 17.2 The ship and the asteroids.

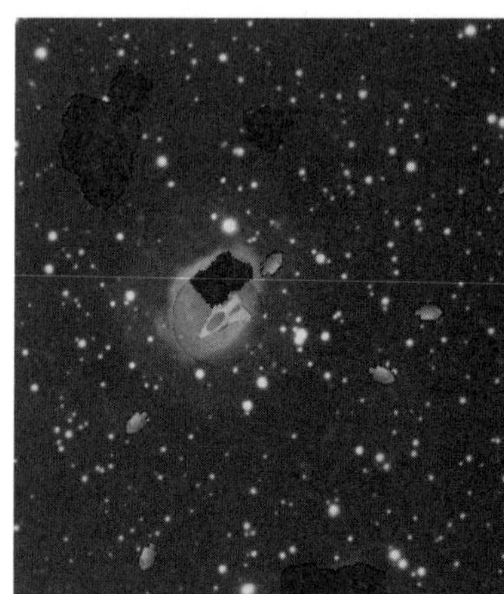

FIGURE 17.3 Shields up!

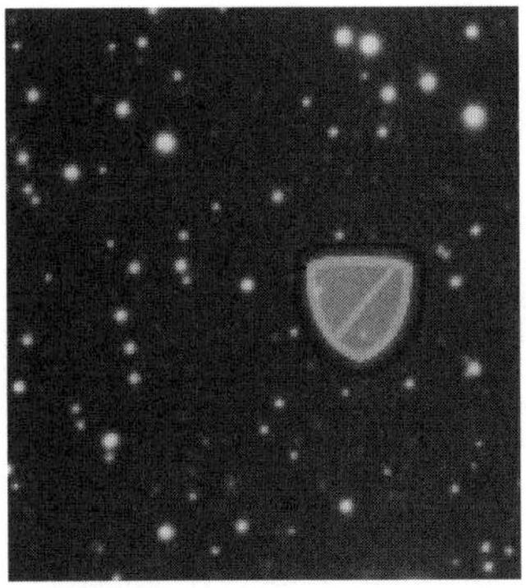

FIGURE 17.4 Time is limited!

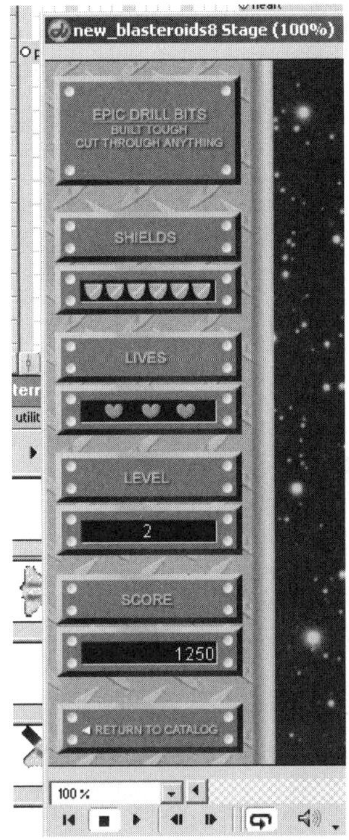

FIGURE 17.5 Useful information.

mum lifetime in the playing area, during which time it can be collected. The prize begins to fade away as it approaches the end of the lifetime. When the lifetime has expired, the prize can no longer be collected; that is, until it is launched again. If the gauge corresponding to the prize is full, collecting the prize then adds to the number of points, with a heart earning 500 points and a shield earning 200 points.

Finally, when the number of lives has run out or the player has finished all the levels the game has to offer, the game goes to the appropriate Game Over screen with a Collect Prize button and a Play Again button. Here, the player is given the opportunity to collect a prize if he has collected enough points, or is given the opportunity to start a new game. In the first case, the game launches an Internet browser pointing to the Web site where the player can collect his prize. Obviously, this requires a secure mechanism to make fraud as difficult as possible. This is where algorithms such as the MD5 checksum come in handy. In the second case, the game starts over back at level 1 with all three lives, full shields, and zero points.

The interface provides several pieces of information to aid the player, as shown in Figure 17.5. These are the points display, the level number display, the lives display containing a set of life icons, and the shields display containing a set of shield icons.

Elements

From the preceding specification, we find the following essential elements of the game:

- Ship
- Playing area
- Drill bit missile
- Asteroid
- Level
- Prize
- Shields
- Explosion
- Collect Prize button
- Start New Game button
- Points display
- Level number display
- Shield strength display
- Shield icon
- Lives display
- Life icon
- Prize screen
- Grand Prize screen

Recognizing How the Game's Elements Interact

The Ship

From the specification, we see that the Ship interacts with four elements: the Playing Area, the Drill Bit Missiles, the Asteroids, and the Explosion. See Figure 17.6 for the graphical representation of these interactions. We can infer that the Ship interacts with the Shields in that the Shields must always be on top of the Ship, so the Ship must tell the Shields where it is. Furthermore, the Ship interacts with the keyboard to find out which action keys are pressed, but the keyboard really is not an element of the game, just a way to control one element of it. There are two parts to the Ship's communication—the part initiated by the Ship and the reactions of the Ship to the communications initiated by other elements. The first part of the communication is done on every frame of the Macromedia Director MX movie:

1. Check the state of the keyboard and adjust the ship accordingly.
2. The Ship moves along a movement vector, a `point` in Lingo, which indicates how far the Ship moves horizontally and vertically.

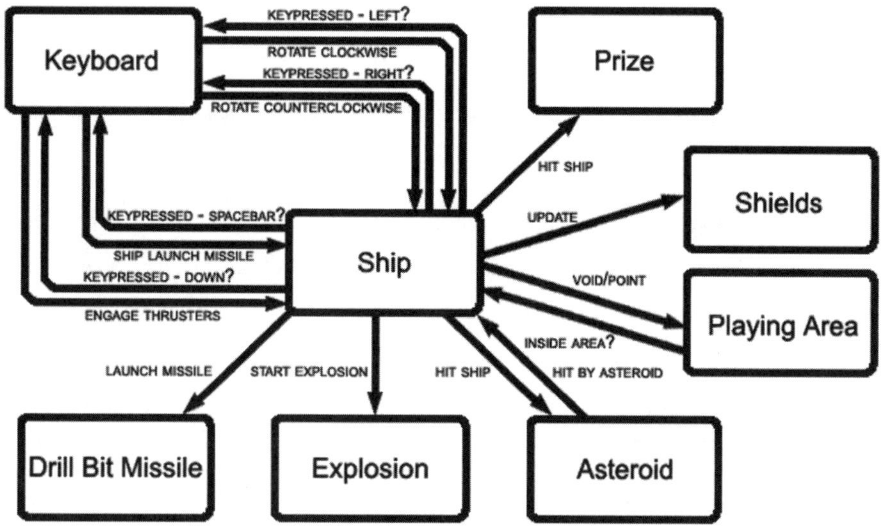

FIGURE 17.6 The relationship diagram for the Ship.

3. The Ship asks the Playing Area if it is still inside. The Playing Area replies with nothing—in Lingo, `void` if the Ship is still inside—or a `point` telling the Ship where to go.
4. Because the Shields and the Ship are separate, and the Shields need to be on top of the Ship, tell the Shields where the Ship is. Also, tell the Shields about the movement vector, so when an Asteroid bounces off the Shields, the Shields can know how much to hit back.
5. Ask the Asteroids or the Prize to check if they are hitting the Ship. If the Prize is not around, it does not answer, but that's okay.
6. Control the firing rate of the Drill Bit Missile. We only allow firing a Missile every few frames so that we do not fire too many. After all, the frame rate of the movie is 30 frames per second, and if we hold down the spacebar, we do not want to launch 30 missiles per second. So, we count down here for the next time we can launch a Missile, so that we end up firing at most six missiles per second by delaying five frames per shot.

The Ship Asks the Keyboard If an Action Key Is Being Pressed

This interaction is broken down further based on the particular action key that is pressed:

1. If the left arrow key is pressed, the Ship rotates clockwise.
2. If the right arrow key is pressed, the Ship rotates counterclockwise.

3. If the down arrow key is pressed, the Ship engages thrusters.
4. If the down arrow key is released, the Ship launches a Drill Bit Missile.

The details behind each of these steps are covered in the *Putting It All Together* section.

The Ship Reacts to the Asteroid Hitting It

The Asteroid asks the Ship if they are in contact, and the ship responds to the message:

1. If there is no contact, no further action needs to be taken.
2. If there is contact and the Shields are gone, the Ship must destroy itself and start the Explosion.

The Asteroids

The specifications tell us that the Asteroid interacts with the Level, the Points Display, the Playing Area, the Shields, the Ship, the Drill Bit Missiles, and the other Asteroids. See Figure 17.7 for the graphical representation of these interactions. For the most part, the Asteroids are mostly reactionary. They initially start idle outside the Playing Area, waiting to be launched. For each frame of the game movie:

1. If the Asteroid has not been launched, do nothing until told to launch.
2. Check if the Asteroid is hitting the Shields to find out if contact is persisting. The Shields tell the Asteroid when contact has been *initiated*, but the Asteroid must check with each frame if the contact *persists*.

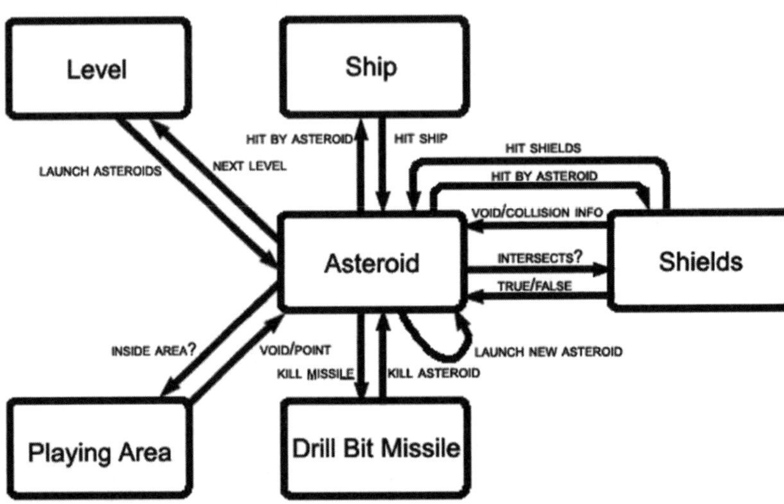

FIGURE 17.7 The relationship diagram for the Asteroid.

3. Move the Asteroid along its movement vector.
4. Ask the Playing Area if the Asteroid has moved outside the Playing Area, moving to the location returned by the Playing Area if the Asteroid is no longer inside.
5. Rotate the Asteroid every few frames.

Every now and again, an object asks the Asteroid to check for collision.

The Drill Bit Missiles Ask for a Collision Check

Now, we must construct the means by which we can allow the Drill Bit Missiles and the Asteroids to interact. To do this, the Drill Bit Missiles check for collisions for each frame of existence.

1. If there is no collision *or* this Asteroid has not been launched, nothing needs to be done.
2. Kill the Drill Bit Missile.
3. Kill the Asteroid.
4. If the Asteroid is large, tell either three smaller Asteroids to launch themselves or two smaller Asteroids and a Prize. Tell the Points Display to add 50 points.
5. If the Asteroid is small, just tell the Points Display to add 100 points.
6. If no Asteroids are left, this level is done, and this last Asteroid can tell the level to move to the next one.

The Shields Asks for a Collision Check

Along the same lines as the Drill Bit Missiles asking for a Missile check, the Shields must check for collisions as well, so that the Shields can raise themselves on collision with an Asteroid. Just like the Drill Bit Missiles, this check is done for each frame of existence.

1. If there is no collision *or* the Asteroid has not been launched, nothing needs to be done.
2. Ask the Shields about the collision.
3. If the Shields tell the Asteroid nothing, they are not around. The Asteroid does not need to do any deflection.
4. If the Asteroid hits the Shields before and is now getting out of the way, again, no need to do any deflection.
5. Otherwise, the Asteroid is going to bounce off the Shields. This requires some vector math. The Shields tell us the *normal* of the collision (the unit vector perpendicular to the Shield surface where the collision occurred)

and the Shield movement vector. We can get the new movement vector using the equation:

movement vector = movement vector + 2 × the collision vector + the shield movement vector

the collision vector = the *projection* of the movement vector onto the unit normal of the collision.

And because we are projecting onto a unit vector, the magnitude of the collision vector is simply the *dot product* of the two vectors.

6. Contact has been initiated, so make note of this. The Asteroid checks on each frame to find out when this contact is finished.

The Ship Asks for a Collision Check

The Ship must also do a collision check, just like the Drill Bit Missiles and the Shields. In case the Shields are completely gone, a collision signals the death of the Ship. Also, just like the Drill Bit Missiles and the Shields, this check is done for each frame of existence.

1. If there is no contact *or* this Asteroid has not been launched, nothing needs to be done.
2. Tell the Ship that an Asteroid has hit it.

Level Tells Asteroids to Launch

With the basic behaviors of the Asteroids implemented, we can move to the original cause of the action—the launching. The initial launch of an Asteroid begins at the start of a level.

1. If there are no more Asteroids to launch *or* this Asteroid has already been launched, nothing else needs to be done.
2. Decrease the count of Asteroids already launched. This tells the next Asteroid whether it needs to launch.
3. Increase the global Asteroid count. After this is equal to zero, the last Asteroid can tell the Level to move to the next one.
4. Set the starting point of the Asteroid randomly on one of the edges of the Playing Area.
5. Set the common properties of the Asteroid, such as the type of Asteroid, its movement, and so on.

A Large Asteroid Tells New Asteroids to Launch Upon Its Destruction

Asteroids are also launched upon the destruction of the large Asteroid. When this happens, small Asteroids are launched.

1. If there are no more new Asteroids to launch *or* this Asteroid has already been launched, nothing more needs to be done.
2. Decrease the new Asteroid launch count.
3. Increase the Asteroid count of the level.
4. Set the common properties of the Asteroid.

The Drill Bit Missile

From the specification, we see that the Drill Bit Missile interacts with the Ship, the Playing Area, and the Asteroid. See Figure 17.8 for the graphical representation of these interactions. The Drill Bit Missile for the most part of its existence asks the Asteroids whether the Drill Bit Missile and some Asteroid are in contact. But until it is launched, however, the Drill Bit Missile sits idly by. For each frame:

1. If the Drill Bit Missile has not been launched, no need to do anything.
2. Move the missile along its movement vector.
3. Ask the Playing Area if the Drill Bit Missile is still inside. If the Playing Area returns with a location, kill the Drill Bit Missile because Drill Bit Missiles do not stick around after leaving the Playing Area.
4. Ask every Asteroid if the Drill Bit Missile has run into it.

The rest of the time, the Drill bit Missile just reacts to messages.

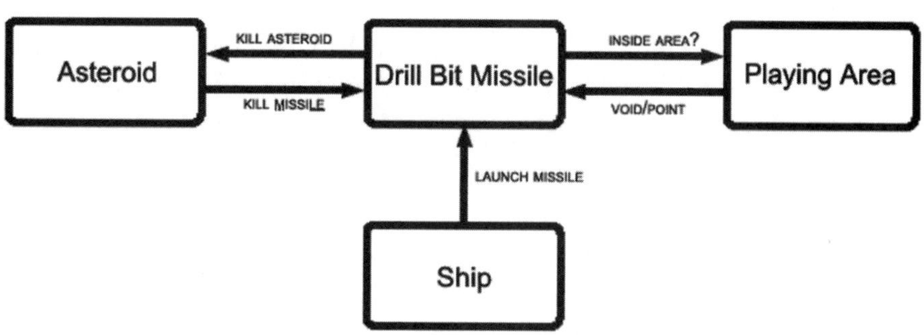

FIGURE 17.8 The relationship diagram for the Drill Bit Missile.

The Ship Tells the Drill Bit Missile to Launch

The Drill Bit Missile receives the launch message sent from the Ship, which causes the Drill Bit Missile to come to life on the screen right underneath the Ship. It then moves away from the Ship, until it hits an Asteroid or leaves the Playing Area.

1. If there are no Drill Bit Missiles left to be launched *or* this Drill Bit Missile has already been launched, do nothing.
2. One less Drill Bit Missile left to launch.
3. Point the Drill Bit Missile in the same direction as the Ship and put it underneath the Ship.
4. The Ship's speed only affects the Drill Bit Missile if the Ship and the Drill Bit Missile are pointed the same way. A positive dot product of the Ship movement vector and the unit vector of the Drill Bit Missile's movement in the direction of the Ship tells us that the two are pointed the same way. The same global table the Ship uses to figure out thrust obtains the Drill Bit Missile's unit vector. The effect of the Ship's motion then is just

ship effect = the *projection* of the Ship's movement vector onto the unit vector of the Drill Bit Missile's movement

Because we are projecting onto a unit vector, the magnitude of the ship effect is simply the dot product of the two vectors.

5. The Drill Bit Missile's total movement vector is the Drill Bit Missile's movement vector due to the launch speed in the direction the Drill Bit Missile is facing added together with the effect of the Ship's movement.

The Asteroid Tells the Missile to Die

After the Drill Bit Missile has been launched, there are two ways for the Drill Bit Missile to die. In one case, the Drill Bit Missile dies when it leaves the Playing Area. The other way is on impact with an Asteroid. In this case, the Asteroid tells the Missile to die.

1. Kill the Drill Bit Missile!

The Explosion

The specification does not say much about the Explosion, other than the Ship starts it when an Asteroid hits it without any Shields left for protection. See Figure 17.9 for the graphical representation of these interactions. The Explosion animation continues for a few frames. After the Explosion is finished, the Ship's life is truly

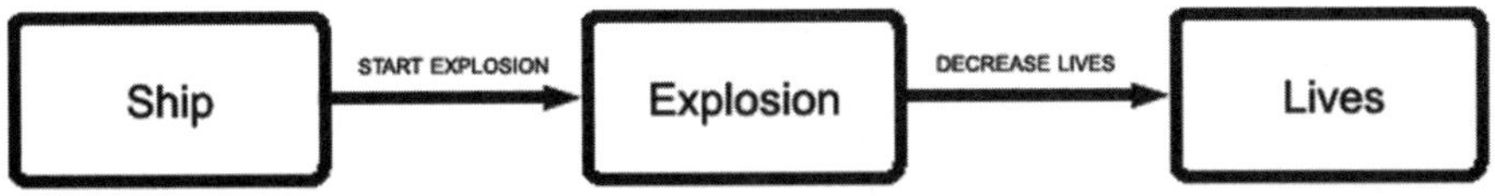

FIGURE 17.9 The relationship diagram for the Explosion.

over, and, thus, the Explosion tells the Lives Display to decrease the number of lives after the Explosion is done.

The Level

The specification does not say much about the Level, other than it launches a set number of asteroids at a set speed every time a new level starts. See Figure 17.10 for the graphical representation of the interactions. We need a *level map* to relate the number of Asteroids and their launch speed to a level number. Then, for every frame of the game movie:

1. If there is a level in progress already, do nothing.
2. After a level has finished, launch the proper number of Asteroids for the next level at the proper speed according to the level map, and mark the level in progress.

We know a level has finished when the number of Asteroids in the Playing Area has reached zero. Thus, the last Asteroid tells the level to move to the next one:

1. Increase the level number to move to the next spot in the level map.
2. If there are no more levels left, the player wins the grand prize, so go to the Grand Prize screen.
3. Mark the level as finished so the game moves on to the next level.

The Lives Display

The specification does not give much detail about the lives display itself. The Lives Display consists of three *Life Icons*, which are individual sprites and independent of one another. When the Shields are exhausted, they send a message to the Lives Display to decrease the number of lives. Because the Lives Display is actually three Life

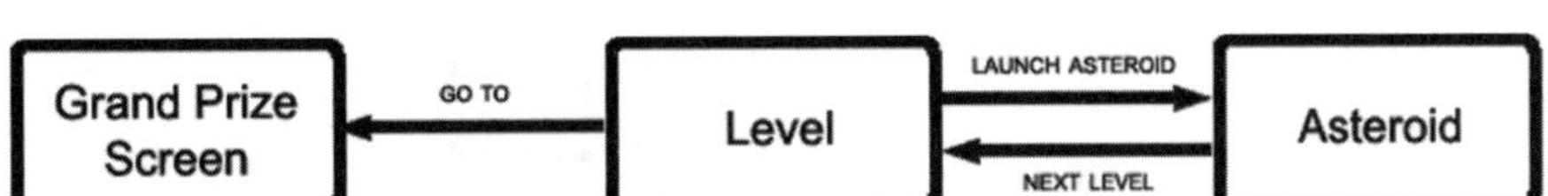

FIGURE 17.10 The relationship diagram for the Level.

Icons, we use a shotgun approach and tell every sprite to decrease the number of lives; only the Life Icon can respond to this request, and the last one disappears. When all the lives are gone, the last Life Icon tells the Points Display to go to the appropriate Prize Screen for the number of points earned. When the Ship passes over a heart Prize, the Prize uses the same shotgun approach to tell all the sprites to increase the number of lives. The Life Icon following the last Life Icon is made visible again. That is, unless all of the Life Icons are already visible, in which case the first Life Icons tells the Points Display to increase the number of points. See Figure 17.11 for the graphical representation of these interactions.

The Playing Area

The specification gives the Playing Area the very specific role of answering the question of whether an object is still inside. It returns nothing, or the Lingo `void`, if the answer to this question is yes. If the answer to this question is no, the Playing Area tells the questioning object where to go with a `point` that identifies where the object should reenter the Playing Area. To give the effect of "wrapping around the screen," reminiscent of the classic Asteroids game, this `point` should be on the side of the Playing Area directly opposite to the side where the Asteroid left.

The Points Display

The specification does not say much on how this element is to be implemented. One notion is to increase the number of points so that in the Points Display, the value increases. Another notion is that when the number of lives drops to zero, the game should go to the appropriate Game Over screen for the number of points accumulated. Because only the Points Display knows how many points have been earned, it is best suited to the job of determining which frame to go to for the appropriate

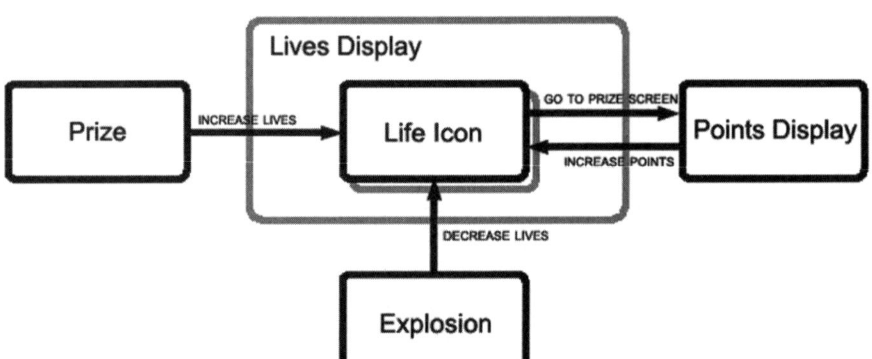

FIGURE 17.11 The relationship diagram for the Lives Display. Note that the "Lives Display" is really a collection of Life Icons.

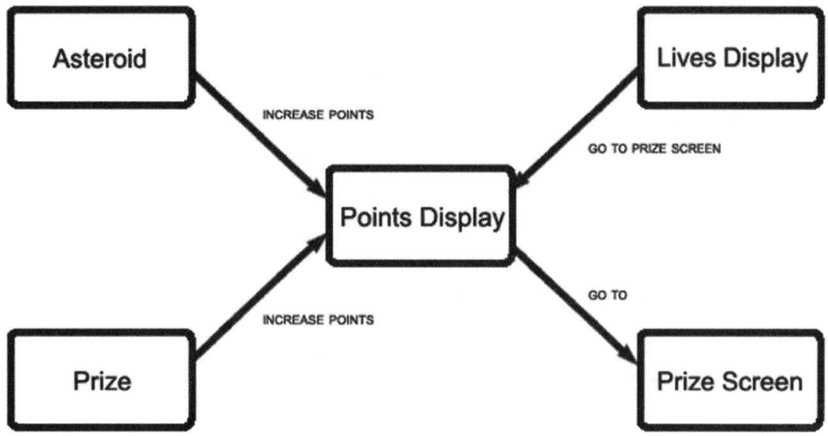

FIGURE 17.12 The relationship diagram for the Points Display.

Game Over screen. Thus, after the Explosion finishes and there are no lives left, the Lives Display simply tells the Points Display to go to the Game Over screen. The diagram of these interactions for the Points Display is shown in Figure 17.12.

The Prize

The specification shows that the Prize is affected by two elements: the Asteroid and the Ship. See Figure 17.13 for the graphical representation of the interactions.

The Asteroid Occasionally Launches the Prize when a Missile Destroys the Larger Asteroid

The Prize initially comes to life only occasionally on the destruction of a large Asteroid being "launched" from the destruction site.

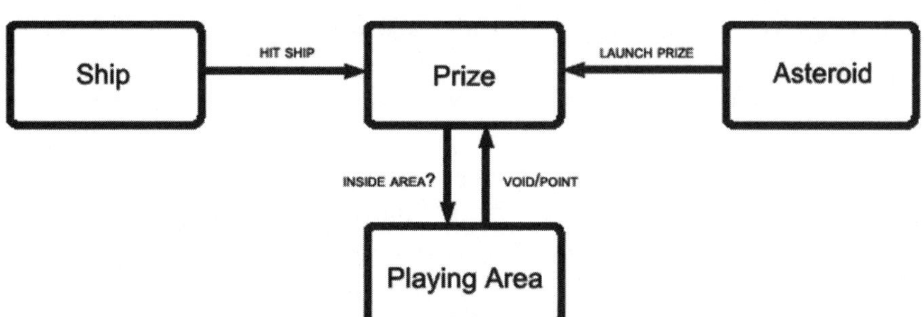

FIGURE 17.13 The relationship diagram for the Prize.

1. If the Prize has not been launched, there is nothing to do.
2. Calculate a movement vector in some random, not too horizontal and not too vertical direction.
3. Make the Prize fully visible.
4. Determine if this Prize is going to be a heart (for extra lives) or a shield (for increasing Shield strength). The odds should be much higher that the Prize should be a shield.

And the Ship Constantly Asks If It Has Come in Contact with a Prize

With the Prize launched, the Ship constantly checks if it has come into contact with the Prize, as the resulting action is its primary concern.

1. If the Prize has not been launched, *or* there is no collision, do nothing, basically ignoring the Ship.
2. If there is a collision, kill the Prize and depending on the Prize, tell the Life Icons or the Shield Icons to increase their value.

The Rest of the Time, the Prize Is Either Sitting Around or Moving Along the Screen with Each Frame of the Game Movie, Ticking Away Its Life

At the same time as the Ship is searching for the Prize, the Prize is living out its lifetime, slowly fading away as it draws near the end of its life.

1. If the Prize has not been launched, do nothing but sit idly by.
2. Tick down on the lifetime of the Prize. After time starts running out, fade the Prize away until time expires and it just disappears.
3. Move the Prize along its movement vector.
4. Ask the Playing Area if the Prize is still inside. If the reply is a point, move there to get back inside.

The Shields

The specification does not say much about the Shields except that they are raised when an asteroid comes in contact, and stay up as long as the contact persists. See Figure 17.14 for the graphical representation of the interactions. The Shields are supposed to stay on top of the Ship, where they do the most good, and because the two are separate objects, they must have a communication link. The Ship sends a message to the Shields telling them to move. It also passes along the movement vector, which becomes useful when an Asteroid hits the Shields and asks for the collision information.

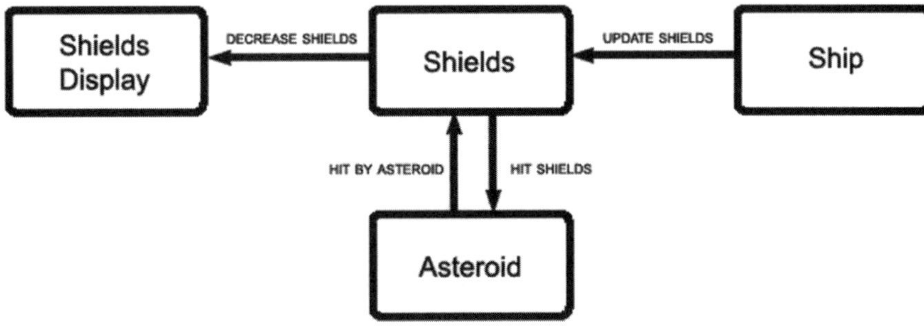

FIGURE 17.14 The relationship diagram for the Shields.

The Shields Go About Each Frame of the Game Movie Assuming Nothing Is Hitting Them

For each frame of the game, the Shields go about their time assuming nothing is hitting them, only raising themselves when they are notified of a hit.

1. Lower the Shields because we are pretending nothing is hitting them.
2. Ask all Asteroids if any of them are hitting the Shields.

If an Asteroid Finds That It Is in Contact with the Shields, It Asks the Shields for the Collision Information Based on Where It Comes in Contact with the Shields

The Asteroid asks the Shields if they are in contact. If they are, this gives the Shields the signal to raise themselves, making the Shield sprite visible on the screen. The Shields receive the message to go up *after* the `enterFrame` handler of the Shields because the Asteroids come after the Shields in the Score. So, by assuming initially that the Shields are down and they get raised in the same frame, we get the illusion that the Shields are up all the time *during contact*. Timing is important! The relationship diagram for the Shields is shown in Figure 17.14.

1. If there are no Shields left, return nothing, the Lingo `void`.
2. Raise the Shields as there is surely a collision when the Asteroid asks for the collision information.
3. Tell the Shields Display to decrease Shield strength.
4. Calculate the unit vector for the normal of the collision.
5. Return the collision information bundled nice and neatly in a property list.

An important note: the Shields receive the message to go up *after* the `enterFrame` handler of the Shields because the Asteroids come after the Shields in the Score. So, by assuming initially that the Shields are down and they get raised in the same frame, we get the illusion that the Shields are up all the time *during contact*. Timing is important!

The Shields Display

The Shields Display works essentially like the Lives Display, with several Shield Icons representing total Shield Strength. However, the important difference to note is that each Shield Icon is not one "Shield strength," but a bucket full of Shield strength. The Shields ask the Asteroids if they are in contact, and if so, the Shields tell the Shields Display to decrease the strength of the Shields, which involves sending a message to all the Shield Icons using a shotgun approach. This causes the last Shield Icon to tap into its "bucket" of Shield Strength. As the Shield strength decreases, the amount of strength in the bucket decreases. The last Shield Icon disappears when the bucket is empty. On the other hand, when the Ship flies over a Prize, the Prize tells the Shields Display to increase the Shield strength, using the shotgun approach as before. If the bucket of the last icon of Shield Strength is not full, it is filled and then a new Shield Icon is added. No new Shield Icon is added if all Shield Icons are currently displayed. Just as with the Life Icon, if the Shield Strength is completely full, the first Shield Icon just tells the Points Display to increase the number of points. The diagram of the interactions for the Shields Display is shown in Figure 17.15.

The Start New Game Button

The specification does not say much regarding this element other than that it makes the game go back to level one, resets the score to zero, resets the number of lives back to three, and restores full Shield strength. This requires sending messages to

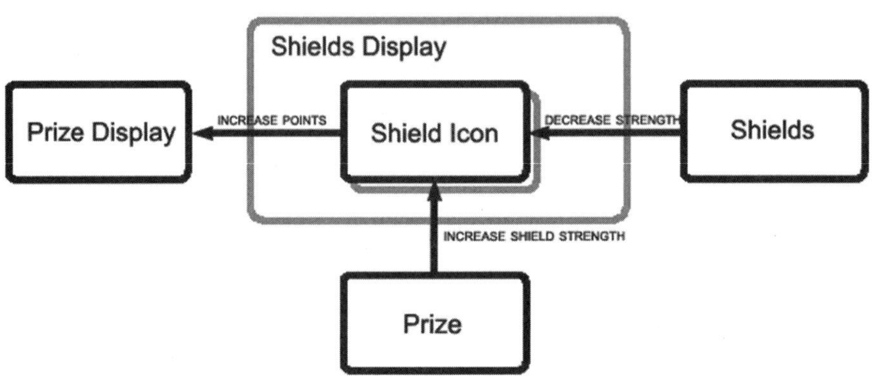

FIGURE 17.15 The relationship diagram for the Shields Display. Note that the "Shields Display" is really a collection of Shield Icons.

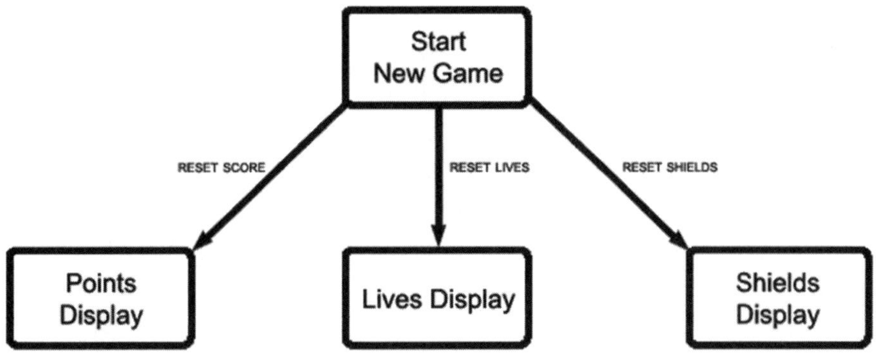

FIGURE 17.16 The relationship diagram for the Start New Game button.

the elements concerned—telling the Level to go back to level 1, telling the Points Display to put a zero in the display, and telling the Lives Display and the Shields Display to reset their values back to full. The diagram of the interactions for the Start New Game button is shown in Figure 17.16.

The Claim Prize Button

The specification says that this button launches a Web browser allowing users to collect their real prize. To minimize on the fraudulent claming of prizes, the button takes three values—the name, e-mail address, and prize name—of the player and blends them together in a not-all-too-obvious way into a single value, so that the MD5 checksum can be calculated. Because the MD5 checksum is only one way (that is, you cannot get the original from the checksum), the final result cannot be reversed to find the original blended text.

Identifying the Scripts of Blasteroids

In listing the handlers, we ignore the usual `beginSprite`, `endSprite`, and `enterFrame` handlers, and list only the custom handlers, which we derive from the analysis in the previous section.

- Asteroid

  `setProperties:` Sets the common properties of an Asteroid; message sent by the Asteroid to itself.

  `launchAsteroid:` Launches a large Asteroid at the start of a level; message sent by the Level

  `killAsteroid:` Checks for collision with the Asteroid; message sent from the Drill Bit Missile.

`launchNewAsteroid:` Launches a new smaller Asteroid when the large Asteroid has been hit by a Drill Bit Missile; message sent from an Asteroid.

`hitShields:` Checks for a collision with the Asteroid; message sent by the Shields.

`hitShip:` Checks for a collision with the Asteroid; message sent by the Ship.

- Drill Bit Missile

  `launchMissile:` Tells the Drill Bit Missile to launch; message sent by the Ship.

  `killMissile:` Tells the Drill Bit Missile to kill itself; message sent by the Asteroid.

- Explosion

  `startExplosion:` Tells the Explosion to start; message sent by the Ship.

- Level

  `startOver:` Resets the level to 1; message sent by the Start New Game button.

  `goToNextLevel:` Tells the Level to go to the next one; message sent by the last Asteroid.

- Life Icon

  `decreaseLives:` Decreases the number of lives; message sent by the Explosion.

  `increaseLives:` Increases the number of lives; message sent by the heart Prize.

  `resetLives:` Resets the life count to full; message sent by the Start New Game button.

- Playing area

  `insideArea:` Asks if they are still inside the Playing Area; message sent by many objects.

- Points Display

  `increasePoints:` Tells the Points Display to increase the score a certain amount; message sent by many objects.

  `resetPoints:` Resets the number of points to zero; message sent by the Start New Game button.

  `goToPrizeScreen:` Asks the Points Display to go to the appropriate score screen; message sent by the Explosion.

- Prize

  `launchPrize:` Launches the Prize; message sent by a large Asteroid hit by a Drill Bit Missile.

  `hitShip:` Checks for collision; message sent by the Ship.

- Shields

  `hitByAsteroid:` Checks for collision; message sent by an Asteroid.

- Shields Icon

  decreaseShields: Takes a notch off the Shield Strength Display; message sent by the shields.

  increaseShields: Adds a notch back onto the Shield StrengthDisplay; message sent by the prize.

- Ship

  keyCheck: Checks the state of the action keys and adjusts the Ship properties accordingly; message sent by the `enterFrame` handler.

  rotateShip: Rotates the ship clockwise or counterclockwise; message sent by the `keyCheck` handler.

  engageThrusters: Engages or disengages the thrusters; message sent by the `keyCheck` handler.

  hitByAsteroid: Informs the Ship that it has been hit; message sent by an Asteroid.

  shipLaunchMissile: Launches one Drill Bit Missile. Note that we place "ship" in front. We don't want this handler called when we actually launch the missiles! Message sent by the `keyCheck` handler.

- Unit Vectors

  Generates the global table of unit vectors for each of the orientations of the Ship and Drill Bit Missiles.; message sent by the `startMovie` handler.

Putting It All Together

ON THE CD

The complete source code for the Blasteroids game can be found on the CD-ROM at /files/templates/chapter17.dir, as it would take up too much space in the book. Instead, we focus on the key concepts and methods used by the game here, to make the source code more clear.

Controlling the Ship

The Player's interface to the game is through the keyboard. To control the Ship, we need to determine the state of each of the *action keys*, namely the left and right arrow keys for rotating the Ship left and right, the down arrow key for engaging and disengaging the thrusters, and the spacebar to launch the Drill Bit Missiles. The `keyCheck` handler in the Ship behavior performs this function. This handler is called from the `enterFrame` handler, so we are checking the keyboard state in every frame. We use the `keyPressed` handler to detect if a key with the specified *scancode* is pressed. Each key on the keyboard is assigned a scancode; those for the action keys are listed in Table 17.1.

TABLE 17.1 Action keys and their scancodes

Key	*Scancode*
Right arrow	124
Left arrow	123
Down arrow	125
Spacebar	49

These scancodes can easily be determined by adding the following frame script to the first frame of a new movie:

```
on enterFrame me
 go to the frame
end
 on keyDown me
 put the keyCode
end
```

As you press keys on the keyboard, the scancodes for the keys appear in the message window.

The basic form of a key check is:

```
if keyPressed(<scancode>) then
   <some action>
end if
```

So, for example, the key check for firing a Drill Bit Missile looks like this:

```
-- check the spacebar key
if keyPressed(49) then
      mySprite.shipLaunchMissile()
end if
```

The thruster controls are a little more complicated because we actually care if the key is up or down. We pass the state of the key to the `engageThrusters` handler of the Ship behavior. If the key is down, we change the image of the Ship to have thrust and we increase the speed of the Ship in the direction it is pointing. Otherwise, we change the image of the Ship to have no thrust.

Animating the Ship

The Ship animation is organized in the cast as a series of images of the Ship in various orientations, starting from with the Ship oriented with the nose pointing up, rotating 360 degrees clockwise over 16 frames, shown in Figure 17.17. These frames are contiguous with the first frame labeled. There are two such sets of frames, one set with the first frame labeled "normal" and the second set with the first frame labeled "thrust." The labeled frames are called the *base frames* and the following, unlabeled frames are simply the *frames*. Each frame is numbered according to its distance from the base frame. Thus, the first frame, the base frame itself, is frame number 0, and each successive frame going clockwise is of increasing frame number. Thus, for the 16-frame animation, the frames are labeled 0 through 15. This also allows us to order the orientations, so that for a particular orientation and a particular state, to get the proper cast member, all we need to do is add the number representing the orientation, which is also the frame number, to the base frame. The following code is from the `keyCheck` handler of the Ship behavior, and demonstrates this idea:

```
-- update the ship image
mySprite.memberNum = myBaseMember.memberNum + myFrame
```

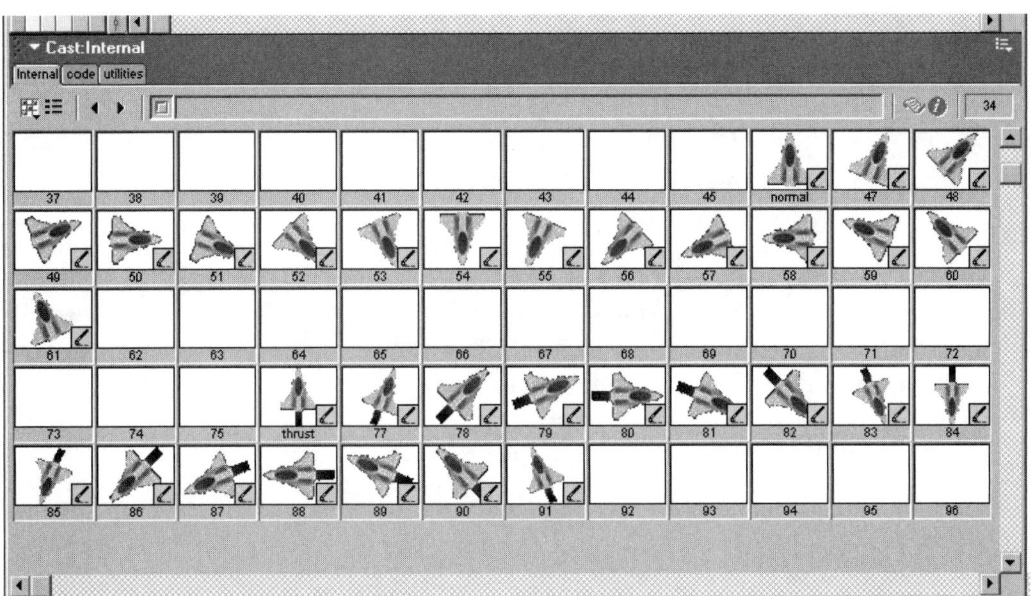

FIGURE 17.17 The ship animation frames.

Arranging the cast members such that the images span a rotation of 360 over 16 frames has the additional advantage of making it easy to cycle through the images repeatedly using the `mod` function. The `mod` function calculates the remainder of division. Thus, if the dividend is smaller than the divisor, the remainder is always the dividend. When the dividend equals the divisor, the `mod` function returns zero. Thus, if the frame number is the dividend and the total number of frames is the divisor, as we increase the frame number by one, as long as the frame number is less than the number of frames, `mod` always returns the next frame number. However, after the frame number equals the number of frames, `mod` returns zero, and we have now started over. This works in principle going forward through the frames. However, the caveat is that the dividend must remain positive because this method does not work with negative numbers. To keep the dividend positive, we need only add the divisor. This does not affect the remainder because:

$$i \bmod n = (n + i) \bmod n, \text{ where } |i| < n.$$

The following code from the `rotateShip` handler of the Ship behavior demonstrates this idea. The variable direction can have a value of +1 or –1.

```
myFrame = (gMaxFrames + myFrame + direction) mod gMaxFrames
```

Another advantage of ordering the orientations of the Ship in this way is the very straightforward creation of a table of unit vectors in which each orientation corresponds to one unit vector that specifies the horizontal and vertical motion that moves the Ship one pixel in the direction the Ship is facing. Thus, to add thrust when the down arrow key is pressed, we can express this in as simple terms as:

```
myMovement = myMovement + gUnitVectors[myFrame + 1]
```

In addition, this arrangement makes it easy to change the way the Ship looks while keeping it oriented the same way, such as when engaging or disengaging the thrusters. In each case, the Ship is pointed the same way, but the appearance changes. All we have to do is change the base frame, and the appearance of the Ship changes and the orientation remains the same:

```
-- engage thrusters
-- switch to the thrust series of images
myBaseMember = member("thrust")
```

and

```
-- disengage thrusters
```

```
-- switch back to the normal series of images
myBaseMember = member("normal")
```

Launching Control

There are many sprites for the Drill Bit Missiles and the Asteroids. However, at any given time in the course of the game, we only need to launch a certain number of them. We only need to launch one Drill Bit Missile each time the spacebar is pressed. We only need to launch a fixed number of Asteroids each time we start a new level. However, each Drill Bit Missile sprite and each Asteroid sprite are independent of one another. Thus, to launch the required number, there must be some form of communication between the sprites to allow them to determine when the required number has been reached. Global variables are very well-suited for this purpose. We can use a shotgun approach, sending the launch message to all sprites using the `sendAllSprites` function. Thus, requests should be unique to the type of object to launch. Thus, only Asteroids respond to the `launchAsteroids` message. Before calling `sendAllSprites`, however, we set a global variable, used by only this message, such as `gAsteroidLaunchCount`, to set the required number of Asteroids to launch. Each Asteroid that can launch decreases the value of this global variable and launches. After the value reaches zero, no other Asteroid launches. So, the Level launches Asteroids in this way:

```
gLaunchCount = gLevelMap[myCurrentLevel].asteroidCount
 sendAllSprites(#launchAsteroid,
      gLevelMap[myCurrentLevel].asteroidSpeed)
```

and the asteroid uses the following code to ensure that only the required number of Asteroids that have not previously been launched are launched by the `launchAsteroid` handler:

```
if gLaunchCount = 0 or myAlive then return
 -- one less Asteroid to launch
 gLaunchCount = gLaunchCount - 1

 ...
end if
```

A more complex application of this principle is in the control of the Life and Shield Strength Displays. Each of these displays is made up of several independently controlled icons. When the Ship collects a prize, we add a free life or a free Shield. We use the same shotgun approach as before, and we must fill only the icon that needs to be filled and then stop. Here again, we use a global variable, `gCollectingPrize`. As long as this variable is `true`, we scan until we find the icon to fill.

However, we must stop there; otherwise, we end up filling up all of the icons, which is definitely not correct. Thus, after we have filled an icon, we set `gCollectingPrize` to `false`, communicating the fact that the prize has been collected. Each subsequent icon sees this fact, and does not fill up:

```
on increaseLives me
-- stop increasing lives once the Prize has been
-- collected
if not gCollectingPrize then return
-- are all Life Icons are displayed?
if gLives = gMaxLives then
-- collect some points
sendSprite(gPointsDisplay, #increasePoints, 500)
-- and that's all
gCollectingPrize = false
return
end if
-- is this Life Icon is the Life Icon to add?
if myLife = gLives + 1 then
-- add a life
gLives = gLives + 1
-- show the Life Icon
mySprite.visible = true
-- and the Prize has been collected
gCollectingPrize = false
end if
end
```

Vectors

Vectors are a very convenient way of representing motion, and all the objects in the Blasteroids game use them. We use the `point` to represent the vector, whereas the `locH` property represents the horizontal motion and the `locV` property represents the vertical motion. Taken together, we can represent motion at any angle. Vectors have a wealth of interesting operations that allow us to do some complex things with very minimum effort. A very good example of this is the deflection the Asteroid off of the Shields. Given the normal of the collision, the movement vector of the Shields, and the movement vector of the Asteroid, we can create the effect of deflection. The normal of the collision is simply the line running perpendicular to the tangent line at the point of collision. This is specified as a unit vector; that is, the motion is just one pixel in the given direction. We lengthen the normal vector to determine how much the Shields are pushing against the Asteroid. The lengthening factor is the dot product, is as follows, and is called the projection of the Ship vector onto the missile normal vector:

```
-- calculate the projection of the movement of the
-- Asteroid onto the normal of the collision
mag = -(unitNormal.locH * myMovement.locH + \
       unitNormal.locV * myMovement.locV)
```

and to calculate deflection, we just add several vectors together:

```
-- calculate the new movement, taking into consideration the
-- deflection effect (2 * mag * unitNormal) and the Shield
-- movement
myMovement = myMovement + 2 * mag * unitNormal +
    info.shieldMovement
```

See Figure 17.18 for a graphical representation of this process. The circle represents the shields. The arrow pointing toward the shields is the movement vector of the asteroid and each red arrow represents the magnitude of the collision with respect to the normal of the collision. The arrow starting from the center of the circle indicates the direction of that normal. Note that the sum of the movement vector and the green vector is the first red vector, and the second red vector completes the path, such that the overall sum is the same as the deflection vector, which is the black arrow pointed away from the shield.

Keeping Things Secure

To limit fraud as much as possible, we use a secure encoding scheme called the *MD5 checksum*. This is a scheme commonly used in encrypting online transactions to keep things secure. An MD5 checksum is calculated from a sequence of charac-

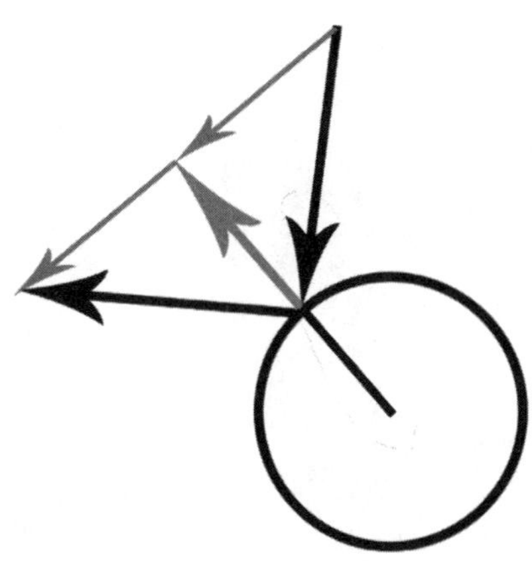

FIGURE 17.18 Graphical relationship of the Asteroid Deflection process.

ters, and thus we combine, or *blend*, several pieces of information together—the prize, the player's name, and the player's e-mail address, as shown in Figure 17.19. The method of blending need not be too elaborate—just hard to guess. On this blended sequence of characters, we compute the MD5 checksum. By making the blending mechanism hard to guess, it makes it much harder for someone to forge an MD5 checksum. Here is the blending process we use illustrated:

```
Prize name:          Prize 1
Name:                Joe Blow
E-mail address:      joeblow@somewhere.net
Blended sequence:    JtPoereni .zBeelr oe1whPJwroeiemz oeBs
                     l@1owPworJliobzeee o Bj1”
MD5 checksum:        1f76c4f0df9260ca0b21b2f8aa99de92
```

ON THE CD

That blended sequence is pretty crazy looking. The blending mechanism is very simple. It goes like this. The first, fourth, seventh, and so on letters come from the player's name going forward. The second, fifth, eight, and so on letters come from the e-mail address going backward. The third, sixth, ninth, and so on letters come from the prize name going forward. The overall length of the blended sequence is

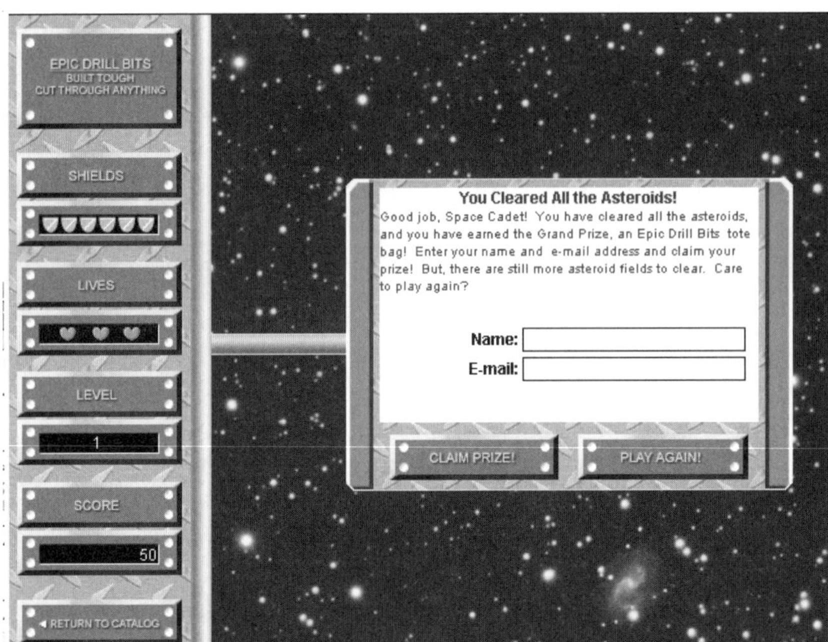

FIGURE 17.19 Claim your prize here! This is how we get the player's name and e-mail address.

the length of the longest of the three values times three. If you run out of letters for any of the shorter two, you start over from the beginning of that value and repeat as many times as necessary to make the required length. It doesn't matter if there are any letters left. In Lingo, the code to do this looks like the following example, and can be found in the `mouseUp` handler of the Claim Prize behavior. The complete code can be found on the CD-ROM at /files/templates/chapter17.dir. Note the return of the `mod` function. This time, instead of cycling through frames, we are cycling through letters. Also note the –1s and the +1s in the expressions involving the `mod` function. Remember, the cycles using `mod` start with 0, whereas the index to a letter in a string starts with 1.

```
-- go through the longest string, and repeat the
-- letters of the shorter strings when out of letters
repeat with charNum = 1 to longest
-- put one character of the name into the blender
blender = blender & \
playerName.char[(charNum - 1) mod \
nameLength + 1]
-- put one character of the e-mail address
-- backward into the blender
blender = blender & \
playerEmail.char[emailLength - \
((charNum - 1) mod emailLength + 1) + 1]
-- put one character of the prize name into the blender
blender = blender & \
gPrizeName.char[(charNum - 1) mod \
prizeLength + 1]
end repeat
```

SUMMARY

ON THE CD

That covers the more complex techniques used by the Blasteroids game, and sheds some light on general techniques that you can use in developing your own game. The source code on the CD-ROM, named chapter17.dir in the \files\templates\ folder, is well-documented, and the comments follow the pseudocode discussed in the *Recognizing How the Game's Elements Interact* section of this chapter. Be certain to take advantage of the full source code on the CD-ROM to fully understand the game.

PART

IV The Real World

In the first three parts of the book, we learned about branding, gameplay, and game development. Using Macromedia Flash MX 2004 and Director MX, we built several Advergames. In the next part of the book, we learn about Advergaming in the real world. We talk to some of the stars in the world of Advergaming along with game developers who may be just a few steps ahead of you.

We begin in Chapter 18 with an Advergaming Developer's Guide. If you are looking to go to work for an Advergaming shop, or hire a top Advergaming company to create a game for you, this is a good place to get started. Chapters 19, 20, and 21 are in-depth case study interviews with three companies that were pioneers and are now leaders in Advergaming—Blockdot, YaYa Media, and AGENCY.COM. In Chapter 22, you'll find a directory of Advergaming development companies, complete with contact information and links to some of their well-known games.

18 Advergaming Developer's Guide

If you are in the market for an Advergame for your company, or are planning to work in the industry, this chapter will help you better understand some of your options.

In this chapter, we begin by learning some of the finer points in selecting a development company. We include a number of tips to help make the selection process go more smoothly. If you are a designer, programmer, artist, or developer, and the world of Advergaming appeals to you, you can apply the information you learn here with the Advergaming companies listed in Chapter 22, A Guide to Advergame Development Companies, to scope out your dream job. We share with you the advice given to us during our interviews with the top executives at both small and large shops.

SELECTING A DEVELOPMENT COMPANY

If you have a vision for a game that goes beyond those examples covered in our book, you may have to hire a development company to build an Advergame for you. Doing your homework prior to selecting a game shop will pay big dividends down the road.

If you have a game in mind, the best way to begin is to create a design specification document. We touched on it in Chapter 5, The Concept: Conceptualizing an Advergame from the Ground Up, and you may remember that the design specification document is like a set of blueprints. In our case, it contains the game genre, storyline, graphics and animation elements, sound and music, tracking information, and most importantly, how the game is used to showcase the brand. Keep in mind that game development is a creative process, and specifications that are not detailed may result in a game that looks nothing like your original vision. "Loose" specifications also tend to cause "mission creep," resulting in delays and budget overruns.

Determining the price of your Advergame does not have to be a "black box" experience, and a professional development shop will take the time to explain and help you formulate your game design specification. Most developers quote a fixed price, so it is in their best interest to work from a well-defined specification. Clients do not like "change orders" that seem to pop up like mushrooms after a warm summer rain, so it is best to take care of these details up front. Sometimes, changes are inevitable, so make sure the project quotes you receive include hourly rates. Watch out for less experienced companies that provide lower initial bids on projects, but don't include some miscellaneous expenses, such as travel, food, and sales tax (which combined can be substantial). A good price is meaningless if you don't get a quality game that does the job. One part of the budget that is easy to overlook is the backend support that comes with the release of any piece of software. The more successful your Advergame, the larger the universe of hardware and conflicting software with which it is bound to come into contact. You'll want to be sure the Advergaming vendor you choose is adequately staffed to handle problems that arise after the game goes live. The old adage "If you don't have good support for your software, you don't have good software!" is especially true for a game designed for mass distribution.

If you have a sizable budget and want a custom game, all Advergaming companies will be happy to design and build a unique game for you. Before you get into custom game development, one area you may want to undertake is a careful review of all of the games created by a vendor to see if any existing games can be repurposed for your application. Sometimes, it can be as easy as putting a new "skin" (changing out the graphical elements) on a game that has already been produced. This can save you quite a bit of money, and you can launch your Advergame in a fraction of the time it takes to build one from scratch.

Whether you create a new game, or reskin an existing game, you'll want all the help you can get when it comes time to launch your Advergame. Some Advergaming shops also host third-party Web sites specifically created as gaming portals and will launch your game from the site as part of their service. For example, Blockdot hosts the *www.kewlbox.com* Web site, which averages over 1.5 million visitors per month. This site is also capable of providing detailed statistics on gameplay and other demographic and tracking information. Even more important, the company has a database of Advergaming enthusiasts and with an e-mail blast can jump-start a promotional campaign instantly.

When you select a game development company, look for one that shares similar values and goals. You may want to look at your choice of vendors as the beginning of an ongoing relationship. Like any good marriage, the two parties involved have to listen, communicate, and work together for the relationship to be successful. If you pick the right partner, you will be working together for years to come.

One perk in selecting a software vendor is that you really need to play some of the Advergames developed by the vendor to help determine if they are the right company to do your job. You may take some added pleasure in knowing that you are actually getting paid to play video games (thus proving your mom wrong). Actually, playing the games will help you decide which features you want to include in your game.

Doing your "due diligence" in selecting a game development company takes on an added weight with an Advergame because a poorly produced game is no fun to play, *and* it casts a shadow on your brand. Ask the game vendor for a list of companies and contacts of recent game customers and call to ask for a candid opinion of their work. With some Advergame budgets well into the six figure range, this level of scrutiny could prevent you from making a career-altering mistake.

WORKING IN THE ADVERGAMING INDUSTRY

So you want to be an Advergame developer? Guess what? So do a lot of other people. If you are not ready to roll up your sleeves and put in the long hours, find another career. The good news is the industry is growing, and there are a number of ways to become part of it. You can work for an established development company (that is, get a job), or start your own Advergaming enterprise. Let's take a closer look at each option.

Working for an Established Developer

There are oodles of books on the art of getting a job, and it's a good idea, if you are just starting out, to do some basic research on the finer points of crafting a cover letter, creating a résumé, preparing for an interview, and conducting research on the company to which you are applying. Getting a job is a job in itself. Talk to veterans and they will tell you there is no such thing as "security" in the world of gaming. Today, a game shop is hot; tomorrow it's nonexistent. So, learning how to get a job is an important skill worth mastering.

In our small company, we are often flooded with job applicants (especially in November and April—just as the school semester is about to end). When we have an opening to fill, we have a process to help us identify and hire new team members. Let's take a closer look at that process.

For any new position, we develop a job specification that outlines the qualifications needed for success in the position. In addition to including the formal education requirements and actual work experience needed for the job, it also includes a salary range. The specification lists who the person in this position reports to and (if applicable) the other team members this person will manage.

We scan all incoming résumés to quickly determine if the applicants have the basic skill set, education, and experience needed for the job at hand. If so, we ask them to send us their transcript (if recently out of school) and a cover letter. The cover letter should be no more than a single page, and it should answer this question: "Please explain your personal goals, what you perceive the mission of the epic software group to be, and how working at this company can help us both achieve success." Their cover letters help us to determine how the candidates express themselves in writing, and if working together makes sense for both the applicants and our company.

Those applicants who make it through this round are invited in for a formal interview. During the visit to our shop, the applicant meets and talks with each member of the group; then, we ask him to show us his portfolio or demo CD/reel. If the applicant looks promising and we feel he can be a productive member of our team, we go to the next phase of the process, which has affectionately been named "the acid test." If we are interviewing a programmer, the acid test might be to write a small application or series of routines in Director MX or Macromedia Flash MX 2004. For a graphic designer, we might ask the applicant to create an interface and provide him with some specific parameters for the way it works. For a 3D artist, we might have him create one or more 3D objects and build a basic animation.

The applicant sets the time for the acid test, which is conducted off-site. Most candidates ask for a week, and we invite them back for the second interview when they are finished. The acid test really helps us understand the skill set of the applicant, along with his ability to meet deadlines and follow instructions. Many applicants simply do not return, and that is a good thing for both parties. If the applicant returns with a successful acid test, usually a job is offered for a trial period of time. An offer of extended employment after successfully completing the trial period usually results.

We look for people who have the skill, the self-motivation, an understanding of the industry, a passion for game development, and the ability to work on a team.

If our hiring process seems long and convoluted, our experience has shown that quick judgments in hiring new team members has sometimes resulted in very poor choices. Because game development in our shop is a team sport, the choice of players is critical to success. Getting hired at other Advergaming development shops may also require you to run a gauntlet of equally challenging obstacles, so you, too, can have a chance to work 60 hours a week doing something you love.

Some things you can do to increase your chances of landing a job in the industry include:

Attend game conventions: Game conventions are offered on both the local (*www.gameconference.com*) and national (E3, SIGGRAPH) levels.

Read game and industry publications: Some examples include *Game Developer Magazine*, *Computer Graphics World*, *Computer Arts*.

Become a regular on game developer Web sites: Some examples include *www.gamedev.net*, *www.gamesutra.com*.

Attend school: Check around your city for courses being offered in game development and design (you can even find some at the community college level). The local Art Institute and Leisure Learning Courses may be another good source of educational resources with classes that can be taken in the evening or on weekends. For those who are really serious, you may want to enroll in a school that specializes in video game development, such as Full Sail or DigiPen. They are not cheap, but when you graduate, you will have the "hands-on" experience that employers find very valuable.

Network: Most game development companies are bombarded with résumés, so anything you can do to get yours to the top of the pile should be considered. One way to get inside the company is to call and ask to interview for "information," not a job. Most developers are more than willing to spend a few minutes with you to discuss the industry and share their success stories. As they get to know you and your talents, they might just mention a problem the company is having with which you can help.

Play games: If you are going to spend hours playing games, why not have fun with a purpose? Visit Advergaming sites and try out the games. You will quickly learn who is building the hot games. Add those names to your list of prospective employers. Use these visits to come up with ideas for building your own game. Developers trying to break into the industry complain, "Everyone wants a person with experience, but how can I get experience if they don't hire me?" The answer: hire yourself and build your own game.

Developing Advergames Solo

The really good news for Advergame developers is that you don't have to join a company to participate in the industry. Some Advergame projects are small enough for you to handle by yourself. If you are a programmer and need help with the graphics, you can find scores of artists wanting to pick up a little extra pocket change to help. The same goes for artists who would never dream of writing source code. Whatever your weak point is, someone is always (for a small fee) willing to step in and help.

Running your own business is not for the faint at heart, but it also can be very rewarding when you see your ideas come to life on the screen and are paid well for them. If you think that running your own business means you don't have to worry about the boss, you are wrong—your clients are your new bosses (more than one client means more than one boss).

Do you have the constitution to stay with a project long after the initial excitement of the startup phase is over? Just having some cool ideas is not enough—game ideas are a dime a dozen. The hard part is making them happen—often with tight budgets and not enough time. Do you have the resources to tide you over when a client takes 90 days to pay an invoice, or worse, cancels the project due to bankruptcy (it has happened to us)?

As an independent Advergame developer, the excitement of having the title "President" or "Founder" on your card may quickly be replaced with the heavy load of problems and challenges you'll face on a daily basis. Are you able to juggle a number of tasks simultaneously, and make decisions on a daily basis that can quickly put you out of business? Are you prepared to do everything from selling the job to creating the application to billing and collecting from the client? If not, there is no shame in working for someone else and having them sweat the details of running a small business. On the other hand, the satisfaction that comes from launching and building a new company can be quite exhilarating (especially when you land a big contract or produce a hot game).

So whether you are looking for a place to go to work, a development company to hire, or just want to learn more about the leaders in Advergaming, the directory in Chapter 22, A Guide to Advergame Development Companies, is a great place to start. For each company, we have listed their contact and general information along with URLs where you will find samples of their games.

ADVERGAMING—ONE DEVELOPER'S SUCCESS STORY

Jeremy Brown (Jer) has made the transition from a game developer working for a successful company to an independent game contractor. He was born and raised in Washington, D.C., and has been living in Sweden for the past six years. His story provides insight into a career path that successful Advergame developers often take, along with his thoughts and philosophy on creating games. Samples of his work can be found in the Gallery section of his Web site—*www.J3R.com.*

Introduction

After gaining a vast amount of experience working as senior Flash developer for one of Europe's largest Internet consultancy agencies, Jeremy decided to break away from a large corporate environment and start his own company. His goal had always been to produce innovative and aesthetically pleasing Flash solutions. His development philosophy includes a dedication to both the external (the graphics) and the internal (the code) elements of the game. Adhering to these principals has allowed him to create Flash solutions that are user-friendly, reliable, and inexpensive to maintain. Jer says that "While high-quality applications are more expensive and time-consuming to create, I believe the long-term benefits of high-quality development are worth the investment."

Moving from HTML to Flash

While working as a network administrator for an Internet café, Jer had the responsibility of creating and maintaining the café's Web site. He found HTML to be extremely limiting. He wanted to grab the user's attention. A friend recommended that he check out Flash, so he picked up a copy of Flash 3 and became absorbed in all the motion that was possible. Jer created several sites with Flash 3 for the owner of the café, mainly focusing on design and the use of motion. Unfortunately, Flash 3 did not provide any real means of programming. When Flash 4 became available, he quit his job and stayed home for six months, immersing himself in the program for over 12 hours each day. The power of the program came with learning object orientation and how it applied to ActionScript (the Flash programming language).

Jer started creating games, but ActionScript language was quite limited, so he continually struggled to come up with tricks to make things work. He turned to VBScript, out of necessity, to create backend systems for his Web sites and games. After six months of experimentation, freelancing, and working on his own projects, he was offered a job at Framfab, one of Europe's largest Internet consultancy companies.

When Flash 5 came out, Jer immediately realized the programming possibilities the program offered and he began developing sophisticated games that were simply not possible before. "The complexity involved in game programming inspired me to focus on further improving my programming skills. I worked all day with Flash on corporate projects, and then continued late into the evenings with personal projects and development; I pushed myself every day to learn new methodologies and to grow as a developer. I studied trigonometry to make up for my lack of attention in high school. I studied object orientation in depth, making my understanding of the subject intuitive. I spent a lot of time reading books, talking with other programmers who were skilled in other programming languages, programming with them, working on projects together, and just hanging out," said Jer.

This intense period of study together with an enormous workload creating dynamic, multilanguage, corporate Web sites and games improved his skills dramatically. His hard work paid off. Jer was promoted to Senior Flash developer at Framfab. This position offered him a great amount of freedom with the games he created. He could focus on all aspects of game development, from the initial brainstorming, concept development, and branding strategy, through to the functional design and specification, and finally the production. Having this overall view of the game development process, he began to focus on the criteria that had a direct relationship to the final success of online games.

Conceptual Design

What follows is a brief overview of the criteria Jer follows when creating Advergames.

How do you go about designing an Advergame to fit a product or company?

I think it is best to start by narrowing down the focus of the game. The first step is to make sure the game has a clear product or service that it is promoting and to be aware of the target group for this product or service. Before getting into actual specifics about the game, it is best to decide what type of game is appropriate for the target group. For example, if the target group for the product is boys ages 8–15, an action game usually works well, whereas if the target group is girls of the same age, a word game, memory game, or coloring game is probably more appropriate. Of course, there are boys who like memory games and girls who like actions games, but we must spend some time investigating our target group in a stereotypical manner to figure out what type of game will most likely attract our target group and keep them coming back.

After we have figured out what type of game to create, it is helpful for the client and developer to try to locate some games online that have interesting characteristics that might work well within the project. By spending some time discussing these games, it is easier for the client and developer to synchronize their efforts.

Next, have a brainstorming session. This should be in a relaxed atmosphere—a chance for both the client representatives and the developer(s) to speak freely about any ideas that come to mind. A great way to do this is to give each person a block of post-it notes and to spend an hour talking and thinking, writing ideas down on these notes, and putting them up on the wall. At this stage, there should be no hesitation, no shooting down of ideas, just a friendly environment in which everyone can participate.

Chances are that after an hour, there will be plenty of ideas on the wall. At this point, it is useful to break up the ideas into categories based on how well each idea might work in an actual implementation, incorporating the product or service and targeting the product or service to the target group. At the same time, the ideas must be organized based on how expensive they would be to implement. The goal is then to find the best idea that is still within budget constraints.

How do you prepare for any possible contingencies that can arise in the later steps of the process?

I think it is important to take each step of development as a separate project and to have final specifications at the end of each stage before moving on to the next. There are usually three main stages to a project:

- Concept development
- Graphic design/system design (can usually be simultaneous)
- Implementation (it is my belief that testing should be part of this stage, not an afterthought)

Changes made late in project development, for example during the implementation, tend to cost much more than changes that are made earlier. It is best to avoid moving on to the next stage if the current stage feels incomplete. In fact, each stage should have formal and final specifications to serve as an outline for the next stage. In reality, time constraints sometimes push teams to jump to the next stage, but I argue that it is far better to hold off on moving to the next stage before the current stage is complete. Spending an extra week designing the system may cause the project to be a week late, but moving on to implementation before the system design is complete will surely add several weeks of delay. This is because if we begin to implement a system without a good design, we will be working in an ad hoc manner. Such improvisational implementation is asking for problems.

I do have one exception to the rule of not jumping ahead. If system design is ready before graphic design, which is often the case on small projects, I usually start the programming implementation with "dummy" graphics, building the system in a way that it is easy to replace these dummy graphics with the real graphics when the real ones are ready. I feel, however, that this is about as far as you want to jump ahead in any stage.

Where are some areas that you look to for creative ideas?

For new game ideas, I tend to look away from the Web. The current possibilities for Web games is really only a few years behind what was possible 5 to 10 years ago with desktop PC games, so I find myself looking at these games more than other current games on the Web. I have a whole list of old games in my mind that I want to create when I find the time; games from my childhood that I played at the arcade. I tend to also look at real-life games and activities and try to imagine how I could simulate them in Flash. After you start looking away from the Web, the possibilities really open up.

When creative ideas start flowing, it can really put strain on a project. When people want to implement too many ideas, a project can come to a halt due to the amount of time it would take to implement everything. How do you achieve a balance between creativity and getting the job done?

I think it is best to break the creative concept development into a formal stage, as I mentioned earlier. In this way, everyone in the project contributes to the creative idea through brainstorming and is involved in working out the final idea. After the final idea is defined, the team must then brainstorm the final idea, and this is when we get trapped in coming up with too many ideas, features, and concepts. It is important that a formal specification for the game is complete before moving on to the graphic design and system design phase. Time and budget are usually the deciding factors here, and it is important that the "features specification" is final before moving on. At the same time, it is usually a good idea to set aside 10% of future project time to unforeseen changes that will need to be made.

The Actual Programming Process

With the conceptual design process finalized, it is time to see the how Jer handles programming and development aspects of his Advergame.

What sort of planning do you do before you actually begin programming an Advergame?

I first make certain that there is a clear game specification, outlining the functionality and features of the game. Assuming that this specification is complete, I begin designing the game system.

I usually design a system from the top down, and then build the system from the bottom up. I start by looking for the main pieces of a game; these pieces are the main classes or components that I use to create the game. For example, if we are building a basic *Asteroids* game, these main pieces might be:

- A `Ship` class
- An `Asteroid` class
- A `Bullet` class
- A `Gameboard` class (current score, current level, ships left, hyperspace left)
- A `Screen` class (where the game takes place)
- A `High Score` class

Then, I write up these classes on post-it notes, listing all their methods, properties, and events, and any other classes that they might need to use in their implementation. For example, the `Ship` class may break down like this:

`UserControl`: Class to handle the user Key events

`fire`: Method

`move`: Method

`onCollision`: Event

`onHyperSpace`: Event

I keep working on the design of my main classes until I come to a solution that works well, meaning that the main classes I have designed enable me to create the system I desire. After I am certain that there is a good design for the main classes, I start designing the classes that these main classes need. For example, I might start by looking at the `Ship` class and design any class that it inherits from or uses through composition, such as the `UserControl` class. In this way, I break down each of the main classes into smaller classes, and keep breaking things down until I have designed the simplest classes the system needs.

There are many methodologies for system design; this is just a summary of my own. The important thing is that I try to design the entire system before I write a line of code. In this way, if I realize I need to make major changes to the system, it is far less time-consuming in the design phase than if I have already committed to the coding process.

When a situation arises that requires you to write a program that's beyond your skill level, how do you manage to get it done?

I am very dedicated to learning, so if time permits I learn what is needed to get the job done. Even if time does not permit, I vow to learn what was needed, so that I will be more prepared the next time. After we have programmed many games and have a good idea how to build an object-oriented system in Flash, there are fewer times when an entire program is beyond our skill level. More often, we have small problems with a certain part of a program. In such a situation, there are many options:

- If time permits, we can learn what is needed. The benefit is obvious here, in that we solve our problem and learn something new at the same time.
- We can look for open source code, articles, and other information on the Internet that will help to solve our problem. We may find the exact code that we need, or we may just find a useful math site that helps us create the one method that was holding us back.
- We can ask around in the Flash community to see if someone is willing to help us with our problem. There are many people out there willing to help; just be careful and do not ask for too much free help. It is unfair to expect other people to do our work for us.

- We can isolate our problem, and hire another developer to solve it for us. If we are under a time constraint, this is probably the best option.

If, however, a project is totally beyond one's grasp, I think it is best to turn the project down, perhaps with a recommendation to another developer who is more capable in solving the client's needs.

You use object-oriented programming (OOP) in all of your games. How do you incorporate OOP and why is it useful?

The most important aspect of object orientation is in the thought process. Often, programmers who are new to object orientation focus too strongly on the actual implementation; it is much more important to learn how to think in an object-oriented manner.

Rather than thinking about functions that manipulate data, object orientation shifts our thought process so that we think in terms of data manipulating itself. In other words, instead of thinking of our program as a bunch of routines that do stuff, we can think of our program as being built of objects, each with properties, behaviors, and events. In this way, we create independent entities that hide the complicated code that makes them work. These entities (objects) should supply easy-to-use interfaces (properties, methods, and events) with which the programmer can work.

If you look at the `MovieClip` class, you see the many properties, methods, and events that this class has. The great thing about all this functionality is that the implementation (how it all works) is hidden from us. To use a `MovieClip` is very easy; we manipulate its public interface, which consists of its properties, methods, and events. We do not need to know how these properties, methods, and events work internally. This allows us to use this class to solve other problems, rather than being bogged down in the code that make our tools work.

Think about a car for a second. The minimum interface you need to drive a car is very simple; it consists of an ignition, clutch, gas pedal, break pedal, gearshift, and steering wheel. Granted, the car has other interface elements, but this minimum set is all you need to drive. Now imagine if you had to know how every aspect of a car worked in order to drive it. There would certainly be far fewer drivers on the road! However, because the implementation of the car is hidden, we are able to use it easily through its simple interface. We are able to think of a car in an abstract manner, as a "transportation device" that works by manipulating a simple set of controls, rather than thinking of it as a complex entity with thousands of parts. This type of thinking is the basis of the object-oriented thought process.

We should build our own classes in the same way. We divide our program into the classes that we need, then we decide what properties, methods, and events will be used to manipulate our classes. Finally, we implement the classes, hiding the complicated programming from ourselves. It sounds a little crazy to be hiding things from ourselves, but this is really a key point. Applications become complicated very quickly; by hiding the complication inside of objects (instances of classes), we reduce the amount of information we need to keep in our minds as we are programming our application. We are able to "use our car" without having to understand "how it works."

Earlier, I mentioned I might build a `Ship` class that breaks down like this:

`UserControl`: Class

`Fire`: Method

`Move`: Method

`onCollision`: Event

`onHyperSpace`: Event

Now, when I write my main game engine, I am not bogged down in all kinds of Key events because the ship has a `UserControl` instance that takes care of this for me. When I want the ship to fire, I simply call the `fire()` method, without having to think about how it works. I call the `move` method once per game engine cycle. I set up listeners or callbacks for the `onCollision` and `onHyperSpace` events. If all of the classes in my game are built with easy-to-use interfaces (properties, methods, and events), then my game engine is going to be easy to write. The code for the game engine is in one control center and is easy to understand and maintain.

At first, some people get confused trying to understand how all this talk of classes is actually related to anything with which they are familiar, such as MovieClips. I think of a MovieClip as a template for any visual representation that might be needed for a class. By default, a MovieClip is the visual representation for the `MovieClip` class, but you can make a MovieClip the visual representation for any class, by assigning an `AS2` class to the MovieClip in the MovieClip linkage properties. When doing this, I consider MovieClips to be "class instance view templates" that can be used to represent any class visually; the default class for this visual template just happens to be MovieClip. In other words, I don't really think of MovieClips as MovieClips anymore, just as "views" for classes.

How important is consistency within your Advergames code? What "quality control" steps do you take with your games?

Consistency is extremely important, as is code readability and system structure. I use coding conventions to enforce a stricter programming environment. For example, I use prefixes on all variable and property names, such as "str" for String and "num" for Number, to keep track of data types. Within classes, I use an underscore at the beginning of a method name to indicate that it is private. I actually went so far as to create my own `Hints` class that writes XML files to provide code hinting on my custom classes to keep track of public properties and methods.

The style of our code has a direct relationship on the quality. Class, property, method, and event names should be contemplated with extreme care. Good naming is the final determining factor in whether our classes are useful. Even if we write the most spectacular classes, if the method, property, and event names are bad, the classes are not useful. As an example, if a car had a keyboard and mouse interface instead of the steering wheel and pedals, it would be far less usable; the usefulness of the car would be undermined by the poor interface design.

We asked Jer to provide us with some final thoughts on his approach to Advergame development:

Do you have any extra programming tips or techniques you would like to add?

- Study object-orientation in depth. Focus particularly on the thought process; do not be bogged down in the actual implementation. Learning to implement things well takes time. For starters, if you begin by understanding the thought process, you gain immediate results.
- Simplify! Any technique or methodology that simplifies your programming is beneficial. Programming is complex; so do not add to that complexity—try to manage it.
- Use coding conventions. For example, you can use prefixes to gain a better understanding of the data types with which you are working. You can use an underscore or a dollar sign in private method names so that you are reminded by the underscore that you should not access them from outside the class. You can give constants names that are all capitalized to signify that they are constant. Even though ActionScript 2 now supports strict typing as well as private and public members, I still find coding conventions to be useful.
- Organize your code. Use white space to separate sections of code. Use one external script per class. If you write good classes with easy-to-use interfaces, you should be able to have one code center, in which you write the program and manipulate your classes through their interfaces. This code center should be very easy to read and understand. The complication should be hidden within the classes.
- Pay attention to the style of your code. Make certain that you and others can read and understand it. Take pride in your work.
- Have fun! Do not become stressed about all the things you feel you need to learn to become a game developer. Enjoy where you are now, and try to learn a little each day.

19 Interview and Case Study—Blockdot

Imagine creating an Advergame that, to date has been played over 25 million times! Well, if you're Blockdot of Dallas, Texas, you don't have to imagine, because your M&M's—*Flip the Mix* game not only holds that distinction, but has also kept players on the site for an average of 35 minutes of gameplay per session. Wow! Talk about hitting a grand slam for your client. And Blockdot is no one-hit-wonder, as several of their other game metrics are equally as impressive and would make some Hollywood executives green with envy.

For over eight years, the Blockdot team has helped some of the world's most recognizable brands successfully execute their online and offline strategies. Billed as a "Different Kind of Creative Group," one visit to their studio and you know that is not hype. Their mission is to build brands, create user databases, and change customer behaviors—tall orders that often involve introducing a new brand, reinforcing an existing brand, or altering the way a prospective client thinks.

Blockdot works with more than a score of Fortune 500 companies, and in 2001, *Brandweek Magazine* selected them as one of the Top 10 Marketers of the Next Generation. Dan Ferguson (see Figure 19.1) and cofounder Mike Bielinski (see Figure 19.2) previously founded NVision Design, the company that released what has to be one of the most successful of all Advergames ever created—*Elf Bowling**. Preceding the hit *Elf Bowling*, they released two other huge successes—*Frogapult* and *Good Willie Hunting*.

Today, their games are showcased on *www.kewlbox.com* ("Log on and Goof Off"; see Figure 19.3), which boasts the Mc Donald's-like tag line "over 150,000,000 game plays and counting!"

Dan Ferguson takes care of the creative direction for Blockdot and Mike Bielinski is the Chief Executive Officer. Dan and Mike were fraternity brothers back at

*Dan Ferguson and Michael Bielinski were the founders of NVision Design. They are the original creators of the games *Elf Bowling*, *Frogapult*, and *Good Willie Hunting*. All trademark and other rights to *Elf Bowling*, *Frogapult*, and *Good Willie Hunting* have been purchased and are currently owned by ComMOTION Interactive.

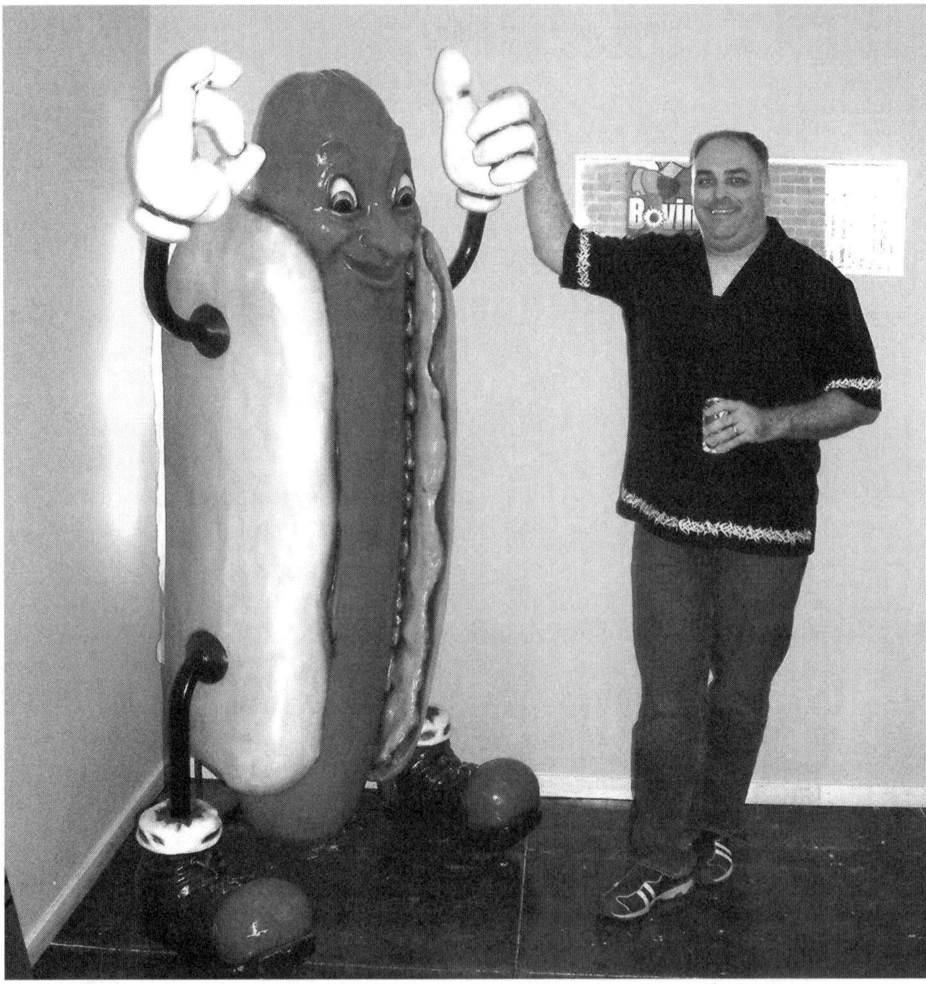

FIGURE 19.1 Dan Ferguson, Blockdot founder and creative director. Photo by Vic Cherubini, epic software group, inc.

University of Texas at Arlington. Mike gained fame immediately after graduation as the inventor of the 3D eye stereogram posters that were the rage in the early 1990s. The growth of this type of 3D art skyrocketed, and prints were sold from kiosks in shopping malls around the country. As the interest for this type of 3D art faded, Mike decided to exit the business and take a year-long sabbatical traveling around Europe. Mike had a great deal of graphics equipment so Dan approached Mike about using it to start a new company. Dan put it to good use and formed NVision Design. When Mike returned, he and Dan decided to focus on producing multi-

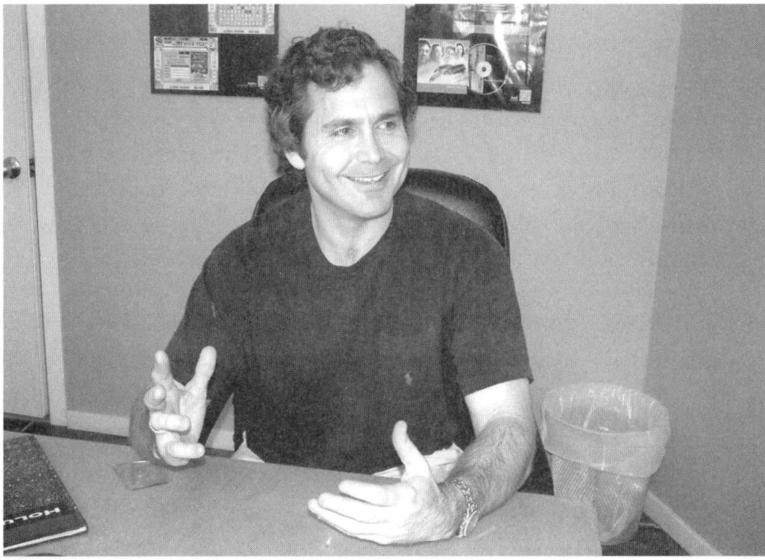

FIGURE 19.2 Mike Bielinski, Blockdot founder and Director of Business. Photo by Vic Cherubini, epic software group, inc.

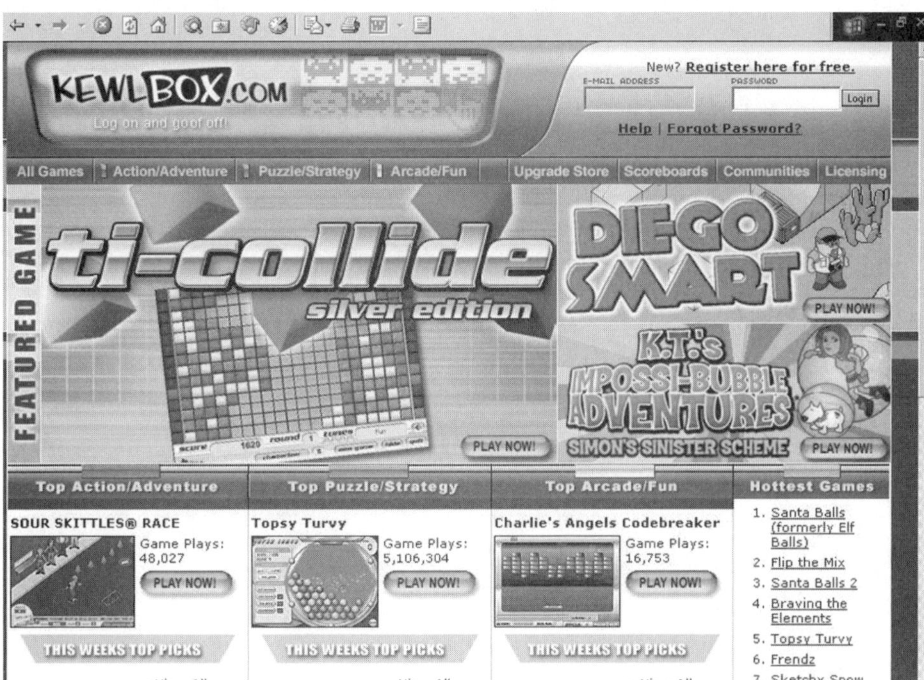

FIGURE 19.3 Home page for the Blockdot game portal, *www.kewlbox.com*. © 2003. Reprinted with permission from Blockdot.

media work. What follows is the story of a roller-coaster ride through the dot-com meltdown and the trip back to reality. Unlike many dot-com disasters, this story has a very happy ending. Both Mike and Dan were kind enough to take some time out of their busy schedules to sit down with us and talk about their work. Their office is in a converted indoor parking garage (you can even see the painted lines for the parking spaces on their conference room floor), in a trendy area in the shadows of the downtown Dallas skyscrapers. Strap on your seatbelts as we take you through a firsthand tour of a company, and meet the visionaries who were developing Advergames before the name had even been invented (see Figure 19.4).

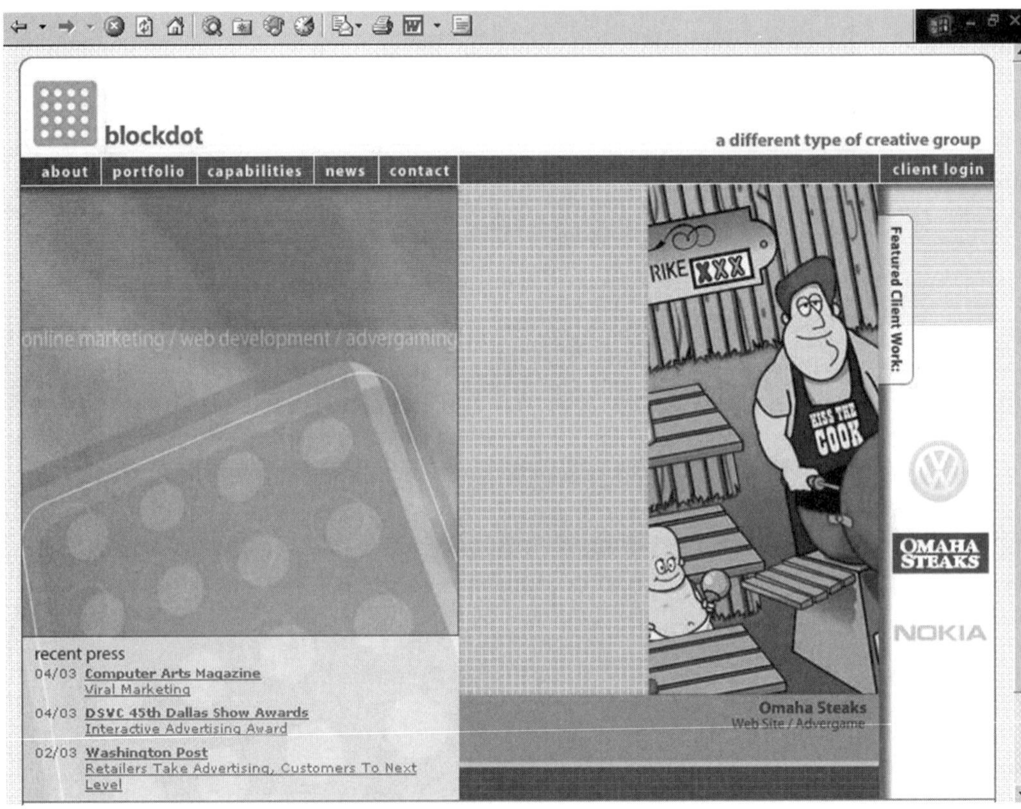

FIGURE 19.4 Home page for Blockdot.com. © 2003. Reprinted with permission from Blockdot.

AN INTERVIEW WITH DAN FERGUSON AND MIKE BIELINSKI

Dan and Mike, you are considered the forefathers of the Advergaming industry. Why Advergaming?

Dan Ferguson: Advergames can reinforce a brand image, keep an online user engaged and entertained, build a database of information about the users, and directly target the market that advertisers want to hit—all very inexpensively when compared to what it costs to advertise in other media. While other Advergame companies boast game plays in the thousands, many Kewlbox.com games have been played in the millions.

Blockdot game development costs range from $5K to $80K and include an unlimited distribution license. When you look at the exposure your brand can get from a successful game, the return on investment is incredible.

Mike Bielinski: With games, people are absolutely absorbed in the event. And by tying the game to a scoreboard system or sweepstakes, you can find out who is playing. Kewlbox.com tracks this activity. We know when and how long people play their games, so that metrics can be compiled and analyzed. We also ask the players to opt-in to a game sponsor's e-mail database, thus helping our clients learn more about their audience and giving them a strong base to use for future, online marketing initiatives.

Who is playing your games?

Dan Ferguson: Our research shows that when boys between the ages of 13 and 17 go online, it's often to play a game. Sixty-two percent of young men between the ages of 18 and 24 play video games, and the numbers for girls and women are growing. Kewlbox.com, our game portal, is split 52% female, 48% male.

Mike Bielinski: Our peak playing hours are during lunch and at the end of the business day, with Thursday and Friday being our most popular days. A new trend is a heavy play on the weekend—sometimes, Saturday activity is equal to or surpasses Wednesday play. That trend says a great deal about the acceptance and quality of an Advergame. If the game is engaging and entertaining, people will make time in their schedules to play it. Adding the "challenge a friend" feature (see Figure 19.5), really improved the numbers as well. When playing an Advergame, most people are not multitasking. They are focused on the game and engaged in the message. Capturing the attention of an online user, for several minutes, is exactly what our clients are seeking.

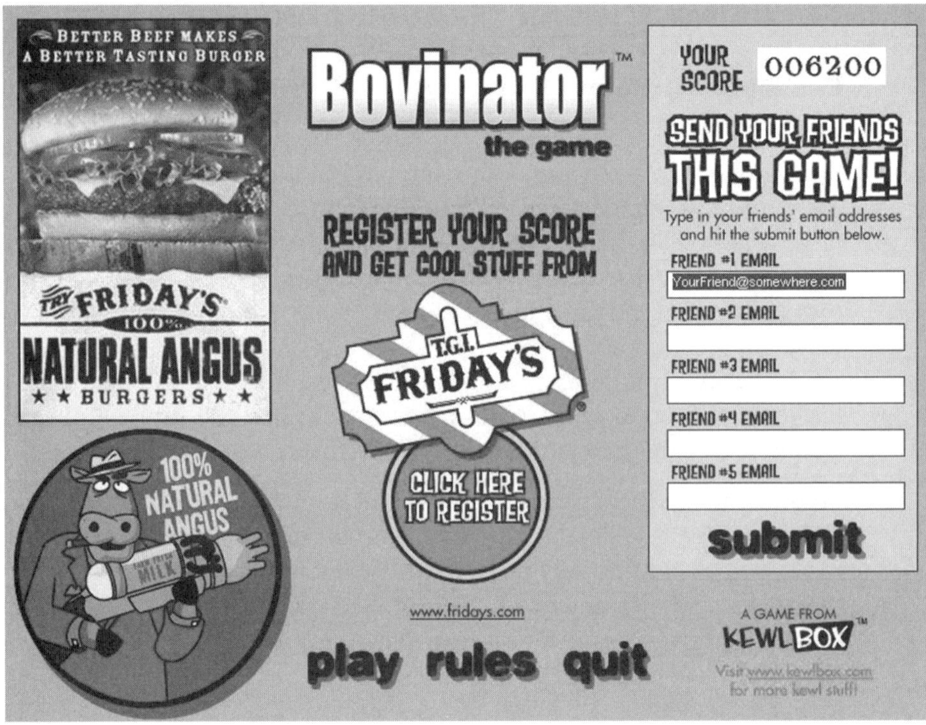

FIGURE 19.5 The "Bovinator" Challenge a Friend exit screen. © 2003. Reprinted with permission from Blockdot.

One of the earliest games you worked on was *Good Willie Hunting*, which was released on April Fool's Day, 1998, while you were still running NVision Design. It helped propel your shop from 5 to 40 people. What was the inspiration for the game, and what happened after it was released?

Mike Bielinski: The inspiration for our first game came to me when I received the famous animated "Dancing Baby" from at least three of my friends as an e-mail attachment. I was amazed that no one had attached their name to the piece, and thought this type of "pass-along" marketing could really call attention to a company. Because we were just getting started, I thought if we could find a topical subject and create a game that was fun and engaging to play, people would pass it around. The Bill Clinton/Monica Lewinsky scandal was brewing, and it looked like it might have some legs, so we decided to do a parody of the *Whack-a-Mole* arcade-style game.

Good Willie Hunting was created in Macromedia Director. I stayed up several days straight writing the code, and used simple stick figures for the graphical elements. At that point in the development cycle, the game was not much to look at, but it gave us a good idea of how it worked and what needed to be tweaked. When Dan saw the stick figures, he went to work and created the "real" graphics. When the graphics were combined with sound effects and music, the game came to life, and we knew we had something special. The last screen of the piece included a listing of all of the services we provided, along with our contact information.

Dan Ferguson: As soon as everything was complete, our next goal was to distribute it as widely as possible. Together, we had about 200 friends in our e-mail directory, so that was the logical place to start. We sent a copy of the game to each of them. Back then, you could attach an .exe (executable file) to an e-mail message and it would not be filtered out. Our mailing went out on April 1, 1998, and we really did not know what to expect. We were shocked when the phone began to ring, and ring, and ring.

We called this approach "endorsement marketing," and we were getting calls from all over the country. We were being offered all kinds of projects, and our little five-man shop was about to explode. Within a year, we had grown to 40, and were working for a number of Fortune 500 companies. Although unlimited growth may sound good, it comes with potential problems. The biggest is cash flow—where you have plenty of work, but not enough cash to cover how fast you are burning through it.

Mike Bielinski: One way to fix the problem is to join forces with another company that has the resources to handle this type of growth. It was the dot-com era, and the concept of the "roll up" (a large company absorbs several smaller companies to gain economies of scale) was hot.

We made the decision to merge with Vectrix Corp and began working on the game that has been called the most successful Advergame ever released—*Elf Bowling*. Released in 1999, *Elf Bowling* was the only non-Microsoft game to make it to the list of the top 10 installed games for the year. For *Elf Bowling*, we wanted a smaller footprint for the size of the game, so I built the game engine from scratch in C++.

Although the game was an incredible success, the dot-com boom was about to go bust, and we decided to leave. After a few months of soul searching, we decided not to do a "startup" but instead a "start over." Blockdot was born in 2001. Our name is our own creation and is based on two basic shapes—a block and a dot. A block is the square shape of a pixel for online work and a dot is the basic element when printing. Understanding the basic principles of media is key to discovering their potential power. We learned a great deal from our earlier efforts. Jason McMinn also joined us as a cofounder to take care of the business elements. We realized we did not need a lot of people, if we just hired the right people.

Describe your first meeting with a client who wants an Advergame to promote his brand, but is not sure exactly what he wants. How do you help him decide what will give him the greatest bang for his buck?

Mike Bielinski: Things are much easier now than they were just a few years ago. Most of the prospective clients we talk with today have good understanding of the Advergaming concept, and may come to us with a specific idea. We do our homework and try to understand the brand, and we listen carefully to their stated objectives. In some cases, we will meet with the client's ad agency so we can better understand how the game fits in with their other marketing campaigns. Budgets often shape the project scope, but in some cases, a simple game is needed and that is what we will suggest.

Dan Ferguson: One advantage we have is a gamer's portal that we created called *www.kewlbox.com*. We learned that far more people will find you if you have your game on a dedicated site. Simply having a game on a client's Web site is like putting up a billboard inside a store. Casual gamers now come to our *www.kewlbox.com* to see what's new, and that really helps the numbers.

What does it take to become part of the Blockdot team? What attributes and skills do you look for in your programmers, artists, and support staff?

Mike Bielinski: We really look for people who understand marketing and who can work well on our team. Several of our key people have worked with us during our days at Nstorm, so we know where their talents lie. Although Dallas has a number of well-known game companies, we have not recruited programmers, artists, or designers from them. One of the best ways to get a job here is as a student intern.

CASE STUDY

Now that we have a better understanding of Blockdot, let's take a closer look at one of their newly released Advergames. In 2003, Blockdot was commissioned by HP to create an adventure game to promote HP's digital imaging products and services. The *Diego Smart* game was targeted to a predominately Latin American audience, and was offered in both Spanish and English versions, as shown in Figure 19.6. It is available as a download for PC and Mac. The game can also be played online at *www.kewlbox.com*. Development time was 90 days.

The Storyline

The Blockdot team played off the idea of creating a hero who was an adventurous photojournalist, and placed him in the Lost City of Machu-Cache. As a photojour-

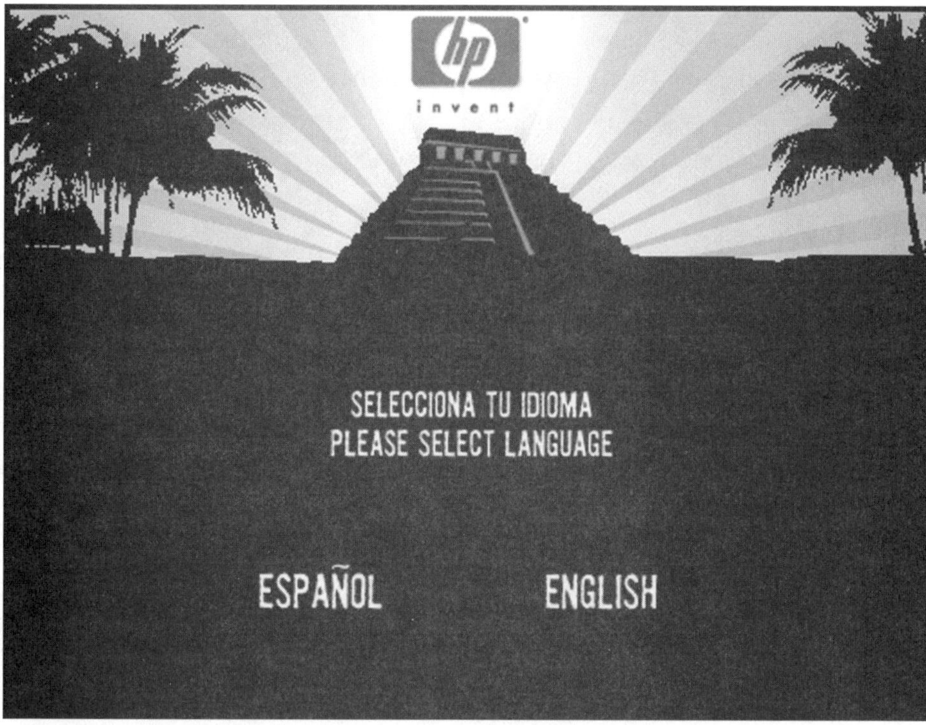

FIGURE 19.6 The *Diego Smart* game can be played in English or Spanish. © 2003. Reprinted with permission from Blockdot.

nalist working for the Historic Relic Society, Diego must explore this treacherous and evil place, and capture evidence of ancient relics (see Figure 19.7). From the "Emperor's Emerald Jaguar" to the "Mystical Collard of Macho-Cache," the relics are hidden within the city and are protected by creatures and historic legends. To make the connection to Latin cultural influences, all the creatures and relics are based on Latin folklore.

Branding

The main challenge was to creatively integrate HP's brand and digital cameras into a game without making the game feel like a commercial. By working directly with the client, HP Latin America, and their advertising agency, Blockdot was able to proactively discuss concepts and ideas. By keeping the game's target audience in the forefront, they created a game that was truly unique and fun to play.

The HP digital cameras were introduced into the game as tools to accomplish a goal. Doing this, without being overly commercial, is the key to the success of the

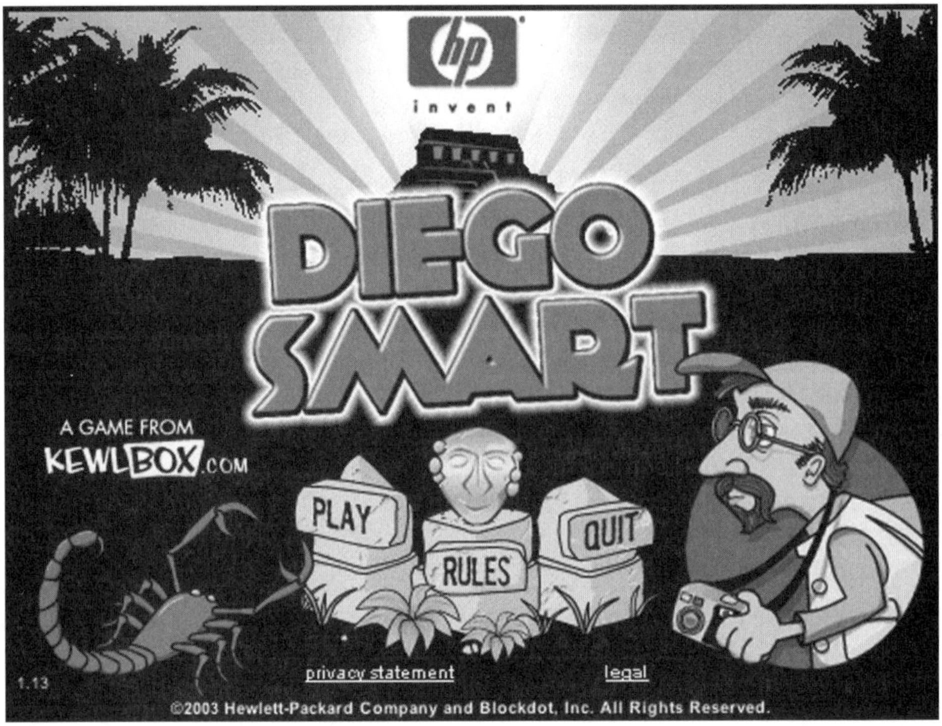

FIGURE 19.7 The splash screen for the *Diego Smart* game. © 2003. Reprinted with permission from Blockdot.

game. As the player advances through the gameplay, the villains become tougher and Diego's equipment gets better, giving them the ideal opportunity to introduce new lines of HP equipment throughout the game. The goal was to present the products in a way that would not distract the player by their presence in the game. If the player thinks he is being marketed to, the overall experience and messaging opportunity is jeopardized.

Gameplay and Design

Blockdot created an environment reminiscent of ancient ruins, deep in the heart of South America. The game was designed to emulate a 3D adventure game, allowing the user to tour the hero's surroundings, as shown in Figure 19.8. The Blockdot artists stylized the characters and environment as illustrations, rather than designing the game with a photorealistic look and feel. This style allowed them to fully develop the characters, giving the hero and villains a comic-book quality. Maintaining the theme of clean, simple appearances, the designers broke down all of the art

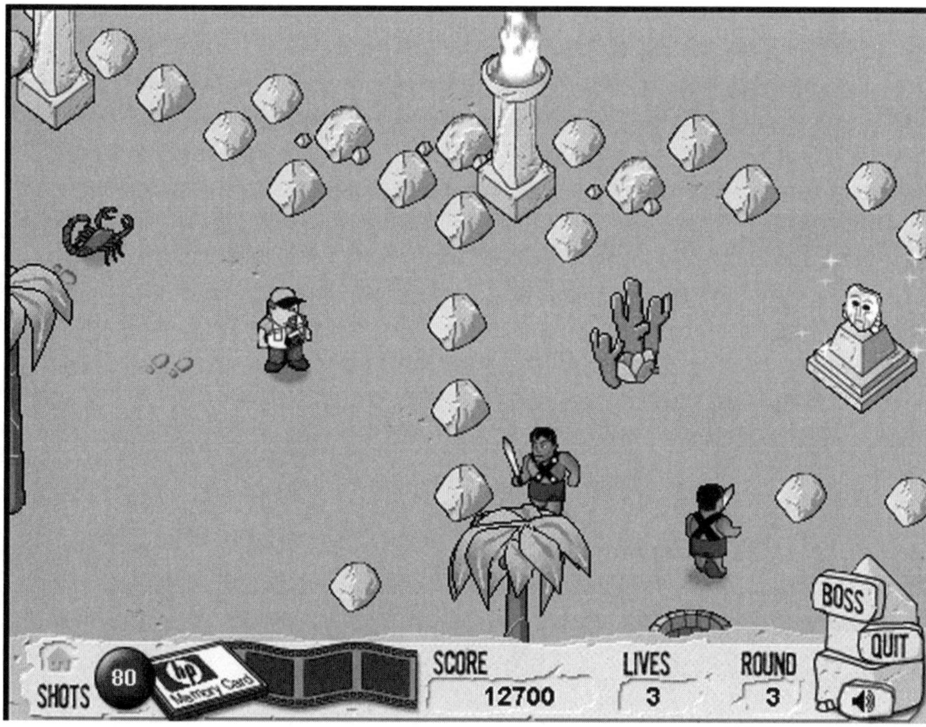

FIGURE 19.8 Game environment—Diego must find the relic and take a photo of it while avoiding the villains. © 2003. Reprinted with permission from Blockdot.

components into basic shapes; that is, spheres, cones, and blocks. These shapes were then given some shading and texture to give them weight and depth. The world in which these characters interact is isometric, giving the player the illusion of a 3D environment, even though the art is flat. Blockdot used the isometric approach as a cost-savings method for HP's budget and as a method to keep the file size at a minimum. This approach is beneficial to the client because the user will not have to download or install any additional 3D plug-ins or drivers to experience the gameplay.

The game was designed using Adobe Illustrator and Adobe Photoshop. Initial character designs were created in Illustrator, and then transferred to Photoshop, in which soft edges and shadowing were added to give them weight and a 3D look.

There are dozens of different game levels, each with a unique layout and landscape. Between rounds, the player receives clues and upgraded equipment, as shown in Figure 19.9. These landscapes were laid out using a custom application developed with Macromedia Director. The map designers used the application to lay out each art element in the game, so each ancient ruin has unique details and

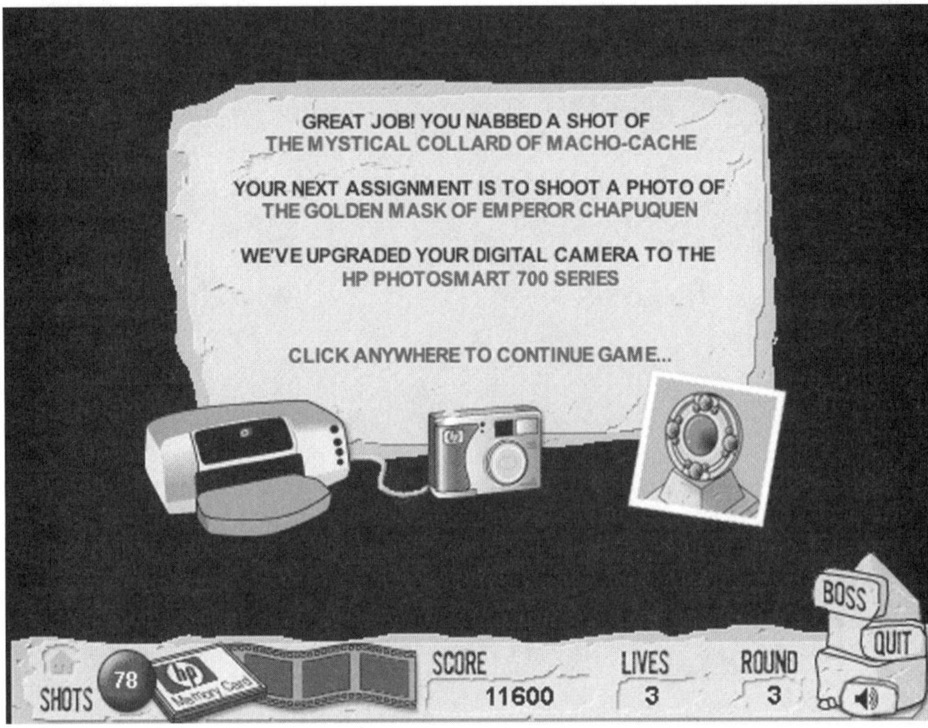

FIGURE 19.9 The player has successfully completed a level and is given a new assignment. © 2003. Reprinted with permission from Blockdot.

hidden things to find. Macromedia Director was also used to build and compile the final game.

The Results

An HP microsite was created, as part of the campaign, so players could post and enter a sweepstakes that was associated with the game, as shown in Figure 19.10. People spent an average of 12 minutes playing the game, and were encouraged to challenge their friends to beat their high score (see Figure 19.11). The response to *Diego Smart* has been a great success. The game was played over 300,000 times during its first month after being released. When players registered their score, 65% opted to join HP's mailing list.

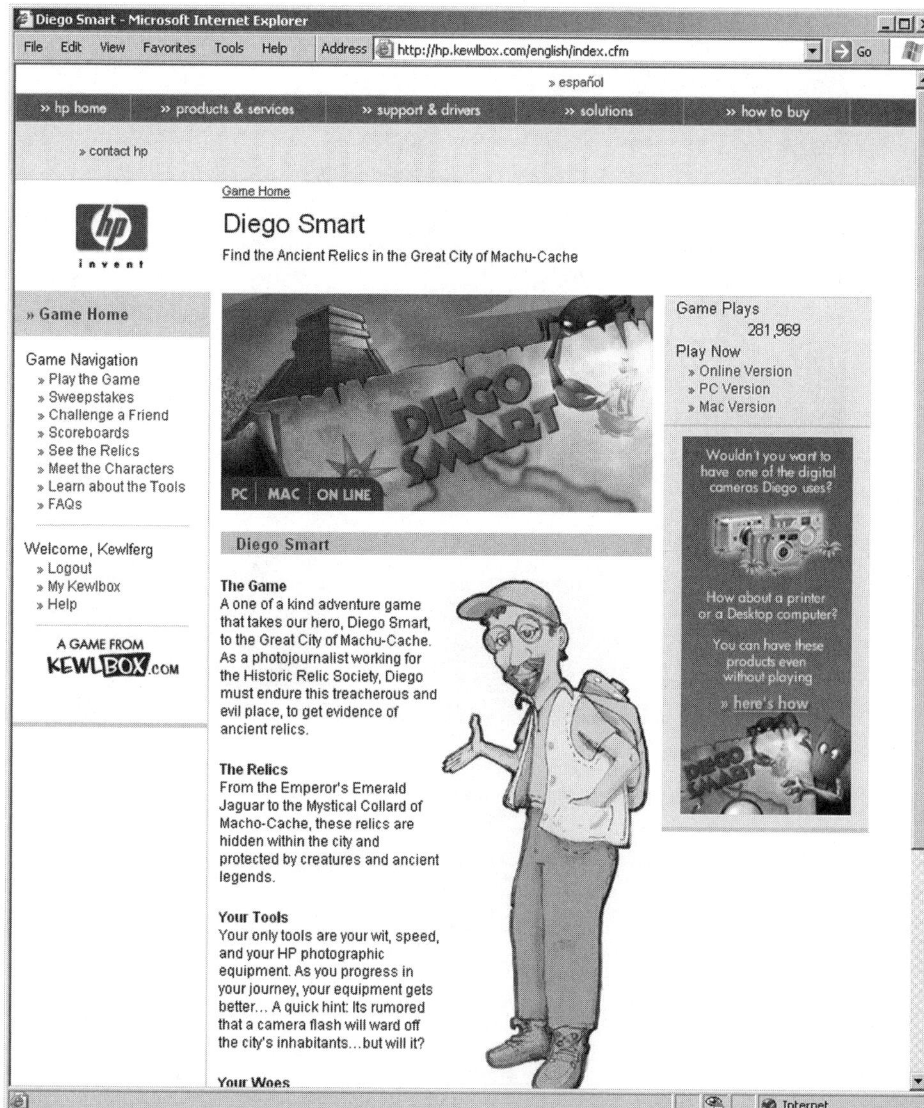

FIGURE 19.10 The HP microsite allows players to post their scores and displays the player's preferred language. © 2003. Reprinted with permission from Blockdot.

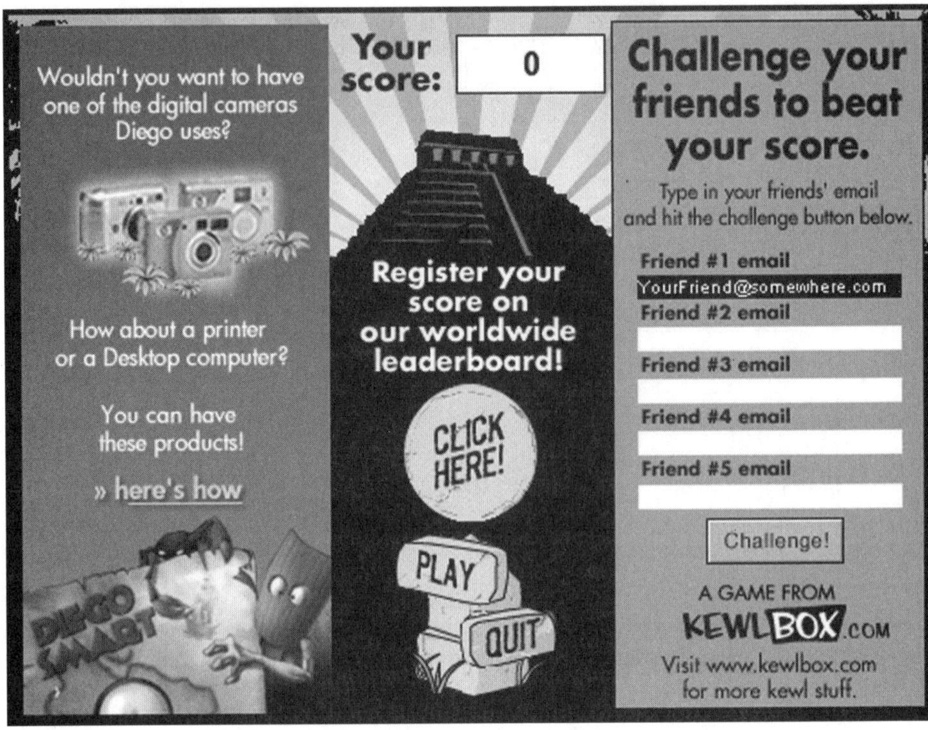

FIGURE 19.11 Traffic to the site was increased using a "challenge a friend" e-mail option. © 2003. Reprinted with permission from Blockdot

20 Interview and Case Study—YaYa Media Inc.

When you are developing programs for clients such as Chrysler, Siemens, Paramount, K-Mart, Burger King, Honda, and Pepsi, you know you have reached the pinnacle of success in the world of Advergaming. And you would expect nothing less from a company employing the person who conceived the word "Advergame" in the first place—Jane Chen (see Figure 20.1). Both Chen and Keith Ferrazzi (see Figure 20.2), the CEO and President of YAYA Media, have made a huge impact on the industry in just three short years. Ferrazzi comes well-equipped with a BA from Yale and an MBA from Harvard, and holds the title as the youngest CMO in a Fortune 500 company. Ferrazzi and his COO James Clarke have brought together a team of highly skilled and experienced programmers,

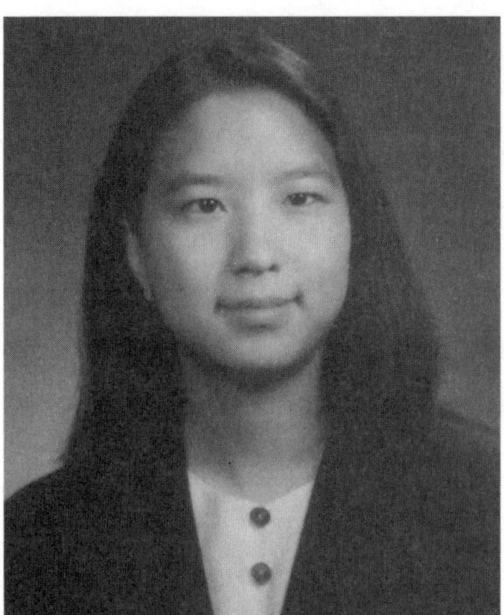

FIGURE 20.1 Jane Chen—coined the name Advergame.

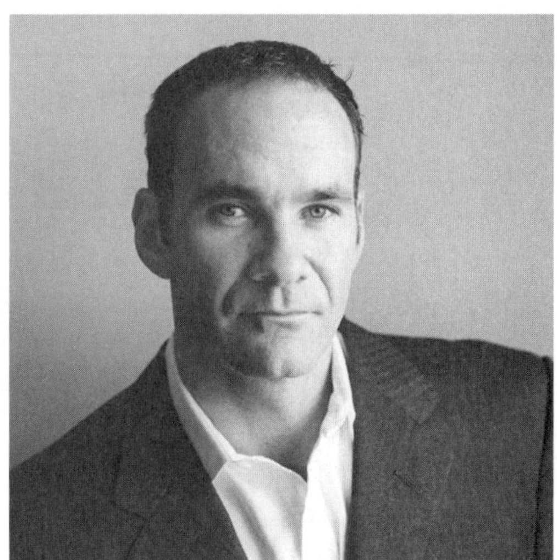

FIGURE 20.2 Keith Ferrazzi—CEO and President of YaYa Media.

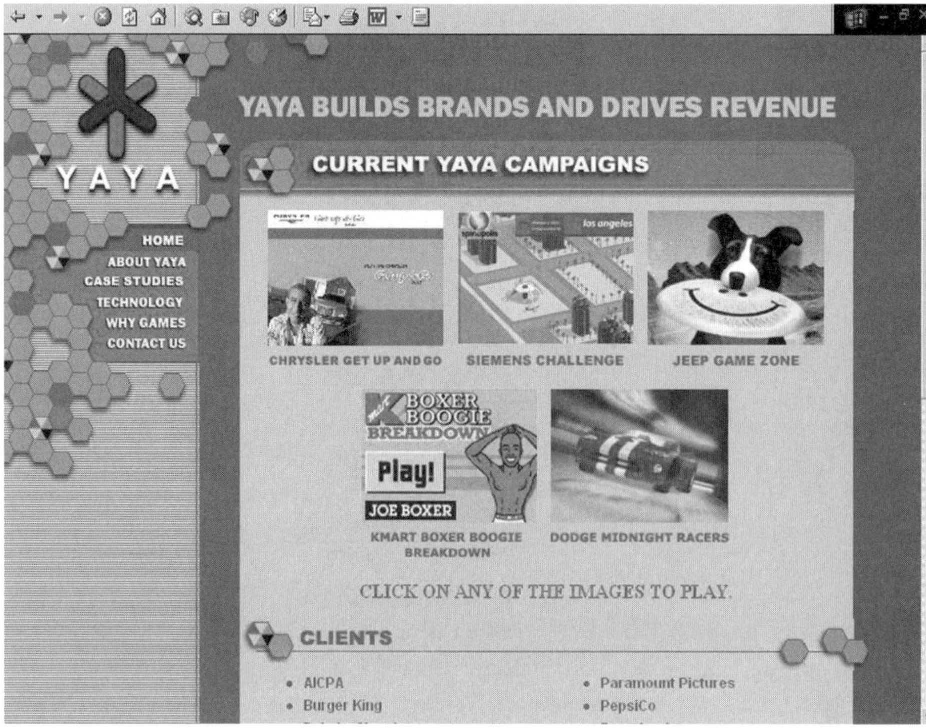

FIGURE 20.3 YaYa Media home page. Image courtesy of YaYa Media.

artists, technology experts, designers, and marketers whose names read like a Who's Who of talent in the games, marketing, and technology communities.

In this chapter, we talk with Chen and Ferrazzi about their work at YAYA Media (see Figure 20.3), and we take a closer look at the *Get Up and Go* game developed by the company for Chrysler.

AN INTERVIEW WITH KEITH FERRAZZI AND JANE CHEN

Keith, YA YA Media is a relatively young company launched at a very challenging time for even traditional advertising agencies. Can you tell us the story behind the company, your name, and your approach to Advergaming?

Keith Ferrazzi: Everybody asks us where the name "YAYA" comes from, but frankly, nobody really remembers anymore. What is more interesting is the "Media" part of our name, which we just added this year. Although we've been working in the interactive games space for the last four years, it's only in the last 18 months or so that we've started to look at, and treat, the games space as a media channel. Fundamentally, games—like any other form of media—are composed of content properties and distribution platforms that aggregate audiences. As such, there are opportunities for brand marketers to participate at all stages of the value chain.

Our approach to Advergaming has always been to bring together competencies in content, technology, and strategy to develop custom solutions for brands that deliver a robust return on marketing investment. Jeff Bell, VP of Marketing at Jeep, once described us as "the connective tissue" that helps their marketing folks to leverage the games space and the game developers to understand brand strategies. That's why we like to lead with strategy. We work with brands to uncover all of their business and marketing objectives first so that game development can maximize end results and metrics that will make the client happy with their investment. For example, do you want people to get so jazzed about your product that they voluntarily request more information? We'll put links to information into the game. Do you have market research questions about the best colors or designs of a product? We'll put the choices in the game. Do you want to reach a particular demographic with a marketing message? We'll create a game in the right genre for your target group and develop a distribution strategy that will put the game in their path.

Most of our clients are not in the games business—they are in the business of selling cars, selling groceries, producing chemicals, and building nuclear reactors. At the end of the day, any investment they make in a marketing property needs to help them sell product. It is our job to shepherd them through game conception and the development of the project, with an eye toward supporting their core business, to maximize the impact of their games-based marketing investment.

In your *Harvard Business Review* article of April 2003, you said that computer games may have some advantages over traditional marketing methods. Can you provide us with some examples?

Keith Ferrazzi: There are many reasons why the gaming medium outshines and outclasses other traditional marketing methods, but the two most prominent ones are interactivity and content on demand.

Games are immersive. Instead of showing product information and attributes via broadcast (or even less engagingly by print), games provide the opportunity to have customers interact with and engage with your brand. Information retention and emotion is engaged at a higher level when you immerse your customers this way. For example, the *America's Army: Operations* game that was used as a recruiting and branding tool by the U.S. Army spurred 1.2 million registered users to participate in 55 million game missions averaging 10 minutes each. Can you imagine 1.2 million people willingly watching a 30-second commercial that many times? Or flipping through a magazine just to linger on the ads? The Army game was so realistic about what life in training was like that boot camps were using the game as prep work before sending cadets out on the obstacle courses.

The second reason Advergames are superior to other forms of traditional media is because it is not dependent upon distribution. In other words, customers can access your games at anytime from anywhere. This is particularly evident with game players at work (where media traditionally has had difficulty penetrating). In a recent study by the Online Publishers Organization, gaming was the fifth most popular at-work online activity. Thirty-nine percent of all at-work respondents visited a gaming site during the workweek. Forty-six percent of at-work women respondents visited a gaming site during the work week. Moreover, the interactive entertainment nature of games keeps customers coming back—for example, new game levels, multiplayer opportunities, high-score recognition. After a brand has established communication with their customers, it opens the door for CRM (Customer Relationship Management) and one-to-one marketing.

Jane, in 2001 while working for <kpe>, you and Matthew Ringel coauthored a groundbreaking white paper titled "Can Advergaming be the Future of Interactive Advertising?" In the article, you talk about online gaming through the lens of three traditional advertising success standards: Message, Medium, and Money. Please explain what you mean.

Jane Chen: We knew that in order for Advergaming to be taken seriously as a marketing solution, we had to redefine the concept of video games. We had to highlight the merits of the medium in the language and numbers that marketers are used to describing traditional marketing solutions to break the stereotype that games are just violent bloodfests played by antisocial teenaged boys.

By message, we refer to the way in which brands communicate product or brand attributes to the customer. For example, in the *Jeep EVO2 4X4* game, users were put behind the virtual driving wheel and taken for an off-road racing experience allowing hands-on product sampling that emphasized the brand attribute of adventure.

Medium identifies the distribution channels that are available to put the game in front of the appropriate audiences—just like the television shows and network's brands have to choose between commercial placement. Different online portals and sites represent unique audience opportunities. In addition, brands have the option of putting games on their own corporate sites, thus driving traffic and increasing stickiness.

Money refers to return-on-investment considerations and metrics of success for the campaign. Depending on what level of the purchase funnel marketers are targeting with games, the metrics of success will differ. For awareness games—such as K-Mart's *Joe Boxer* game that emulated the popular TV spot with the guy in boxers dancing around in wild abandon—game plays and time engaged are important factors. For purchase-oriented games—such as the *Jimmy Neutron* radio-controlled car game from Radio Shack—conversion rates of those who played the game and then clicked a link to buy is the key metric. ROI is, therefore, a relative measure. If a game can outperform the equivalent traditional media solution (that is, CPM for awareness games, acquisition cost for purchase-oriented games), then it is the right solution.

Now, let's take a closer look at each of these three elements. Let's start with "Message." You say that Advergames can be Associative, Illustrative, or Demonstrative. Can you define each term and provide us with an example?

Jane Chen: Associative, illustrative, and demonstrative refer to the degree in which the brand is integrated into the game content. Associative games usually feature the brand rather than the product, and the objective is to link a lifestyle or essence to the brand. An example is the Jack Daniel's *Real Pool* game, which integrated logos into a 3D pool hall environment. Although there is no whiskey or drinking in the game, the placement served to identify the Jack Daniel's brand with an old-style nostalgic billiards feel that would appeal to men aged 21 to 34.

Illustrative games feature the product in gameplay as a prop or tool. For example, the numerous Lifesavers® games on Candystand.com feature Lifesaver pucks in hockey games and candy-themed tiles in mah-jongg solitaire. Although the products themselves are featured, they tend to be incidental to gameplay.

Demonstrative games are the deepest in terms of product integration. In these games, the products are engaged in a realistic and integral way to gameplay. Driving games such as *Jeep EVO2 4x4* and *Honda Adventure Race* are clear examples of demonstrative gaming. Realistic use of the product is integral to gameplay and, therefore, brands have the opportunity of making their products "heroes" in the game.

One of the first questions that every Advergame development company asks is, "How much is this going to cost us," and "What kind of return can we expect for our investment?" How do you go about establishing a budget?

Keith Ferrazzi: The budget for any Advergame should always be determined after a thorough analysis of the client's needs and sensitivity. That's why we always emphasize strategy first. The most important thing is to evaluate budgets and costs "all-in." That means taking into consideration distribution and promotion in addition to development. The Advergame should always be put in a position to succeed. There is nothing worse than charging a client $500,000 to build a beautiful game that no one plays because it is buried three pages deep on a client's corporate Web site.

Work backward from a client's established baselines. How much do they spend on TV, print, and banner ads? What returns do they get from those investments and how do they measure it? If possible, custom design the game to mimic these metrics of success. If a television commercial costs a company $15 CPM (Cost Per Thousand), then a game, all-in, should achieve at least the same CPM level calculated off of gameplays or site visits.

One way of boosting a game's ROI (Return on Investment) is to add other value-enhancing functions. Does the client have a CRM infrastructure? If so, what is the value of a new name, address, and phone number to add to their database? If these are of value to a client, then adding a registration function to the game provides value beyond the traditional media metrics of the game.

Another ROI-enhancing solution is to leverage existing game assets. If you have access to a game engine that can be easily reskinned for a client, that lowers costs, which lowers the hurdle of success. A client who may not have the budget to build a custom game for several hundreds of thousands of dollars may be much more willing to spring for a reskinned game that only costs a fraction of that.

Keith, it has been reported that one of your personal favorites is the *Get Up and Go* game YAYA Media created for Chrysler. Please describe the game and tell us how you and your team took it from concept to creation.

Keith Ferrazzi: Chrysler wanted to create a game targeting adult women that would increase their awareness of all the different vehicles in the line. Strategically, we did a lot of up-front research to identify what kind of games women prefer to play. We found out a couple things. First of all, women tend to be collaborative rather than competitive players. They like thinking and learning and strategy games, rather than "twitch" games. They predominantly game online. We took these findings and developed the concept of a travel personality test that would play a lot like an online Cosmo Quiz.

People answer a series of 21 fun questions related to travel and get matched to a personality, such as "City Slicker" or "Beach Bum." At the end of the quiz, you are also matched to the Chrysler car that most closely reflects your personality. In terms of the collaborative community aspect, if you invite a friend to play, you can determine how compatible the two of you are as travel-mates.

For the development stage, we wanted to create a visually stunning and beautiful game (see Figure 20.4) that would far transcend the typical checklist format of online personality tests. We wanted the look and feel to be brand-consistent with Chrysler and the female audience we were targeting. As a result, we decided to go with a Flash-based game with lots of pictures and travel-themed visual assets.

After the development and launch, our team switched into analytical mode. Another advantage of Advergames is the ability to track all sorts of campaign metrics (see Figure 20.5). Detailed reports can be generated about which vehicles were the most popular and the demographics and psychographics of consumers who

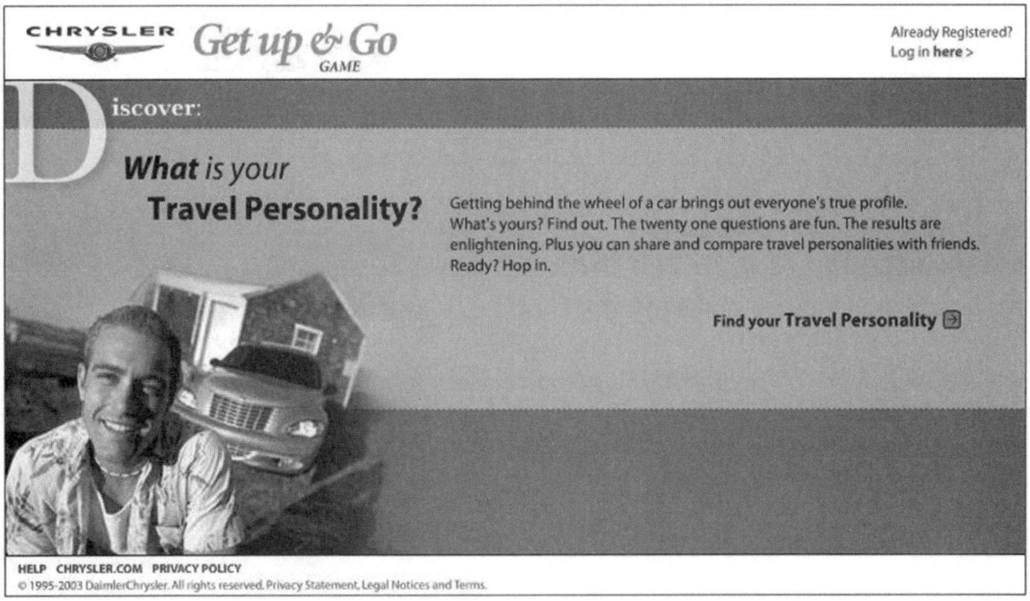

FIGURE 20.4 Splash screen of the Chrysler *Get Up And Go* game. Image courtesy of YaYa Media.

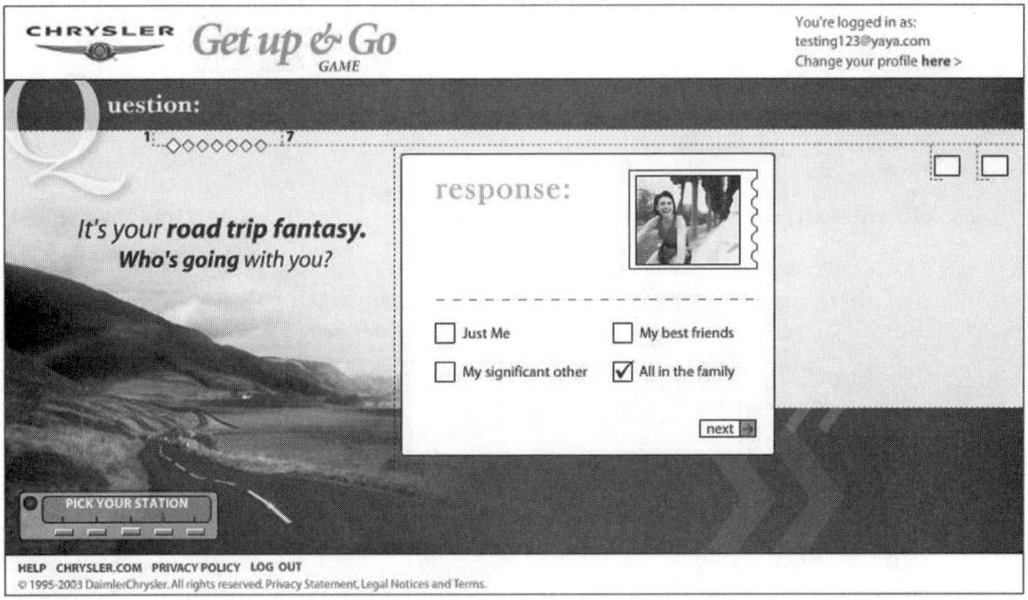

FIGURE 20.5 Chrysler *Get Up And Go* road trip fantasy response page. Image courtesy of YaYa Media.

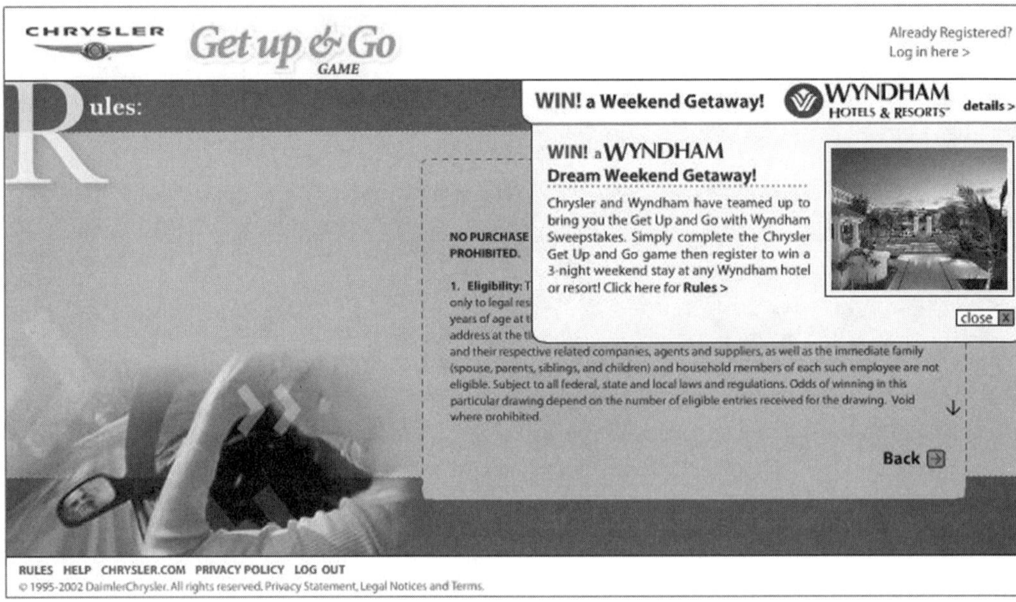

FIGURE 20.6 Chrysler and Wyndham sweepstakes—just complete the game and register to win a three-night stay. Image courtesy of YaYa Media.

chose which vehicle. We provided monthly reports on the findings of the game data and recommended next steps. All of this data can be used for future direct marketing or market research.

How was the game distributed?

Keith Ferrazzi: The game was placed on the Chrysler.com Web site. An e-mail was sent out to the Chrysler mailing list. A copromotional partnership was formed with Wyndham Hotels (see Figure 20.6) who provided a weekend getaway as a sweepstakes prize. Wyndham also e-mailed the URL to their mailing list and promoted the game on their Web site.

Can you share some of the metrics with us? For example, how were you able to measure gameplay and determine the return on the client's investment?

Keith Ferrazzi: On average, players spent 7.6 minutes playing the game with 32% of all players engaged for 20 minutes or more. Twenty-two percent of players invited a friend to play (see Figure 20.7) and 66% of invited players clicked through (versus 40% open rates for similar types of e-mail direct marketing). Most impor-

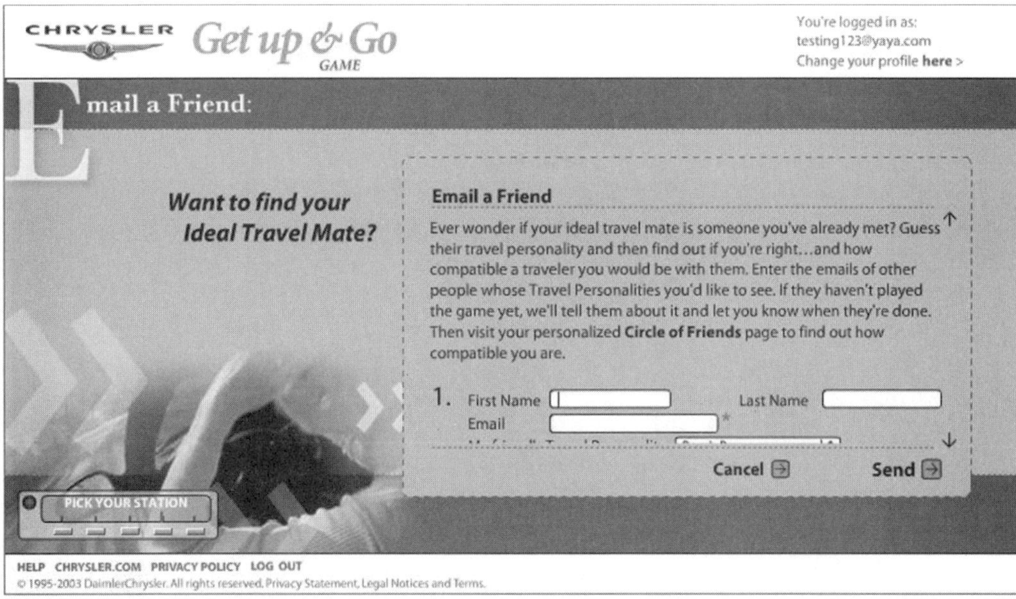

FIGURE 20.7 YaYa boosted traffic with an "e-mail a friend" option. Image courtesy of YaYa Media.

tantly, 15% of players requested brochures on vehicles in the game. This is a significant increase above the less than 1% of Web site visitors who request brochures.

What do you see for the future of Advergames?

Jane Chen: I see Advergames as being a standard part of a brand's marketing mix. Currently, 10% of American leisure time is spent playing games, but the percentage of advertising spending directed toward games is nowhere near that amount. The relevance and prevalence of games as a media product is just too dominant and compelling to ignore. As more high-profile Advergames such as *America's Army* start to dominate marketing industry and mainstream press, we believe that brands will start to move into the medium in a big way.

Furthermore, I believe that there will be significant platform expansion opportunities. Besides online gaming on PCs, gaming consoles are becoming networked, download-capable mobile phones are increasing penetration in the United States, and interactive television is slowly gaining a foothold. All of these represent platforms where Advergaming can—and will—take root.

21 Interview and Case Study–AGENCY.COM

AGENCY.COM is an interactive marketing and technology agency. Since 1995, the company has built world-class, customer-focused Web sites, intranets, and extranets, supported by interactive marketing and advertising campaigns for Fortune 1000 companies. AGENCY.COM is headquartered in New York, and has offices in Amsterdam, Chicago, Dallas, London, and San Francisco. AGENCY.COM serves a broad and diversified global client base in a variety of industries, including 3M, British Airways, Hewlett-Packard, and Heineken UK.

In this chapter, we take a closer look at two unique and innovative Advergames developed by AGENCY.COM. The Heinenken UK *Text Message Trivia* game uses cell phone technology, whereas the Miller Lite *VRL* (Virtual Racing League) involves a massive cross-medium ad campaign that pushes the creative and technical envelope for Advergames.

CASE STUDY 1–HEINEKEN UK *TEXT MESSAGE TRIVIA* GAME

Advergames are not limited to personal computers as you see in this very creative cellular application produced by the UK office of AGENCY.COM for their client Heineken UK. The game was played by pub-goers on their mobile phones, in the hopes of winning free beer. Let's take a closer look at the Heineken *TMT* (Text Message Trivia) game.

AGENCY.COM's creative and technology staff brainstormed an idea to use the text message feature of a cell phone to create an interactive trivia game. Players have an opportunity to show off their trivia knowledge and quench their thirst in the process. The game uses text message (SMS) technology to allow patrons to play pub trivia at any time and potentially win free pints of Heineken beer. It was the first game of its kind, dubbed as "contextual mobility," meaning the service relates directly to the user's environment.

To let players know about the game, AGENCY.COM created point-of-sale materials that were prominently placed throughout the pub to promote and explain the game. These promotional items included tent cards, shown in Figure 21.1 and Figure 21.2, beer mats, posters, and staff T-shirts.

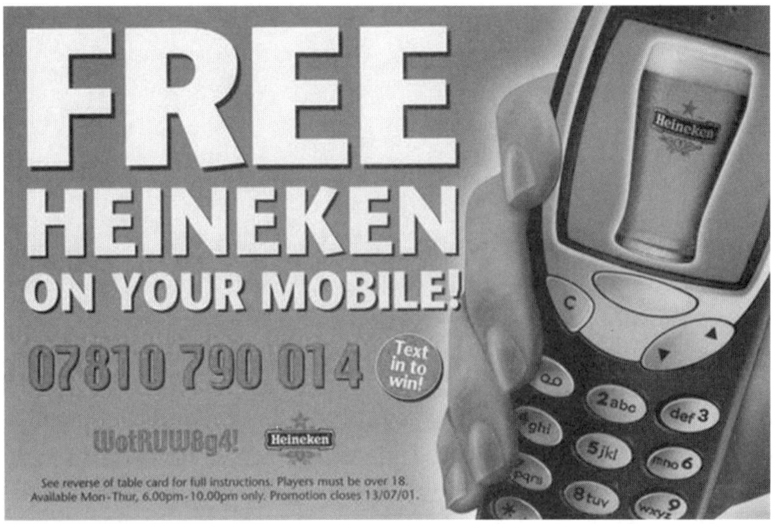

FIGURE 21.1 The "Call to Action" side of the tent card. © 2003. Reprinted with permission from AGENCY.COM.

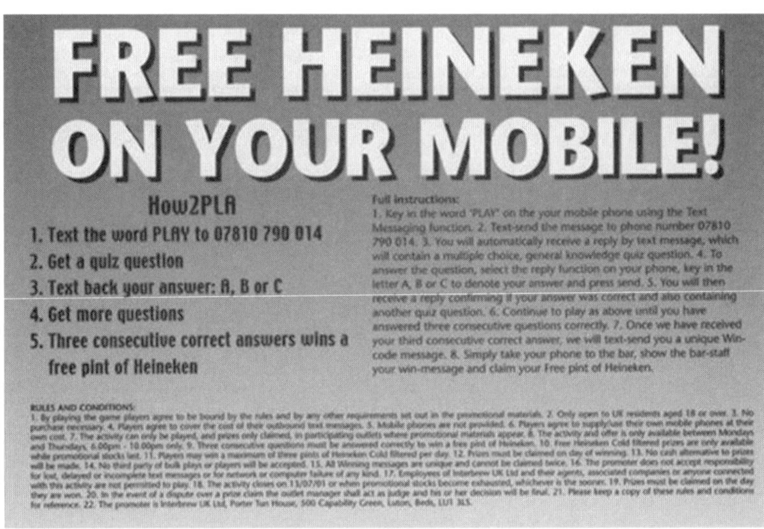

FIGURE 21.2 The "step-by-step" instruction side of the tent card. © 2003. Reprinted with permission from AGENCY.COM.

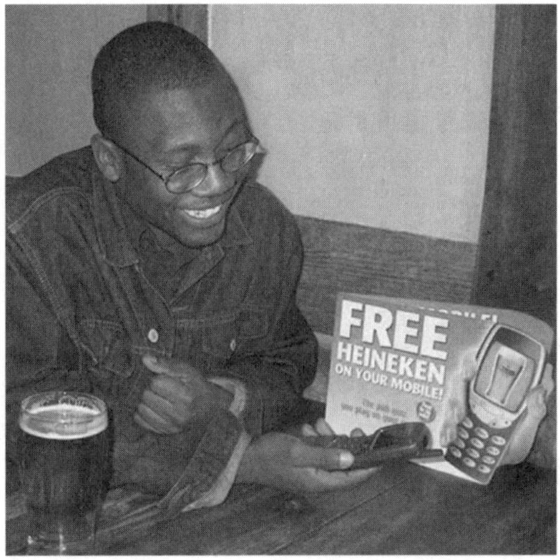

FIGURE 21.3 A player begins the game. © 2003.
Reprinted with permission from AGENCY.COM.

The game begins with the player dialing the phone number shown on the tent card as our player in Figure 21.3 is doing.

The player sends a text message to the telephone number provided. It contains the word *play*, as seen in Figure 21.4.

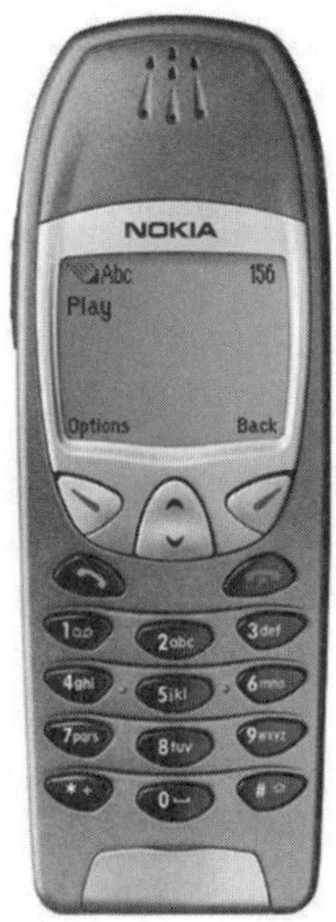

FIGURE 21.4 A player initiates the game. © 2003.
Reprinted with permission from AGENCY.COM.

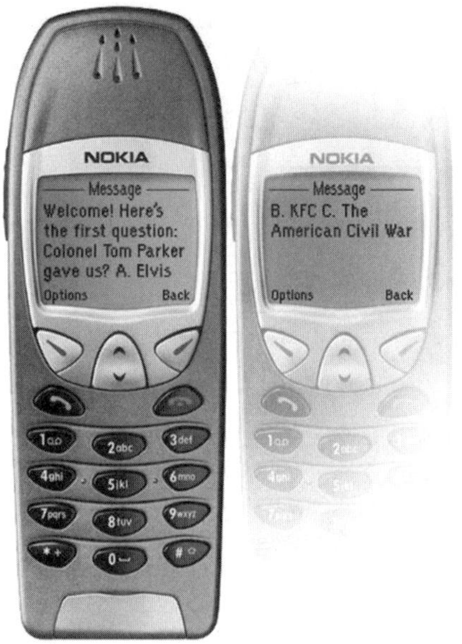

FIGURE 21.5 The first trivia question appears. © 2003. Reprinted with permission from AGENCY.COM.

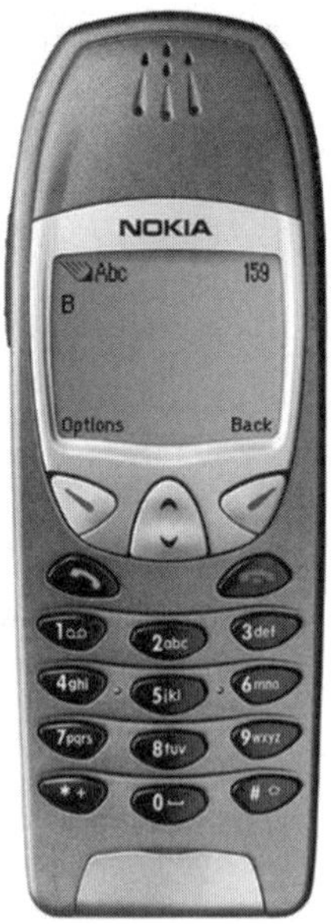

FIGURE 21.6 The player chooses "B" for the answer. © 2003. Reprinted with permission from AGENCY.COM.

Moments later, the customer receives a text message containing a random trivia question, as shown in Figure 21.5.

In Figure 21.6, the player makes his selection by replying to the text message with the letter representing his answer from the keypad.

If the player's answer is correct (see Figure 21.7), another text message containing the second question is sent, in the same format.

To answer the second question, the player sends another text message to the number containing the letter representing his answer, as shown in Figure 21.8.

Figure 21.9 shows that the player has again given the correct answer. The player now receives a third and final question.

The player responds by again replying with a text message containing his letter choice, as shown in Figure 21.10.

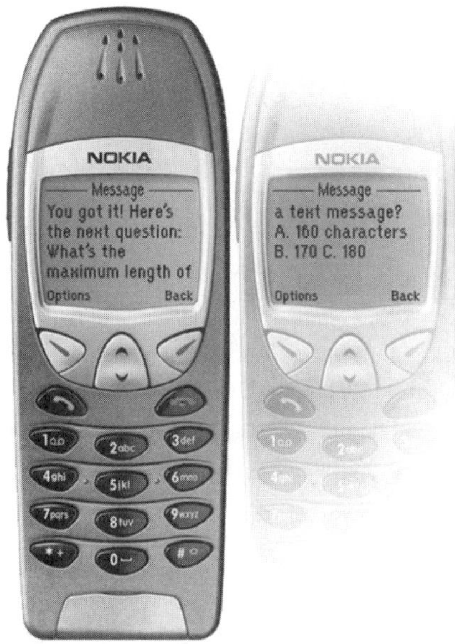

FIGURE 21.7 Question 2. © 2003. Reprinted with permission from AGENCY.COM.

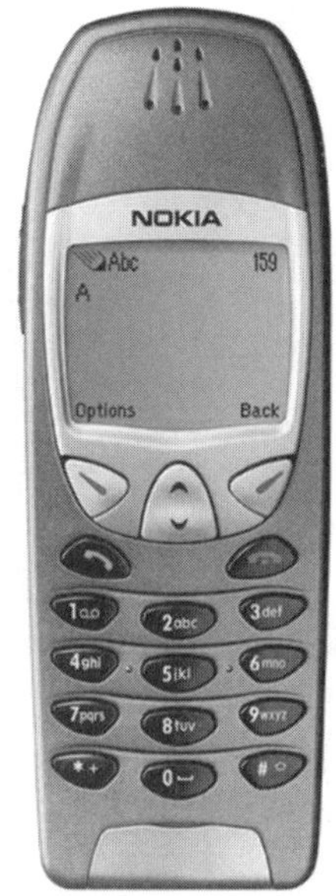

FIGURE 21.8 Answer 2. © 2003. Reprinted with permission from AGENCY.COM.

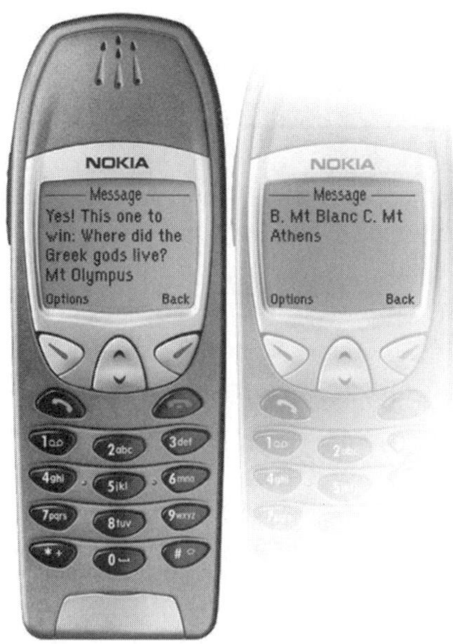

FIGURE 21.9 Final question. © 2003. Reprinted with permission from AGENCY.COM.

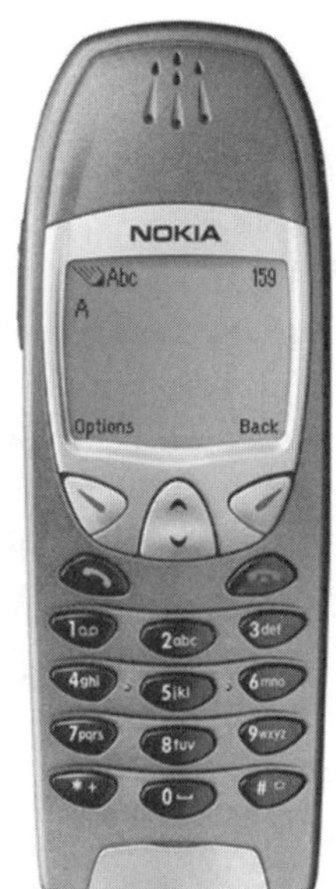

FIGURE 21.10 Final answer. © 2003. Reprinted with permission from AGENCY.COM.

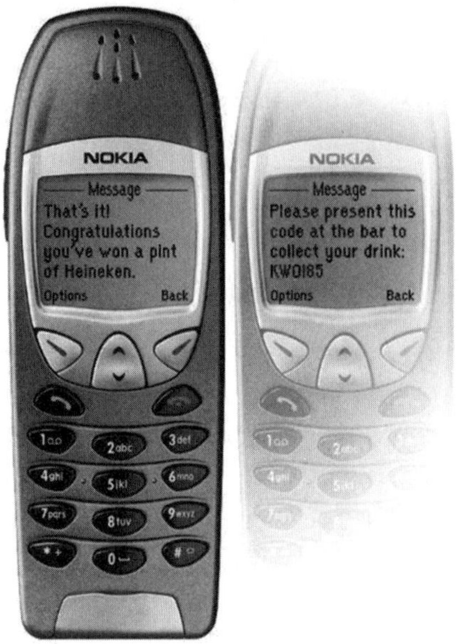

FIGURE 21.11 Winning message. © 2003. Reprinted with permission from AGENCY.COM.

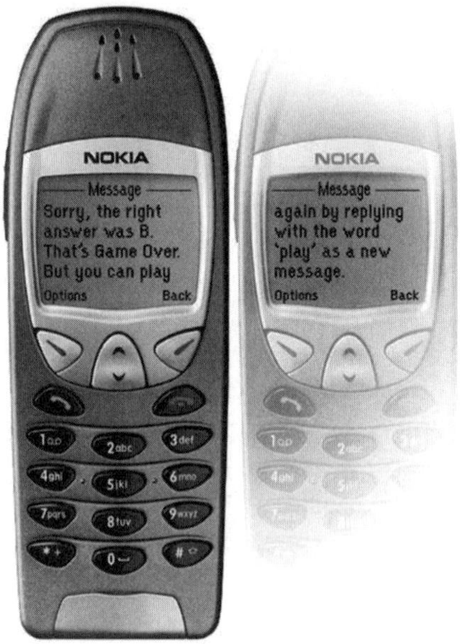

FIGURE 21.12 Wrong answer display. © 2003. Reprinted with permission from AGENCY.COM.

The player wins by answering three consecutive questions correctly. He presents the "text message coupon," shown in Figure 21.11, at the bar to collect his free pint of Heineken.

When a player answers the question wrong, as shown in Figure 21.12, he receives a text message commiserating and offering the chance to play again.

Interbrew, which brews Heineken in the UK, implemented the game in the summer of 2001, in 500 pubs throughout the United Kingdom. The rules were:

- Customers could win a maximum of three pints per night—this was enforced by the game system.
- Customers could play as many times as they wanted.
- The game was available Monday through Thursday from 6 p.m. to 10 p.m.

Customers paid for their outgoing text messages and Heineken UK paid for the incoming messages.

In most pubs, nothing creates a buzz quite like the chance to win free drinks. Iain Newell, Interbrew's Marketing Manager said, "We are always looking for new ways to attract and retain our customers. *Text Message Trivia* capitalizes on the increasing popularity of text messaging while also allowing us to develop a direct, one-to-one relationship with our customers."

The game allowed sophisticated statistical tracking. Heineken UK was able to determine the following.

- Average game length: 7 minutes
- Average number of games per player, per night: 3
- Percentage of games ending in a win: 20%
- Percentage of games abandoned: 4%

CASE STUDY 2—MILLER BREWING COMPANY—*VIRTUAL RACING LEAGUE*

To stand out from the crowd, Miller Brewing Company knew it needed something more powerful than a simple 30-second spot to connect NASCAR car racing fans to their flagship Miller Lite brand. Miller brought together its agency partners to create an integrated campaign strategy based on a single message: *Only Miller Lite gets you behind the wheel in stock car racing.* To determine the best way to make this happen, AGENCY.COM's team, including Dan Simmons (see Figure 21.13), Creative Director, conducted a series of individual and group interviews. From these interviews, the team learned that a stock car racing fan is motivated by more than just the speed and adrenaline of the race itself. It's the behind-the-scenes activities that transform the casual spectator into an avid fan. When you know the "story-be-

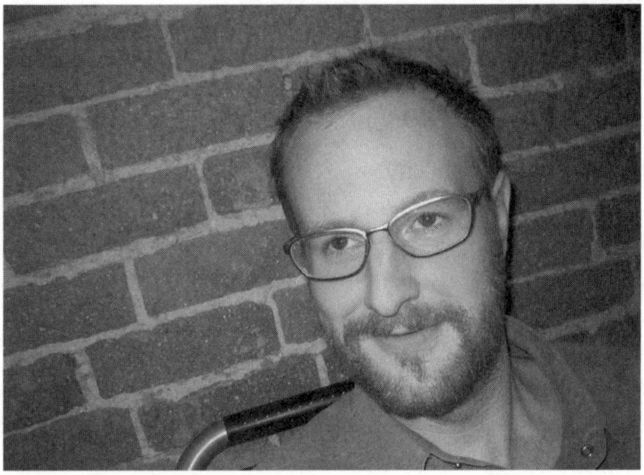

FIGURE 21.13 Dan Simons—Creative Director—AGENCY.COM.

hind-the-story" of the drivers, owners, pit crews, and sponsors, blended with the story lines (rivalries, track types, weather conditions, qualifying races, garages, team colors), and plot twists (crashes, standings, prizes, victory, and defeat), it takes the sport to a new level. If Miller could capitalize on the subtleties and intricacies of the race and allow the viewer to vicariously become part of the action, it could immerse a fan in the brand far deeper than a simple 30-second spot.

Based on these findings, AGENCY.COM decided that an interactive online game could be developed to empower the fans and engage them in a Miller Lite-branded stock car racing experience. AGENCY.COM created the Miller Lite *Virtual Racing League* (VRL; see Figure 21.14), a fantasy game that allows consumers to run their own fantasy stock car racing team, complete with a stock car, a garage, and a bank account with a lump sum of sponsorship money. By making decisions about their race team, which could include a custom paint job for the stock car, hiring a crew chief, recruiting and training a driver, buying new tires, and so on, participants get to simulate the thrills of real racing.

AGENCY.COM used the *VRL* game for a marketing technique called a "cross-medium strategy," in which information from one medium is combined with information from another. In this case, players could collect additional sponsorship money by recording codes displayed in Miller-sponsored broadcasts of actual stock

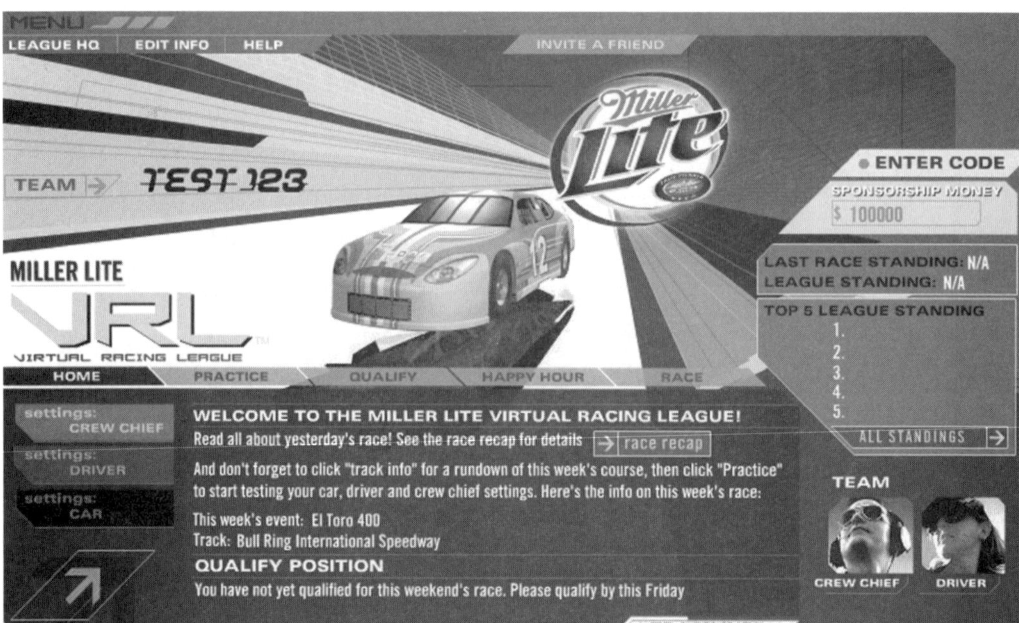

FIGURE 21.14 Miller Lite–*Virtual Racing League* (VRL) splash page. © 2003. Reprinted with permission from AGENCY.COM.

car racing events, as well as in print and online ads, and in Miller Lite packaging. When players entered these codes into the appropriate fields of the online game, additional funds were added to their sponsorship account.

You start off the season with $800,000 to hire your team and get your car ready for the race (see Figure 21.15). When you register for the game, you receive an e-mail with your first code. Mine looked like this:

```
>>>>>>>>> MILLER LITE VRL CODE <<<<<<<<<
          VRL49N2N66
>>>>>>>>> MILLER LITE VRL CODE <<<<<<<<<
```

Every week, a player competes against other league members to determine starting grid placement, and there is even a "happy hour" before the race to fine-tune your car. At the conclusion of each race, a personalized summary of the race highlights and results is sent to each participant, along with details of how his or her team fared.

The Miller Lite *VRL* was conceived at Red Sky in 2001, and has grown into an annual game that runs the entire NASCAR season (February to November). When Red Sky became part of AGENCY.COM, one of the major accounts that came on-board was Miller. Red Sky's creative talents, along with AGENCY.COM's technical

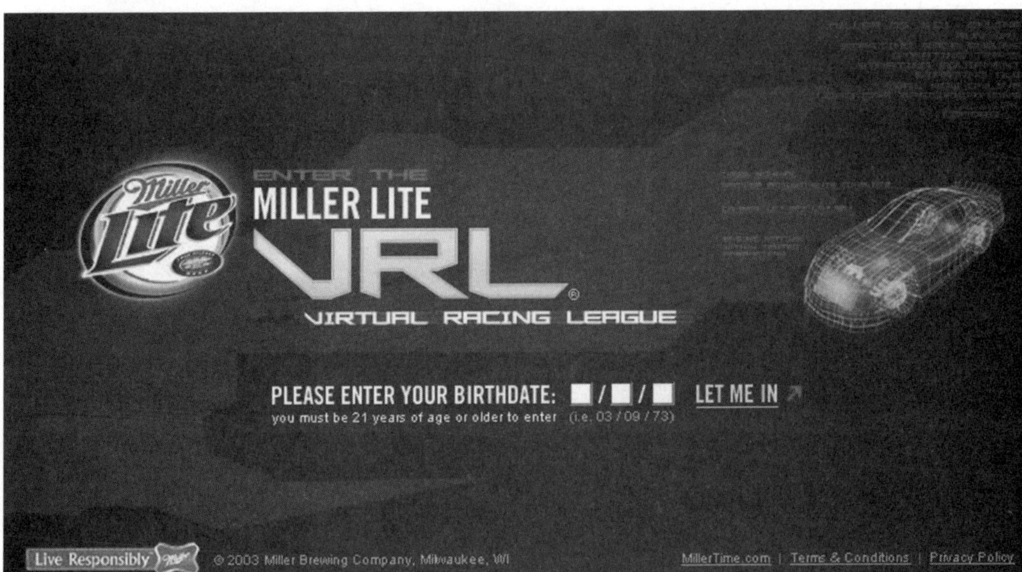

FIGURE 21.15 Entry screen for the Miller Lite *VRL* game—players must be over 21. © 2003. Reprinted with permission from AGENCY.COM.

experts advanced the initial concept in a far more robust *VRL* for the 2002 season. The game was enhanced for the 2003 season due to the game's popularity with a very loyal fan base. Currently, the development team for the *VRL* game at AGENCY.COM is headed up by Dan Simmons. We had a chance to talk with Dan about his work on the game, and what's in store for the future.

Dan, can you tell us about some of the technical and creative challenges you and your team faced in producing the Miller *VRL* game?

Dan Simmons: We had another difficult challenge of balancing the competition between die-hard fans with in-depth understanding of cars and racing with fans that were new to the sport and may only have limited knowledge. Because they would end up playing together in the same leagues, we needed to make the game fair and fun for everyone.

For instance, when players make adjustments to their cars, we don't expect them to know what diameter cylinders they should be using in their engines for a particular size track, or what their specific mileage should be in a 500-mile race. Instead, we focused on variables that most everyone would know about from watching a race or could figure out with a little trial and error. Then, we made a few careful decisions on what to include that would make the game realistic for true-blooded fans—always making sure the average player could understand the cause and effect, and that it wasn't so deep that they'd need a Chilton Manual to fix their cars.

I think the other thing we had going for us was the male psyche, which is notoriously curious and has a penchant for tinkering. A big part of any game is overcoming the learning curve, and this gave players just enough of a challenge to make things interesting.

We also had a huge barrier to overcome in terms of what stock car racing means to these fans. There's a big expectation for action and excitement with this sport—speeds in excess of 200 mph and exchanges of paint that can lead to 20-car pile-ups. There's also a lot of drama from long-held rivalries—the personalities are half the sport. Because Miller Lite wasn't the official sponsor of NASCAR, we needed to fabricate much of this drama and the cast of characters playing in it (see Figure 21.16). Plus, this isn't a video game, so we were at a big disadvantage in terms of showing any action.

So we focused instead on the things we could do best, which was telling a great story and creating an environment in which people could get emotionally involved. We needed to create a competitive, lively environment. Basically, what we wanted in the end was to generate fodder for trash talking! We realized early on that this would be the biggest attraction to the game, and the thing that would keep players coming back for more—a true sense of competition.

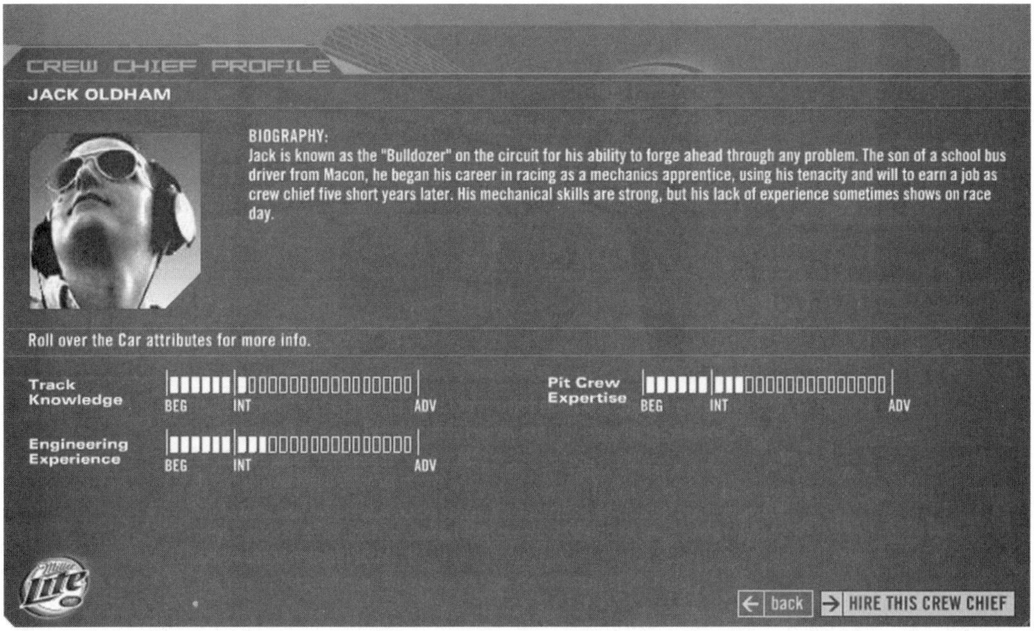

FIGURE 21.16 The Crew Chief profile of one of the many characters you can choose from in the *VRL* game.

We blew out things that would make people want to root for their teams and create a feeling of ownership, such as allowing players to name their teams anything thing they wanted, paint their cars (see Figure 21.17), and choose who their team members would be.

Then, we looked at other ways people access the world of racing. It's not always through television with motion and sound. A lot of people just read about it in the paper or online. So, we developed a story engine that generates a race cap in the vein of a news article. Each article is unique to each league and every race being run by each system throughout the series.

That's actually my favorite part of the game. Just imagining hundreds of thousands of players, divided into leagues of 43 teams/cars, all making individual adjustments to win, entering them into these races, all of those different variables coming together in different ways, all of the possible outcomes—somehow, we managed to create a tool that takes all of that chaos, all of that raw data, and forms it into a dramatic news article with quotes, detailed accounts of crashes, and some serious "hero time" for winners. It's an article that's different for every person playing each week, and has been surprisingly effective in terms of depicting that high-octane excitement that people love about this sport.

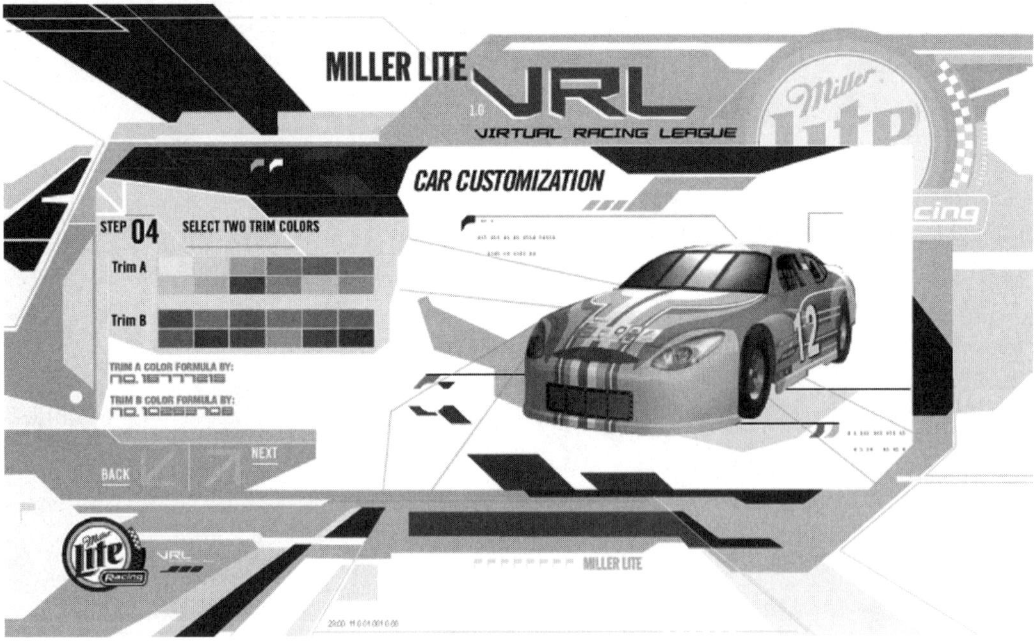

FIGURE 21.17 You can customize your race car color and trim.

As an Advergame, the Miller Lite *Virtual Racing League* exceeded every goal established for it. In 2002, the site attracted nearly 305,000 registrants—a 290% increase over the previous year and over double the goal of 150,000 established for 2002 (see Figure 21.18). And perhaps the best endorsement of any branding effort comes from a happy client—Gina Shaffer, Miller Brewing Company's senior manager of digital marketing said, "Interactive marketing is an integral part of our overall brand-building strategy, helping us connect and build relationships with our legal-drinking-age consumers in new and innovative ways. We are thrilled that our partnership with AGENCY.COM has yielded such noteworthy results."

Dan, what comes next? What can *VRL* fans expect for the 2004 season, and what are your thoughts about the future of the Advergaming industry?

Dan Simmons: We're currently in talks with Miller about next season, so we're not sure what will be in store right now. Part of any good Advergame is the anticipation of "what comes next."

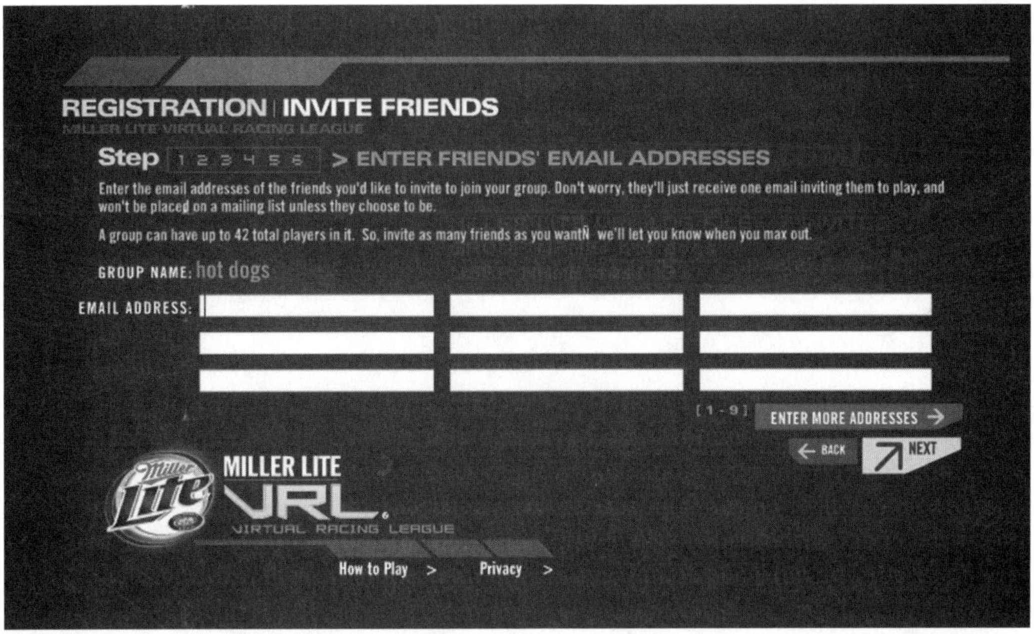

FIGURE 21.18 Up to 42 players can register in a group. AGENCY.COM made it easy to get the word out about the game.

Dan, you have a great deal of experience in both marketing and game development. Please share with us the unique niche that Advergames fill in both worlds.

Dan Simmons: Advertisers must understand the space they're playing in—it's all of gaming, not just Advergaming. They're competing with cutting-edge content from online fantasy sports games to beautifully rendered, immersive experiences on TV consoles and PCs. They have the potential to engage big partners, such as EA, Sega, Activision—some already are—as well as creating uniquely branded content they own for themselves.

The spectrum is wide, the choices are many, and the advertisers need to understand that to be effective, they can't create the equivalent of a cheap, unsophisticated ad. Consumers see through it, particularly when you ask them to interact with you. When was the last time you willingly returned a phone call from someone you found bland or annoying?

And that's really the core of the issue. You're asking people to get involved with a brand, to make a commitment. Games are about spending time, actively participating, and getting feedback. It's like any other relationship you have in the real world; people expect a positive return on their experience. Even if they don't win the game, they want to leave feeling like they had fun.

Let's be honest, people are busy, they have a lot of things vying for their attention, and they'll ignore what appears to be clutter. When we look to the future, we need to forge new ground, set high standards, and deliver entertainment that's valued. Mascot Whacking and Logo Tetris won't cut it. Advergaming isn't just a logo slap, it is branded entertainment and it's competing with everything else out there.

Advertisers need to face the fact that a bad experience with a lame game can be far more detrimental to a consumer's brand relationship than an ineffective print campaign that everyone ignored. Like everything in life, Advergaming's biggest asset, active participation with a brand for more than 30 seconds, is also its biggest liability—if you foul it up, the stakes can be high.

But the potential is too great to ignore. People want this stuff. They're eating it up! Look at the level of participation in games, the growth in the gaming industry during the current economic downturn. It's amazing to think of what is ahead for product placement, branded modules within video games, Easter eggs that unlock new features, character endorsements, and the dimension that real-world products can bring to a gaming environment. It's just the beginning, and we need to handle this delicate egg with care until it's hatched.

22 A Guide to Advergame Development Companies

This chapter 22 contains a directory with some of the top Advergaming development shops in the world. By no means is this an exhaustive listing because Advergaming is in its infancy, and game companies, in general, come and go rather quickly. When we started working on this book, a Google search on Advergaming returned a manageable number of "hits." Not any more. Wading through the pages of links can be both time-consuming and frustrating. Even so, you'll want to use your favorite search tool to research which Advergaming companies are today's hot shops. Use the information below to get started—but remember—this is fun with a purpose, so try not to get too distracted playing the games!

2pixel8 Design Studio

Federico Salmón, 1
Madrid 28016 (Spain)
(ph): +34 625 067 671
(fax): +34 913 509 276
www.2pixel8.com
jal@2pixel8.com

Company Overview

2pixel8 is a design studio specializing in Flash and interactive contents, with a multidisciplinary team that works hard to achieve new ways of expression, using all kinds of media in a creative fusion.Table 22.1 shows a sampling of games that 2pixel8 has developed.

TABLE 22.1 A sampling of games from 2pixel8

Game	***Client***	***Application and URL***
Blanca Island	Blanca de Navarra (La Navarra)	In this game, the user must help the main character of the game get off of a desert island, through different stages in which hints were granted to the user, to finish the game. The users who finished the game won different prizes. See Figure 22.1. *http://portfolio.2pixel8.com/blanca*
Mission in Lapland	Addiction to the Net	This game was an interactive Christmas e-card created in Flash, for the clients of Addiction to the Net, to greet the season in a humorous and enjoying way. The aim of the game is to successfully package the gifts for the kids at Santa's factory. See Figure 22.2. *http://portfolio.2pixel8.com/laponia*

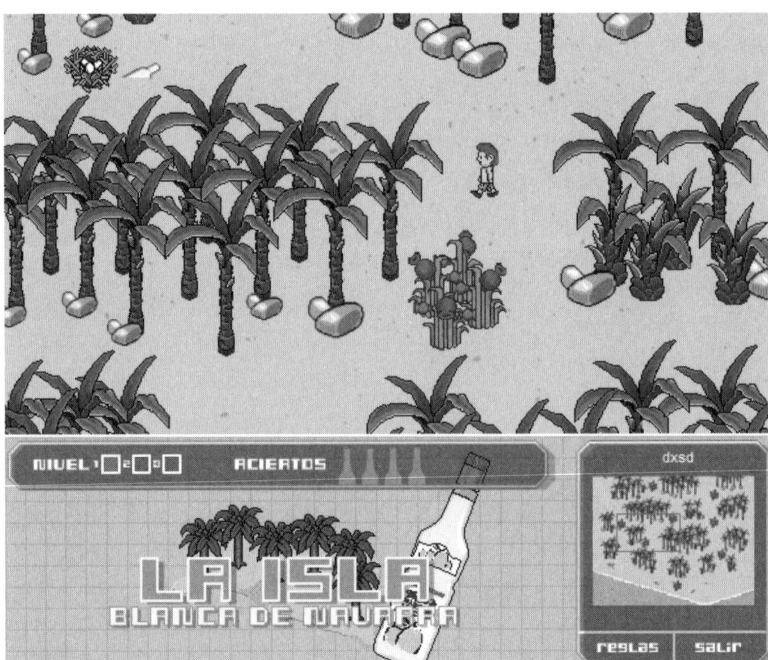

FIGURE 22.1 2pixel8 Blanca Island game. © 2003. Reprinted with permission from 2pixel8 Design Studio.

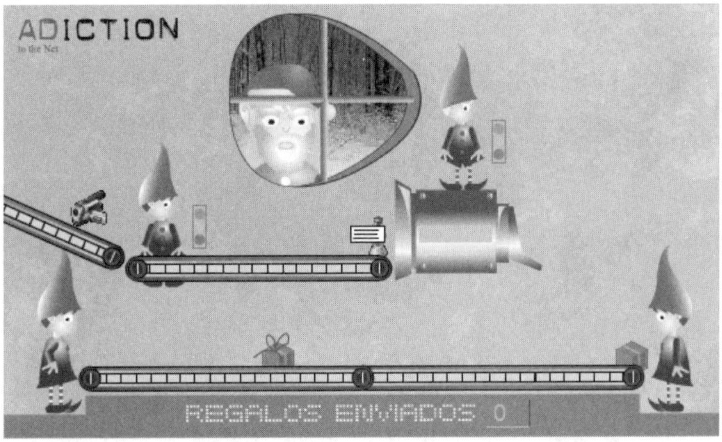

FIGURE 22.2 2pixel8 Mission in Lapland game. © 2003. Reprinted with permission from 2pixel8 Design Studio.

8Legged Entertainment

1535 Huddersfield Ct.
San Jose, CA 95126
(ph): 408-439-9540
(fax): 253-541-5269
www.8legged.com
info@8legged.com

Company Overview

8Legged Entertainment is a new media content company that is dedicated to creating original properties, rich in character, story, and production values for emerging and traditional media environments. Their initial foray in Advergaming came as a way to add value to the award-winning animated series, *Deep Fried, Live!* (see Figure 22.3) with Tako the Octopus, an interactive cooking show hosted by an accident-prone octopus chef. By inserting three levels of gameplay into the Thanksgiving episode, 8Legged Entertainment was able to make it even more engaging for the on-line viewer.

8Legged's primary focus has always been on story and character, and this is the same approach they take to Advergaming. They specialize in creating characters, environments, and situations that tie directly to established narrative elements to provide a more immersive experience for the player. Table 22.2 shows a sampling of games that 8Legged Entertainment has developed. Figure 22.4 shows the 8Legged Entertainment home page.

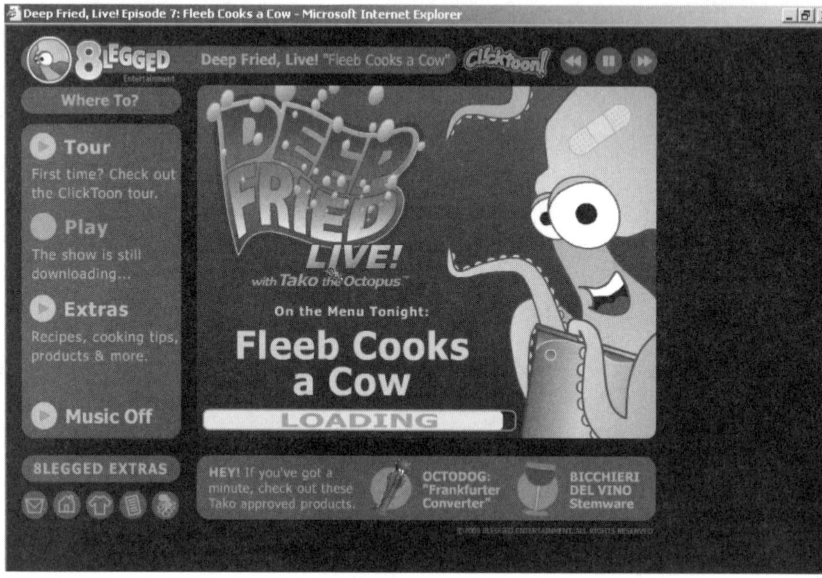

FIGURE 22.3 8Legged Entertainment Deep Fried Turkey cartoon. © 2003. 8Legged Entertainment. Reprinted with permission.

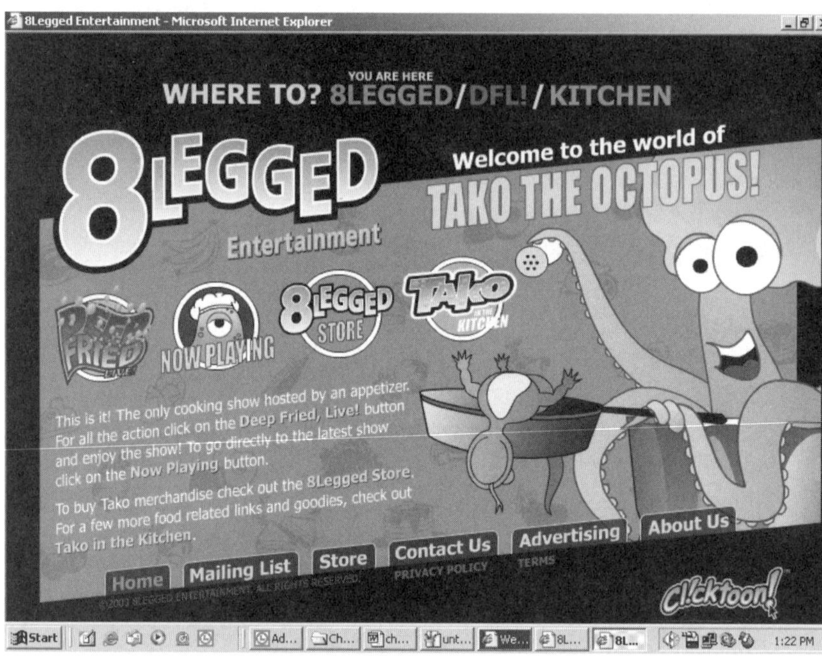

FIGURE 22.4 8Legged Entertainment home page. © 2003. 8Legged Entertainment. Reprinted with permission.

TABLE 22.2 A sampling of games from 8Legged Entertainment

Game	*Client*	*Application and URL*
Deep Fried Turkey Game	8Legged Entertainment	Episode 4 of the *Deep Fried, Live!* series was also a game. As the story unfolded, we asked viewers to help the host (an octopus in a bucket) keep Thanksgiving dinner on track. Tasks included catching the turkey, collecting ingredients, and protecting the deep fryer from renegade birds. *www.deepfriedlive.com* (click the "turkey" icon)
FindLaw "Court of Justice" Game	Unleashed Media (& FindLaw)	8Legged created character and sound designs, animation, and music for an online Advergame based on the "Who Wants to Be a Millionaire" format. The game was used by the online law resource, FindLaw, as a way to entertain, as well as enter players into a contest (after they completed the game). The URL is no longer online.

Blockdot

824 Exposition, Suite 2
Dallas, TX 75226
(ph): 214-823-0500
(fax): 214-823-0535
www.blockdot.com
dferguson@blockdot.com

Company Overview

Blockdot, Inc. is a privately owned Dallas-based company that specializes in game development. Samples of their work can be found at *www.kewlbox.com* (pronounced "Cool Box"), a game site that receives about 2 million gameplays per week. Kewlbox.com was built to serve as a launching pad for the games created by Blockdot, an award-winning creative and technology firm. Two of the founders of Kewlbox.com/Blockdot, Mike Bielinski and Dan Ferguson, are considered the forefathers of Advergaming and Viral Marketing, having launched the first popular Advergame on April Fool's Day, 1998. They have created some of the most successful Advergames on the Internet for companies such as AT&T®, Motorola®, M&M's®, Skittles®, T.G.I. Friday's®, and Nokia®. They are most recognized for creating the holiday elf game—*Santa Balls*, which has been played over 25 million times. In March 2001, *Brandweek Magazine* recognized Dan Ferguson and Mike Bielinski as two of the Top 10 Marketers of the Next Generation. Table 22.3 shows a sampling of games that Blockdot has developed.

TABLE 22.3 A sampling of games from Blockdot

Game	*Client*	*Application and URL*
M&M's—Flip The Mix	Mars Candy	Game was used to promote M&M's candies. The game is a tremendous success with average gameplay of 35 minutes per game session; over 8 million hours of brand exposure have been logged. Game Plays: over 16 million.
AT&T—Frendz	AT&T	Game was used to promote AT&T's Unlimited Long Distance Plan. The game is based on connecting little alien "Frendz" to help illustrate the client's message (see Figure 22.5). The game was also built with peak call, holiday reminders that would go off to remind players to call their loved ones. Game Plays: over 3 million.
Santa Balls	Kewlbox	Game was used as a holiday greeting card for Kewlbox.com (see Figure 22.6), which has become a tradition with Blockdot. The game features the now infamous Oliver the Elf, who cracks wise comments during the game. Game Plays: over 25 million.
T.G.I. Friday's—Bovinator	T.G.I. Friday's	Game was used to promote T.G.I. Friday's Angus Beef Burgers, and featured Bob the Bovinator. Client reported that the campaign doubled their Web traffic and tripled their registration database. Game Plays: over 1.5 million.
Nokia—Sketchy Snow Sledding	Nokia	Game was used to promote Nokia's text messaging features of their 3300 series phones. The game enables the audience to interact with the text messaging system by sending codes, which unlocks features in the game, or to receive SMS score notifications to notify them

TABLE 22.3 *(Continued)*

Game	***Client***	***Application and URL***
		of changes to the scoreboards. Over half a million hours of brand exposure have been logged. Game Plays: over 3 million.
SBC–Braving the Elements	SBC	Game was used to promote SBC's online bill payment system. The game shows the outrageous perils and pitfalls of trying to mail your bill payments. Over 2 million hours of brand exposure have been logged. Game Plays: over 8 million.

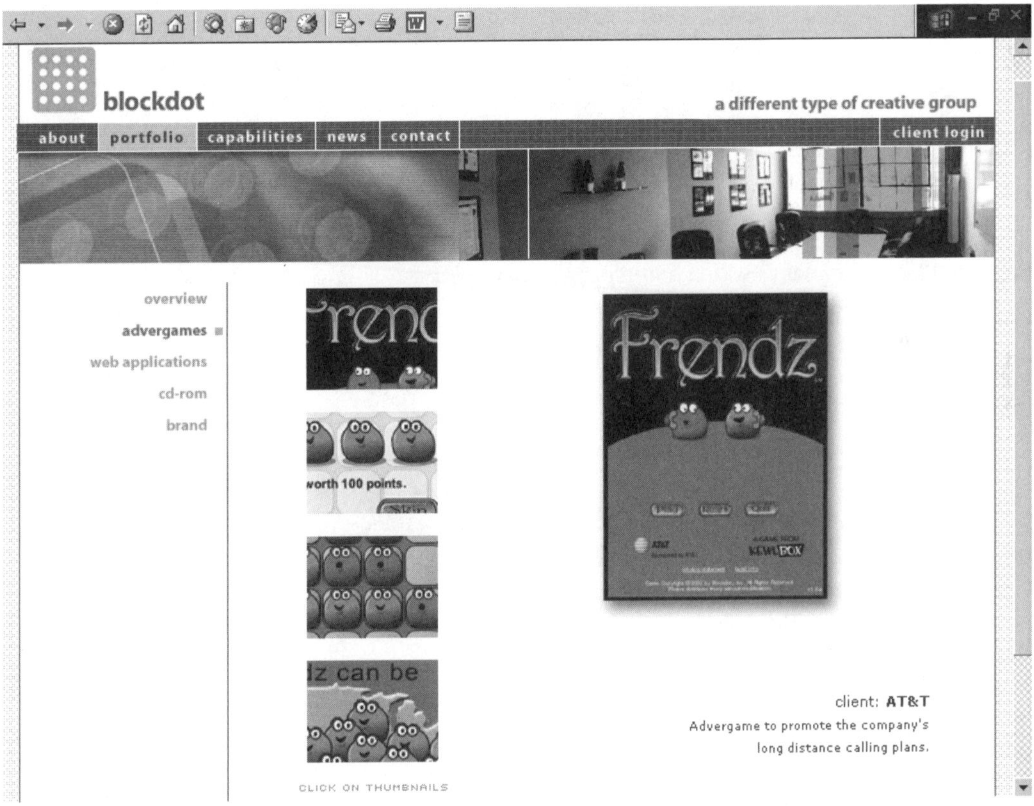

FIGURE 22.5 Blockdot Frenz game. © 2003. Reprinted with permission from Blockdot.

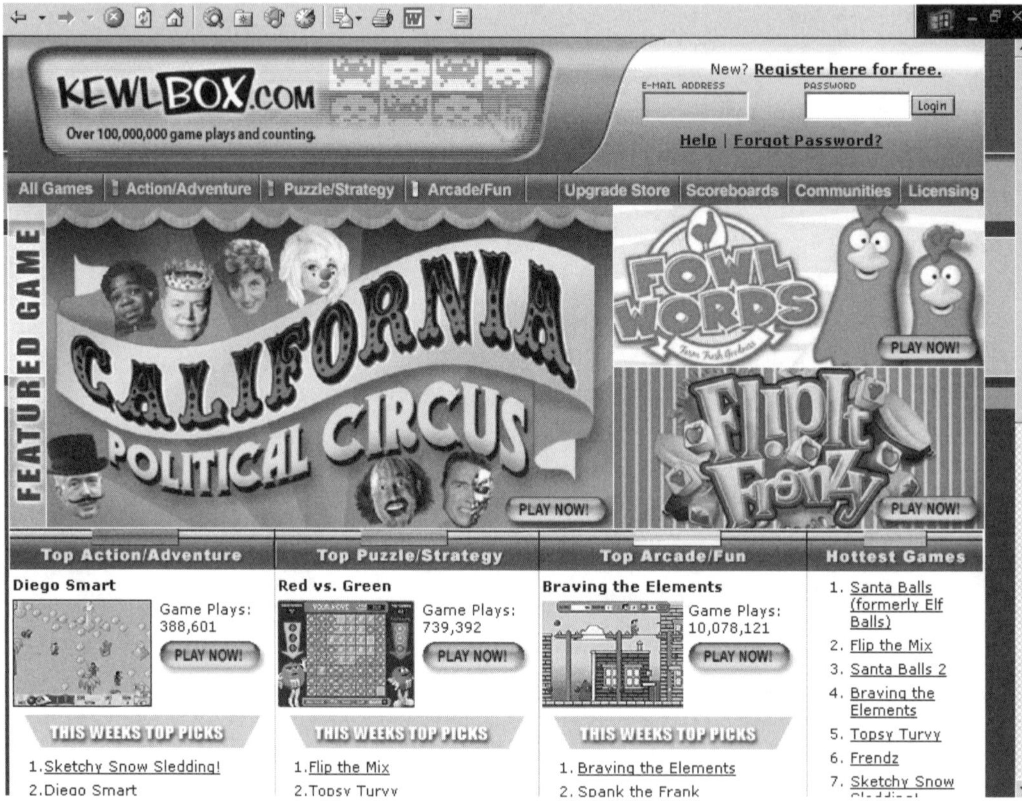

FIGURE 22.6 Blockdot Kewlbox home page.

Choice Internet

17785 Center Court Drive Suite 280
Cerritos, CA 90703
(ph): 562-865-6886
(fax): 562-865-6889
www.choiceinternet.com
info@choiceinternet.com

Company Overview

Choice is an interactive agency that specializes in building engaging digital experiences that help companies connect with youth audiences.

For Advergaming, the Choice philosophy is to use Advergaming as part of an integrated marketing effort that enables their clients to accomplish multiple objec-

TABLE 22.4 A sampling of games from Choice Internet

Game	*Client*	*Application and URL*
Nitto 1320 Challenge	Nitto Tire Corporation and other game sponsors	The Nitto 1320 Challenge online drag racing game (see Figure 22.8) has developed a large fan-base of heavily active game players who participate in both the gameplay and community aspects of the online game. Choice developed the Nitto 1320 Challenge with enough depth to draw users back to the game several times each day. The game has a devoted following, and uses and includes exclusive features and hidden codes designed to: • Capture extensive user demographic data • Build an e-mail database of hundreds of thousands of active users • Drive traffic to specific Web destinations • Drive retail sales • Educate consumers about our client's products *www.nitto1320.com*

tives. Rather than place brands within simple games, the goal is to build games that have enough gameplay and sophistication to draw a captive audience and to incorporate the client's brands as an integral component of the game experience.

In short, Choice is pushing the envelope to develop Advergaming strategies that deliver much more than brand impressions. Table 22.4 shows an example of a game that Choice Internet has developed. Figure 22.7 shows the Choice Internet Web site.

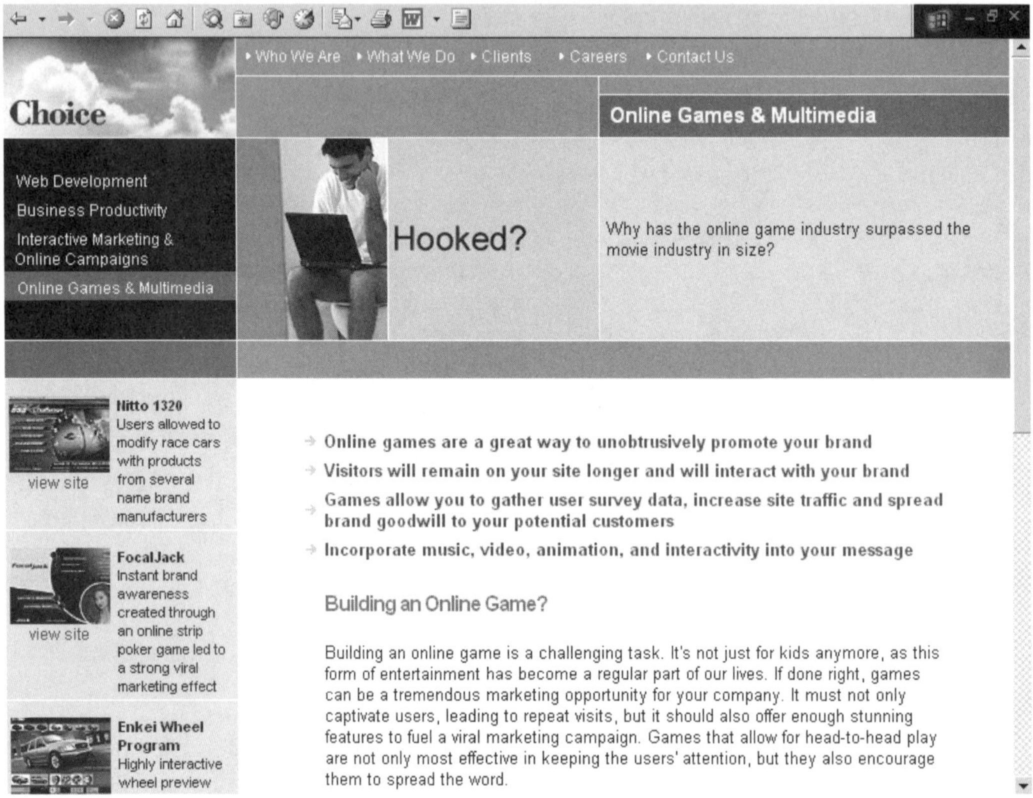

FIGURE 22.7 Choice Internet Web site. © 2003. Reprinted with permission from Choice Internet.

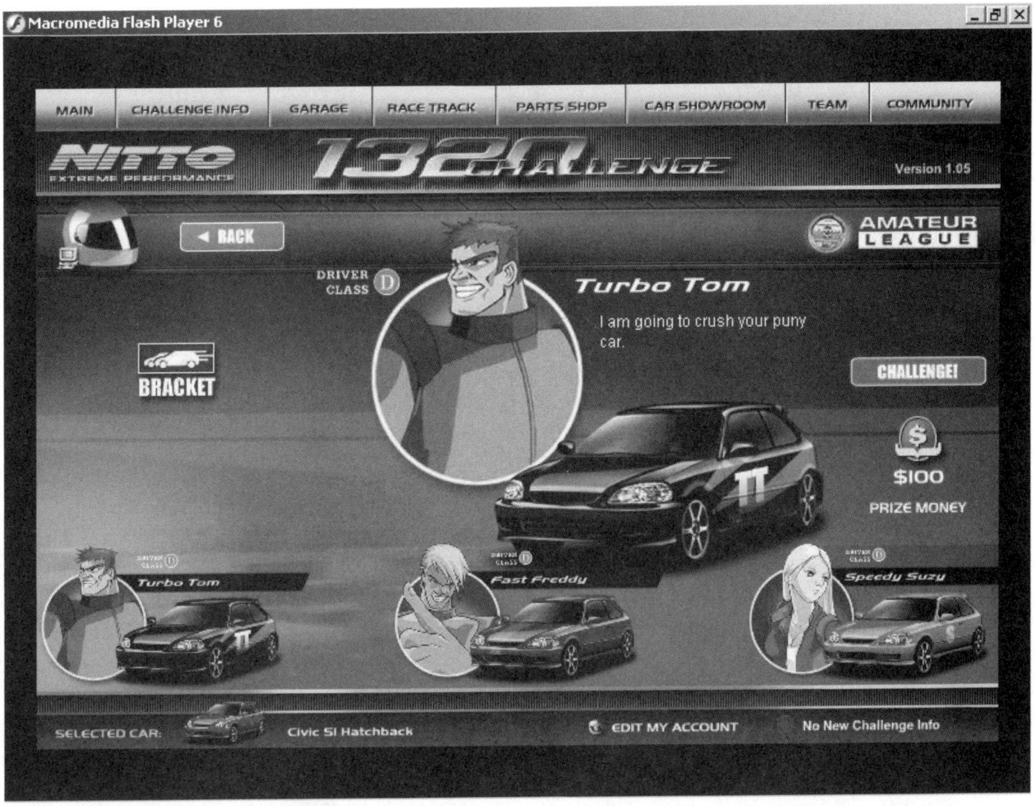

FIGURE 22.8 Choice Internet Nitto Tire game. © 2003. Reprinted with permission from Choice Internet.

Deepend New York

813 Broadway, Floor 2
New York, NY, 10003
(ph): 212-253-1974
(fax): 212-253-2375
www.deepend.com
james@deepend.com

Company Overview

Driven by creative vision and technical innovation, Deepend New York's award-winning team has established a global brand renowned for its creativity and excellence. The Deepend studio offers creative digital communication services and strategic brand planning, with a skill base that covers Web development, brand and graphics design, multimedia, games development, 3D visualization, interactive TV, moving image, and convergent media, including broadband, handheld, and wireless technologies. In the year 1999–2000, Deepend won 17 major international awards, culminating in being named "Number One Creative Interactive Agency in the World" by *Advertising Age International.* It is Deepend's unerring commitment to pushing the boundaries of creative and technical development, while focusing intensely on user experience that maintains this award-winning status.

The multimedia team at Deepend has produced a portfolio of award-winning online games. These Advergames are used in promoting, supporting, and enhancing a brand through innovative and addictive online games, ranging from small promotional tools to ambitious, multilevel, networked games. Table 22.5 shows a sampling of games that Deepend has developed.

TABLE 22.5 A sampling of games from Deepend

Game	*Client*	*Application and URL*
Gotan Goes Fizzy	Michaelides & Bednash; Tango	See the Case Study section of Chapter 1. www.playerthree.net/portfolio.php?f=4
Wirefighter	BT	BT Wirefighter was a game created to drive traffic to the then newly designed Wire Play site, which contained gaming content. The game opened from a link in an e-mail, allowing the player to play the game and record his high score. After completing the game, the player was prompted to submit an e-mail address to challenge a friend. This simple viral campaign created an extremely successful marketing platform for BT Wire Play and the game itself remained in the top 10 games played on Wire Play for over two years, an achievement in that its estimated shelf life was three months. www.playerthree.net/playgames.php

GameSpy Industries

18002 Skypark Circle
Irvine, CA 92614
(ph): 949-798-4200
(fax): 949-798-4299
www.gamespy.com
pubservices@gamespy.com

Company Overview

GameSpy is the Web's #1 location for online information and entertainment for the "connected gamer"—online game playing enthusiasts. GameSpy has more than 300,000 subscribers and 20 million registered users. GameSpy is also the leading provider of technology for online gameplay in video games, enabling more than 80% of today's titles that can be played online. Founded in 1995, privately held GameSpy is headquartered in Irvine, California, and can be found at *www.gamespy.com*. The GameSpy home page is featured in Figure 22.9.

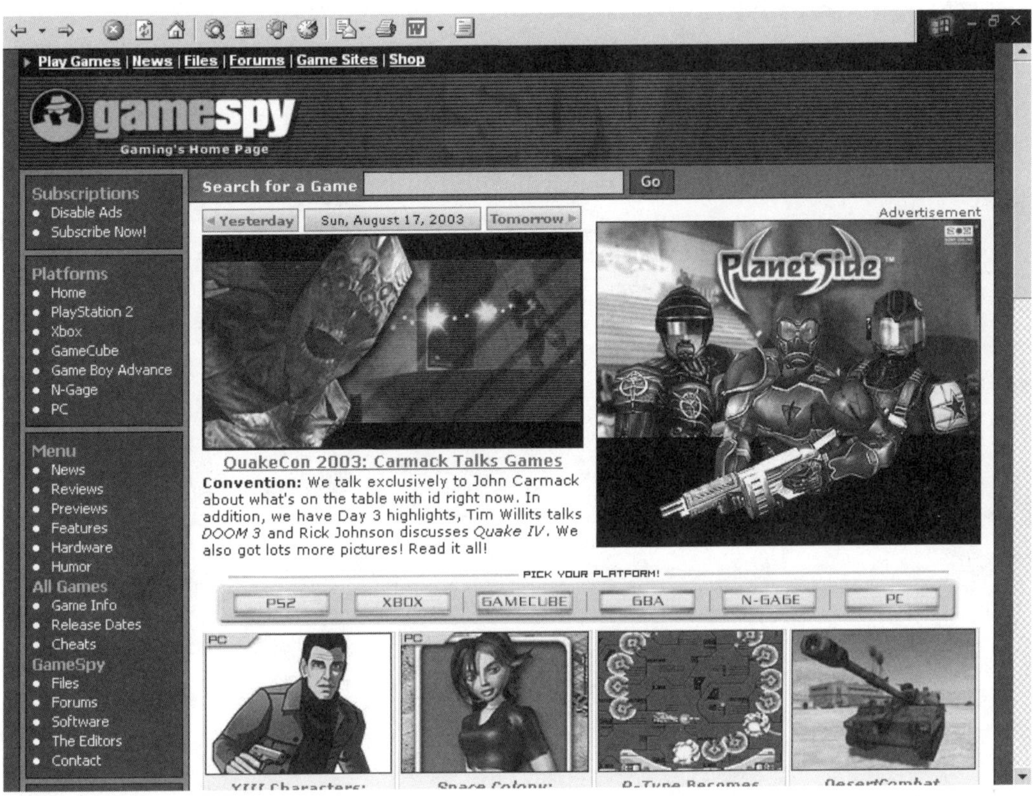

FIGURE 22.9 GameSpy home page.

GameSpy content development is focused on two areas: providing middleware that enables online gameplay in PC, PS2, and Xbox video games and customized games and game modifications (mods) on behalf of advertisers and strategic partners.

HSR Business to Business, Inc.

300 E-Business Way, Suite 500
Cincinnati, OH 45241
(ph): 513-671-3811
(fax): 513-671-8163
www.hsr.com
rsegal@hsr.com

Company Overview

HSR Business to Business is an integrated marketing communications firm specializing in the needs of business-to-business clients. HSR Business to Business' complete offering includes strategy, advertising, sales promotion, public relations, and Internet services.

"Advergames are designed to educate the target audience on evidence supporting brand position, benefits, and features," says Mike Hensley, executive vice president, Internet Division. HSR utilizes exciting new forms of e-marketing, such as Advergames, to build traffic to Web sites. Establishing this dialogue with customers is vital, as is creating an experience that brings them back repeatedly. When potential customers enjoy visiting a Web site, you are one step closer to winning their business. Table 22.6 shows an example game that HSR Business to Business has developed. The HSR home page can be seen in Figure 22.10.

TABLE 22.6 A sampling of games from HSR Business to Business

Game	*Client*	*Application and URL*
Seedy Rom	AMD	Designed to get the word out about AMD's new high-speed processors, this game enables players to maneuver through a moving maze, while battling villains and picking up product information along the way. The URL is no longer available.

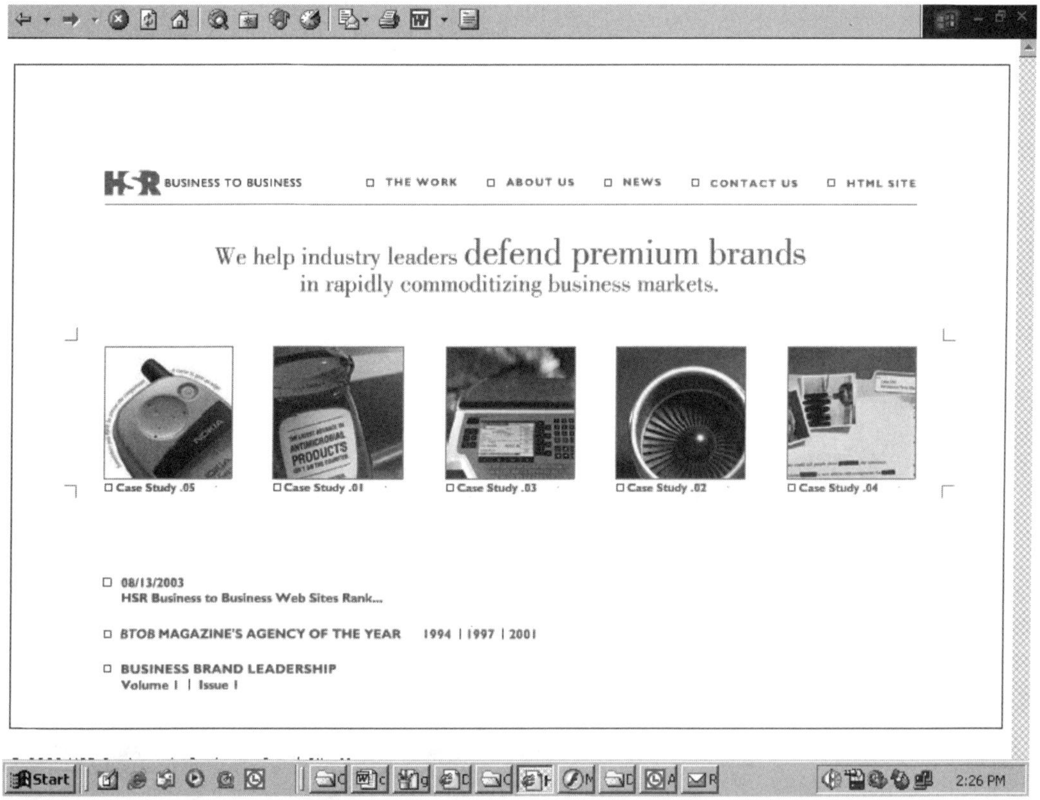

FIGURE 22.10 HSR home page. © 2003. Reprinted with permission from HSR.

Leviathan Games

14013 24th Ave. NE
Seattle, WA 98125
(ph): 206-361-5113
www.leviathangames.com
info@leviathangames.com

Company Overview

Leviathan Games makes online 3D games for advertisers. Free and quick for players to download, these properties are known in the industry as Advergames. As the name suggests, Advergames are video game hybrids that carry a branded message or theme. Although a relatively new method of advertising, Advergames are quickly gaining momentum as sponsors realize the value of having their target not only notice, but also actively engage with the brand. Results prove that gamers are willing to register, or "opt in" to mailing lists in exchange for downloading a high-quality, free Advergame. That translates to an eager, receptive audience. With more than 60 million online gamers, with equal distribution among sexes and age ranges, many of the most desirable target demographics are represented. Plus, Advergames encourage players to recommend the games to others in the demographic, creating a viral marketing component on which only the Internet can capitalize.

Currently there are a wide range of products and developers making Advergames; Leviathan Games represents the most technologically sophisticated tier.

Far beyond Flash games, or even Java applets, Leviathan Games utilizes 3D Web technologies, such as the WildTangent Web Driver and the Virtools Web Player to interface directly with Microsoft DirectX.

Leviathan engineers, artists, and game designers have more than 30 years experience building successful 3D products for PC-CDROM, X-Box, and PlayStation®. Leviathan has created products for numerous Fortune 500 companies, including Sony® and Coca-Cola. Table 22.7 shows a sampling of games that Leviathan Games has developed. The Leviathan Games home page is shown in Figure 22.11.

TABLE 22.7 A sampling of games from Leviathan Games

Game	*Client*	*Application and URL*
Sprite® One-on-One Challenge	Sprite	See Figure 22.12. *www.spritemadness.com*
BellSouth FastAccess DSL Racing	BellSouth	See Figure 0.1 from Introduction. *www.dsl-playground.com/*

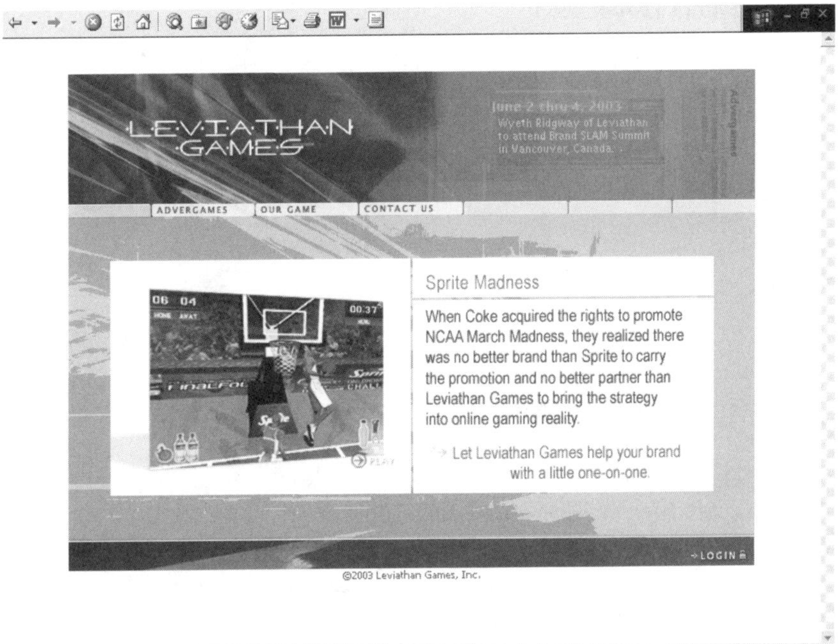

FIGURE 22.11 Leviathan Games home page. © 2003. Reprinted with permission from Leviathan Games.

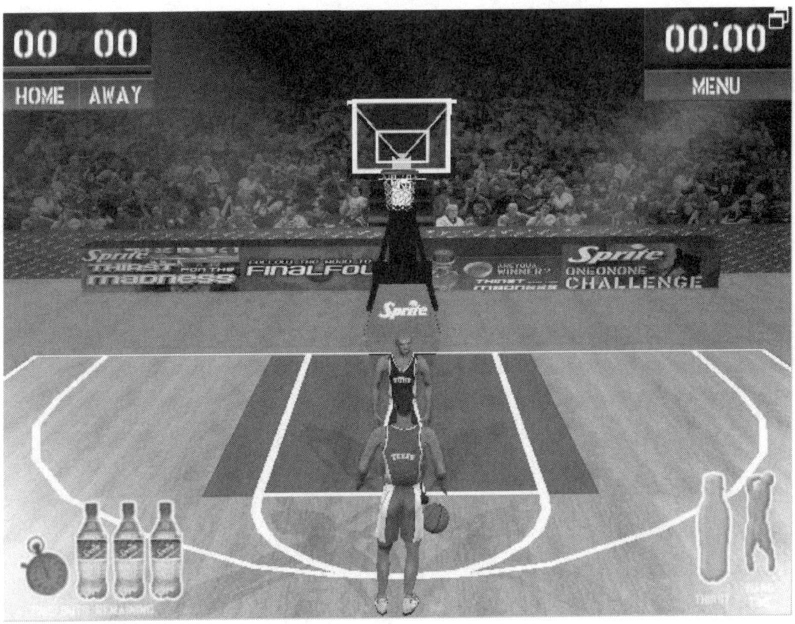

FIGURE 22.12 Leviathan Games Sprite One-on-One Challenge. © 2003. Reprinted with permission from Leviathan Games.

MindComet Corporation

500 Winderely Place, Suite 115
Maitland, FL 32751
(ph): 407-838-1010
(fax): 407-838-1011
www.mindcomet.com
info@mindcomet.com

Company Overview

MindComet is a multidisciplinary global solutions developer offering a complete array of digital media development services designed to build brand equity, to create a positive return on investment, and to address the needs of the connected consumer.

Their Advergame development philosophy focuses on user-friendly applications with high-quality graphics designed to gather user data. A key factor in choosing a solution provider is the provider's ability to grow with the solution and take advantage of new trends in technology as they develop.

MindComet is a recognized pioneer of digital content creation and excels in the development of rich media solutions, in addition to being one of the leading developers of comprehensive marketing-centric interactive solutions that consistently deliver results.

MindComet is competent in a wide array of technologies, applications, and media. Examples of these include Web application development, which covers all project phases from discovery to maintenance, rich media marketing and sales, and custom-built solutions and Advergames. MindComet's Advergames act as a powerful user-profiling application that allows a company to track and analyze user interaction with specific modules of the game. Disc-based media are CD and DVD marketing and sales tools with rich media content in either nonlinear or linear presentation formats. MindComet's proprietary technology allows advanced tracking of user interaction with the CD and DVD content when users are connected to the Internet. MindComet's kiosk systems fuse the best of interactive and industrial design into a physically captivating, powerful interactive solution. Table 22.8 shows an example game that MindComet has developed. The MindComet home page can be seen in Figure 22.13.

TABLE 22.8 A sampling of games from MindComet

Game	*Client*	*Application and URL*
NEXTEL® Front Nine	Nextel	As part of Nextel's golf association with CBS Sportsline.com and PGATour.com, MindComet launched the Nextel Front Nine prior to the Master's Tournament to reach both avid and casual golf fans. Developed in Director MX, this game allows users to play the first nine holes of golf, employing a viral marketing component in addition to capturing valuable demographic information. See Figure 22.14. *http://games.mindcomet.net/nextel/golf/*

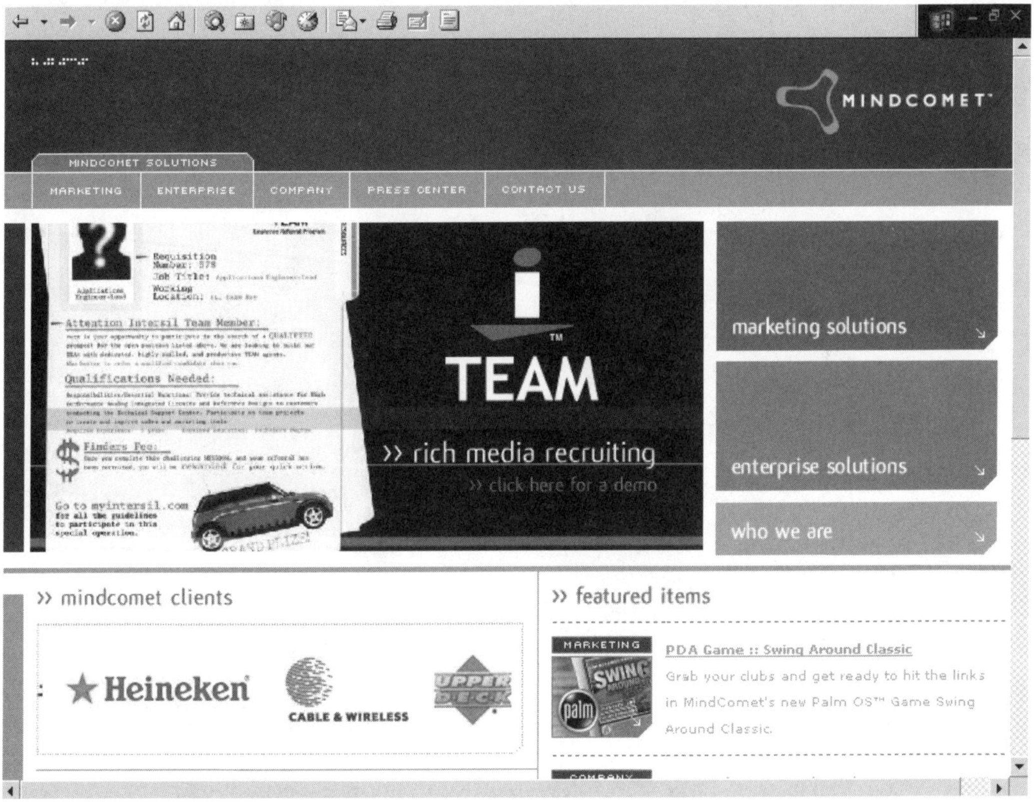

FIGURE 22.13 MindComet home page. © 2003. Reprinted with permission from MindComet.

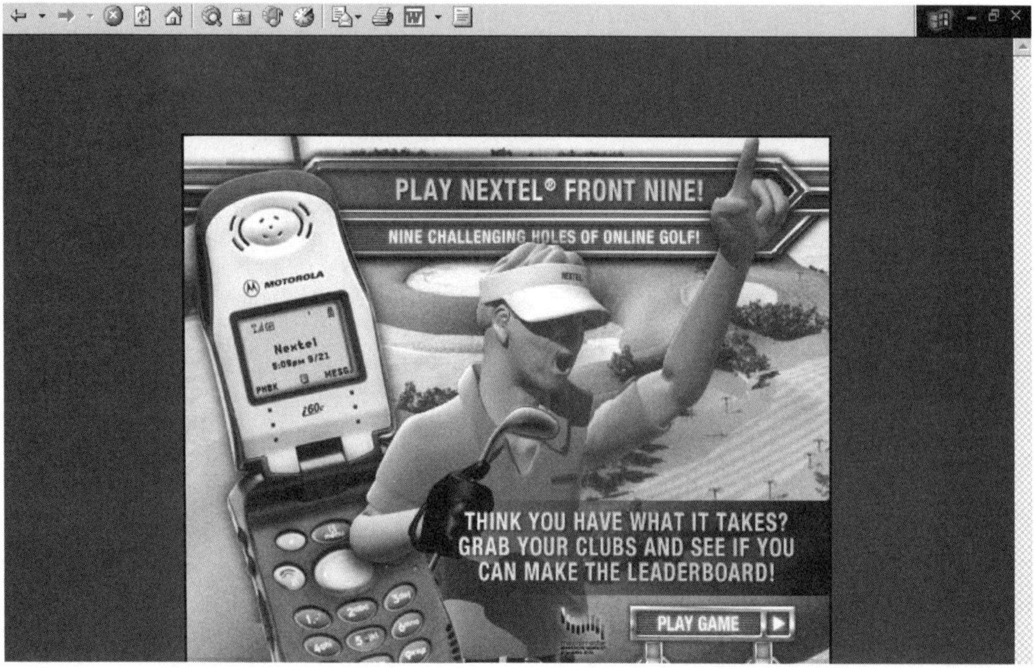

FIGURE 22.14 MindComet NEXTEL Front Nine game. © 2003. Reprinted with permission from MindComet.

Playerthree

7 Topham House, Prior Street
Greenwich, London, SE10 8ST
(ph): 0208 469 0471
(fax): 0208 469 0471
www.playerthree.net
info@playerthree.net

Company Overview

Playerthree creates interactive digital games and toys—enjoyable, challenging, and rewarding, just as they should be. Having met at Deepend, we've worked together producing games for six years, forming Playerthree in 2001. We've generated award-winning concepts, designs, and code on Web sites and mobile phones for clients including Cartoon Network®, De-construct, Deepend, Kelloggs®, Nestle®, Nokia, Panasonic®, Poke, Sky Interactive, Supernoodles, Swatch®, Tango, and Technics®. Table 22.9 shows a sampling of games that Playerthree has developed. The Playerthree home page can be seen in Figure 22.15.

TABLE 22.9 A sampling of games from Playerthree

Game	*Client*	*Application and URL*
Planet Prostate	Publicis Networks for the Prostate Cancer Society	Playerthree was commissioned to produce a viral game to act as the sole promotional tool to raise awareness of prostate cancer and the charity among young men and women online. We created a staged game within which the main character, Sammy Sperm, takes a surreal, but factually correct journey from the testes to the prostate gland, highlighting the dangers and medical processes that occur along the way. However, the whole look of the game was intended to be fun and tongue-in-cheek and very arcadelike. A high score table reflected the successes of the many thousands of gamers who took part. The game received superb coverage throughout Europe in digital and traditional media. See Figure 22.16. *www.playerthree.net*
Panasonic F1 Games	De-construct for Panasonic Europe	Playerthree worked closely with de-construct (*www.de-construct.com*) to develop a series of challenging games to promote Panasonic products and their sponsorship of the Toyota® F1 team. The games sat within a larger microsite developed by de-construct. Because image rights are very restrictive in F1 and we were consciously not trying to create the next best racing game, the games took a unique approach, distilling the essence of the challenges faced by F1 drivers and turning them into accurately focused skill games. The skills being assessed were racing line, gear change, wheel change, engine tune, aerodynamics, and braking. A new game was released for each Grand Prix race in Europe and excellent prizes were offered to the individually best registered players for each game, including the chance to drive a formula one car for the overall best player. The competition has proved so successful that is now in its second year. *www.playerthree.net*

TABLE 22.9 *(Continued)*

Game	*Client*	*Application and URL*
Swatch: Soul City	Deepend Italy for Swatch Europe	Playerthree created a snowboarding "big air" game to sit within a microsite developed by Deepend Italy for Swatch. The game needed to promote their Soul City event in Austria and attract European users. The main prize was two holiday tickets to the event. We created a simple and very addictive game of skill that appealed to a youthful audience and both sexes. You had three runs to launch yourself off a big ramp and perform as many tricks as possible before making as good a landing as possible. Your three scores were totaled together to give your competition score. *www.playerthree.net*

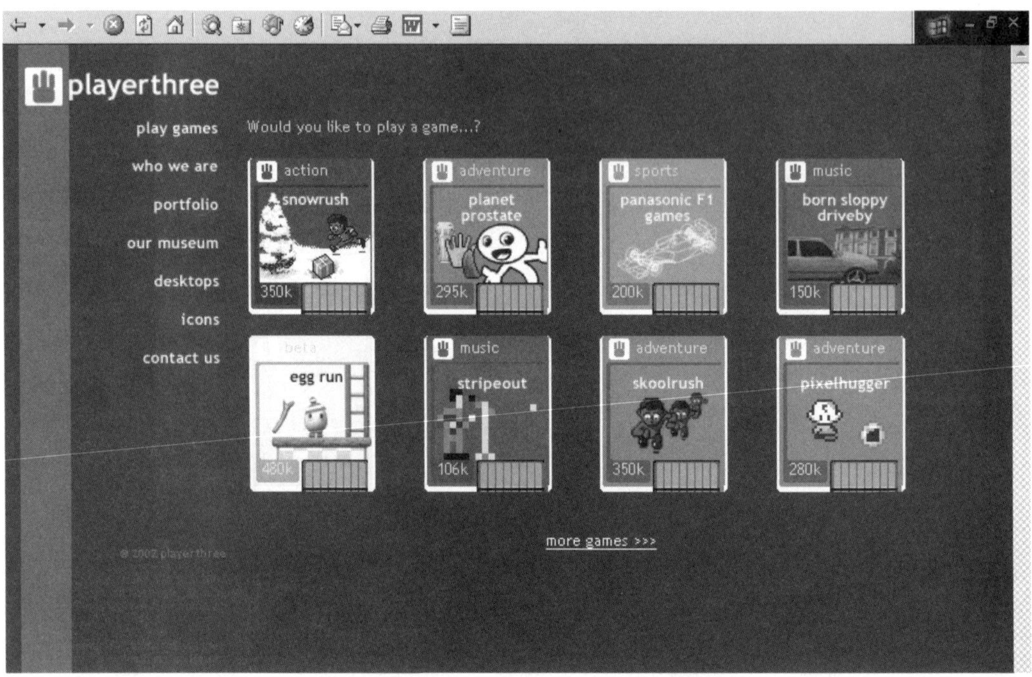

FIGURE 22.15 Playerthree home page. © 2003. Reprinted with permission from Playerthree.

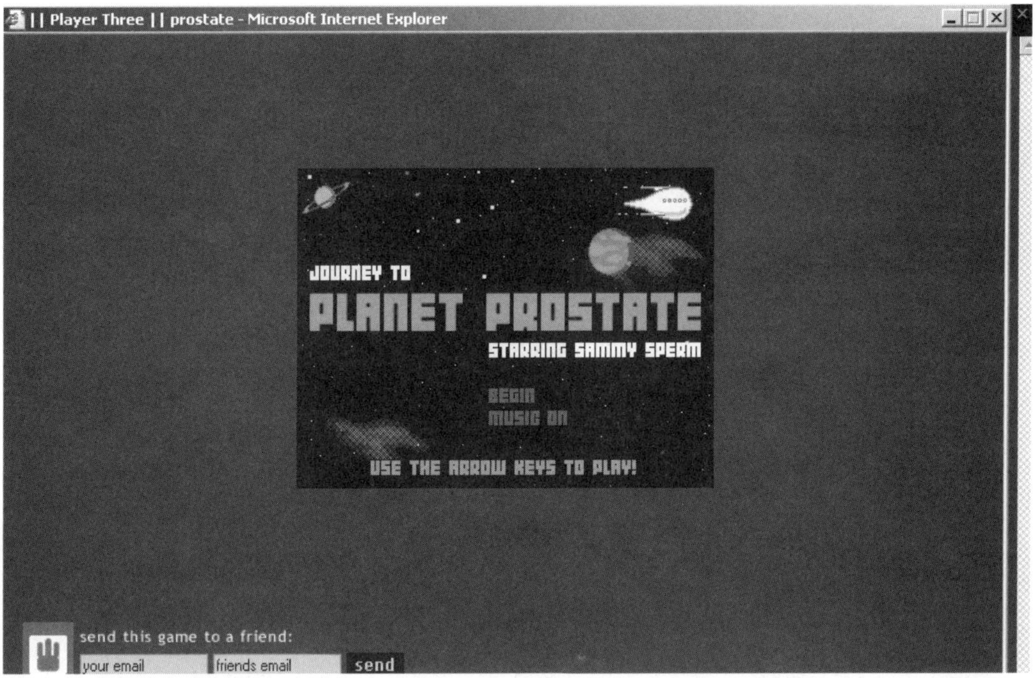

FIGURE 22.16 Planet Prostate. © 2003. Reprinted with permission from Playerthree.

The Groove Alliance, Inc.

3351-D Riverside Drive #406
Sherman Oaks, CA 91423
(ph): 866-245-4235
(fax): 305-574-2499
www.3dgroove.com
sales@3dgroove.com

Company Overview

The Groove Alliance designs, develops, and publishes custom Advergames, and licenses its 3D Groove™ game development and distribution platform to third-party Advergame developers.

3D Groove enables narrowband broadcasting of console-quality 3D video games directly to any Windows or Macintosh Web browser, even over 56K. Whereas other 3D gaming technologies exclude the majority of Web users by requiring 3D hardware cards and high-end PCs, 3D Groove enables console-quality Web games for everyone—without any need for 3D hardware. In development since 1997, 3D Groove has been downloaded more than 50 million times since it was first released in 1999.

3D Groove games provide a unique solution for advertisers, portals, destination sites, and game publishers who need to deliver compelling and profitable online content that cuts through the clutter of the Web. Dozens of 3D Groove-powered original games and branded Advergames have been deployed by publishers and advertisers, including AT&T, Cartoon Network, Cisco®, DaimlerChrysler®, Intel®, Jack Daniel's®, Mars®/M&M's, Mazda®, Microsoft®/MSN®, Nestle, Nickelodeon®, PepsiCo®, Procter & Gamble, Warner Bros.®, and Radio Shack®. Winner of the 2001 Webby Award for best online games, The Groove Alliance was also nominated for a 2001 BAFTA Interactive Entertainment Award.

The Groove Alliance's latest GX™ technology incorporates seven years and millions of dollars in research and development. GX is architected to deliver the maximum possible gaming performance to the broadest possible audience, with support for both Windows and Mac OS as a self-contained 550Kb browser plug-in. GX features the fastest software rendering technology available, for high performance even without 3D hardware cards. For those users with 3D hardware, GX takes full advantage of DirectX and OpenGL. Table 22.10 shows a sampling of games that The Groove Alliance has developed. The Groove Alliance home page can be seen in Figure 22.17, as well as the Mountain Dew® game in Figure 22.18 and a Groove Alliance Web site in 22.19.

TABLE 22.10 A sampling of games from The Groove Alliance

Game	*Client*	*Application and URL*
Mountain Dew Code Red Street Hoops: Nothin' But Net	Tribal DDB/PepsiCo	See Figure 19.18. *www.mountaindew.com/code_red/nuthinbutnet/net_game.html*
RadioShack RC Stuntmachine Showdown	MSN/Radio Shack	*http://zone.msn.com/stuntmachine*
Nestlé's Nesquik Chocolate Mountain Challenge	Ayzenberg Group/ Nestle	*www.nesquik.com/games.asp?game=bunnychallenge*
Warner Bros. presents *Eight Legged Freaks*: Let the Squashing Begin	Warner Bros. Pictures	*http://letthesquashingbegin.warnerbros.com*
AT&T Unlimited Challenge 2	AT&T	*http://att.3dgroove.com/*

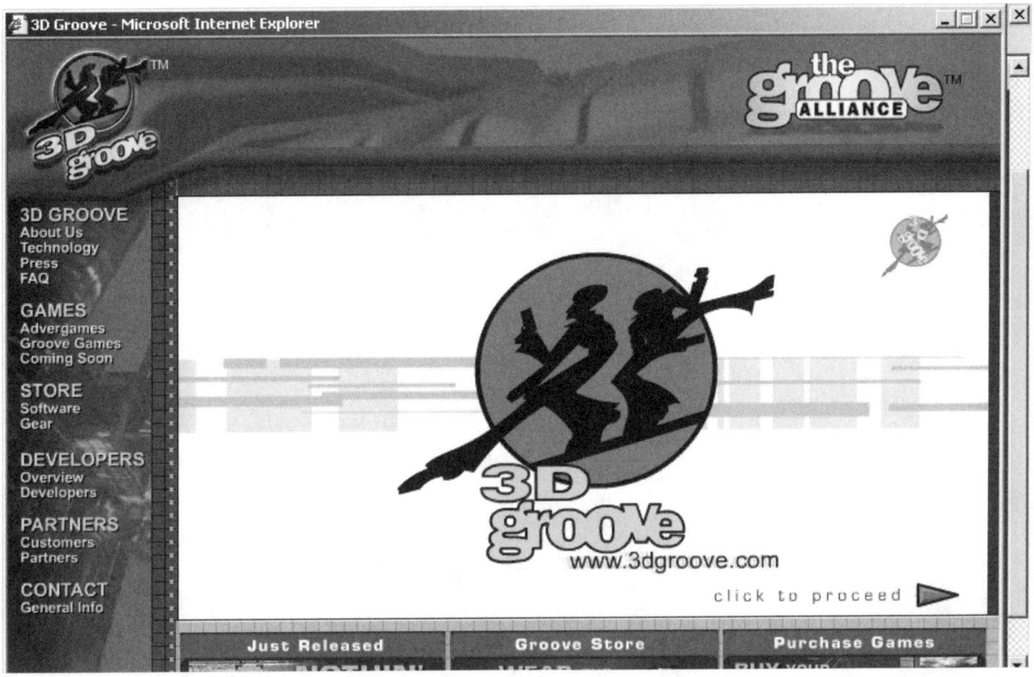

FIGURE 22.17 The Groove Alliance home page. © 2003. Reprinted with permission from The Groove Alliance, Inc.

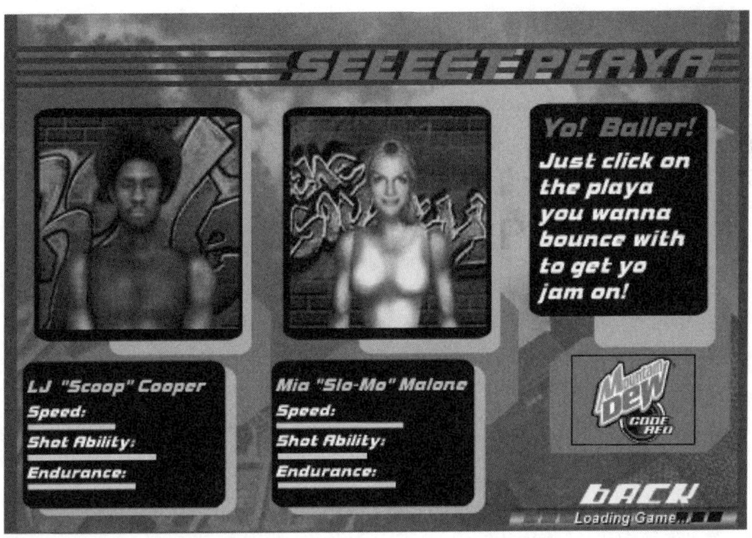

FIGURE 22.18 The Groove Alliance Mountain Dew game. © 2003. Reprinted with permission from The Groove Alliance, Inc.

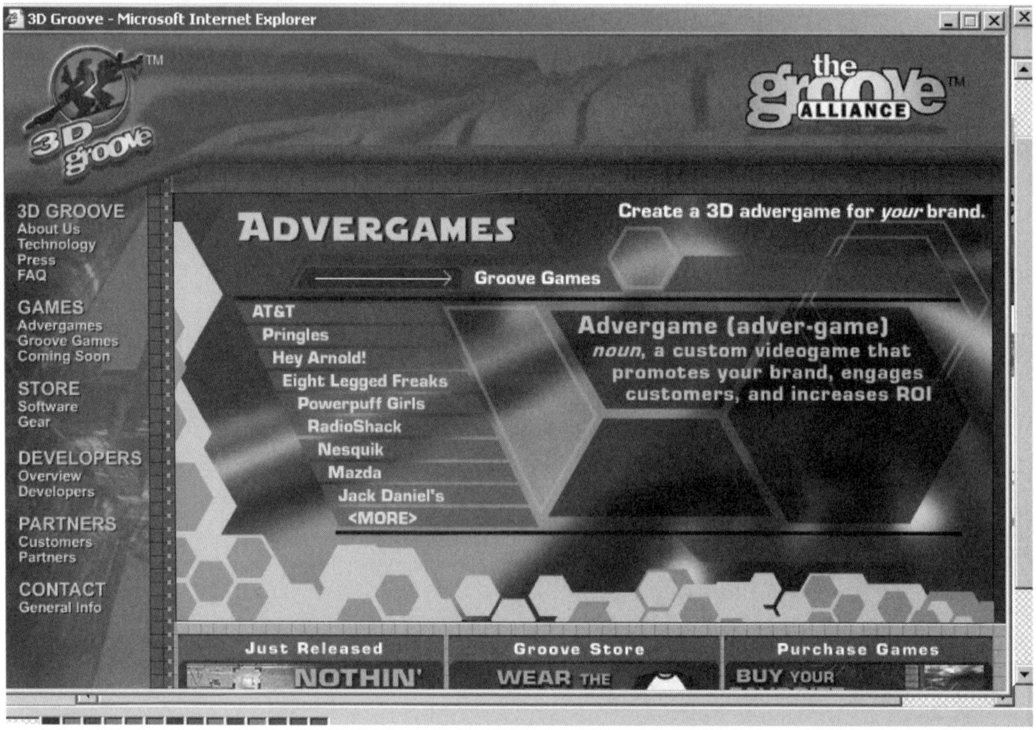

FIGURE 22.19 The Groove Alliance Web site. © 2003. Reprinted with permission from The Groove Alliance, Inc.

Unleashed Media, Inc.

510 S. Mathilda Ave #9
Sunnyvale, Ca. 94086
(ph): 408-773-1347
(fax): 408-773-1408
www.unleashedmedia.com
marketing@unleashedmedia.com

Company Overview

Unleashed Media™ creates extraordinary results by providing a superior level of expertise in Advergaming and viral marketing techniques. The Unleashed Media team is committed to increasing your response rates and viral marketing effectiveness with award-winning customized Advergames for the Web or theatrical trade shows. Table 22.11 shows a sampling of games that Unleashed Media has developed. The Unleashed Media home page can be seen in Figure 22.20.

TABLE 22.11 A sampling of games from Unleashed Media

Game	*Client*	*Application and URL*
Who Wants to Save the Holidays	Internal	A take-off on the game show "Who Wants to Be a Millionaire," this Flash cartoon parity was created for branding and lead generation. Successfully completing the game results in an e-mail invitation to become a certified Elf. See Figure 22.21. *www.unleashedmedia.com/who.html*
The Find Law Court	Findlaw.com	A take-off on the game show "Who Wants to Be a Millionaire" and "Judge Judy," this Flash cartoon parity was created for branding and marketing exposure. Successfully completing the game results in an e-mail invitation to subscribe to several of their newsletters and enter to win a cash prize. *www.findlaw.com/game/*
The Sopranelves	Internal	A take-off on the show "Sopranos," this Flash cartoon parity was created for branding and lead generation. Successfully completing the game results in an e-mail invitation to become a certified FBI Agent. *www.unleashedmedia.com/meezy/cardgame.html*
Palm Las Vegas	Palm	A Roulette game used for generating leads at a trade show, this Flash game was created for branding and lead generation. Successfully completing the game results in several types of prizes, as well as a chance to win a grand prize. *www.unleashedmedia.com/portfolio/interactive_media/palm_vm.html*
On the Spot	*TV Guide Magazine*	A take-off on the game show "Who Wants to Be a Millionaire," this game is used for generating leads at trade shows. This game was created for branding and lead generation. Successfully completing the game results in several types of prizes, as well as a chance to win a grand prize. There is no URL, as it is too heavy for the Web.

TABLE 22.11 *(Continued)*

Game	***Client***	***Application and URL***
Fudin' & Fools	*TV Guide Magazine*	A take-off on the game show "Family Feud," this game is used for generating leads at trade shows. This game was created for branding and lead generation. Successfully completing the game results in winning a large, color screen TV. There is no URL, as it is too heavy for the Web.
Quiz O' Rama	Hewlett-Packard, Microsoft, Bank Of America	A take-off on the game show "Jeopardy," this game is used for generating leads at trade shows. This game was created for branding and lead generation. Successfully completing the game results in several types of prizes, as well as a chance to win a grand prize. There is no URL, as it is too heavy for the Web.

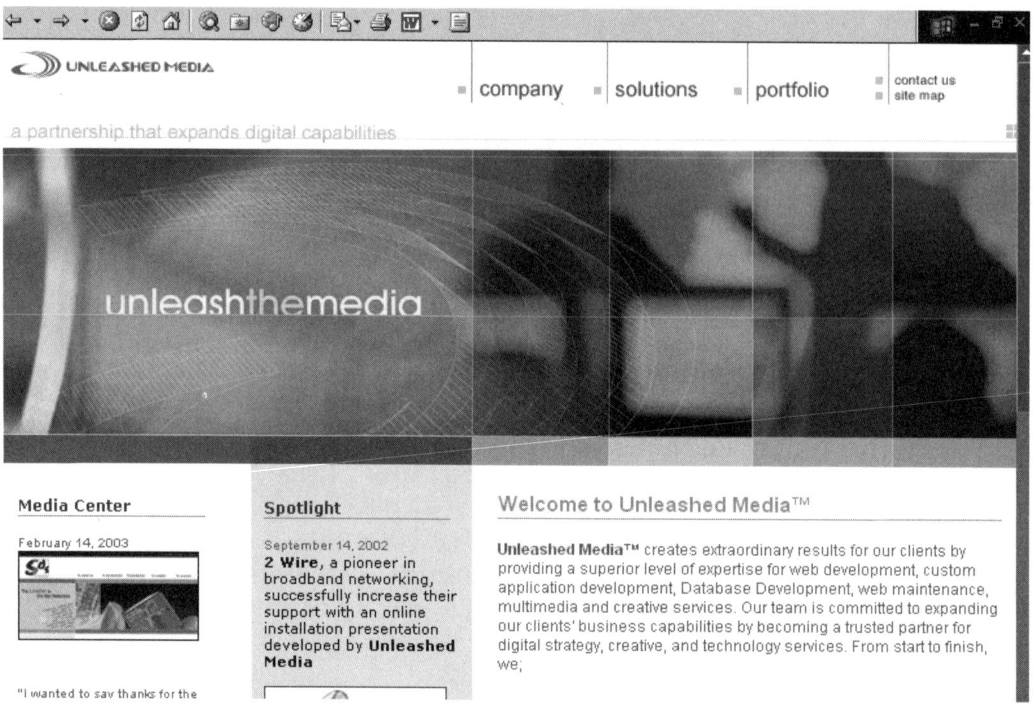

FIGURE 22.20 Unleashed Media home page. © 2003. Reprinted with permission from Unleashed Media.

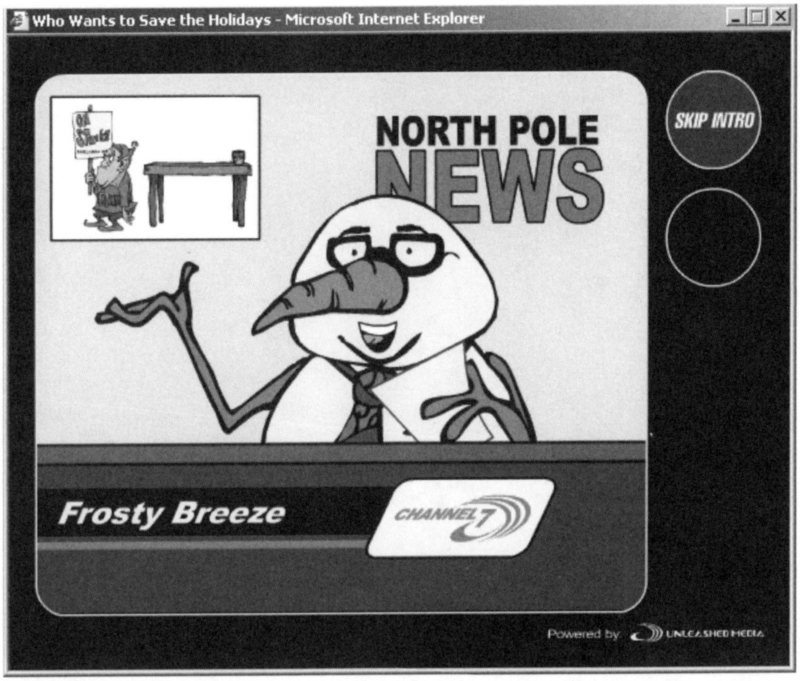

FIGURE 22.21 Unleashed Media, Who Wants to Save the Holidays game.

YAYA Media, Inc.

12300 Wilshire Boulevard, Suite 400
Los Angeles, CA 90025
(ph): 310-207-2702
(fax): 310-207-2727
www.yaya.com
jane@yaya.com

Company Overview

YAYA Media is a pioneer in games-based marketing solutions, providing a broad range of products spanning Advergames, recruiting games, Edutainment, and games strategy to Fortune 500 brands. YAYA's unique approach to Advergaming blends traditional advertising with entertainment marketing and CRM to maximize return on investment. YAYA has had great success in helping clients such as Chrysler, Siemens, Paramount, K-Mart, Burger King, Honda, and Safeway® realize their marketing objectives. They have helped companies, large and small, by building branding awareness, driving revenue, motivating trial, and maximizing their CRM initiatives with compelling custom content.

About the CD-ROM

The *Advergaming Developer's Guide* includes a companion CD-ROM filled with the games, source code, and graphics from the sample applications used in the book. You will also find trial versions of both Macromedia Flash 2004 and Macromedia Director MX. From the CD-ROM, you can play any of the sample games or take a look behind the scenes at how each game was developed. Mix the code and concepts from different applications to create your own unique Advergame. On the CD-ROM, you will find games that are perfect for beginners, as well as experienced developers.

ON THE CD

On the CD-ROM, you will also find many online resources that include dozens of games and Advergame sites, industry links, and other helpful tips, tools, and techniques used by game developers around the world. This CD-ROM plays on a Mac or PC.

The following is a brief description of what is included in the CD-ROM:

Chapters: From the main menu of the program, you have the option to play the game or reference the source code and graphics used to create it.

Online Resources: Click the Online Resource option from the main menu and a file loads showing dozens of Advergames, separated into genres such as Action Adventure Games, Puzzle/Quiz/Strategy Games, and Arcade/Casino Games. Scroll through this file to find reference articles and information about various industry conferences and meetings.

Macromedia Flash MX 2004, Trial Version: From the main menu, click the Macromedia Flash 2004 icon to load a trial version on your computer. Use the trial version to create the Macromedia Flash 2004 applications shown in the book or your own. If you want to buy the complete version, visit the Macromedia Web site at *www.macromedia.com*.

Macromedia Director MX, Trial Version: With Director MX, you can create interactive content that integrates long video streams, photo-quality images, audio, animation, 3D models, text, and Macromedia Flash content. Create accessible content for people with disabilities. Then deploy on CD-ROM, DVD, kiosks, or the Web. Install this trial version by clicking the Director MX icon on the main menu to build the Director MX games shown in the book.

SYSTEM REQUIREMENTS

Windows

- Intel Pentium III 600MHz or higher
- Windows 2000 or Windows XP
- 128 MB of free available system RAM (256 MB recommended)
- 275 MB available disk space

Macintosh

- Power Macintosh G3 500 MHz or Higher
- Mac OS X 10.2.6 or 10.3
- 128 MB or more of free available system RAM (256 MB recommended)
- 215 MB available disk space

Glossary

action: A piece of code placed on an object within a Macromedia Flash 2004 movie.

ActionScript: The scripting language used within Macromedia Flash 2004.

alignment: The idea that all interface elements should be connected by their locations relative to screen edges and each other.

antialiasing: The process of smoothing an image to avoid the appearance of jagged edges due to sharp changes in the colors of pixels.

applet: An application that can only be viewed through an Internet browser with the proper plug-in.

application: See *program.*

argument: See *parameter.*

array: See *list.*

ASCII: The American Standard Code for Information Interchange.

awareness: The knowledge gained through one's own perception. For a brand, awareness is the number of people (measured in percent) who recall a brand.

behavior script: A Lingo script designed to affect only the sprite or sprites to which it has been applied, as opposed to affecting an entire Director MX movie.

bitmap: An array of values that make up an image of one or more colors.

Boolean: A variable or statement having to do with the values True and False.

brand: A name given to a product or service; it is composed of a mixture of attributes, tangible and intangible. Brands are symbolized by a trademark, and can create value in the mind of the consumer. From a legal standpoint, brands are considered intellectual property and are protected by law.

brand associations: The beliefs, knowledge, and feelings that consumers develop over time about brands. When these experiences are consistent with the brand position, the customer is able to differentiate one brand from another.

brand equity: The sum total of the assets and liabilities of a brand and equals the brand's value to the consumer. Brands that have high brand loyalty, name awareness, perceived quality, along with strong trademarks and strategic distributor relations are said to have high brand equity.

brand loyalty: The strength of preference consumers have for a brand versus the competition. Brand loyalty is typically measured in price sensitivity or repeat purchase behavior.

brand management: The management of the packaging, price, and product, as well as all aspects of the customer experience with buying and using the brand.

cast: A panel that stores scripts, images, sounds, and other media to be used within a Director MX movie.

cast member: A script, image, sound, or other medium stored within a cast to be used within a Director MX movie.

cell: A section of a channel that holds the contents of that channel for exactly one frame.

channel: A numbered row of cells that represents a single layer of a Director MX movie.

character: A single letter, numerical digit, or symbol that could be a component of a string.

color: The predefined Lingo type consisting of a red value, a green value, and a blue value that indicate a single color.

command: Any line of Lingo programming code. Generally refers to built-in Lingo functions.

commenting: The process of hiding a line of source code from the rest of the Director MX movie for the purpose of clarifying unclear source code or debugging a movie.

conditional: A structure that keeps one or several lines of code from being executed unless a specified condition is met

constant: A value that is incapable of changing its worth.

contrast: The idea that interface elements that do not appear exactly alike should appear very different.

Customer Relationship Management (CRM): A system of managing the ongoing relationship between a company and its customers. CRM software programs are designed to track customer behavior and increase the bond between the consumer and the brand.

demographics: The characteristics that characterize a group of people, such as nationality, sex, age, education, marital status, occupation, or income. Decisions on Advergame design and deployment are often based on demographic data.

Director MX: The multimedia development utility created by Macromedia designed to make multimedia programming easy.

dot syntax: The new style of Lingo programming that resembles mathematical equations.

effects channels: The six channels that can hold effects, such as transitions, sounds, and behaviors, as opposed to visual sprites.

event handler: A function built into Director MX and Flash 2004 that executes at set intervals or based on user interaction.

feedback: The information provided to the user about his interaction with an interface.

film loop: A sort of cast member that can contain multiple frames and/or sprites within itself.

float: The predefined Lingo type indicating decimal, or floating-point, numbers.

font: A style in which text is graphically displayed.

frame: A numbered column of cells that represents a single point in a Director MX movie.

frame rate: The number of frames that a movie displays per second.

function: A section of code that executes only when it is specifically told to do so.

future feedback: The feedback given to the user before an interaction occurs.

global variable: A variable that exists from the point it was first assigned a value to the end of the handler or function in which it began.

graphic: A visual representation of an item either directly or indirectly made up of pixels.

handler: See *event handler.*

hard return: A break in a block of text caused by the user pressing the Enter key to insert a carriage return.

icon: An image or symbol that is used to represent an action or idea.

integer: The predefined Lingo type indicating numbers that do not contain any decimal fractions.

interface: An interactive means of bringing information to the user.

keyframe (Director MX): A frame of a movie that is designated to signify a change in a sprite channel.

keyframe (Flash MX 2004): A frame of a Flash 2004 movie that contains objects.

launch: The initial introduction of a new product or service. The launch is part of the rollout that includes a plan to introduce the new product or service to different geographical markets or consumer segments. An Advergame may be during the launch of a new product to promote the product's unique features and benefits.

layer: A row of frames that represents a single layer of a Flash 2004 movie.

library: A panel that stores symbols, images, videos, sounds, and other media to be used within a Macromedia Flash 2004 movie.

linear list: A list variable that contains only a list of ordered values.

Lingo: The programming language used to create scripts within Director MX.

list: A single variable that holds zero or more values within itself.

local variable: A variable that exists from the point it was first assigned a value to the end of the handler or function in which it began.

loop: A structure that makes a group of code execute repeatedly as long as a specified condition is met.

Macromedia Flash 2004: The Web multimedia development utility created by Macromedia designed to make multimedia programming easy.

marker: A special kind of frame that can be accessed by its given name.

market segment: A group of customers who share the same needs and values. Consumers in a specific market segment can be expected to respond in much the same way to a company's offering. An Advergame might be targeted at college-bound high school seniors.

mask: An image that indicates (usually with only two colors) a certain portion of another image that is active, clickable, or visible.

member: See *cast member*.

metaphor: A representation of a physical object that is meant to give the user an idea of how an interface operates.

movie: Any application, presentation, or game created within Director MX.

movie script: A Lingo script designed to alter an entire Director MX movie.

nested: A conditional or loop that is enclosed within another conditional or loop.

niche marketing: The marketing designed to fill the needs, wants, and expectations of a small group of individuals.

opacity: The amount of visibility a visual item conveys.

opaque: The characteristic of a visual item to be completely visible.

operating system: The shell application required to run all other applications on a computer.

operator: A term or function indicating some operation to be performed.

parameter: A value passed to a function or behavior to be used as an internal variable.

past feedback: The feedback that is given to the user after an interaction has occurred.

pixel: A single dot of color within a raster image or video buffer.

platform: See *operating system*.

point: The predefined Lingo type consisting of a horizontal value and a vertical value that indicate a single 2D location.

present feedback: The feedback that is given to the user as an interaction is taking place.

positioning statement: A written description that identifies how a company wants its products or brand to be perceived in the minds of its target audience. Typically used to identify how the brand differs from the competition.

program: A series of ordered instructions that tell the computer what to do.

programmer: The person writing a particular application.

property list: A list variable that contains not only values, but also property names.

property variable: A variable that exists only within a single script or as an attribute of a specified sprite.

proximity: The idea that the positioning of interface elements close together indicates a relationship.

puppet: A sound or sprite that is under Lingo control as opposed to Score control.

raster graphics: The graphics that work directly with pixels instead of shapes.

registration point: The point on a graphic element upon which positioning and rotation is based.

repetition: The idea that similar styles should be reused throughout an interface to convey a sense of continuity.

rotating: The process of distorting a graphic element by changing its angular orientation.

runtime: The point in the development of a program at which the program is actually executed.

Score: The visual display of all frames, channels, and cells within a Director MX movie.

script: A section of Lingo code that makes up exactly one member of a cast.

share of mind: The way a consumer often thinks about a specific brand in a particular category.

Shockwave: The name given to all Internet content created with Director MX.

simplicity: The idea that an interface should not contain so many elements as to confuse the user.

skewing: The process of distorting a graphic element by slanting it horizontally.

soft return: A break in a block of text caused by a line of text being too long and wrapping onto the next line.

sprite: A representation of a visual cast member after it has been placed on the Stage or within the Score.

sprite channel: See *channel.*

Stage: The visual area of a Director MX movie where all the action takes place.

string: The predefined Lingo type indicating a group of zero or more characters organized in a specific order.

tick: One sixtieth of a second.

top-of-mind: The brand that comes to mind first when a consumer is asked about a product or service.

trademark: "Any sign capable of being represented graphically which is capable of distinguishing goods or services of one undertaking from those of another undertaking" (UK Trade Marks Act 1994).

translucent: The characteristic of a visual item to be partially visible.

transparent: The characteristic of a visual item to be completely invisible.

type: A classification of a value, such as integer, string, color, and so forth.

user: The person using a particular application.

value: A number, section of text, or other item of a set worth.

variable: A constant letter or word that can represent a changing value.

vector graphics: The graphics that work with shapes instead of directly with pixels.

verbose syntax: The old style of Lingo programming that resembles English sentences.

visual channels: The channels that can hold visual sprites, as opposed to transitions, sounds, or behaviors.

visual identity: The visual components of a brand, which may include its logo, typography, and how it is packaged, as well as photographic and illustrative elements. Advergame developers study the visual identity of a brand and often incorporate these elements into their games.

void: Without any set value.

white space: The screen area in an interface that does not contain any active elements.

word wrap: The characteristic of a text field that allows entire words to move to the next line when the preset width of the field would otherwise be exceeded.

Xtra: A plug-in application that is designed to expand the functionality of Director MX in some way.

Index